I0575303

William Warburton, Pope Alexander

The Works of Alexander Pope

With his last corrections, additions, and improvements - together with all his notes, as they were delivered to the editor a little before his death - Vol. 5

William Warburton, Pope Alexander

The Works of Alexander Pope
With his last corrections, additions, and improvements - together with all his notes, as they were delivered to the editor a little before his death - Vol. 5

ISBN/EAN: 9783337100759

Printed in Europe, USA, Canada, Australia, Japan

Cover: Foto ©Lupo / pixelio.de

THE

WORKS

OF

Alexander Pope, Esq.

IN NINE VOLUMES, COMPLETE.

WITH

NOTES AND ILLUSTRATIONS

By JOSEPH WARTON, D.D.

AND OTHERS.

VOLUME THE FIFTH.

LONDON:

Printed for B. Law, J. Johnson, C. Dilly, G. G. and J. Robinson, J. Nichols, R. Baldwin, H. L. Gardner, F. and C. Rivington, J. Sewell, T. Payne, J. Walker, R. Faulder, J. Scatcherd, B. and J. White, Ogilvy and Son, T. N. Longman, Cadell jun. and Davies, and E. Pote.

1797.

CONTENTS

OF THE

FIFTH VOLUME.

[*The Article marked thus* † *was not inserted in* Dr. WARBURTON's Edition.]

	Page
A LETTER to the PUBLISHER, occasioned by the first correct Edition of the DUNCIAD -	3
MARTINUS SCRIBLERUS's Prolegomena and Illustrations to the DUNCIAD, with the Hypercritics of ARISTARCHUS - - -	15
The DUNCIAD, in FOUR BOOKS.	
Book I. - - -	75
Book II. - - -	123
Book III. - - -	177
Book IV. - - -	227

APPENDIX.

I. A Preface prefixed to the five first imperfect Editions of the DUNCIAD -	301
II. A List of Books, Papers, and Verses in which our Author was abused - -	307
III. Advertisement to the first Edition with NOTES, in quarto - - -	314

IV. Adver-

Page

IV. Advertiſement to the firſt Edition of the FOURTH BOOK when printed ſeparately 316

V. Advertiſement to the complete Edition of 1743 318

VI. Advertiſement printed in the Journals, 1730 319

VII. A Parallel of the Characters of Mr. DRYDEN and Mr. POPE - - - 321

† The DUNCIAD, as it ſtood in the quarto Edition, 1728.

† Book I. - - - 337

† Book II. - - - 349

† Book III. - - - 365

THE

DUNCIAD,

IN FOUR BOOKS,

WITH THE

PROLEGOMENA OF SCRIBLERUS,

THE

HYPERCRITICS OF ARISTARCHUS,

AND

NOTES VARIORUM.

A LETTER TO THE PUBLISHER,

OCCASIONED BY

THE FIRST CORRECT EDITION

OF THE

DUNCIAD.

IT is with pleasure I hear, that you have procured a correct copy of the Dunciad, which the many surreptitious ones have rendered so necessary; and it is yet with more, that I am informed it will be attended with a Commentary: A work so requisite, that I cannot think the Author himself would have omitted it, had he approved of the first appearance of this poem.

Such notes as have occurred to me I herewith

of my life, and a much greater reſpect to Truth, than to him or any man living, engaged me in enquiries, of which the encloſed Notes are the fruit.

I perceived that moſt of theſe Authors had been (doubtleſs very wiſely) the firſt aggreſſors. They had tried, till they were weary, what was to be got by railing at each other: Nobody was either concerned or ſurprized if this or that ſcribler was proved a dunce: But every one was curious to read what could be ſaid to prove Mr. Pope one, and was ready to pay ſomething for ſuch a diſcovery: A ſtratagem, which, would they fairly own, it might not only reconcile them to me, but ſcreen them from the reſentment of their lawful Superiors, whom they daily abuſe, only (as I charitably hope) to get that *by* them, which they cannot get *from* them.

I found this was not all: Ill ſucceſs in that had tranſported them to Perſonal abuſe, either of himſelf, or (what I think he could leſs forgive) of his Friends. They had called men of virtue and honour bad men, long before he had either leiſure or inclination to call them bad writers: And ſome had been ſuch old offenders, that he had quite forgotten their perſons as well as their ſlanders, till they were pleaſed to revive them.

Now what had Mr. Pope done before, to incenſe them? He had publiſhed thoſe works which are in the hands of every body, in which not the leaſt

mention

mention is made of any of them. And what has he done ſince? He has laughed, and written the Dunciad. What has that ſaid of them? A very ſerious truth, which the public had ſaid before, that they were dull: And what it had no ſooner ſaid, but they themſelves were at great pains to procure, or even purchaſe room in the prints, to teſtify under their hands to the truth of it.

I ſhould ſtill have been ſilent, if either I had ſeen any inclination in my friend to be ſerious with ſuch accuſers, or if they had only meddled with his Writings; ſince whoever publiſhes, puts himſelf on his trial by his Country. But when his moral character was attacked, and in a manner from which neither truth nor virtue can ſecure the moſt innocent; in a manner, which, though it annihilates the credit of the accuſation with the juſt and impartial, yet aggravates very much the guilt of the accuſers; I mean by authors without names; then I thought, ſince the danger was common to all, the concern ought to be ſo; and that it was an act of juſtice to detect the authors, not only on this account, but as many of them are the ſame who for ſeveral years paſt have made free with the greateſt names in church and ſtate, expoſed to the world the private misfortunes of families, abuſed all, even to women, and whoſe proſtituted papers (for one or other Party, in the unhappy diviſions of their country) have inſulted the fallen, the friendleſs, the exil'd, and the dead.

Besides this, which I take to be a public concern, I have already confessed I had a private one. I am one of that number, who have long loved and esteemed Mr. Pope; and had often declared it was not his capacity or writings (which we ever thought the least valuable part of his character) but the honest, open, and beneficent man, that we most esteemed, and loved in him Now, if what these people say were believed, I must appear to all my friends either a fool, or a knave; either imposed on myself, or imposing on them; so that I am as much interested in the confutation of these calumnies, as he is himself.

I am no author, and consequently not to be suspected either of jealousy or resentment against any of the men, of whom scarce one is known to me by sight; and as for their writings, I have sought them (on this one occasion) in vain, in the closets and libraries of all my acquaintance. I had still been in the dark, if a Gentleman had not procured me (I suppose from some of themselves, for they are generally much more dangerous friends than enemies) the passages I send you. I solemnly protest I have added nothing to the malice or absurdity of them; which it behoves me to declare, since the vouchers themselves will be so soon and so irrecoverably lost. You may in some measure prevent it, by preserving at least their titles [a], and discovering (as far as you can

[a] Which we have done in a list printed in the Appendix.

can depend on the truth of your information) the names of the concealed authors.

The firſt objection I have heard made to the poem is, that the perſons are too obſcure for ſatire. The perſons themſelves, rather than allow the objection, would forgive the ſatire; and if one could be tempted to afford it a ſerious anſwer, were not all aſſaſſinates, popular inſurrections, the inſolence of the rabble without doors, and of domeſtics within, moſt wrongfully chaſtiſed, if the meanneſs of offenders indemnified them from puniſhment? On the contrary, obſcurity renders them more dangerous, as leſs thought of: Law can pronounce judgment only on open facts; morality alone can paſs cenſure on intentions of miſchief; ſo that for ſecret calumny, or the arrow flying in the dark, there is no public puniſhment left, but what a good writer inflicts.

The next objection is, that theſe ſort of authors are poor. That might be pleaded as an excuſe at the Old Bailey, for leſſer crimes than defamation, (for 'tis the caſe of almoſt all who are tried there), but ſure it can be none here: For who will pretend that the robbing another of his Reputation ſupplies the want of it in himſelf? I queſtion not but ſuch authors are poor, and heartily wiſh the objection were removed by any honeſt livelihood. But poverty is here the accident, not the ſubject: He who deſcribes malice and villainy to be pale and meagre, expreſſes not the leaſt anger againſt paleneſs or leanneſs, but againſt malice and villainy. The Apothecary in Romeo and Juliet is poor; but is he therefore juſtified in vending poiſon? Not but poverty itſelf becomes a juſt ſubject of ſatire, when it is the conſequence of vice, prodigality, or neglect of one's lawful calling; for then it increaſes the public burden, fills the ſtreets and highways with robbers, and the garrets with clippers, coiners, and weekly journaliſts.

But admitting that two or three of theſe offend leſs in their morals than in their writings; muſt poverty make nonſenſe ſacred? If ſo, the fame of bad authors would be much better conſulted than that of all the good ones in the world; and not one of an hundred had ever been called by his right name.

They miſtake the whole matter: It is not charity to encourage them in the way they follow, but to get them out of it; for men are not bunglers becauſe they are poor, but they are poor becauſe they are bunglers.

Is it not pleaſant enough, to hear our authors crying out on the one hand, as if their perſons and characters were too ſacred for ſatire; and the public objecting on the other, that they are too mean even for ridicule? But whether bread or fame be their end, it muſt be allowed, our author, by and in this poem, has mercifully given them a little of both.

There are two or three, who by their rank and fortune have no benefit from the former objections, ſuppoſing them good, and theſe I was ſorry to ſee in

ſuch

ſuch company. But if, without any provocation, two or three gentlemen will fall upon one, in an affair wherein his intereſt and reputation are equally embarked; they cannot certainly, after they have been content to print themſelves his enemies, complain of being put into the number of them.

Others, I am told, pretend to have been once his friends. Surely they are their enemies who ſay ſo, ſince nothing can be more odious than to treat a friend as they have done. But of this I cannot perſuade myſelf, when I conſider the conſtant and eternal averſion of all bad writers to a good one.

Such as claim a merit from being his admirers, I would gladly aſk, if it lays him under a perſonal obligation? At that rate he would be the moſt obliged humble ſervant in the world. I dare ſwear for theſe in particular, he never deſired them to be his admirers, nor promiſed in return to be theirs: That had truly been a ſign he was of their acquaintance; but would not the malicious world have ſuſpected ſuch an approbation of ſome motive worſe than ignorance, in the author of the Eſſay on Criticiſm? Be it as it will, the reaſons of their admiration and of his contempt are equally ſubſiſting, for his works and theirs are the very ſame that they were.

One, therefore, of their aſſertions I believe may be true, "That he has a contempt for their writings." And there is another, which would probably be ſooner allowed by himſelf than by any good judge beſide,

beſide, "That his own have found too much ſucceſs with the public." But as it cannot conſiſt with his modeſty to claim this as a juſtice, it lies not on him, but entirely on the public, to defend its own judgment.

There remains what in my opinion might ſeem a better plea for theſe people, than any they have made uſe of. If obſcurity or poverty were to exempt a man from ſatire, much more ſhould folly or dulneſs, which are ſtill more involuntary; nay, as much ſo as perſonal deformity. But even this will not help them: Deformity becomes an object of ridicule when a man ſets up for being handſome; and ſo muſt Dulneſs when he ſets up for a Wit. They are not ridiculed becauſe ridicule in itſelf is, or ought to be, a pleaſure; but becauſe it is juſt to undeceive and vindicate the honeſt and unpretending part of mankind from impoſition, becauſe particular intereſt ought to yield to general, and a great number who are not naturally fools, ought never to be made ſo, in complaiſance to thoſe who are. Accordingly we find that in all ages, all vain pretenders, were they ever ſo poor, or ever ſo dull, have been conſtantly the topics of the moſt candid ſatiriſts, from the Codrus of Juvenal to the Damon of Boileau.

Having mentioned Boileau, the greateſt Poet and moſt judicious critic of his age and country, admirable for his talents, and yet perhaps more admirable for his judgment in the proper application of them; I cannot

cannot help remarking the reſemblance betwixt him and our author, in qualities, fame, and fortune; in the diſtinctions ſhewn them by their ſuperiors, in the general eſteem of their equals, and in their extended reputation amongſt foreigners; in the latter of which ours has met with the better fate, as he has had for his tranſlators perſons of the moſt eminent rank and abilities in their reſpective nations [b]. But the reſemblance holds in nothing more, than in their being equally abuſed by the ignorant pretenders to poetry of their times; of which not the leaſt memory will remain but in their own writings, and in the notes made upon them. What Boileau has done in almoſt all his poems, our author has only in this: I dare anſwer for him he will do it in no more; and on this principle, of attacking few but who had ſlandered him, he could not have done it at all, had he been confined from cenſuring obſcure and worthleſs perſons, for ſcarce any other were his enemies. However, as the parity is ſo remarkable, I hope it will continue to the laſt; and if ever he ſhould

[b] Eſſay on Criticiſm, in French verſe, by General Hamilton; the ſame, in verſe alſo, by Monſieur Roboton, Counſellor and Privy Secretary to King George I. after by the Abbé Reynel, in verſe, with notes. Rape of the Lock, in French, by the Princeſs of Conti, Paris, 1728, and in Italian verſe, by the Abbé Conti, a noble Venetian; and by the Marquis Rangoni, Envoy extraordinary from Modena to King George II. Others of his works by Salvini of Florence, &c. His Eſſays and Diſſertations on Homer, ſeveral times tranſlated into French. Eſſay on Man, by the Abbé Reynel, in verſe; by Monſieur Silhouette, in proſe, 1737, and ſince by others in French, Italian, and Latin.

ſhould give us an edition of this poem himſelf, I may ſee ſome of them treated as gently, on their repentance or better merit, as Perrault and Quinault were at laſt by Boileau.

In one point I muſt be allowed to think the character of our Engliſh poet the more amiable. He has not been a follower of fortune or ſucceſs; he has lived with the great without flattery; been a friend to men in power, without penſions, from whom, as he aſked, ſo he received, no favour, but what was done him in his friends. As his ſatires were the more juſt for being delayed, ſo were his panegyrics; beſtowed only on ſuch perſons as he had familiarly known, only for ſuch virtues as he had long obſerved in them, and only at ſuch times as others ceaſe to praiſe, if not begin to calumniate them, I mean when out of power, or out of faſhion [c]. A ſatire, therefore, on writers ſo notorious for the contrary practice, became no man ſo well as himſelf; as none, it is plain, was ſo little in their friendſhips, or ſo much in that of thoſe whom they had moſt abuſed, namely, the greateſt and beſt of all parties. Let me add a further reaſon, that, though engaged in their friendſhips, he never eſpouſed their animoſities; and can

[c] As Mr. Wycherley, at the time the town declaimed againſt his book of poems; Mr. Walſh, after his death; Sir William Trumball, when he had reſigned the office of Secretary of State; Lord Bolingbroke, at his leaving England, after the Queen's death; Lord Oxford, in his laſt decline of life; Mr. Secretary Craggs, at the end of the South-Sea year, and after his death; Others only in Epitaphs.

can almoſt ſingly challenge this honour, not to have written a line of any man, which, through guilt, through ſhame, or through fear, through variety of fortune, or change of Intereſts, he was ever unwilling to own.

I ſhall conclude with remarking what a pleaſure it muſt be to every reader of humanity, to ſee all along, that our Author in his very laughter is not indulging his own ill-nature, but only puniſhing that of others. As to his Poem, thoſe alone are capable of doing it juſtice, who, to uſe the words of a great writer, know how hard it is (with regard both to his ſubject and his manner) VETUSTIS DARE NOVITATEM, OBSOLETIS NITOREM, OBSCURIS LUCEM, FASTIDITIS GRATIAM.

I am

Your moſt humble ſervant,

St. James's,
Dec. 22, 1728.

WILLIAM CLELAND[d].

---

[d] This Gentleman was of Scotland, and bred at the univerſity of Utrecht, with the Earl of Mar. He ſerved in Spain under Earl Rivers. After the peace, he was made one of the commiſſioners of the cuſtoms in Scotland, and then of Taxes in England; in which, having ſhewn himſelf for twenty years diligent, punctual, and incorruptible, though without any other aſſiſtance of fortune, he was ſuddenly diſplaced by the Miniſter, in the ſixty-eighth year of his age; and died two months after, in 1741. He was a perſon of univerſal learning, and an enlarged converſation; no man had a warmer heart for his friend, or a ſincerer attachment to the conſtitution of his country.—And yet, for all this, the public would never believe him to be the author of this letter. P. W.

Many reaſons have been alledged to prove it was written by our author himſelf.

MARTINUS SCRIBLERUS

His Prolegomena and Illuſtrations

TO THE

DUNCIAD:

WITH THE

HYPER-CRITICS OF ARISTARCHUS.

Dennis, Remarks on Pr. Arthur.

I CANNOT but think it the moſt reaſonable thing in the world, to diſtinguiſh good writers, by diſcouraging the bad. Nor is it an ill-natured thing, in relation even to the very perſons upon whom the reflections are made. It is true, it may deprive them, a little the ſooner, of a ſhort profit and a tranſitory reputation; but then it may have a good effect, and oblige them (before it be too late) to decline that for which they are ſo very unfit, and to have recourſe to ſomething in which they may be more ſucceſsful.

Character of Mr. P. 1716.

THE Perſons whom Boileau has attacked in his writings, have been for the moſt part Authors, and moſt of thoſe Authors, Poets: And the cenſures he hath paſſed upon them have been confirmed by all Europe.

Gildon, Pref. to his New Rehearſal.

IT is the common cry of the Poetaſters of the town, and their fautors, that it is an ill-natured thing to expoſe the Pretenders to wit and poetry. The Judges and Magiſtrates may with full as good reaſon be reproached with Ill-nature for putting the laws in execution againſt a thief or impoſtor—The ſame will hold in the republic of Letters, if the Critics and Judges will let every ignorant pretender to ſcribbling paſs on the world.

 Theobald,

Theobald, Lett. to Mist, June 22, 1728.

ATTACKS may be levelled, either againſt Failures in Genius, or againſt the Pretenſions of writing without one.

Concanen, Ded. to the Author of the Dunciad.

A Satire upon Dullneſs is a thing that has been uſed and allowed in all ages.

Out of thine own Mouth will I judge thee, wicked Scribbler!

TESTIMONIES OF AUTHORS

CONCERNING

OUR POET AND HIS WORKS.

M. SCRIBLERUS Lectori S.

BEFORE we present thee with our exercitations on this most delectable poem (drawn from the many volumes of our Adversaria on modern authors) we shall here, according to the laudable usage of editors, collect the various judgments of the learned concerning our Poet: Various indeed, not only of different authors, but of the same author at different seasons. Nor shall we gather only the testimonies of such eminent wits, as would of course descend to posterity, and consequently be read without our collection; but we shall likewise with incredible labour seek out for divers others, which, but for this our diligence, could never at the distance of a few months appear to the eye of the most curious. Hereby thou may'st not only receive the delectation of variety, but also arrive at a more certain judgment, by a grave and circumspect comparison of the witnesses with each other, or of each with himself. Hence also thou wilt be enabled to draw reflections, not only of a critical but a moral nature, by being let into many particulars of the perſon as well as genius, and of the fortune as well as merit, of our Author: In which if I relate ſome things of little concern peradventure to thee, and ſome of as little even to him; I entreat thee to conſider how minutely all true critics and commentators are wont to inſiſt upon ſuch, and how material they ſeem to themſelves, if to none other. Forgive me, gentle reader, if (following learned example) I ever and anon become tedious: allow me to take the ſame pains to find whether my author were good or bad, well or ill-natured, modeſt or arrogant; as another, whether his author was fair or brown, ſhort or tall, or whether he wore a coat or a caſſock.

We purpoſed to begin with his Life, Parentage, and Education: But as to theſe, even his contemporaries do exceedingly differ. One ſaith [a], he was educated at home; another [b], that he was bred at St. Omer's by Jeſuits; a third [c], not at St. Omer's, but at Oxford; a fourth [d], that he had no univerſity education at all. Thoſe who allow him to be bred at home, differ as much concerning his Tutor: One ſaith [e], he was kept by his father on purpoſe; a ſecond [f], that he was an itinerant prieſt; a third [g], that

---

[a] Giles Jacob's Lives of Poets, vol. ii. in his Life.
[b] Dennis's Reflections on the Eſſay on Criticiſm, p. 4.
[c] Dunciad diſſected, p. 4.
[d] Guardian, No 40.
[e] Jacob's Lives, &c. vol. ii.
[f] Dunciad diſſected, p. 4.
[g] Farmer P. and his ſon.

that he was a parson; one [h] calleth him a secular clergyman of the church of Rome; another [i], a monk. As little do they agree about his father, whom one [k] supposeth, like the father of Hesiod, a tradesman or merchant; another [l], a husbandman; another [m], a hatter, &c. Nor has an author been wanting to give our poet such a father, as Apuleius hath to Plato, Jamblichus to Pythagoras, and divers to Homer, namely a Demon: For thus Mr. Gildon [n]: "Certain it is, that his original is not from Adam, but the Devil; and that he wanted nothing but horns and tail to be the exact resemblance of his infernal Father." Finding therefore such contrariety of Opinions, and (whatever be ours of this sort of generation) not being fond to enter into controversy, we shall defer writing the Life of our Poet, till authors can determine among themselves what parents or education he had, or whether he had any education or parents at all.

Proceed we to what is more certain, his Works, though not less uncertain the judgments concerning them;

---

[h] Dunciad dissected. [i] Characters of the times, p. 45.

[k] Female Dunciad, p. ult. [l] Dunciad dissected.

[m] Roome, Paraphrase on the ivth of Genesis, printed 1729.

[n] Character of Mr. P. and his Writings, in a Letter to a Friend, printed for S. Popping, 1716, p. 10. Curl, in his Key to the Dunciad, (first edit. said to be printed for A. Dodd), in the 10th page, declared Gildon to be author of that libel; though in the subsequent editions of his Key he left out this assertion, and affirmed (in the Curliad, p. 4. and 8.) that it was written by Dennis only.

them; beginning with his Eſſay on Criticiſm, of which hear firſt the moſt ancient of Critics,

Mr. John Dennis.

"His precepts are falſe or trivial, or both; his thoughts are crude and abortive, his expreſſions abſurd, his numbers harſh and unmuſical, his rhymes trivial and common:—inſtead of majeſty, we have ſomething that is very mean; inſtead of gravity, ſomething that is very boyiſh; and inſtead of perſpicuity and lucid order, we have but too often obſcurity and confuſion." And in another place: "What rare numbers are here! Would not one ſwear that this youngſter had eſpouſed ſome antiquated muſe, who had ſued out a divorce from ſome ſuperannued ſinner, upon account of impotence, and who being poxed by her former ſpouſe, has got the gout in her decrepid age, which makes her hobble ſo damnably [o]."

No leſs peremptory is the cenſure of our hypercritical Hiſtorian,

Mr. Oldmixon.

"I dare not ſay any thing of the Eſſay on Criticiſm in verſe; but if any more curious reader has diſcovered in it ſomething new which is not in Dryden's prefaces, dedications, and his Eſſay on Dramatic Poetry, not to mention the French critics, I ſhould be very glad to have the benefit of the diſcovery [p]."

He

[o] Reflections critical and ſatirical on a Rhapſody, called an Eſſay on Criticiſm. Printed for Bernard Lintot, octavo.

[p] Eſſay on Criticiſm in proſe, octavo, 1728, by the author of The Critical Hiſtory of England.

He is followed (as in fame, so in judgment) by the modest and simple-minded

MR. LEONARD WELSTEAD;

Who, out of great respect to our poet not naming him, doth yet glance at his Essay, together with the Duke of Buckingham's, and the Criticisms of Dryden, and of Horace, which he more openly taxeth [q]: "As to the numerous treatises, essays, arts, &c. both in verse and prose, that have been written by the moderns on this ground-work, they do but hackney the same thoughts over again, making them still more trite. Most of their pieces are nothing but a pert, insipid heap of common-place. Horace has even in his Art of Poetry thrown out several things which plainly shew he thought an Art of Poetry was of no use, even while he was writing one."

To all which great Authorities, we can only oppose that of

MR. ADDISON.

"[r] The Art of Criticism (saith he) which was published some months since, is a master-piece in its kind. The observations follow one another, like those in Horace's Art of Poetry, without that methodical regularity which would have been requisite in a prose writer. They are some of them uncommon, but such as the reader must assent to, when he sees them explained with that ease and perspicuity in which

[q] Preface to his Poems, p. 18, 53. [r] Spectator, No 253.

which they are delivered. As for thoſe which are the moſt known and the moſt received, they are placed in ſo beautiful a light, and illuſtrated with ſuch apt alluſions, that they have in them all the graces of novelty; and make the reader, who was before acquainted with them, ſtill more convinced of their truth and ſolidity. And here give me leave to mention what Monſieur Boileau has ſo well enlarged upon in the preface to his works: That wit and fine writing doth not conſiſt ſo much in advancing things that are new, as in giving things that are known an agreeable turn. It is impoſſible for us who live in the latter ages of the world, to make obſervations in criticiſm, morality, or any art or ſcience, which have not been touched upon by others; we have little elſe left us, but to repreſent the common ſenſe of mankind in more ſtrong, more beautiful, or more uncommon lights. If a reader examines Horace's Art of Poetry, he will find but few precepts in it which he may not meet with in Ariſtotle, and which were not commonly known by all the poets of the Auguſtan age. His way of expreſſing and applying them, not his invention of them, is what we are chiefly to admire.

"Longinus, in his reflections, has given us the ſame kind of ſublime, which he obſerves in the ſeveral paſſages that occaſioned them: I cannot but take notice that our Engliſh author has after the ſame manner exemplified ſeveral of the precepts in

the

the very precepts themſelves." He then produces ſome inſtances of a particular beauty in the numbers, and concludes with ſaying, that "there are three poems in our tongue of the ſame nature, and each a maſter-piece in its kind; The Eſſay on Tranſlated Verſe; the Eſſay on the Art of Poetry; and the Eſſay on Criticiſm."

Of Windſor Foreſt, poſitive is the judgment of the affirmative

Mr. JOHN DENNIS.

"[s] That it is a wretched rhapſody, impudently writ in emulation of the Cooper's Hill of Sir John Denham: The author of it is obſcure, is ambiguous, is affected, is temerarious, is barbarous."

But the author of the Diſpenſary,

Dr. GARTH,

in the preface to his poem of Claremont[t], differs from this opinion; "Thoſe who have ſeen theſe two excellent poems of Cooper's Hill, and Windſor Foreſt, the One written by Sir John Denham, the other by Mr. Pope, will ſhew a great deal of candour if they approve of this."

Of the Epiſtle of Eloiſa, we are told by the obſcure writer of a poem called Sawney, "That becauſe Prior's Henry and Emma charmed the fineſt taſtes, our author writ his Eloiſe in oppoſition to it; but forgot innocence and virtue: if you take away her tender

[s] Letter to B. B. at the end of the Remarks on Pope's Homer, 1717. [t] Printed 1728, p. 12.

tender thoughts, and her fierce desires, all the rest is of no value." In which, methinks, his judgment resembles that of a French taylor on a villa and gardens by the Thames: "All this is very fine, but take away the river, and it is good for nothing."

But very contrary hereunto was the opinion of

Mr. PRIOR

himself, saying in his Alma [u],

"O Abelard! ill-fated youth,
Thy tale will justify this truth.
But well I weet, thy cruel wrong
Adorns a nobler Poet's song:
Dan Pope, for thy misfortune griev'd,
With kind concern and skill has weav'd
A silken web; and ne'er shall fade
Its colours: gently has he laid
The mantle o'er thy sad distress,
And Venus shall the texture bless," &c.

Come we now to his translation of the Iliad, celebrated by numerous pens, yet shall it suffice to mention the indefatigable

Sir RICHARD BLACKMORE, Kt.

Who (though otherwise a severe censurer of our author) yet styleth this a "laudable translation [w]."

That ready writer

Mr. OLDMIXON,

in his forementioned essay, frequently commends the same. And the painful

Mr.

---

[u] Alma, Cant. ii.   [w] In his Essays, Vol. i. printed for E. Curl.

Mr. Lewis Theobald

thus extolls it[x]: "The ſpirit of Homer breathes all through this tranſlation.—I am in doubt, whether I ſhould moſt admire the juſtneſs to the original, or the force and beauty of the language, or the ſounding variety of the numbers: But when I find all theſe meet, it puts me in mind of what the poet ſays of one of his heroes, That he alone raiſed and flung with eaſe a weighty ſtone, that two common men could not lift from the ground; juſt ſo, one ſingle perſon has performed in this tranſlation, what I once deſpaired to have ſeen done by the force of ſeveral maſterly hands." Indeed the ſame gentleman appears to have changed his ſentiment in his Eſſay on the Art of ſinking in Reputation, (printed in Miſt's Journal, March 30, 1728), where he ſays thus: "In order to ſink in Reputation, let him take it into his head to deſcend into Homer (let the world wonder, as it will, how the devil he got there) and pretend to do him into Engliſh, ſo his verſion denote his neglect of the manner how." Strange variation! We are told in

Mist's Journal, June 8,

"That this tranſlation of the Iliad was not in all reſpects conformable to the fine taſte of his friend Mr. Addiſon; inſomuch that he employed a younger muſe, in an undertaking of this kind, which he ſuperviſed

[x] Cenſor, Vol. ii. N° 33.

ſupervifed himſelf." Whether Mr. Addiſon did find it conformable to his taſte, or not, beſt appears from his own teſtimony the year following its publication, in theſe words:

Mr. ADDISON, FREEHOLDER, N° 40.

"When I conſider myſelf as a Britiſh freeholder, I am in a particular manner pleaſed with the labours of thoſe who have improved our language with the tranſlations of old Greek and Latin authors.—We have already moſt of their Hiſtorians in our own tongue, and, what is more for the honour of our language, it has been taught to expreſs with elegance the greateſt of their poets in each nation. The illiterate among our own countrymen may learn to judge from Dryden's Virgil of the moſt perfect epic performance. And thoſe parts of Homer which have been publiſhed already by Mr. Pope, give us reaſon to think that the Iliad will appear in Engliſh with as little diſadvantage to that immortal poem."

As to the reſt, there is a ſlight miſtake, for this younger muſe was an elder: Nor was the gentleman (who is a friend of our author) employed by Mr. Addiſon to tranſlate it after him, ſince he ſaith himſelf that he did it before [y]. Contrariwiſe that Mr. Addiſon engaged our author in this work appeareth by declaration thereof in the preface to the Iliad, printed ſome time before his death, and by his own letters

[y] Vid. pref. to Mr. Tickel's tranſlation of the firſt book of the Iliad, 4to.

letters of October 26, and November 2, 1713. Where he declares it is his opinion, that no other perſon was equal to it.

Next comes his Shakeſpear on the ſtage: "Let him (quoth one, whom I take to be Mr. Theobald, Miſt's Journal, June 8, 1728), publiſh ſuch an author as he has leaſt ſtudied, and forget to diſcharge even the dull duty of an editor. In this project let him lend the bookſeller his name (for a competent ſum of Money) to promote the credit of an exorbitant ſubſcription." Gentle reader, be pleaſed to caſt thine eye on the propoſal below quoted, and on what follows (ſome months after the former aſſertion) in the ſame Journaliſt of June 8: "The bookſeller propoſed the book by ſubſcription, and raiſed ſome thouſands of pounds for the ſame: I believe the gentleman did not ſhare in the profits of this extravagant ſubſcription.

"After the Iliad, he undertook (ſaith

MIST'S JOURNAL, June 8, 1728)

the ſequel of that work, the Odyſſey; and having ſecured the ſucceſs by a numerous ſubſcription, he employed ſome underlings to perform what, according to his propoſals, ſhould come from his own hands." To which heavy charge we can in truth oppoſe nothing but the words of

MR. POPE'S PROPOSAL for the ODYSSEY, (printed for J. Watts, Jan. 10, 1724.)

"I take this occaſion to declare that the ſubſcription for Shakeſpear belongs wholly to Mr. Tonſon: And

that

that the benefit of this Propoſal is not ſolely for my own uſe, but for that of two of my friends, who have aſſiſted me in this work." But theſe very gentlemen are extolled above our poet himſelf in another of Miſt's Journals, March 30, 1728, ſaying, "That he would not adviſe Mr. Pope to try the experiment again of getting a great part of a book done by aſſiſtants, leſt thoſe extraneous parts ſhould unhappily aſcend to the ſublime, and retard the declenſion of the whole." Behold! theſe Underlings are become good writers!

If any ſay, that before the ſaid propoſals were printed, the ſubſcription was begun without declaration of ſuch aſſiſtance; verily thoſe who ſet it on foot, or (as the term is) ſecured it, to wit, the right honourable the Lord Viſçount HARCOURT, were he living, would teſtify, and the right honourable the Lord BATHURST, now living, doth teſtify, the ſame is a falſhood.

Sorry I am, that perſons profeſſing to be learned, or of whatever rank of authors, ſhould either falſely tax, or be falſely taxed. Yet let us, who are only reporters, be impartial in our citations, and proceed.

MIST'S JOURNAL, June 8, 1728.

"Mr. Addiſon raiſed this author from obſcurity, obtained him the acquaintance and friendſhip of the whole body of our nobility, and transferred his powerful intereſts with thoſe great men to this riſing bard, who frequently levied by that means unuſual

contributions

contributions on the public." Which ſurely cannot be, if, as the author of the Dunciad diſſected reporteth; "Mr. Wycherley had before introduced him into a familiar acquaintance with the greateſt Peers and brighteſt Wits then living."

"No ſooner (ſaith the ſame Journaliſt) was his body lifeleſs, but this author reviving his reſentment, libelled the memory of his departed friend; and what was ſtill more heinous, made the ſcandal public." Grievous the accuſation! unknown the accuſer! the perſon accuſed no witneſs in his own cauſe; the perſon, in whoſe regard accuſed, dead! But if there be living any one nobleman whoſe friendſhip, yea any one gentleman whoſe ſubſcription Mr. Addiſon procured to our author; let him ſtand forth, that truth may appear! "Amicus Plato, amicus Socrates, ſed magis amica veritas." In verity the whole ſtory of the libel is a lie; witneſs thoſe perſons of integrity, who ſeveral years before Mr. Addiſon's deceaſe, did ſee and approve of the ſaid verſes, in no wiſe a libel, but a friendly rebuke, ſent privately in our author's own hand to Mr. Addiſon himſelf, and never made public, till after their own Journals, and Curl had printed the ſame. One name alone, which I am here authoriſed to declare, will ſufficiently evince the truth, that of the right honourable the Earl of Burlington.

Next is he taxed with a crime (in the opinion of ſome authors, I doubt, more heinous than any in morality),

morality), to wit, plagiarism, from the inventive and quaint-conceited

JAMES MOORE SMITH, Gent.

"[a] Upon reading the third volume of Pope's Miscellanies, I found five lines which I thought excellent; and happening to praise them, a gentleman procured a modern comedy, (the Rival Modes), published last year, where were the same verses to a tittle.

"These gentlemen are undoubtedly the first plagiaries that pretend to make a reputation by stealing from a man's works in his own life-time, and out of a public print." Let us join to this what is written by the author of the Rival Modes, the said Mr. James Moore Smith, in a letter to our author himself, who had informed him, a month before that play was acted, Jan. 27, 1726-7, that "These verses, which he had before given him leave to insert in it, would be known for his, some copies being got abroad. He desires, nevertheless, that since the lines had been read in his comedy to several, Mr. P. would not deprive it of them;" &c. Surely if we add the testimonies of the Lord Bolingbroke, of the lady to whom the said verses were originally addressed, of Hugh Bethel Esq. and others who knew them as our author's long before the said gentleman composed his play; it is hoped, the ingenuous that affect not error, will rectify their opinion by the suffrage of so honourable personages.

And

[a] Daily Journal, March 18, 1728.

And yet followeth another charge, inſinuating no leſs than his enmity both to Church and State, which could come from no other informer than the ſaid

Mr. JAMES MOORE SMITH.

"[a] The Memoirs of a Pariſh Clerk was a very dull and unjuſt abuſe of a perſon who wrote in defence of our Religion and Conſtitution, and who has been dead many years." This ſeemeth alſo moſt untrue; it being known to divers that theſe Memoirs were written at the ſeat of the Lord Harcourt in Oxfordſhire, before that excellent perſon (biſhop Burnet's) death, and many years before the appearance of that hiſtory, of which they are pretended to be an abuſe. Moſt true it is that Mr. Moore had ſuch a deſign, and was himſelf the man who preſt Dr. Arbuthnot and Mr. Pope to aſſiſt him therein; and that he borrowed thoſe Memoirs of our author, when that hiſtory came forth, with intent to turn them to ſuch abuſe. But being able to obtain from our author but one ſingle hint, and either changing his mind, or having more mind than ability, he contented himſelf to keep the ſaid Memoirs, and read them as his own to all his acquaintance. A noble perſon there is, into whoſe company Mr. Pope once chanced to introduce him, who well remembereth the converſation of Mr. Moore to have turned upon the "Contempt he had for the work of that reverend prelate,

[a] Daily Journal, April 3, 1728.

prelate, and how full he was of a design he declared himself to have of exposing it." This noble person is the Earl of Peterborough.

Here in truth should we crave pardon of all the foresaid right honourable and worthy personages, for having mentioned them in the same page with such weekly riff-raff railers and rhymers; but that we had their ever-honoured commands for the same; and that they are introduced not as witnesses in the controversy, but as witnesses that cannot be controverted; not to dispute, but to decide.

Certain it is, that dividing our writers into two classes, of such who were acquaintance, and of such who were strangers to our author; the former are those who speak well, and the other those who speak evil of him. Of the first class, the most noble

JOHN Duke of BUCKINGHAM

sums up his character in these lines;

"[b] And yet so wond'rous, so sublime a thing,
As the great Iliad, scarce could make me sing;
Unless I justly could at once commend
A good companion, and as firm a friend.
One moral, or a mere well-natur'd deed,
Can all desert in sciences exceed."

So also is he decyphered by the honourable

SIMON HARCOURT.

"[c] Say

---

[b] Verses to Mr. P. on his translation of Homer.

" [c] Say, wondrous youth, what column wilt thou chuſe,
What laurel'd arch for thy triumphant Muſe?
Tho' each great ancient court thee to his ſhrine,
Tho' ev'ry laurel through the dome be thine,
Go to the good and juſt, an awful train!
Thy ſoul's delight."——

Recorded in like manner for his virtuous diſpoſition, and gentle bearing, by one ingenious

Mr. WALTER HART,

in this apoſtrophe:

" [d] O! ever worthy, ever crown'd with praiſe!
Bleſt in thy life, and bleſt in all thy lays.
Add, that the Siſters ev'ry thought refine,
And ev'n thy life be faultleſs as thy line.
Yet envy ſtill with fiercer rage purſues,
Obſcures the virtue, and defames the Muſe.
A ſoul like thine, in pain, in grief, reſign'd,
Views with juſt ſcorn the malice of mankind."

The witty and moral ſatiriſt

Dr. EDWARD YOUNG,

wiſhing ſome check to the corruption and evil manners of the times, calleth out upon our poet to undertake a taſk ſo worthy of his virtue:

" [e] Why ſlumbers Pope, who leads the Muſes' train,
Nor hears that virtue, which he loves, complain?"

Mr.

---

[c] Poem prefixed to his works. [d] In his poems, printed for B. Lintot. [e] Univerſal Paſſion, Sat. I.

Mr. Mallet,

in his epiftle on Verbal Criticifm:

" Whofe life feverely fcan'd, tranfcends his lays;
For wit fupreme, is but his fecond praife."

Mr. Hammond,

that delicate and correct imitator of Tibullus, in his Love Elegies, Elegy xiv.

" Now, fir'd by Pope and Virtue, leave the age,
In low purfuit of felf-undoing wrong,
And trace the author through his moral page,
Whofe blamelefs life ftill anfwers to his fong."

Mr. Thomson,

in his elegant and philofophical poem of the Seafons:

" Altho' not fweeter his own Homer fings,
Yet is his life the more endearing fong."

To the fame tune alfo fingeth that learned clerk of Suffolk

Mr. William Broome.

" [f] Thus, nobly rifing in fair Virtue's caufe,
From thy own life tranfcribe th' unerring laws."

And, to clofe all, hear the reverend Dean of St. Patrick's:

" A foul with ev'ry virtue fraught,
By Patriots, Priefts, and Poets taught.
Whofe filial piety excells
Whatever Grecian ftory tells.
A genius for each bus'nefs fit,
Whofe meaneft talent is his wit," &c.

Let

[f] In his poems, and at the end of the Odyffey.

Let us now recreate thee by turning to the other ſide, and ſhewing his character drawn by thoſe with whom he never converſed, and whoſe countenances he could not know, though turned againſt him: Firſt again commencing with the high voiced and never enough quoted

MR. JOHN DENNIS;

who, in his Reflections on the Eſſay on Criticiſm, thus deſcribeth him: "A little affected hypocrite, who has nothing in his mouth but candour, truth, friendſhip, good-nature, humanity, and magnanimity. He is ſo great a lover of falſehood, that whenever he has a mind to calumniate his cotemporaries, he brands them with ſome defect which is juſt *contrary to ſome good quality*, for which all their *friends and their acquaintance* commend them. He ſeems to have a particular pique to *people of quality*, and authors of that rank. He muſt derive his religion from St. Omer's."—But in the Character of Mr. P. and his writings, (printed by S. Popping 1716), he ſaith, "though he is a profeſſor of the worſt religion, yet he *laughs at it*;" but that "nevertheleſs, he is a *virulent Papiſt*; and yet a *pillar* for the *church of England*."

Of both which opinions

MR. LEWIS THEOBALD

ſeems alſo to be; declaring, in Miſt's Journal of June 22, 1718, "That if he is not ſhrewdly abuſed, he made it his buſineſs to cackle to both Parties in

 their

their own ſentiments."[a] But, as to his *pique* againſt *people of quality*, the ſame Journaliſt doth not agree, but ſaith, (May 8, 1728), "He had, by ſome means or other, the *acquaintance and friendſhip of the whole body of our nobility*."

However contradictory this may appear, Mr. Dennis and Gildon, in the character laſt cited, make it all plain, by aſſuring us, "That he is a creature that reconciles all contradictions; he is a beaſt, and a man; a Whig and a Tory; a writer (at one and the ſame time) of [g] Guardians and Examiners; an aſſerter of liberty, and of the diſpenſing power of kings; a Jeſuitical profeſſor of truth; a baſe and a foul pretender to candour." So that, upon the whole account, we muſt conclude him either to have been a great hypocrite, or a very honeſt man; a terrible impoſer upon both parties, or very moderate to either.

Be it as to the judicious reader ſhall ſeem good. Sure it is, he is little favoured of certain authors, whoſe wrath is perilous: for one declares he ought to have a *price ſet on his head*, and to be hunted down as a *wild beaſt* [h]. Another proteſts that he does not know *what may happen*; adviſes him to *inſure his perſon*; ſays he has *bitter enemies*, and expreſly declares it will be well if he *eſcapes with his life* [i].

One

[g] The names of two weekly papers.

[h] Theobald, letter in Miſt's Journal, June 22, 1728.

[i] Smedley, Pref. to Gulliveriana, p. 14, 16.

One desires he would *cut his own throat, or hang himself* [k]. But Pasquin seemed rather inclined it should be done by the government, representing him engaged in grievous designs with a Lord of Parliament, then under prosecution [l]. Mr. Dennis himself hath written to a *Minister*, that he is one of the most *dangerous persons in this kingdom* [m]; and assureth the public, that he is an *open* and *mortal enemy* to his country; a monster, that *will*, one day, shew as *daring a soul* as a *mad Indian*, who runs a *muck* to kill the first Christian he meets [n]. Another gives information of *Treason* discovered in his poem [o]. Mr. Curl boldly supplies an imperfect verse with *Kings* and *Princesses* [p]. And one Matthew Concanen, yet more impudent, publishes at length the two most SACRED NAMES in this nation, as members of the Dunciad [q]!

This is prodigious! yet it is almost as strange, that in the midst of these invectives his greatest enemies have (I know not how) born testimony to some merit in him.

Mr.

---

[k] Gulliveriana, p. 332. [l] Anno 1723. [m] Anno 1729.

[n] Pref. to Rem. on the Rape of the Lock, p. 12. and in the last page of that treatise.

[o] Page 6, 7. of the Preface, by Concanen, to a book intitled, A collection of all the Letters, Essays, Verses, and Advertisements, occasioned by Pope and Swift's Miscellanies. Printed for A. Moore, octavo, 1712.

[p] Key to the Dunciad, 3d edit. p. 18.

[q] A list of persons, &c. at the end of the forementioned Collection of all the Letters, Essays, &c.

Mr. THEOBALD,

in cenſuring his Shakeſpear, declares, "He has ſo great an *eſteem* for Mr. Pope, and ſo high an *opinion* of his *genius* and *excellencies*; that notwithſtanding he profeſſes a *veneration almoſt riſing to Idolatry* for the writings of this inimitable poet, he would be very loth even to do *him* juſtice, at the expence of that *other gentleman*'s character [r]."

Mr. CHARLES GILDON,

after having violently attacked him in many pieces, at laſt came to wiſh from his heart, "That Mr. Pope would be prevailed upon to give us Ovid's Epiſtles by his hand, for it is certain we ſee the original of Sappho to Phaon with much more life and likeneſs in his verſion, than in that of Sir Car. Scrope. And this (he adds) is the more to be wiſhed, because in the Engliſh tongue we have ſcarce any thing truly and naturally written upon Love [s]." He alſo, in taxing Sir Richard Blackmore for his heterodox opinions of Homer, challengeth him to anſwer what Mr. Pope hath ſaid in his preface to that poet.

Mr. OLDMIXON

calls him a great maſter of our tongue; declares "the purity and perfection of the Engliſh language to be found in his Homer; and, ſaying there are more good verſes in Dryden's Virgil than in any other work, excepts this of our author only [t]."

The

---

[r] Introduction to his Skakeſpear reſtored, in quarto, p. 3.

[s] Commentary on the Duke of Buckingham's Eſſay, octavo, 1721, p. 97, 98.

[t] In his proſe Eſſay on Criticiſm.

The author of a Letter to Mr. Cibber ſays, "[u] Pope *was* ſo good a verſifier [*once*] that his predeceſſor Mr. Dryden, and his cotemporary Mr. Prior excepted, the harmony of his numbers *is* equal to any body's. And, that he *had* all the merit that a man can have that way." And

Mr. THOMAS COOKE,

after much blemiſhing our author's Homer, crieth out,

"But in his other works what beauties ſhine,
While ſweeteſt muſic dwells in ev'ry line!
Theſe he admir'd, on theſe he ſtamp'd his praiſe,
And bade them live to brighten future days [w]."

So alſo one who takes the name of

H. STANHOPE,

the maker of certain verſes to Duncan Campbell [x], in that poem, which is wholly a ſatire on Mr. Pope, confeſſeth,

"'Tis true, if fineſt notes alone could ſhow
(Tun'd juſtly high, or regularly low)
That we ſhould fame to theſe mere vocals give;
Pope more than we can offer ſhould receive:
For when ſome gliding river is his theme,
His lines run ſmoother than the ſmootheſt
ſtream," &c.

MIST'S JOURNAL, June 8, 1728.

Although

[u] Printed by J. Roberts, 1742, p. 11.

[w] Battle of Poets, folio, p. 15.

[x] Printed under the title of the Progreſs of Dulneſs, duodecimo, 1728.

Although he says, "The smooth numbers of the Dunciad are all that recommend it, nor has it any other merit;" yet that same paper hath these words: "The author is allowed to be a perfect master of an easy and elegant versification. *In all his works* we find the most *happy turns* and *natural similies*, wonderfully short and thick sown."

The Essay on the Dunciad also owns, p. 25. it is very full of *beautiful images*. But the panegyric, which crowns all that can be said on this poem, is bestowed by our laureate,

Mr. COLLEY CIBBER,

who "grants it to be a better poem of its kind than ever was writ:" but adds, "it was a victory over a parcel of poor wretches, whom it was almost cowardice to conquer.—A man might as well triumph for having killed so many silly flies that offended him. Could he have let them alone, by this time, poor souls! they had been buried in oblivion [y]." Here we see our excellent Laureate allows the justice of the satire on every man in it, but *himself*; as the great Mr. Dennis did before him.

The said

Mr. DENNIS and GILDON,

in the most furious of all their works the forecited character (p. 5.) do in concert [z] confess, "That some men

[y] Cibber's Letter to Mr. Pope, p. 9, 12.

[z] *in concert*] Hear how Mr. Dennis hath proved our mistake in this place. "As to my writing in *concert* with Mr. Gildon, I declare

men of *good understanding* value him for his rhymes." And (p. 17) "That he has got, like Mr. Bays in the Rehearsal, (that is, like Mr. Dryden) a notable knack at rhyming, and writing smooth verse."

Of his Essay on Man, numerous were the praises bestowed by his avowed enemies, in the imagination that the same was not written by him, as it was printed anonymously.

Thus sang of it even

BEZALEEL MORRIS.

"Auspicious bard! while all admire thy strain,
All but the selfish, ignorant, and vain;
I, whom no bribe to servile flatt'ry drew,
Must pay the tribute to thy merit due:

Thy

I declare upon the honour and word of a gentleman, that I never wrote so much as one line in *concert* with any one man whatsoever. And these two Letters from Gildon will plainly shew that we are not writers in *concert* with each other.

"Sir,

—— "The height of my ambition is to please men of the best judgment; and finding that I have entertained my master agreeably, I have the extent of the reward of my labour."

"Sir,

"I had not the opportunity of hearing of your excellent pamphlet till this day. I am infinitely satisfied and pleased with it, and hope you will meet with that encouragement your admirable performance deserves, &c.

"CH. GILDON."

"Now is it not plain, that any one who sends such compliments to another, has not been used to write in partnership with him to whom he sends them?" Dennis, Rem. on the Dunc. p. 50. Mr. Dennis is therefore welcome to take this piece to himself.

Thy muſe ſublime, ſignificant, and clear,
Alike informs the Soul, and charms the Ear."

And

Mr. Leonard Welsted

thus wrote [a] to the unknown author on the firſt publication of the ſaid Eſſay: "I muſt own, after the reception which the vileſt and moſt immoral ribaldry hath lately met with, I was ſurprized to ſee what I had long deſpaired, a performance deſerving the name of a poet. Such, Sir, is your work. It is, indeed, above all commendation, and ought to have been publiſhed in an age and country more worthy of it. If my teſtimony be of weight any where, you are ſure to have it in the ampleſt manner," &c. &c. &c.

Thus we ſee every one of his works hath been extolled by one or other of his moſt inveterate enemies; and to the ſucceſs of them all they do unanimouſly give teſtimony. But it is ſufficient, inſtar omnium, to behold the great critic, Mr. Dennis, ſorely lamenting it, even from the Eſſay on Criticiſm to this day of the Dunciad! "A moſt notorious inſtance (quoth he) of the depravity of genius and taſte, the *approbation* this Eſſay meets with [b].—I can ſafely affirm, that I never attacked any of theſe writings, unleſs they had *ſucceſs* infinitely beyond their merit.—This, though an empty, has been

[a] In a letter under his hand, dated March 12, 1733.
[b] Dennis, Pref. to his Reflect. on the Eſſay on Criticiſm.

been a *popular* scribler. The epidemic madness of the times has given him *reputation* [c].—If, after the the cruel treatment so many extraordinary men (Spencer, Lord Bacon, Ben. Johnson, Milton, Butler, Otway, and others) have received from this country, for these last hundred years, I should shift the scene, and shew all that penury changed at once to riot and profuseness; and more squandered away upon *one object*, than would have satisfied the greater part of those extraordinary men; the reader to whom this one creature should be unknown, would fancy him a prodigy of art and nature, would believe that all the great qualities of these persons were centered in him alone:—But if I should venture to assure him, that the PEOPLE of ENGLAND had made such a choice—the reader would either believe me a *malicious enemy*, and *slanderer*; or that the reign of the last (Queen Anne's) *Ministry* was designed by fate to encourage *Fools* [d]."

But it happens, that this our poet never had any place, pension, or gratuity, in any shape, from the said glorious Queen, or any of her Ministers. All he owed, in the whole course of his life, to any court, was a subscription for his Homer of 200*l.* from King George I, and 100*l.* from the Prince and Princess.

However, lest we imagine our author's Success was constant and universal, they acquaint us of certain

[c] Pref. to his Rem. on Homer. [d] Rem. on Hom. p. 8, 9.

certain works in a less degree of repute, whereof, although owned by others, yet do they assure us he is the writer. Of this sort Mr. DENNIS [e] ascribes to him *two farces*, whose names he does not tell, but assures us that *there is not one jest in them*: And an imitation of Horace, whose title he does not mention, but assures us *it is much more execrable than all his works* [f]. The DAILY JOURNAL, May 11, 1728, assures us, "He is below Tom Durfey in the Drama, because (as that writer thinks) the Marriage-Hater matched, and the Boarding-School, are better than the What-d'ye-call-it;" which is not Mr. P's, but Mr. Gay's. Mr. GILDON assures us, in his New Rehearsal, p. 48. "That he was writing a *play* of the Lady Jane Grey;" but it afterwards proved to be Mr. Rowe's. We are assured by another, "He wrote a pamphlet called Dr. Andrew Tripe [g];" which proved to be one Dr. Wagstaff's. Mr. THEOBALD assures, in Mist of the 27th of April, "That the treatise of the *Profound* is very dull, and that Mr. Pope is the author of it." The writer of Gulliveriana is of another opinion; and says, "the whole, or greatest part, of the merit of this treatise must and can only be ascribed to Gulliver [h]." [Here, gentle reader! cannot I but smile at the strange blindness and positiveness of men; knowing the said treatise to appertain to none other but to me Martinus Scriblerus.]

We

[e] Rem. on Homer, p. 8. [f] Character of Mr. Pope, p. 7.
[g] Ibid. p. 6. [h] Gulliv. p. 336.

We are aſſured in Miſt of June 8, "That his own *plays* and *farces* would better have adorned the Dunciad, than thoſe of Mr. Theobald; for he had neither genius for tragedy nor comedy." Which, whether true or not, it is not eaſy to judge; in as much as he had attempted neither. Unleſs we will take it for granted, with Mr. Cibber, that his being once very angry at hearing a friend's Play abuſed, was an infallible proof the play was his own; the ſaid Mr. Cibber thinking it impoſſible for a man to be much concerned for any but himſelf: "Now let any man judge (ſaith he) by this concern, who was the true mother of the child [i]?"

But from all that hath been ſaid, the diſcerning reader will collect, that it little availed our author to have any candour, ſince when he declared he did not write for others, it was not credited; as little to have any modeſty, ſince, when he declined writing in any way himſelf, the preſumption of others was imputed to him. If he ſingly enterprized one great work, he was taxed of boldneſs and madneſs to a prodigy [k]: If he took aſſiſtants in another, it was complained of, and repreſented as a great injury to the publick [l]. The loftieſt heroics, the loweſt ballads, treatiſes againſt the ſtate or church, ſatires on lords and ladies, raillery on wits and authors, ſquabbles with

[i] Cibber's Letter to Mr. P. p. 19.

[k] Burnet's Homerides, p. 1. of his tranſlation of the Iliad.

[l] The London and Miſt's Journals, on his undertaking the Odyſſey.

with bookſellers, or even full and true accounts of monſters, poiſons, and murders; of any hereof was there nothing ſo good, nothing ſo bad, which had not at one or other ſeaſon been to him aſcribed. If it bore no author's name, then lay he concealed; if it did, he fathered it upon that author to be yet better concealed: If it reſembled any of his ſtyles, then it was evident; if it did not, then diſguiſed he it on ſet purpoſe. Yea, even direct oppoſitions in religion, principles, and politics, have equally been ſuppoſed in him inherent. Surely a moſt rare and ſingular character! Of which let the reader make what he can.

Doubtleſs moſt commentators would hence take occaſion to turn all to their author's advantage, and from the teſtimony of his very enemies would affirm, That his capacity was boundleſs, as well as his imagination; that he was a perfect maſter of all ſtyles, and all arguments; and that there was in thoſe times no other writer, in any kind, of any degree of excellence, ſave he himſelf. But as this is not our own ſentiment, we ſhall determine on nothing; but leave thee, gentle reader, to ſteer thy judgment equally between various opinions, and to chuſe whether thou wilt incline to the Teſtimonies of Authors avowed, or of Authors concealed; of thoſe who knew him, or of thoſe who knew him not. P.

MARTINUS SCRIBLERUS

OF THE POEM*.

THIS poem, as it celebrateth the moſt grave and ancient of things, Chaos, Night, and Dulneſs; ſo is it of the moſt grave and ancient kind. Homer (ſaith Ariſtotle) was the firſt who gave the *form*, and (ſaith Horace) who adapted the *meaſure*, to heroic poeſy. But even before this, may be rationally preſumed from what the ancients have left written, was a piece by Homer compoſed, of like nature and matter with this of our poet. For of epic ſort it appeareth to have been, yet of matter ſurely not unpleaſant, witneſs what is reported of it by the learned archbiſhop Euſtathius, in Odyſſ. x. And accordingly Ariſtotle, in his Poetic, chap. iv. doth further ſet forth, that as the Iliad and Odyſſey gave example to tragedy, ſo did this poem to comedy its firſt idea.

From theſe authors alſo it ſhould ſeem, that the Hero, or chief perſonage of it was no leſs *obſcure*, and his underſtanding and ſentiments no leſs quaint and ſtrange (if indeed not more ſo) than any of the actors of our poem. MARGITES was the name of this perſonage, whom Antiquity recordeth to have been

* All this diſcourſe was written by Pope.

been *Dunce the first*; and surely from what we hear of him, not unworthy to be the root of so spreading a tree, and so numerous a posterity. The poem therefore celebrating him was properly and absolutely a *Dunciad*; which though now unhappily lost, yet is its nature sufficiently known by the infallible tokens aforesaid. And thus it doth appear, that the first Dunciad was the first epic poem, written by Homer himself, and anterior even to the Iliad or Odyssey.

Now, forasmuch as our poet hath translated those two famous works of Homer which are yet left, he did conceive it in some sort his duty to imitate that also which was lost; and was therefore induced to bestow on it the same form which Homer's is reported to have had, namely that of epic poem; with a title also framed after the ancient Greek manner, to wit, that of *Dunciad*.

Wonderful it is, that so few of the moderns have been stimulated to attempt some Dunciad! since in the opinion of the multitude, it might cost less pain and toil than an imitation of the greater epic. But possible it is also, that, on due reflection, the maker might find it easier to paint a Charlemagne, a Brute, or a Godfrey, with just pomp and dignity heroic, than a Margites, a Codrus, or a Fleckno.

We shall next declare the occasion and the cause which moved our poet to this particular work. He lived in those days, when (after Providence had permitted the invention of printing as a scourge for

the

the ſins of the learned) paper alſo became ſo cheap, and printers ſo numerous, that a deluge of authors covered the land: whereby not only the peace of the honeſt unwriting ſubject was daily moleſted, but unmerciful demands were made of his applauſe, yea of his money, by ſuch as would neither earn the one, nor deſerve the other. At the ſame time, the licence of the preſs was ſuch, that it grew dangerous to refuſe them either: for they would forthwith publiſh ſlanders unpuniſhed, the authors being anonymous, and ſkulking under the wings of publiſhers, a ſet of men who never ſcrupled to vend either calumny or blaſphemy, as long as the town would call for it.

[a] Now our author, living in thoſe times, did conceive it an endeavour well worthy an honeſt ſatyriſt, to diſſuade the dull, and puniſh the wicked, *the only way that was left.* In that public-ſpirited view he laid the plan of this poem, as the greateſt ſervice he was capable (without much hurt or being ſlain) to render his dear country. Firſt taking things from their original, he conſidereth the cauſes creative of ſuch authors, namely *Dulneſs* and *Poverty*; the one born with them, the other contracted by neglect of their proper talents, through ſelf-conceit of greater abilities. This truth he wrappeth in an *allegory* [b] (as the conſtruction of epic poeſy requireth), and feigns that

[a] Vide Boſſu, Du Poeme Epique, ch. viii.

[b] Boſſu, chap. vii.

that one of these Goddesses had taken up her abode with the other, and that they jointly inspired all such writers and such works. [c] He proceedeth to shew the *qualities* they bestow on these authors, and the *effects* they produce [d]; then the *materials*, or *stock*, with which they furnish them [e]; and (above all) that *self-opinion* [f], which causeth it to seem to themselves vastly greater than it it, and is the prime motive of their setting up in this sad and sorry merchandise. The great power of these Goddesses acting in alliance (whereof as the one is the mother of Industry, so is the other of Plodding) was to be exemplified in some *one, great and remarkable action* [g]: And none could be more so than that which our poet hath chosen, *viz.* the restoration * of the reign of Chaos and Night, by the ministry of Dulness their daughter, in the removal of her imperial seat from the city to the polite world; as the action of the Aeneid is the restoration of the empire of Troy, by the removal of the race from thence to Latium. But as Homer singing only the wrath of Achilles, yet includes in his poem the whole history of the Trojan war; in like manner our author hath drawn into this *single action* the whole history of Dulness and her children.

A *person* must next be fixed upon to support this action. This *phantom* in the poet's mind must have a *name*:

---

[c] Book I. ver. 32. &c.
[d] Ver. 45 to 54.
[e] Bossu, B. I. ver. 57 to 77.
[f] Ver. 80.
[g] Ibid. chap. vii, viii.

* Altered from the edition 1729. See the note at the beginning of B. IV. of the Dunciad.

a *name*[h]: He finds it to be ——; and he becomes of courſe the Hero of the poem.

The *fable* being thus, according to the beſt example, one and entire, as contained in the propoſition; the *machinery* is a continued chain of allegories, ſetting forth the whole power, miniſtry, and empire of Dulneſs, extended through her ſubordinate inſtruments, in all her various operations.

This is branched into *Epiſodes*, each of which hath its Moral apart, though all conducive to the main end. The crowd, aſſembled in the ſecond book, demonſtrates the deſign to be more extenſive than to bad poets only, and that we may expect other epiſodes of the Patrons, Encouragers, or Paymaſters of ſuch authors, as occaſion ſhall bring them forth. And the third book, if well conſidered, ſeemeth to embrace the whole world. Each of the games relateth to ſome or other vile claſs of writers: The firſt concerneth the plagiary, to whom he giveth the name of More; the ſecond the libelous Noveliſt, whom he ſtyleth Eliza; the third, the flattering Dedicator; the fourth, the bawling Critic, or noiſy Poet; the fifth, the dark and dirty Party-writer; and ſo of the reſt; aſſigning to each ſome *proper name* or other, ſuch as he could find.

As for the *Characters*, the public hath already acknowledged how juſtly they are drawn: The manners

---

[h] Boſſu, chap. viii. Vide Ariſtot. Poetic. ix chap.

manners are ſo depicted, and the ſentiments ſo peculiar to thoſe to whom applied, that ſurely to transfer them to any other or wiſer perſonages, would be exceeding difficult: And certain it is, that every perſon concerned, being conſulted apart, hath readily owned the reſemblance of every portrait, his own excepted. So Mr. Cibber calls them, "a parcel of *poor wretches*, ſo many *ſilly flies*[1]: but adds, our Author's wit is remarkably more bare and barren, whenever it would fall foul on *Cibber*, than upon any other perſon whatever."

The *deſcriptions* are ſingular, the *compariſons* very quaint, the *narration* various, yet of one colour: The purity and chaſtity of *diction* is ſo preſerved, that in the places moſt ſuſpicious, not the *words* but only the *images* have been cenſured, and yet are thoſe images no other than have been ſanctified by ancient and claſſical authority, (though, as was the manner of thoſe good times, not ſo curiouſly wrapped up), yea, and commented upon by the moſt grave Doctors, and approved Critics.

As it beareth the name of *Epic*, it is thereby ſubjected to ſuch ſevere indiſpenſible rules as are laid on all Neoterics, a ſtrict imitation of the Ancients; inſomuch that any deviation, accompanied with whatever poetic beauties, hath always been cenſured by the ſound Critic. How exact that imitation hath been in this piece, appeareth not only by its general ſtructure,

[1] Cibber's Letter to Mr. P. p. 9, 12, 41.

ſtructure, but by particular alluſions infinite, many whereof have eſcaped both the commentator and poet himſelf, yea divers by his exceeding diligence are ſo altered and interwoven with the reſt, that ſeveral have already been, and more will be, by the ignorant abuſed, as altogether and originally his own.

In a word, the whole poem proveth itſelf to be the work of our Author, when his faculties were in full vigour and perfection: at that exact time when years have ripened the judgment, without diminiſhing the imagination: which, by good critics is held to be punctually at *forty*. For at that ſeaſon it was that Virgil finiſhed his Georgics; and Sir Richard Blackmore, at the like age compoſing his Arthurs, declared the ſame to be the very *Acme* and pitch of life for epic poeſy: Though ſince he hath altered it to *ſixty*, the year in which he publiſhed his Alfred [k]. True it is, that the talents for *criticiſm*, namely ſmartneſs, quick cenſure, vivacity of remark, certainty of aſſeveration, indeed all but acerbity, ſeem rather the gifts of youth than of riper age: But it is far otherwiſe in *poetry*; witneſs the works of Mr. Rymer and Mr. Dennis, who beginning with Criticiſm, became afterwards ſuch poets as no age hath paralleled. With

[k] See his Eſſays.

With good reaſon therefore did our author chuſe to write his Eſſay on that ſubject at twenty, and reſerve for his maturer years this great and wonderful work of the Dunciad. P.

RICHARDUS ARISTARCHUS

OF THE

HERO OF THE POEM *.

Of the nature of Dunciad in general, whence derived, and on what authority founded, as well as of the art and conduct of this our poem in particular, the learned and laborious Scriblerus hath, according to his manner, and with tolerable ſhare of judgment, diſſertated. But when he cometh to ſpeak of the person of the Hero fitted for ſuch poem, in truth he miſerably halts and hallucinates. For, miſled by one Monſieur Boſſu, a Gallic critic, he prateth of I cannot tell what phantom of a Hero, only raiſed up to ſupport the fable. A putid conceit! As if Homer and Virgil, like modern Undertakers, who firſt build their houſe, and then ſeek out for a tenant, had contrived the ſtory of a war and a wandring, before they once thought either of Achilles or Aeneas. We ſhall therefore ſet our good brother and the world alſo right in this particular, by aſſuring them,

* It is a ſingular circumſtance, that the hero of the Rehearſal, as well as of the Dunciad, ſhould have been changed. Howard, not Dryden, was the original hero of the former. And perhaps theſe changes, in both pieces, were for the worſe.

them, that, in the greater epic, the prime intention of the muſe is to exalt heroic virtue, in order to propagate the love of it among the *children* of men; and conſequently that the poet's firſt thought muſt needs be turned upon a real ſubject meet for laud and celebration; not one whom he is to make, but one whom he may find, truly illuſtrious. This is the primum mobile of his poetic world, whence every thing is to receive life and motion. For, this ſubject being found, he is immediately ordained, or rather acknowledged, an *Hero*, and put upon ſuch action as befitteth the dignity of his character.

But the Muſe ceaſeth not here her eagle-flight. For ſometimes, ſatiated with the contemplation of theſe *ſuns of glory*, ſhe turneth downward on her wing, and darts, with Jove's lightning, on the *gooſe* and *ſerpent* kind. For we apply to the Muſe in her various moods, what an ancient maſter of wiſdom affirmeth of the Gods in general: "Si Dii non iraſcuntur impiis et injuſtis, nec pios utique juſtoſque diligunt. In rebus enim diverſis, ut in utramque partem moveri neceſſe eſt, aut in neutram. Itaque qui bonos diligit, et malos odit; et qui malos non odit, nec bonos diligit. Quia et diligere bonos ex odio malorum venit; et malos odiſſe ex bonorum caritate deſcendit." Which in our vernacular idiom may be thus interpreted: "If the gods be not provoked at evil men, neither are they delighted with the good and juſt. For contrary objects muſt

either

either excite contrary affections, or no affections at all. So that he who loveth good men, muſt at the ſame time hate the bad; and he who hateth not bad men, cannot love the good; becauſe to love good men proceedeth from an averſion to evil; and to hate evil men, from a tenderneſs to the good." From this delicacy of the Muſe aroſe the *little Epic*, more lively and choleric than her elder ſiſter, (whoſe bulk and complexion incline her to the flegmatic). And for this, ſome notorious vehicle of vice and folly was ſought out, to make thereof an EXAMPLE. An early inſtance of which (nor could it eſcape the accurate Scriblerus) the Father himſelf of Epic-poem, affordeth us. From him the practice deſcended to the Greek dramatic Poets, his Offspring; who in the compoſition of their *Tetralogy* *, or ſet of four pieces, were wont to make the laſt a *Satiric Tragedy*. Happily one of theſe ancient *Dunciads* (as we may well term it) is come down unto us, amongſt the Tragedies of the poet Euripides. And what doth the reader ſuppoſe may be the ſubject thereof? Why in truth, and it is worthy obſervation, the unequal conteſt of an *old, dull, debauched buffoon Cyclops*, with the heaven-directed *Favourite of Minerva*: who, after

* Richardus Ariſtarchus is fond of bringing things, however improper and incongruous, into a ſyſtem. Our Dunciad is to be added to the epics of Homer, Virgil, and Milton, as a ſatiric piece, to make, as it were, a complete Tetralogy, as the Cyclops of Euripides was added to ſerious tragedies. This conceit is extremely ſtrained and tortured.

after having quietly born all the monſter's obſcene and impious ribaldry, endeth the farce in puniſhing him with the mark of an indelible brand in his *forehead.* May we not then be excuſed, if for the future we conſider the Epics of Homer, Virgil, and Milton, together with this our poem, as a complete *Tetralogy*; in which, the laſt worthily holdeth the place or ſtation of the *ſatiric* piece?

Proceed we therefore in our ſubject. It hath been long, and, alas for pity! ſtill remaineth a queſtion, whether the Hero of the *greater Epic* ſhould be an *honeſt Man*; or, as the French Critics expreſs it, *un honnête homme* [a]: but it never admitted of any doubt, but that the Hero of the *little Epic* ſhould be his very oppoſite. Hence, to the advantage of our Dunciad, we may obſerve, how much juſter the *Moral* of that poem muſt needs be, where ſo important a queſtion is previouſly decided.

But then it is not every knave, nor (let me add) every fool that is a fit ſubject for a Dunciad. There muſt ſtill exiſt ſome analogy, if not reſemblance of qualities, between the Heroes of the two poems; and this, in order to admit what neoteric Critics call the *Parody*, one of the livelieſt graces of the little Epic. Thus it being agreed, that the conſtituent qualities of the greater Epic Hero, are *Wiſdom*, *Bravery*, and *Love*, from whence ſpringeth *heroic Virtue*;

---

[a] Si un Heros Poetique doit etre un honnête homme. Boſſu, du Poeme Epique, liv. v. ch. 5.

Virtue; it followeth, that thoſe of the leſſer Epic Hero ſhould be *Vanity*, *Aſſurance*, and *Debauchery*, from which happy aſſemblage reſulteth *heroic Dulneſs*, the never-dying ſubject of this our Poem.

This being ſettled, come we now to particulars. It is the character of true *Wiſdom*, to ſeek its chief ſupport and confidence within itſelf; and to place that ſupport in the reſources which proceed from a conſcious rectitude of Will.—And are the advantages of *Vanity*, when ariſing to the heroic ſtandard, at all ſhort of this ſelf-complacence? Nay, are they not, in the opinion of the enamoured owner, far beyond it? "Let the world (will ſuch a one ſay) impute to me what *Folly* or weakneſs they pleaſe; but till *Wiſdom* can give me ſomething that will make me more heartily happy, I am content to be GAZED AT [b]." This, we ſee, is *Vanity* according to the *heroic* gage or meaſure; not that low and ignoble ſpecies which pretendeth to *virtues* we *have not*; but the laudable ambition of being *gazed at* for glorying in thoſe *vices*, which every body knows *we have*. "The world may aſk (ſays he) why I make my follies public? Why not? I have paſſed my time very pleaſantly with them [c]." In ſhort, there is no ſort of Vanity ſuch a Hero would ſcruple to exult in, but that which might go near to degrade him from his high ſtation in this our Dunciad; namely,

[b] Dedication to the Life of COLLY CIBBER.

[c] Life, p. 2. octavo edit.

namely, "Whether it would not be *Vanity* in him, to take ſhame to himſelf *for not being a wiſe man*[d]?"

Bravery, the ſecond attribute of the true Hero, is Courage, manifeſting itſelf in every limb; while its correſpondent virtue in the mock Hero, is, that ſame Courage all collected into the FACE. And as Power, when drawn together, muſt needs have more force and ſpirit than when diſperſed, we generally find this kind of courage in ſo high and heroic a degree, that it inſults not only Men, but Gods. Mezentius is, without doubt, the braveſt character in all the Aeneis: But how? His bravery, we know, was an high courage of blaſphemy. And can we ſay leſs of this brave man's, who having told us that he placed "his *Summum bonum* in thoſe follies, which he was not content barely to poſſeſs but would likewiſe glory in," adds, "*If I am miſguided*, 'TIS NATURE'S FAULT, *and I follow* HER[e]." Nor can we be miſtaken in making this happy quality a ſpecies of *Courage*, when we conſider thoſe illuſtrious marks of it, which made his FACE "more known (as he juſtly boaſteth) than moſt in the kingdom;" and his *Language* to conſiſt of what we muſt allow to be the moſt *daring* Figure of Speech, that which is taken from the *Name of God*.

Gentle Love, the next ingredient in the true Hero's compoſition, is a mere bird of paſſage, or (as Shakeſpear

[d] Life, p. 2. octavo edit.

[e] Life, p. 23. octavo.

Shakeſpear calls it) *Summer-teeming Luſt*, and evaporates in the heat of *Youth*; doubtleſs by that refinement it ſuffers in paſſing through thoſe *certain ſtrainers* which our Poet ſomewhere ſpeaketh of *. But when it is let alone to work upon the *Lees*, it acquireth ſtrength by *Old age*; and becometh a laſting ornament to the little Epic. It is true, indeed, there is one objection to its fitneſs for ſuch an uſe: For not only the ignorant may think it *common*, but it is admitted to be ſo, even by him who beſt knoweth its value. "Don't you think, (argueth he) to ſay only *a man has his Whore* [f], ought to go for little or nothing? Becauſe *defendit numerus*, take the firſt ten thouſand men you meet, and, I believe you would be no loſer if you betted ten to one, that every ſingle ſinner of them, one with another, had been guilty of the ſame frailty [g]." But here he ſeems not to have done juſtice to himſelf; † the man is ſure enough a Hero, who hath his Lady at fourſcore. How doth his modeſty herein leſſen the merit of a *whole well-ſpent* Life: not taking to himſelf the commendation (which *Horace* accounted the

---

* "Luſt, through ſome certain ſtrainers well refin'd,
Is gentle love, and charms all womankind."

[f] Alluding to theſe lines in the Epiſt. to Dr. Arbuthnot.
"And has not COLLY *ſtill* his Lord and Whore,
His Butchers Henley, his Free-Maſons Moore?"

[g] C. Cibber's Letter to Mr. P. p. 46.

† Here Ariſtarchus deſcends improperly from his gravity into a ſtrain a little ludicrous.

the greatest in a theatrical character) of continuing, to the very *dregs*, the same he was from the beginning,

—— " Servetur ad IMUM
Qualis ab incepto processerat."——

But here, in justice both to the Poet and the Hero, let us farther remark, that the calling her *his* Whore, implieth she was *his own* and not his *neighbour's*. Truly a commendable Continence! and such as Scipio himself must have applauded. For how much Self-denial was exerted not to covet his neighbour's whore? and what disorders must the coveting her have occasioned in that Society, where (according to this political calculator) *nine* in *ten* of all ages have their *concubines!*

We have now, as briefly as we could devise, gone through the three constituent qualities of either Hero. But it is not in any, nor in all of these, that Heroism properly or essentially resideth. It is a lucky result rather from the collision of these lively qualities against one another. Thus, as from Wisdom, Bravery, and Love, ariseth *Magnanimity* the object of *Admiration*, which is the aim of the greater Epic; so from Vanity, Impudence, and Debauchery, springeth *Buffoonry*, the source of *Ridicule*, that " laughing ornament," as the owner well termeth it [h], of the little Epic.

He

---

[h] Colly Cibber's Letter to Mr. P. p. 31.

He is not aſhamed (God forbid he ever ſhould be aſhamed!) of this character; who deemeth that not *Reaſon* but *Riſibility* diſtinguiſheth the human ſpecies from the brutal. "As Nature (ſaith this profound philoſopher) diſtinguiſhed our ſpecies from the mute creation by our Riſibility, her deſign muſt have been by that faculty as evidently to raiſe our *happineſs*, as by *our Os ſublime*, OUR ERECTED FACES, to lift the dignity of our *form* above them[i]." All this conſidered, how complete a Hero * muſt he be, as well as how happy a Man, whoſe Riſibility lieth not barely in his *muſcles*, as in the common ſort, but (as himſelf informeth us) in his very *ſpirits?* And whoſe *Os ſublime* is not ſimply an ERECT FACE, but a *brazen head*; as ſhould ſeem by his preferring it to one of *Iron*, ſaid to belong to the late king of Sweden[k].

But whatever perſonal qualities a Hero may have, the examples of Achilles and Aeneas ſhew us, that all theſe are of ſmall avail, without the conſtant *aſſiſtance of the* GODS: for the ſubverſion and erection of Empires have never been adjudged the work of Man. How greatly ſoever then we may eſteem of his high talents, we can hardly conceive his perſonal prowes alone ſufficient to reſtore the decayed empire of

---

[i] Cibber's Life, p. 23, 24. [k] Letter, page 8.

* In this and many other paſſages of this diſcourſe, the attempts of Ariſtarchus, at ſatire and ridicule, are very frigid and awkward indeed.

of DULNESS. So weighty an atchievement muſt require the particular favour and protection of the GREAT; who being the natural patrons and ſupporters of *Letters*, as the ancient Gods were of *Troy*, muſt firſt be drawn off, and engaged in another Intereſt, before the total ſubverſion of them can be accompliſhed. To ſurmount, therefore, this laſt and greateſt difficulty, we have, in this excellent man, a profeſſed Favourite and Intimado of the GREAT. And look, of what force ancient piety was to draw the Gods into the party of Aeneas, that, and much ſtronger is modern incenſe, to engage the Great in the party of Dulneſs.

Thus have we eſſayed to pourtray or ſhadow out this noble Imp of Fame. But now the impatient reader will be apt to ſay, if ſo many and various graces go to the making up a Hero, what mortal ſhall ſuffice to bear his character? Ill hath he read, who ſeeth not, in every trace of this picture, that *individual*, ALL-ACCOMPLISHED PERSON, in whom theſe rare virtues and lucky circumſtances have agreed to meet and concentre, with the ſtrongeſt luſtre and fulleſt harmony.

The good Scriblerus indeed, nay the World itſelf, might be impoſed on, in the late ſpurious editions, by I can't tell what *Sham Hero*, or *Phantom*: But it was not ſo eaſy to impoſe on HIM whom this egregious error moſt of all concerned. For no ſooner had the fourth book laid open the high and ſwelling

ſwelling ſcene, but he recognized his own heroic Acts: And when he came to the words,

Soft on her lap her Laureat ſon reclines,

(though *Laureat* imply no more than *one crown'd with laurel*, as befitteth any aſſociate or Conſort in Empire) he loudly reſented this indignity to violated Majeſty. Indeed not without cauſe, he being there repreſented as *faſt aſleep*; ſo miſbeſeeming the Eye of Empire, which, like that of Jove, ſhould never doze nor ſlumber. "Hah! (ſaith he) faſt aſleep, it ſeems! that's a little too ſtrong. Pert and dull at leaſt you might have allowed me, but as ſeldom aſleep as any fool[l]." However, the injured Laureat may comfort himſelf with this reflection, that tho' it be a *ſleep*, yet it is not the *ſleep of death*, but of *immortality*. Here he will [m] *live* at leaſt, tho' not *awake*; and in no worſe condition than many an enchanted Hero before him. The famous *Durandarte*, for inſtance, was, like him, caſt into a long ſlumber by *Merlin* the *Britiſh Bard* and Necromancer: and his example, for ſubmitting to it with a good grace, might be of ſervice to our Hero. For that diſaſtrous knight being ſorely preſſed or driven to make his anſwer by ſeveral *perſons of quality* [n], only replied with a ſigh, *Patience, and ſhuffle the cards* [o].

But

[l] Colly Cibber's Letter to Mr. P. p. 53. [m] Ibid. p. 1.
[n] See Cibber's Letter to Mr. P.
[o] Don Quixote, Part ii. Book ii. chap. 22.

But now, as nothing in this world, no not the moſt ſacred or perfect things either of Religion or Government, can eſcape the ſtings of Envy, methinks I already hear theſe carpers objecting to the clearneſs of our Hero's title.

It would never (ſay they) have been eſteemed ſufficient to make an Hero for the Iliad or Aeneis, that Achilles was brave enough to overturn one Empire, or Aeneas pious enough to raiſe another, had they not been Goddeſs-born, and Princes-bred. What then did this Author mean, by erecting a Player inſtead of one of his Patrons, (a perſon, "never a Hero even on the ſtage [p]") to this dignity of Colleague in the empire of Dulneſs; and Atchiever of a work that neither old Omar, Attila, nor John of Leiden, could entirely bring to paſs.

To all this we have, as we conceive, a ſufficient anſwer from the Roman hiſtorian, *Fabrum eſſe ſuae quemque fortunae: That every man is the* Carver *of his own fortune.* The politic Florentine, Nicholas Machiavel, goeth ſtill further, and affirmeth that a man needeth but to *believe himſelf a Hero* to be one of the worthieſt that ever breathed. "Let him (ſaith he) but fancy himſelf capable of high things, and he will of courſe be able to atchieve the higheſt." From this principle it followeth, that nothing can exceed our Hero's proweſs; as nothing ever equalled the

[p] See Cibber's Life, p. 148.

the greatneſs of his conceptions. Hear how he conſtantly paragons himſelf; at one time, to ALEXANDER the Great and CHARLES the XII. of Sweden, for the exceſs and delicacy of his Ambition[q]; to HENRY the IV. of FRANCE, for honeſt Policy[r]; to the firſt BRUTUS, for love of Liberty[s]; to Sir ROBERT WALPOLE, for good Government while in power[t]: At another time, to the godlike SOCRATES, for his Diverſions and Amuſements[u]; to HORACE, MONTAIGNE, and Sir WILLIAM TEMPLE, for an elegant Vanity that maketh them for ever read and admired[w]; to TWO Lord CHANCELLORS, for Law, from whom, when confederate againſt him at the bar, he carried away the prize of Eloquence[x]; and, to ſay all in a word, to the right reverend the Lord BISHOP of LONDON himſelf, in the art of writing *Paſtoral letters*[y].

Nor did his *Actions* fall ſhort of the ſublimity of his Conceit. In his early youth, he *met the Revolution*[z] face to face in Nottingham; at a time when other Patriots contented themſelves to *follow* her. It was here he got acquainted with *Old Battle-array*, of whom he hath made ſo honourable mention in one of his immortal Odes[a]. But he ſhone

[q] See Cibber's Life, p. 149. [r] Ibid. p. 424. [s] Ibid. p. 366. [t] Ibid. p. 457. [u] Ibid. p. 18. [w] Ibid. p. 425. [x] Ibid. p. 436, 437. [y] Ibid. p. 52. [z] Ibid. 47.

[a] "Old BATTLE-ARRAY in confuſion is fled;
And olive-rob'd Peace is come in his ſtead," &c.
Colly Cibber's Birth-day Ode, or New-year's Ode, (I don't know which) on the Peace.

ſhone in Courts as well as Camps: He was *called up* when *the Nation fell in labour* of this *Revolution*[b]: and was a goſſip at her chriſtening, with the Biſhop and the Ladies[c].

As to his *Birth*, it is true he pretendeth no relation either to heathen God or Goddeſs; but, what is as good, he was deſcended from a *Maker* of both[d]. And that he did not paſs himſelf on the world for a Hero, as well by birth as education, was his own fault: For, his lineage he bringeth into his life as an Anecdote, and is ſenſible he had it in his power *to be thought no body's ſon at all*[e]: And what is that, I pray you, but coming into the world a Hero?

But be it (the punctilious Laws of Epic Poeſy ſo requiring) that a Hero of more than mortal birth muſt needs be procured for this atchievement: Even for this we have a reſource. We can eaſily derive our Hero's pedigree from a Goddeſs of no ſmall power and authority amongſt men; and legitimate and inſtall him after the right claſſical and authentic faſhion: For, like as the ancient Sages found a ſon of Mars in a mighty Warrior; a ſon of Neptune in a ſkilful Seaman; a ſon of Phoebus in a harmonious Poet; ſo have we here, if need be, a ſon of FORTUNE * in an artful *Gameſter*. And who, I pray you,

[b] Colly Cibber's Life, p. 57.
[c] Ibid. 58, 59.
[d] A Statuary.
[e] Cibber's Life, p. 6.
* A very pitiful jeſt indeed!

you, fitter than the Offspring of *Chance*, to aſſiſt in reſtoring the Empire of *Night* and *Chaos*?

There is in truth another objection of greater weight, namely, "That this Hero ſtill exiſteth, and hath not yet finiſhed his earthly courſe. For if Solon ſaid well, that no man could be called happy till his death, ſurely much leſs can any one, till then, be pronounced a Hero: this ſpecies of men being far more ſubject than others to the caprices of Fortune and Humour." But to this alſo we have an anſwer, which will (we hope) be deemed deciſive. It cometh from *himſelf*; who, to cut this matter ſhort, hath ſolemnly proteſted that HE WILL NEVER CHANGE OR AMEND.

With regard to his *Vanity*, he declareth that nothing ſhall ever part them. "Nature (ſaith he) hath amply ſupplied me in *Vanity*; a pleaſure which neither the pertneſs of Wit, nor the gravity of Wiſdom, will ever perſuade me to part with[f]." Our poet had charitably endeavoured to adminiſter a cure to it: But he telleth us plainly, "My ſuperiors perhaps may be mended by him; but for my part I own myſelf incorrigible. I look upon my *Follies* as the beſt part of my Fortune[g]." And with good reaſon: We ſee to what they have brought him!

Secondly, as to *Buffoonry*, "Is it (ſaith he) a time of day for me to leave off theſe fooleries, and ſet up a new

[f] Cibber's Life, p. 424. [g] Ibid. p. 19.

a new character? I can no more put off my *Follies* than my Skin; I have often tried, but they ſtick too cloſe to me; nor am I ſure my friends are diſpleaſed with them, for in this light I afford them frequent matter of mirth, &c. &c.[h]" Having then ſo publickly declared himſelf INCORRIGIBLE, he is become *dead in law*, (I mean the *law Epopoeian*) and devolveth upon the Poet; is now his property; and may be taken and dealt with like an old Egyptian Hero; that is to ſay, *emboweled* and *embalmed* for Poſterity.

Nothing therefore (we conceive) remaineth to hinder his own prophecy of himſelf from taking immediate effect. A rare felicity! and what few Prophets have had the ſatisfaction to ſee, alive! Nor can we conclude better than with that extraordinary one of his, which is conceived in theſe Oraculous words, MY DULNESS WILL FIND SOMEBODY TO DO IT RIGHT[i].

* *Tandem* PHOEBUS *adeſt, morſuſque inferre parentem*
Congelat, et patulos, ut erant, INDURAT *hiatus*[k].

W.

---

[h] Cibber's Life, p. 17. [i] Ibid. p. 243, octavo edit.
[k] Ovid, of the ſerpent biting at Orpheus's head.

* It is difficult to ſee the propriety and juſtneſs of this application from Ovid.

By AUTHORITY.

By virtue of the Authority in Us veſted by the * Act for ſubjecting Poets to the Power of a Licenſer, we have reviſed this Piece; where finding the ſtyle and appellation of KING to have been given to a certain Pretender, Pſeudo-Poet, or Phantom, of the name of TIBBALD; and apprehending the ſame may be deemed in ſome ſort a Reflection on Majeſty, or at leaſt an inſult on that Legal Authority which has beſtowed on another Perſon the Crown of Poeſy: We have ordered the ſaid Pretender, Pſeudo-Poet, or Phantom, utterly to vaniſh and evaporate out of this work: And do declare the ſaid Throne of Poeſy from henceforth to be abdicated and vacant, unleſs duly and lawfully ſupplied by the LAUREATE himſelf. And it is hereby enacted, that no other perſon do preſume to fill the ſame.

ƆC Ch.

---

* A ſtroke of ſatire againſt the act for licenſing plays, which was oppoſed with equal wit and vehemence, by many of our poet's friends, and particularly by the Earl of Cheſterfield.

By AUTHORITY.

By virtue of the Authority in Us vested by the Act for subjecting Poets to the Power of a Licenser, we have revised this Piece; Where finding the style and appellation of King to have been given to a certain Pretender, Pseudo-Poet, or Phantom, of the name of Tibbald; and apprehending the same may be deemed in some sort a Reflection on Majesty, or at least an insult on that Legal Authority which has bestowed on another Person the Crown of Poesy: We have ordered the said Pretender, Pseudo-Poet, or Phantom, utterly to vanish and evaporate out of this work: And do declare the said Throne of Poesy from henceforth to be abdicated and vacant, unless duly and lawfully supplied by the Laureate himself. And it is hereby enacted, that no other person do presume to fill the same.

OC. Ch.

[illegible] of late [illegible] the following pages, which [illegible] which could not [illegible] by want of our poets [illegible] substituted.

THE

DUNCIAD:

TO

DR. JONATHAN SWIFT.

BOOK THE FIRST.

ARGUMENT.

THE Propoſition, the Invocation, and the Inſcription. Then the Original of the great Empire of Dulneſs, *and cauſe of the continuance thereof. The College of the* Goddeſs *in the City, with her private Academy for Poets in particular; the Governors of it, and the four Cardinal Virtues. Then the Poem* haſtes into the midſt of things, *preſenting her on the evening of a Lord Mayor's day revolving the long ſucceſſion of her Sons, and the glories paſt and to come. She fixes her eye on* Bays *to be the Inſtrument of that great Event which is the Subject of the Poem. He is deſcribed penſive among his Books, giving up the Cauſe, and apprehending the Period of her Empire: After debating whether to betake himſelf to the Church, or to Gaming, or to Party-writing, he raiſes an Altar of proper books, and (making firſt his ſolemn prayer and declaration) purpoſes thereon to ſacrifice all his unſucceſsful writings. As the pile is kindled, the Goddeſs, beholding the flame from her ſeat, flies and puts it out by caſting upon it the*

the poem of Thulé. *She forthwith reveals herſelf to him, tranſports him to her Temple, unfolds her Arts, and initiates him into her Myſteries; then announcing the death of* Euſden *the Poet Laureate, anoints him, carries him to Court, and proclaims him ſucceſſor.*

BOOK I.

THE Mighty Mother, and her Son, who brings
The Smithfield Muſes to the ear of Kings,
I ſing. Say you, her inſtruments the Great!
Call'd to this work by Dulneſs, Jove, and Fate;
You

REMARKS.

The DUNCIAD, ſic MS. It may well be diſputed whether this be a right reading: Ought it not rather to be ſpelled *Dunceiad*, as the Etymology evidently demands? *Dunce* with an *e*, therefore *Dunceiad* with an *e*. That accurate and punctual Man of Letters, the Reſtorer of *Shakeſpeare*, conſtantly obſerves the preſervation of this very Letter *e*, in ſpelling the name of his beloved Author, and not like his common careleſs Editors, with the omiſſion of one, nay ſometimes of two *ee's* (as *Shakſpear*) which is utterly unpardonable. "Nor is the neglect of a *Single Letter* ſo trivial as to ſome it may appear; the alteration whereof in a learned language is an Atchievement that brings honour to the Critic who advances it; and Dr. Bentley will be remembered to poſterity for his performances of this ſort, as long as the world ſhall have any eſteem for the remains of Menander and Philemon." THEOBALD.

VARIATIONS.

VER. 1. *The Mighty Mother, &c.*] In the firſt Edit. it was thus,

Books and the Man I ſing, the firſt who brings
The Smithfield Muſes to the Ear of Kings.
Say, great Patricians! ſince yourſelves inſpire
Theſe wond'rous works (ſo Jove and Fate require)
Say, for what cauſe, in vain decry'd and curſt,
Still——

IMITATIONS.

Say, great Patricians! ſince yourſelves inſpire
Theſe wond'rous works—
— "Dii coeptis (nam vos mutaſtis et illas.)" OVID. Met. I.

You by whose care, in vain decry'd, and curst,
Still Dunce the second reigns like Dunce the first;
Say,

REMARKS.

This Poem was written in the year 1726. In the next year an imperfect Edition was published at Dublin, and reprinted at London in twelves; another at Dublin, and another at London in octavo; and three others in twelves the same year. But there was no perfect Edition before that of London in quarto; which was attended with Notes. We are willing to acquaint Posterity, that this Poem was presented to King George the second and his Queen, by the hands of Sir Robert Walpole, on the 12th of March 1728-9. SCHOL. VET.

It was expresly confessed in the Preface to the first edition, that this Poem was not published by the Author himself. It was printed originally in a foreign Country. And what foreign Country? Why, one notorious for blunders; where finding blanks only instead of proper names, these blunderers filled them up at their pleasure.

The very *Hero* of the Poem hath been mistaken to this hour; so that we are obliged to open our Notes with a discovery who he really was. We learn from the former Editor, that this Piece was presented by the hands of Sir Robert Walpole to King George II. Now the author directly tells us, his Hero is the Man

——— "who brings
The Smithfield Muses to the ear of Kings."

And it is notorious who was the person on whom this Prince conferred the honour of the *Laurel*.

It appears as plainly from the *Apostrophe* to the *Great* in the third verse, that Tibbald could not be the person, who was never an author in fashion, or caressed by the Great; whereas this single characteristic is sufficient to point out the true Hero; who, above all other Poets of his time, was the *Peculiar Delight* and *Chosen Companion* of the Nobility of England; and wrote, as he himself tells us, certain of his Works at the *earnest Desire of Persons of Quality*.

Lastly

IMITATIONS.

VER. 6. Alluding to a verse of Mr. Dryden, not in Mac Fleckno (as is said ignorantly in the Key to the *Dunciad*, p. 1.) but in his verses to Mr. Congreve,

"And Tom the second reigns like Tom the first."

Say, how the Goddeſs bade Britannia ſleep,
And pour'd her Spirit o'er the land and deep.

In

REMARKS.

Laſtly, the ſixth verſe affords full proof; this Poet being the only one who was univerſally known to have had a *Son* ſo exactly like him, in his poetical, theatrical, political, and moral Capacities, that it could juſtly be ſaid of him

"Still Dunce the ſecond reigns like Dunce the firſt." BENTL.

VER. 1. *The Mighty Mother and her Son, &c.*] The Reader ought here to be cautioned, that the *Mother*, and not the *Son*, is the principal Agent in this Poem: The latter of them is only choſen as her colleague, (as was anciently the cuſtom in Rome before ſome great expedition), the main action of the Poem being by no means the Coronation of the Laureate, which is performed in the very firſt book, but the Reſtoration of the Empire of Dulneſs in Britain, which is not accompliſhed till the laſt. *

Ibid.—*her Son, who brings, &c.*] Wonderful is the ſtupidity of all the former Critics and Commentators on this work! It breaks forth at the very firſt line. The author of the Critique prefixed to *Sawny*, a Poem, p. 5. hath been ſo dull as to explain *the Man who brings, &c.* not of the Hero of the piece, but of our Poet himſelf, as if he vaunted that *Kings* were to be his readers; an honour, which tho' this Poem hath had,, yet knoweth he how to receive it with more modeſty.

We remit this Ignoraut to the firſt lines of the *Aeneid*, aſſuring him that Virgil there ſpeaketh not of himſelf, but of *Aeneas*:

"Arma virumque cano, Trojae qui primus ab oris
Italiam, fato profugus, Lavinaque venit
Littora: multum ille et terris jactatus et alto," &c.

I cite the whole three verſes, that I may by the way offer a *Conjectural Emendation*, purely my own, upon each: Firſt, *oris* ſhould be read *aris*, it being, as we ſee, *Aen.* ii. 513. from the *altar* of *Jupiter Hercaeus* that *Aeneas* fled as ſoon as he ſaw *Priam* ſlain. In the ſecond line I would read *flatu* for *fato*, ſince it is moſt clear it was by *Winds* that he arrived at the *ſhore* of Italy. *Jactatus*, in the third, is ſurely as improperly applied to *terris*, as proper to *alto*; to ſay a man is *toſt on land*, is much at one with ſaying *he walks at ſea: Riſum teneatis, amici?* Correct it, as I doubt not it ought to be, *vexatus*. SCRIBLERUS.

VER. 2. *The Smithfield Muſes*] *Smithfield* is the place where Bartholomew Fair was kept, whoſe ſhews, machines, and

dramatical

In eldeſt time, ere mortals writ or read,
Ere Pallas iſſu'd from the Thund'rer's head,
Dulneſs o'er all poſſeſs'd her ancient right,
Daughter of Chaos and eternal Night:
Fate in their dotage this fair Ideot gave,
Groſs as her ſire, and as her mother grave,
Laborious, heavy, buſy, bold, and blind,
She rul'd, in native Anarchy, the mind.
Still her old Empire to reſtore ſhe tries,
For, born a Goddeſs, Dulneſs never dies.
O Thou! whatever title pleaſe thine ear,
Dean, Drapier, Bickerſtaff, or Gulliver!
Whether thou chuſe Cervantes' ſerious air,
Or laugh and ſhake in Rab'lais' eaſy chair,

Or

REMARKS.

dramatical entertainments, formerly agreeable only to the taſte of the Rabble, were, by the Hero of this poem, and others of equal genius, brought to the Theatres of Covent Garden, Lincolns-inn-fields, and the Haymarket, to be the reigning pleaſures of the Court and Town. This happened in the reigns of King George I. and II. See Book iii.

VER. 12. *Daughter of Chaos, &c.*] The beauty of the whole Allegory being purely of the poetical kind, we think it not our proper buſineſs, as a Scholiaſt, to meddle with it: but leave it (as we ſhall in general all ſuch) to the reader; remarking only that *Chaos* (according to *Heſiod's* Θεογονία) was the Progenitor of all the Gods. SCRIBLERUS.

VER. 20. *Drapier, Bickerſtaff, or Gulliver!*] The ſeveral Names and Characters he aſſumed, in his ludicrous, his ſplenetic, or his party writings; which take in all his works. *

VER. 21.—Cervantes' *ſerious air,*] In the *Travels of Gulliver*; written to decry the *Lying Vanities* of Travellers, juſt as Don Quixote's adventures were to expoſe the abſurdities of Books of Chivalry; and with the ſame ſerious and ſolemn air.—The *laughing* with *Rab'lais*, in the next line, alludes to the *Tale of a Tub,*

Or praise the Court, or magnify Mankind,
Or thy griev'd Country's copper chains unbind;
From

VARIATIONS.

After ver. 22. in the MS.

Or in the graver Gown instruct mankind,
Or silent let thy morals tell thy mind.

But this was to be understood, as the Poet says, *ironicè*, like the 23d Verse.

REMARKS.

Tub, which is in the manner of the satirical and more regular parts of that famous French droll. Dr. S. Clarke in the first Edition of his Boyle's Lectures gives this book for an example of scoffing Atheism. And tho' I think there be neither impiety nor irreligion in the conduct of his *Tale*, yet surely it was impossible for a man really penetrated with a serious sense of Religion, ever to prevail on himself to expose the abuses of it in the manner he has done. *

The Travels of Gulliver were not written to decry the lying vanities of travellers, but chiefly and principally to expose the politics and measures of the English government, as well as the pride and depravity of human nature in general. Nor are they carried on or conceived in the manner of Cervantes. Voltaire called Swift, for writing the Tale of a Tub, Rabelais in his senses. When so many undeserving persons have been persecuted, particularly under the arbitrary government of France, for the freedom of their opinions, it is marvellous that Rabelais, who levelled his bitter satire against so many haughty princes, and as haughty priests, could possibly escape their vengeance. Garagantua certainly meant Francis I.; Louis XII. is Grand Gousier; Henry II. Pantagruel; Charles V. Picrocole. The Monks of that time are disguised under the name of Brother John des Entomures. The genealogy of Christ is ridiculed by that of Garagantua. The Treatises of Theology were laughed at under the titles of the books found in the Library of St. Victor; such as Biga Salutis, Braguelta Juris, Pentouffle Decentorun; and by such questions as, utrùm chimera in vacuo bombinans possit comedere secundas intentiones. Lord Peter's Loaf is minutely copied from Rabelais. Scarron had a master named J. Moreau, who wrote in Heroic verse a comic poem called The Pigmeid; which Scarron copied in

From thy Boeotia tho' her Pow'r retires,
Mourn not, my SWIFT! at ought our Realm acquires.
Here pleas'd behold her mighty wings outſpread
To hatch a new Saturnian age of Lead.
Cloſe to thoſe walls where Folly holds her throne,
And laughs to think Monroe would take her down,
Where

VARIATIONS.

VER. 29. *Cloſe to thoſe walls, &c.*] In the former Edd. thus,

Where wave the tatter'd enſigns of Rag-fair,
A yawning ruin hangs and nods in air;
Keen, hollow winds howl through the bleak receſs,
Emblem of muſic caus'd by Emptineſs;
Here in one bed two ſhiv'ring Siſters lie,
The Cave of Poverty and Poetry.

Var. *Where wave the tatter'd enſigns of Rag-fair,*] *Rag-fair* is a place near the *Tower of London*, where old clothes and frippery are ſold. W.

REMARKS.

his Gigantomachei. Had Swift ever ſeen theſe poems which bear ſo near a reſemblance to his Liliput and Brobdignac? Lord Orford obſerved to me, that he thought Swift had been guilty of an uſeleſs repetition of the ſame ſatire in theſe two Voyages, by only changing great into ſmall. And he alſo was of opinion, that Cervantes had continued his work to too great a length. After his hero had attacked a Windmill for a Giant, and had miſtaken a mean Inn for a magnificent Caſtle, all that followed was only the ſelf ſame idea varied, and new-modelled. I pretend not to determine on the juſtneſs of this criticiſm; becauſe I am unwilling to hint any thing that can in the ſmalleſt degree depreciate this original writer, Cervantes. But it is with difficulty I can bring myſelf to doubt of the juſtneſs of any of Lord Orford's critical opinions.

VER. 23. *Or praiſe the Court, or magnify Mankind,*] *Ironicè*, alluding to *Gulliver's* repreſentations of both.——The next line relates to the papers of the *Drapier* againſt the currency of *Wood's* Copper coin in *Ireland*, which, upon the great diſcontent of the People, his Majeſty was graciouſly pleaſed to recal. W.

Where o'er the gates, by his fam'd father's hand,
Great Cibber's brazen, brainless brothers stand;
One Cell there is, conceal'd from vulgar eye,
The Cave of Poverty and Poetry.
Keen, hollow winds howl through the bleak recess
Emblem of Music caus'd by Emptiness.
Hence Bards, like Proteus long in vain ty'd down,
Escape in Monsters, and amaze the town.

Hence

REMARKS.

VER. 31. *By his fam'd father's hand,*] Mr. Caius-Gabriel Cibber, father of the Poet Laureate. The two Statues of the Lunatics over the gates of Bedlam-hospital were done by him, and (as the son justly says of them) are no ill monuments of his fame as an Artist. W.

VER. 34. *Poverty and Poetry.*] I cannot here omit a remark that will greatly endear our Author to every one, who shall attentively observe that Humanity and Candor, which every where appears in him towards those unhappy objects of the ridicule of all mankind, the bad Poets. He here imputes all scandalous rhymes, scurrilous weekly papers, base flatteries, wretched elegies, songs, and verses, (even from those sung at Court, to ballads in the streets), not so much to malice or servility as to Dulness; and not so much to Dulness as to Necessity. And thus, at the very commencement of his Satire, makes an apology for all that are to be satirized. W.

VER. 37. *Hence Bards, like Proteus long in vain ty'd down,*
Escape in Monsters, and amaze the town.]

Ovid has given us a very orderly account of these *escapes*;

"Sunt quibus in plures jus est transire figuras:
Ut tibi, complexi terram maris incola, PROTEU;
Nunc violentus *Aper*; nunc, quem tetigisse timerent,
Anguis eras; modo te faciebant *cornua Taurum*:
Saepe *Lapis* poteras." Met. viii.

Neither Palaephatus, Phurnutus, nor Heraclides give us any steady light into the mythology of this mysterious fable. If I be not deceived in a part of learning which has so long exercised my pen, by *Proteus* must certainly be meant a hacknied Town scribler;

and

Hence Miſcellanies ſpring, the weekly boaſt
Of Curl's chaſte preſs, and Lintot's rubric poſt:

Hence

REMARKS.

and by his transformations, the various diſguiſes ſuch a one aſſumes, to elude the purſuit of his natural enemy, the Bailiff. And in this light, doubtleſs, Horace underſtood the fable, where, ſpeaking of *Proteus*, he ſays,

> " Quum RAPIES in JUS *malis ridentem alienis,*
> Fiet aper;" &c.

Proteus is repreſented as one bred of the mud and ſlime of Egypt, the original ſoil of Arts and Letters; and what, I pray you, is a Town-ſcribbler, but a creature made up of the excrements of luxurious Science? By the change then into a *Boar*, is meant his character of a *furious and dirty Party-writer;* the *Snake* ſignifies a *Libeller*; and the *Horns of the Bull*, the *Dilemmas* of a *Polemical Anſwerer*. Theſe are the three great Parts he aſſumes; and when he has completed his circle, he ſinks back again (as the laſt change into a *Stone* denotes) into his natural ſtate of immoveable Stupidity. Hence it is, that the Poet, where ſpeaking at large of all theſe various Metamorphoſes in the ſecond Book, deſcribes MOTHER OSBORNE, the great Antitype of our Proteus, in ver. 312. after all her changes, as at laſt quite *ſtupified to Stone*. If I may expect thanks of the learned world for this diſcovery, I would by no means deprive that excellent Critic of his ſhare, who diſcovered before me, that in the character of Proteus was deſigned *Sophiſtam, Magum, Politicum, praeſertim rebus omnibus ſeſe accommodantem.* Which in Engliſh is, A political Writer, a Libeller, and a Diſputer, writing indifferently for or againſt every Party in the ſtate, every Sect in religion, and every Character in private life. See my Fables of Ovid explained. ABBE BANIER. *

A very cloſe reſemblance to the following lines of Dr. Young, in his firſt epiſtle on the Authors of the Age, addreſt to Mr. Pope.

> " How juſtly Proteus' tranſmigrations fit
> The monſtrous changes of a modern wit?
> Now, ſuch a gentle ſtream of eloquence
> As ſeldom riſes to the verge of ſenſe;
> Now, by mad rage transform'd into a flame,
> Which yet fit engines well apply'd can tame;
> Now, on immodeſt traſh the ſwine obſcene
> Invites the town to ſup at Drury Lane;

A dreadful

Hence hymning Tyburn's elegiac lines,
Hence Journals, Medleys, Merc'ries, MAGAZINES:
Sepulchral

VARIATIONS.

VER. 41. In the former Edd.

Hence hymning Tyburn's elegiac Lay,
Hence the soft sing-song on Cecilia's Day.

VER. 42. Alludes to the annual Songs composed to Music on St. Cecilia's Feast. W.

REMARKS.

A dreadful Lyon, now, he roars at Pow'r,
Which sends him to his brothers at the Tow'r;
He's, now, a Serpent, and his double tongue
Salutes, nay licks the feet of those he stung."

VER. 40. *Curl's chaste press, and Lintot's rubric post:*] Two booksellers, of whom see Book ii. The former was fined by the Court of King's Bench for publishing obscene Books; the latter usually adorned his shop with titles in red letters. W.

VER. 41. *Hence hymning Tyburn's elegiac lines,*] It is an ancient English custom, for the Malefactors to sing a Psalm at their execution at Tyburn; and no less customary to print Elegies on their deaths, at the same time, or before. W.

VER. 42. MAGAZINES:] The common names of those monstrous collections in prose and verse; where Dulness assumes all the various shapes of Folly to draw in, and cajole the Rabble. The eruption of every miserable Scribbler; the dirty scum of every stagnant Newspaper; the rags of worn-out Nonsense and Scandal, picked up from every Dunghill; under the title of *Essays, Reflections, Queries, Songs, Epigrams, Riddles, &c.* equally the disgrace of Wit, Morality, and Common Sense. P. *

It is but justice to add, that the Gentleman's Magazine, the first of its kind, does by no means deserve this severe sarcasm; but has been a means of preserving many useful and fugitive pieces on many interesting subjects.

IMITATIONS.

VER. 41, 42. *Hence hymning Tyburn's—Hence, &c.*

——— "Genus unde Latinum,
Albanique patres, atque altae moenia Romae."

VIRG. Aeneid. i.

Sepulchral Lies, our holy Walls to grace,
And New-year Odes, and all the Grub-ſtreet race.
  In clouded Majeſty here Dulneſs ſhone;
Four guardian Virtues, round, ſupport her throne:
Fierce champion Fortitude, that knows no fears
Of hiſſes, blows, or want, or loſs of ears:
Calm Temperance, whoſe bleſſings thoſe partake
Who hunger and who thirſt for ſcribbling ſake:

Prudence

REMARKS.

VER. 43. *Sepulchral Lies,*] Is a juſt ſatire on the Flatteries and Falſhoods admitted to be inſcribed on the walls of Churches, in Epitaphs; which occaſioned the following Epigram:

"FRIEND! in your Epitaphs, I'm griev'd,
  So very much is ſaid:
One half will never be believ'd,
  The other never read." W.

The Epigram here inſerted, alludes to the too long, and ſometimes, fulſome Epitaphs, written by Dr. FRIEND, in pure Latinity indeed, but full of Antitheſes.

VER. 44. *New-year Odes,*] Made by the Poet Laureate for the time being, to be ſung at court on every New-year's-day, the words of which are happily drowned in the voices and inſtruments. W.

VER. 50. *Who hunger and who thirſt, &c.*] "This is an alluſion to a text in Scripture, which ſhews, in Mr. *Pope*, a delight in prophaneneſs," ſaid Curl upon this place. But it is very familiar with Shakeſpear to allude to paſſages of Scripture. Out of a great number I will ſelect a few, in which he not only alludes to, but quotes the very Text from holy Writ. In All's

well

IMITATIONS.

VER. 45. *In clouded Majeſty*]
——— "the Moon
Riſing in clouded Majeſty"——— MILTON, book iv.

VER. 48. ——— *that knows no fears*
Of hiſſes, blows, or want, or loſs of ears:]
"Quem neque pauperies, neque mors, neque vincula terrent."
HOR.

Prudence, whoſe glaſs preſents th' approaching jail:
Poetic Juſtice, with her lifted ſcale,
Where, in nice balance, truth with gold ſhe weighs,
And ſolid pudding againſt empty praiſe.
  Here ſhe beholds the Chaos dark and deep,
Where nameleſs Somethings in their cauſes ſleep,
Till genial Jacob, or a warm Third day,
Call forth each maſs, a Poem, or a Play:

How

REMARKS.

well that ends well, *I am no great Nebuchadnezzar, I have not much ſkill in graſs.* Ibid. *They are for the flowery way that leads to the broad gate and the great fire,* Matt. vii. 13. In Much ado about nothing, *All, all, and moreover God ſaw him when he was hid in the Garden,* Gen. iii. 8. (in a very jocoſe ſcene). In Love's Labour Loſt, he talks of Samſon carrying the gates on his back; in the Merry Wives of Windſor, of Goliah and the weaver's beam; and in Henry IV. Falſtaff's ſoldiers are compared to Lazarus and the prodigal ſon.——The firſt part of this note is Mr. CURL's, the reſt is Mr. Theobald's, Appendix to Shakeſpear reſtor'd, p. 144. W.

It ſeems to be rather an odd and a weak defence of uſing a phraſe of Scripture lightly and profanely, to ſay that Shakeſpear did ſo.

VER. 55. *Beholds the Chaos*] This paſſage from hence down to verſe 78, is an inſtance of great power and elegance of Style on a ſubject that with ſuch difficulty admits of either.

VER. 57. *Jacob,*] A race of bookſellers, that did honor to their profeſſion, for integrity and encouragement of authors. Jacob Tonſon was admitted to the familiarity and friendſhip of the moſt eminent writers of his time; who made him a preſent of their portraits by good maſters.

IMITATIONS.

VER. 55. *Here ſhe beholds the Chaos dark and deep,*
Where nameleſs Somethings, &c.]

That is to ſay, unform'd things, which are either made into Poems or Plays, as the Bookſellers or the Players bid moſt.

 These

How hints, like ſpawn, ſcarce quick in embryo lie,
How new-born nonſenſe firſt is taught to cry,
Maggots half form'd in rhyme exactly meet,
And learn to crawl upon poetic feet.
Here one poor word an hundred clenches makes,
And ductile Dulneſs new meanders takes;
There motley Images her fancy ſtrike,
Figures ill pair'd, and Similes unlike.
She ſees a Mob of Metaphors advance,
Pleas'd with the madneſs of the mazy dance!

How

REMARKS.

Ver. 63. *Here one poor word an hundred clenches makes,*] It may not be amiſs to give an inſtance or two of theſe operations of *Dulneſs* out of the Works of her Sons, celebrated in the Poem. A great Critic formerly held theſe clenches in ſuch abhorrence, that he declared, "he that would pun, would pick a pocket." Yet Mr. Dennis's works afford us notable examples in this kind; "*Alexander Pope* hath ſent abroad into the world as many *Bulls* as his nameſake Pope *Alexander*.——Let us take the initial and final letters of his name, *viz.* *A. P—E*, and they give you the idea of an *Ape*.—*Pope* comes from the Latin word *Popa*, which ſignifies a little wart: or from *poppyſma*, becauſe he was continually *popping* out ſquibs of wit, or rather *Popyſmata* or *Popyſmus*." Dennis on *Hom.* and Daily Journal, *June* 11, 1728. P.

IMITATIONS.

Theſe lines allude to the following in Garth's Diſpenſary, Cant. vi.

"Within the chambers of the globe they ſpy
The beds where ſleeping vegetables lie,
Till the glad ſummons of a genial ray
Unbinds the glebe, and calls them out to day." W.

Ver. 64. *And ductile Dulneſs, &c.*] A parody on a verſe in Garth, Cant. i.

"How ductile matter new meanders takes." W.

How Tragedy and Comedy embrace;
How Farce and Epic get a jumbled race;
How Time himſelf ſtands ſtill at her command,
Realms ſhift their place, and Ocean turns to land.
Here gay Deſcription Egypt glads with ſhow'rs,
Or gives to Zembla fruits, to Barca flow'rs;
Glitt'ring with ice here hoary hills are ſeen,
There painted vallies of eternal green,
In cold December fragrant chaplets blow,
And heavy harveſts nod beneath the ſnow.
All theſe, and more, the cloud-compelling Queen
Beholds through fogs that magnify the ſcene.

She

REMARKS.

VER. 70, &c. *How Farce and Epic—How Time himſelf, &c.*] Allude to the tranſgreſſions of the *Unities* in the Plays of ſuch poets. For the miracles wrought upon *Time* and *Place*, and the mixture of Tragedy and Comedy, Farce and Epic, ſee Pluto and Proſerpine, Penelope, &c. if yet extant. W.

VER. 73. *Egypt glads with ſhow'rs,*] In the Lower Egypt rain is of no uſe, the overflowing of the Nile being ſufficient to impregnate the ſoil.—Theſe ſix verſes repreſent the inconſiſtences in the deſcriptions of poets, who heap together all glittering and gaudy images, though incompatible in one ſeaſon, or in one ſcene.

See the Guardian, N° 40. parag. 6. See alſo *Euſden*'s whole works, if to be found. It would not have been unpleaſant to have given examples of all theſe ſpecies of bad writing from theſe Authors, but that it is already done in our Treatiſe of the *Bathos*. SCRIBL.

VER. 79. *The cloud-compelling*] Gray has left a very fine fragment of an hymn to Ignorance, very much in the manner of the Dunciad; " Many of the lines of this fragment (ſays Mr. Maſon)

are

IMITATIONS.

VER. 79. *The cloud-compelling Queen*] From Homer's Epithet of Jupiter, νεφεληγερέτα Ζεύς. W.

She tinſel'd o'er in robes of varying hues,
With ſelf-applauſe her wild creation views;
Sees momentary monſters riſe and fall,
And with her own fools-colours gilds them all.
'Twas on the day, when * * rich and grave,
Like Cimon, triumph'd both on land and wave:
(Pomps without guilt, of bloodleſs ſwords and maces,
Glad chains, warm furs, broad banners, and broad faces)

Now

VARIATIONS.

VER. 85. in the former Editions,

'Twas on the day when Thorold, rich and grave.

Sir George Thorold, Lord Mayor of London in the year 1720. W.

REMARKS.

are ſo ſtrong, and the general caſt of the verſification ſo muſical, that I believe it will give the generality of readers a higher opinion of his poetical talents, than many of his lyrical productions have done. I ſpeak of the generality; becauſe it is a certain fact, that their taſte is founded upon the ten-ſyllable couplets of Dryden and Pope, and upon theſe only." P. 176.

VER. 85, 86. *'Twas on the day, when * * rich and grave, Like Cimon, triumph'd*] Viz. a Lord Mayor's Day, his name the author had left in blanks, but moſt certainly could never be that which the Editor foiſted in formerly, and which no way agrees with the chronology of the poem. BENTL.

The proceſſion of a Lord Mayor is made partly by land, and partly by water.—Cimon, the famous Athenian General, obtained a victory by ſea, and another by land, on the ſame day, over the Perſians and Barbarians. W.

VER. 88. *Glad chains,*] The ignorance of theſe Moderns! This was altered in one edition to *Gold chains*, ſhewing more regard to the metal of which the chains of Aldermen are made, than to the beauty of the Latiniſm and Graeciſm, nay of figurative ſpeech itſelf: *Laetas ſegetes*, glad, for making glad, &c. SCRIBL.

Now Night descending, the proud scene was o'er,
But liv'd, in Settle's numbers, one day more.
Now May'rs and Shrieves all hush'd and satiate lay,
Yet eat, in dreams, the custard of the day;
While pensive Poets painful vigils keep,
Sleepless themselves to give their readers sleep.
Much to the mindful Queen the feast recalls
What City Swans once sung within the walls;
Much she revolves their arts, their ancient praise,
And sure succession down from Heywood's days.
She saw, with joy, the line immortal run,
Each sire imprest and glaring in his son:
So watchful Bruin forms, with plastic care,
Each growing lump, and brings it to a Bear.

She

REMARKS.

Ver. 90. *But liv'd, in Settle's numbers one day more.*] A beautiful manner of speaking, usual with poets in praise of poetry, in which kind nothing is finer than those lines of Mr. Addison:

> " Sometimes, misguided by the tuneful throng,
> I look for streams immortaliz'd in song,
> That lost in silence and oblivion lie,
> Dumb are their fountains, and their channels dry;
> Yet run for ever by the Muses skill,
> And in the smooth description murmur still."

Ibid. *But liv'd, in Settle's numbers, one day more.*] Settle was poet to the City of London. His office was to compose yearly panegyrics upon the Lord Mayors, and verses to be spoken in the Pageants: But that part of the shows being at length frugally abolished, the employment of City-poet ceased; so that upon Settle's demise there was no successor to that place. W.

Ver. 98. *John Heywood,* whose Interludes were printed in the time of Henry VIII.

She ſaw old Pryn in reſtleſs Daniel ſhine,
And Euſden eke out Blackmore's endleſs line;
She

REMARKS.

VER. 103. *Reſtleſs Daniel*] I am ſorry to find De Foe placed in ſuch company. He was a writer of uncommon genius and fertility of fancy. Witneſs his Robinſon Cruſoe, in which a wonderful reach of invention is diſplayed; his Hiſtory of the Plague in London which for a long time impoſed on Dr. Mead, who thought it genuine; and his Memoirs of a Cavalier, a favourite book of the great Earl of Chatham, who ſpoke of it as the beſt account of the Civil Wars extant; and who, when he was at laſt convinced that it was all a fiction, cried out,

—— Sic extorta voluptas,
Et demptus per vim mentis gratiſſimus error.

Among other entertaining works, De Foe wrote, in priſon, 1703, a Review, conſiſting of a Scandal Club, as he entitled it, on queſtions of Theology, Morals, Politics, Trade, Language, Poetry, Love, &c. which Mr. Chalmers thinks gave a hint for the plan of the Tatler and Spectator.

VER. 104. *And Euſden eke out, &c.*] Laurence Euſden Poet Laureate. Mr. Jacob gives a catalogue of ſome few only of his works, which were very numerous. Mr. Cook, in his Battle of Poets, ſaith of him,

"Euſden, a laurel'd Bard, by fortune rais'd,
By very few was read, by fewer prais'd."

Mr. Oldmixon, in his Arts of Logic and Rhetoric, p. 413, 414, affirms, "That of all the Galimatia's he ever met with, none comes up to ſome verſes of this poet, which have as much of the Ridiculum and the Fuſtian in them as can well be jumbled together, and are of that ſort of nonſenſe, which ſo perfectly confounds all ideas, that there is no diſtinct one left in the mind." Further he ſays of him, "That he hath propheſied his own poetry ſhall be ſweeter than Catullus, Ovid, and Tibullus; but we have little hope of the accompliſhment of it, from what he hath lately publiſhed." Upon which Mr. Oldmixon has not ſpared a reflection, "That the putting the Laurel on the head of one who writ ſuch verſes, will give futurity a very lively idea of the judgment and juſtice of thoſe who beſtow'd it." Ibid. p. 417. But the well-known learning of that noble Perſon, who was then Lord Chamberlain, might have ſcreen'd him from this unmannerly reflection

She ſaw ſlow Philips creep like Tate's poor page,
And all the mighty Mad in Dennis rage.

REMARKS.

reflection. Nor ought Mr. Oldmixon to complain, ſo long after, that the Laurel would have better become his own brows, or any others: It were more decent to acquieſce in the opinion of the Duke of *Buckingham* upon this matter:

—— "In ruſh'd Euſden, and cry'd, Who ſhall have it,
But I, the true Laureate, to whom the King gave it?
Apollo begg'd pardon, and granted his claim,
But vow'd that till then he ne'er heard of his name."

Seſſion of Poets.

The ſame plea might alſo ſerve for his ſucceſſor, Mr. Cibber; and is further ſtrengthened in the following Epigram, made on that occaſion:

"In merry Old England it once was a rule,
The King had his Poet and alſo his Fool:
But now we're ſo frugal, I'd have you to know it,
That Cibber can ſerve both for Fool and for Poet."

Of Blackmore, ſee Book ii. Of Philips, Book i. ver. 262. and Book iii. *prope fin.*

Nahum Tate was Poet Laureate, a cold writer of no invention; but ſometimes tranſlated tolerably when befriended by Mr. Dryden. In his ſecond part of Abſalom and Achitophel are above two hundred admirable lines together of that great hand, which ſtrongly ſhine through the inſipidity of the reſt. Something parallel may be obſerved of another author here mentioned. W.

VER. 106. *And all the mighty Mad in Dennis rage.*] Mr. Theobald, in the Cenſor, vol. ii. N. 33. calls Mr. Dennis by the name of Furius. "The modern Furius is to be looked upon as more an object of pity, than of that which he daily provokes, laughter and contempt. Did we really know how much this *poor* man [*I wiſh that reflection on* poverty *had been ſpared*] ſuffers by being contradicted, or which is the ſame thing in effect, by hearing another praiſed; we ſhould in compaſſion, ſometimes attend to him with a ſilent nod, and let him go away with the triumphs of his ill-nature.—*Poor* Furius [*again*] when any of his cotemporaries are ſpoken well of, quitting the ground of the preſent diſpute, ſteps back a thouſand years to call in the ſuccour of the Ancients. His very panegyric is ſpiteful, and he uſes it for the ſame reaſon

In each ſhe marks her Image full expreſt,
But chief in BAYS's monſter-breeding breaſt;

Bays,

VARIATIONS.

VER. 108. *But chief in Bays's, &c.*] In the former Editions thus,

> But chief, in Tibbald's monſter-breeding breaſt;
> Sees Gods with Demons in ſtrange league engage,
> And earth, and heav'n, and hell, her battles wage.
> She ey'd the Bard, where ſupperleſs he ſate,
> And pin'd, unconſcious of his riſing fate;
> Studious he ſate, with all his books around,
> Sinking from thought to thought, &c.

Var. *Tibbald*] Author of a pamphlet intitled, *Shakeſpear reſtor'd.* During two whole years while Mr. Pope was preparing his Edition of Shakeſpear, he publiſhed Advertiſements, requeſting aſſiſtance, and promiſing ſatisfaction to any who could contribute to its greater perfection. But this Reſtorer, who was at that time ſoliciting favours of him by letters, did wholly conceal his deſign, till after its publication: (which he was ſince not aſhamed to own, in a *Daily Journal* of *Nov.* 26, 1728.) And then an outcry was made in the Prints, that our Author had joined with the Bookſeller to raiſe an *extravagant ſubſcription*; in which he had no ſhare, of which he had no knowledge, and againſt which he had publicly advertiſed in his own propoſals for *Homer*. Probably that proceeding elevated *Tibbald* to the dignity he holds in this Poem, which he ſeems to deſerve no other way better than his brethren; unleſs we impute it to the ſhare he had in the Journals, cited among the *Teſtimonies of Authors* prefixed to this work.

REMARKS.

as ſome Ladies do their commendations of a dead beauty, who would never have had their good word, but that a living one happened to be mentioned in their company. His applauſe is not the tribute of his *Heart*, but the ſacrifice of his *Revenge*," &c. Indeed his pieces againſt our poet are ſomewhat of an angry character, and as they are now ſcarce extant, a taſte of his ſtyle may be ſatisfactory to the curious. "A young, ſquab, ſhort gentleman, whoſe outward form, though it ſhould be that of downright monkey, would not differ ſo much from human ſhape as his unthinking immaterial part does from human underſtanding.—

He

Bays, form'd by nature Stage and Town to bleſs,
And act, and be, a Coxcomb with ſucceſs.

Dulneſs

REMARKS.

He is as ſtupid and as venomous as a hunch-back'd toad.—A book through which folly and ignorance, thoſe brethren ſo lame and impotent, do ridiculouſly look very big and very dull, and ſtrut and hobble, cheek by jowl, with their arms on kimbo, being led and ſupported, and bully-back'd by that blind Hector, Impudence." Reflect. on the Eſſay on Criticiſm, p. 26, 29, 30.

It would be unjuſt not to add his reaſons for this Fury, they are ſo ſtrong and ſo coercive: "I regard him (ſaith he) as an *Enemy*, not ſo much to me, as to my King, to my Country, to my Religion, and to that Liberty which has been the ſole felicity of my life. A vagary of Fortune, who is ſometimes pleaſed to be frolickſome, and the epidemic *Madneſs of the times* have given him *Reputation*, and Reputation (as Hobbes ſays) is *Power*, and *that has made him dangerous*. Therefore I look on it as my duty to *King George*, whoſe faithful ſubject I am; to my *Country*, of which I have appeared a conſtant lover; to the *Laws*, under whoſe protection I have ſo long lived; and to the *Liberty* of my *Country*, more dear to me than life, of which I have now for forty years been a conſtant aſſertor, &c. I look upon it as my duty, I ſay, to do—*you ſhall ſee what*—to pull the lion's ſkin from this little Aſs, which popular error has thrown round him; and to ſhew that this Author, who has been lately ſo much in vogue, has neither Senſe in his thoughts, nor Engliſh in his expreſſions." DENNIS, Rem. on Hom. Pref. p. 2, 91, &c.

Beſides theſe public-ſpirited reaſons, Mr. D. had a private one; which by his manner of expreſſing it in p. 92. appears to have been equally ſtrong. He was even in bodily fear of his life from the machinations of the ſaid Mr. P. "The ſtory (ſays he) is too long to be told, but who would be acquainted with it, may hear it from Mr. Curl, my Bookſeller.—However, what my reaſon has ſuggeſted to me, that I have with a juſt confidence ſaid, in defiance of his two clandeſtine weapons, his *Slander* and his *Poiſon*." Which laſt words of his book plainly diſcover Mr. D's ſuſpicion was that of being *poiſoned*, in like manner as Mr. Curl had been before him: Of which fact ſee *A full and true account of a horrid and barbarous revenge, by poiſon, on the body of Edmund Curl*, printed in 1716, the year antecedent to that wherein theſe Remarks of

Mr.

Dulneſs with tranſport eyes the lively Dunce,
Remembering ſhe herſelf was Pertneſs once.

Now

REMARKS.

Mr. Dennis were publiſhed. But what puts it beyond all queſtion, is a paſſage in a very warm treatiſe, in which Mr. Dennis was alſo concerned, price two-pence, called *A true character of Mr. Pope and his Writings*, printed for S. Popping, 1716: in the tenth page whereof he is ſaid "to have inſulted people on thoſe calamities and diſeaſes which he himſelf gave them, by adminiſtring *Poiſon* to them:" and is called (p. 4.) "a lurking way-laying coward, and a ſtabber in the dark." Which (with many other things moſt lively ſet forth in that piece) muſt have rendered him a terror, not to Mr. Dennis only, but to all chriſtian people. This charitable warning only provoked our incorrigible Poet to write the following Epigram:

Should Dennis publiſh, you had ſtabb'd your Brother,
Lampoon'd your Monarch, or debauch'd your Mother;
Say, what revenge on Dennis can be had?
Too dull for laughter, for reply too mad:
On one ſo poor you cannot take the law;
On one ſo old your ſword you ſcorn to draw:
Uncag'd then let the harmleſs monſter rage,
Secure in dulneſs, madneſs, want, and age.

For the reſt; Mr. John Dennis was the ſon of a Sadler, in London, born in 1657. He paid court to Mr. Dryden: and having obtained ſome correſpondence with Mr. Wycherley and Mr. Congreve, he immediately obliged the public with their Letters. He made himſelf known to the Government by many admirable ſchemes and projects; which the Miniſtry, for reaſons beſt known to themſelves, conſtantly kept private. For his character, as a writer, it is given us as follows: "Mr. Dennis is *excellent* at Pindaric writings, *perfectly regular* in all his performances, and a perſon of *ſound Learning*. That he is maſter of a great deal of *Penetration* and *Judgment*, his criticiſms (particularly on *Prince Arthur*) do ſufficiently demonſtrate." From the ſame account it alſo appears that he writ Plays "more to get *Reputation* than *Money*." DENNIS of himſelf. See Giles Jacob's Lives of Dram. Poets, p. 68, 69. compared with p. 286. W.

The moſt candid and ample account of Dennis is given in the New Edition of the Biographia Britannica by Dr. Kippis.

Now (ſhame to Fortune!) an ill Run at Play
Blank'd his bold viſage, and a thin Third day:
Swearing

VARIATIONS.

Var. *Tibbald*] Yet this Tibbald, contemptible as he is here repreſented to be, was aſſiſted in his edition of Shakeſpeare by Warburton, publiſhed in ſix volumes octavo; and he mentions, as he well might, Warburton's aſſiſtance, as a great ſupport of his work. This edition of Tibbald was juſtly eſteemed the beſt, till thoſe of Malone and Stevens appeared. W.

REMARKS.

VER. 109. *Bays, form'd by nature, &c.*] It is hoped the poet here hath done full juſtice to his Hero's character, which it were a great miſtake to imagine was wholly ſunk in ſtupidity: he is allowed to have ſupported it with a wonderful mixture of Vivacity. This character is heightened according to his own deſire, in a Letter he wrote to our author. "Pert and dull at leaſt you might have allowed me. What! am I only to be dull, and dull ſtill, and again, and for ever?" He then ſolemnly appealed to his own conſcience, "that he could not think himſelf ſo, nor believe that our Poet did; but that he ſpoke worſe of him than he could poſſibly think; and concluded it muſt be merely to ſhow his *Wit*, or for ſome *Profit* or *Lucre* to himſelf." Life of C. C. chap. vii. and Letter to Mr. P. pag. 15, 40, 53. And to ſhew his claim to what the Poet was ſo unwilling to allow him, of being *pert* as well as *dull*, he declares he will have the *laſt word*; which occaſioned the following Epigram:

Quoth Cibber to Pope, Tho' in verſe you foreclose,
I'll have the laſt Word; for, by G—, I'll write proſe.
Poor Colly, thy reas'ning is none of the ſtrongeſt,
For know, the laſt Word is the Word that laſts longeſt. W.

It is a ſingular fact in the Hiſtory of the Engliſh Stage, that the very firſt comedy, acted after the libertine times of the reſtoration, in which any decency, purity of manners, and reſpect to the honour of the marriage-bed, were preſerved, was this very Cibber's Love's Laſt Shift. It was received with the greateſt applauſe, particularly the ſcene of reconcilement in the laſt act. The candid Abbè d'Olivet in tom. ii. of his pleaſing Hiſtory of the French Academy, page 145. has zealouſly defended the abilities and character of Chapelain, the Cibber of Boileau. It was at the deſire of Malherbe and Vaugelas that Chapelain wrote

Swearing and ſupperleſs the Hero ſate,
Blaſphem'd his Gods, the Dice, and damn'd his Fate.
Then gnaw'd his Pen, then daſh'd it on the ground,
Sinking from thought to thought, a vaſt profound!
Plung'd for his ſenſe, but found no bottom there,
Yet wrote and flounder'd on, in mere deſpair.
Round him much Embryo, much Abortion lay,
Much future Ode, and abdicated Play;

Nonſenſe

VARIATIONS.

VER. 121. *Round him much Embryo, &c.*] In the former Editions thus,

He roll'd his eyes that witneſs'd huge diſmay,
Where yet unpawn'd, much learned lumber lay;
Volumes, whoſe ſize the ſpace exactly fill'd,
Or which fond authors were ſo good to gild,
Or where, by ſculpture made for ever known,
The page admires new beauties not its own.
Here ſwells the ſhelf, &c.—— W.

IMITATIONS.

Var. *He roll'd his eyes that witneſs'd huge diſmay,*]

—— "round he throws his eyes,
That witneſs'd huge affliction and diſmay." MILT. b. i.

The progreſs of a bad poet in his thoughts being (like the progreſs of the Devil in Milton) through a *Chaos*, might probably ſuggeſt this imitation. W.

REMARKS.

the famous preface to the Adone of Marino. And it was he who corrected the very firſt compoſition of Racine, whoſe Ode to the new Queen introduced him to Colbert, and procured him a penſion. And it is remarkable, that Chapelain ſhould be the perſon who firſt pointed out to Cardinal Richlieu, and the poets whom he employed, the neceſſity of obſerving the Three Unities in a drama. It is obſervable that Boileau at firſt had introduced Pelletier into his ſatires; and afterwards inſerted the name of Collitet, in lines inapplicable to the latter. So unlucky were both theſe great poets, in the changes they made of the objects of their ſatire!

Nonſenſe precipitate, like running Lead,
That ſlip'd thro' Cracks and Zig-zags of the Head;
All that on Folly Frenzy could beget,
Fruits of dull Heat, and Sooterkins of Wit.
Next o'er his Books his eyes began to roll,
In pleaſing memory of all he ſtole,
How here he ſipp'd, how there he plunder'd ſnug,
And ſuck'd all o'er, like an induſtrious Bug.
Here lay poor Fletcher's half-eat ſcenes, and here
The Frippery of crucify'd Moliere;
There hapleſs Shakeſpear, yet of Tibbald ſore,
Wiſh'd he had blotted for himſelf before.

The

REMARKS.

VER. 118. *Sinking from thought*] From Lord Rocheſter on man, "Stumbling from thought to thought."——

VER. 125. *All that on Folly*] "To dwell too much on the Follies, Blunders, and Blemiſhes, of bad and deſpicable Dunces, (ſays Plutarch with his uſual humanity), reminds one of Philip's project of collecting together all the moſt abandoned and incorrigible villains he could find, to people a new city which he had built, and called Poneropolis."

VER. 129. *How here he ſipp'd,*] Congreve borrowed much from Ben Johnſon, (of whom he was remarkably fond), particularly the character of Bluff, and the firſt ſcene of the fifth Act of the Way of the World, betwixt Lady Wiſhfort and her Maid Foible; where ſhe minutely deſcribes her former way of life, and upbraids her for ingratitude, evidently from the ſcene betwixt the two ſharpers, Subtle and Face, in the Alchymiſt.

VER. 131. *Poor Fletcher's half-eat ſcenes,*] A great number of them taken out to patch up his plays. W.

VER. 132. *The Frippery*] "When I fitted up an old play, it was as a good houſewife will mend old linen, when ſhe has not better employment." Life, p. 217, Octavo. W.

VER. 133. *Hapleſs Shakeſpear, &c.*] It is not to be doubted but Bays was a ſubſcriber to Tibbald's Shakeſpear. He was

The reſt on Out-ſide merit but preſume,
Or ſerve (like other Fools) to fill a room;
Such with their ſhelves as due proportion hold,
Or their fond Parents dreſt in red and gold;
Or where the pictures for the page atone,
And Quarles is ſav'd by Beauties not his own.

Here

REMARKS.

frequently liberal this way; and, as he tells us, "ſubſcribed to Mr. Pope's Homer, out of pure Generoſity and Civility; but when Mr. Pope did ſo to his Nonjuror, he concluded it could be nothing but a joke." Letter to Mr. P. p. 24.

This Tibbald, or Theobald, publiſhed an edition of Shakeſpear, of which he was ſo proud himſelf as to ſay, in one of Miſt's Journals, June 8, "That to expoſe any errors in it was impracticable." And in another, April 27, "That whatever care might for the future be taken by any other Editor, he would ſtill give above five hundred Emendations, that *ſhall* eſcape them all." W.

VER. 134. *Wiſh'd he had blotted*] It was a ridiculous praiſe which the Players gave to Shakeſpear, "that he never blotted a line." Ben Johnſon honeſtly wiſhed he had blotted a thouſand; and Shakeſpear would certainly have wiſhed the ſame, if he had lived to ſee thoſe alterations in his works, which, not the Actors only (and eſpecially the daring Hero of this Poem) have made on the *Stage*, but the preſumptuous Critics of our days in their *Editions*. W.

VER. 135. *The reſt on Out-ſide merit, &c.*] This Library is divided into three parts; the firſt conſiſts of thoſe authors from whom he ſtole, and whoſe works he mangled; the ſecond, of ſuch as fitted the ſhelves, or were gilded for ſhew, or adorned with pictures; the third claſs our author calls ſolid learning, old Bodies of Divinity, old Commentaries, old Engliſh Printers, or old Engliſh Tranſlations; all very voluminous, and fit to erect altars to Dulneſs. W.

Theſe ſix lines are below the uſual vein of our author; and the note upon them is very forced and unnatural. The prints in Ogilby's China, many of them by Hollar, atone for the page. Dryden uſed to ſay that Quarles excelled him in a facility of rhyming.

Here ſwells the ſhelf with Ogilby the great;
There, ſtamp'd with arms, Newcaſtle ſhines complete:
Here

REMARKS.

VER. 141. *Ogilby the great*;] "John Ogilby was one who, from a late initiation into literature, made ſuch a progreſs as might well ſtyle him the prodigy of his time! ſending into the world ſo many *large volumes!* His tranſlations of Homer and Virgil *done to the life*, and *with ſuch excellent ſculptures:* And (what added great grace to his works) he printed them all on *ſpecial good paper*, and in a *very good letter*." WINSTANLY, Lives of Poets. W.

VER. 142. *There, ſtamp'd, &c.*] "A liſt of her works, which fill many folio's, (ſays Mr. Walpole), here follows:

"The World's Olio.—Nature's Picture drawn by Fancy's pencil to the life. In this volume (ſays the title) are ſeveral feigned ſtories of natural deſcriptions, as comical, tragical, and tragi-comical, poetical, romantical, philoſophical, and hiſtorical, &c. &c. Lond. 1656. folio. One may gueſs how like this portrait of Nature is, by the fantaſtic bill of the features.—Orations of divers ſorts, accommodated to divers places. Lond. 1662. folio.—Plays. Lond. 1662.—Philoſophical and Phyſical Opinions. Lond. 1663. folio.—Obſervations upon Experimental Philoſophy; to which is added, the Deſcription of a New World. Lond. 1668. folio. One Mr. James Briſtow began to tranſlate ſome part of theſe philoſophic diſcourſes into Latin.—Philoſophical Letters. Lond. 1664. folio.—Poems and Phancies. Lond. 1664. folio.—Sociable Letters. Lond. 1664. folio.—The Life of the Duke her huſband, &c. Lond. 1667. folio. It was tranſlated into Latin.—Plays never before printed. Lond. 1668. folio." Her plays alone are nineteen in number, and ſome of them in two parts. One of them, The Blazing World, is unfiniſhed, her Grace (which ſeems never elſe to have happened to her) finding her genius not tend to the proſecution of it. To another, called The Preſence, are nine and twenty ſupernumerary ſcenes. In another, The Unnatural Tragedy, is a whole ſcene written againſt Cambden's

IMITATIONS.

VER. 140. In the former Edd.

The page admires new beauties not it's own.]

"Miraturque novas frondes et non ſua poma."

VIRG. Georg. ii.

Here all his suff'ring brotherhood retire,
And 'scape the martyrdom of jakes and fire:
A Gothic Library! of Greece and Rome
Well purg'd, and worthy Settle, Banks, and Broome.
But,

VARIATIONS.

VER. 146. In the first Edit. it was,

Well purg'd, and worthy W—y, W—s, and Bl—

And in the following altered to Withers, Quarles, and Blome, on which was the following note:

It was printed in the surreptitious editions, *Westly*, *Watts*, who were persons eminent for good life: the one writ the Life of Christ in verse, the other some valuable pieces in the lyric kind on pious subjects. The line is here restored according to its original.

" *George Withers* was a great pretender to poetical zeal against the vices of the times, and abused the greatest personages in power, which brought upon him *frequent Correction*. The *Marshalsea* and *Newgate* were no strangers to him." WINSTANLY. *Quarles* was as dull a writer, but an honester man. *Blome*'s books are remarkable for their cuts. W.

REMARKS.

Cambden's Britannia; her Grace thought, I suppose, that a geographic satire in the middle of a play, was mixing the *utile* with the *dulci*. Three volumes more, in folio, of her poems are preserved in manuscript. Whoever has a mind to know more of this fertile pedant, will find a detail of her works in Ballard's Memoirs, from whence I have taken this account."

VER. 146. *Worthy Settle, Banks, and Broome.*] The Poet has mentioned these three authors in particular, as they are parallel to our Hero in his three capacities: 1. Settle was his Brother Laureate; only indeed upon half-pay, for the City instead of the Court; but equally famous for unintelligible flights in his poems on public occasions, such as Shows, Birth-days, &c. 2. Banks was his Rival in *Tragedy* (tho' more successful) in one of his Tragedies, the *Earl of Essex*, which is yet alive: *Anna Boleyn*, the *Queen of Scots*, and *Cyrus the Great*, are dead and gone. These he drest in a sort of *Beggar's Velvet*, or a happy mixture of the *thick Fustian*, and *thin Prosaic*; exactly imitated in *Perolla and Isidora*, *Cæsar in Egypt*, and the *Heroic Daughter*. 3. Broome was

But, high above, more solid Learning shone,
The Classics of an Age that heard of none;
There Caxton slept, with Wynkyn at his side,
One clasp'd in wood, and one in strong cow-hide;
There,

REMARKS.

was a serving man of Ben Johnson, who once picked up a *Comedy* from his Betters, or from some cast scenes of his Master, not entirely contemptible. W.

VER. 149. *Caxton*] A Printer in the time of Edw. IV. Rich. III. and Hen. VII. Wynkyn de Word, his successor, in that of Hen. VII. and VIII. The former, whom Bale intitles, *Vir non omnino stupidus*, translated into prose Virgil's Aeneis, as a history; of which he speaks, in his Proeme, in a very singular manner, as of a book hardly known. "Happened that to my hande cam a lytyl book in frenche, whiche late was translated out of latyn by some noble clerke of fraunce, whiche booke is named *Eneidos*, (made in latyn by that noble poete & grete clerk Vyrgyle:) whiche booke I sawe over and redde therein, How after the generall destruccyon of the grete Troy, Eneas departed berynge his old fader anchises upon his sholdres, his lytyl son yolas on his hande, his wyse with moche other people followynge, and how he shipped and departed; wythe all thystorye of his adventures that he had er he came to the atchievement of his conquest of ytalye, as all alonge shall be shewed in this present booke. In whiche booke I had grete playsyr, by cause of the fayr and honest termes & wordes in frenche, whiche I never sawe to fore lyke, ne none so playsaunt ne so well ordred; whiche booke as me semed sholde be moch requsiyte to noble men to see, as wel for the eloquence as the hystoryes. How wel that many hondred yerys passed was the sayd booke of Eneydos wyth other workes made and lerned dayly in scholis, especyally in ytalye and other places, whiche historye the sayd Vyrgyle made in metre." *Tibbald* quotes a rare passage from him in *Mist's Journal* of *March* 16, 1728, concerning a *straunge and mervyllouse beaste called Sagittarye*, which he would have *Shakespear* to mean rather than *Teucer*, the Archer celebrated by *Homer*. W.

An undeserved piece of ridicule, on an industrious man, whose labours introduced literature into this country. See what is said of him by one who was a real and rational lover of antiquity, in the History of English Poetry, vol. ii.

There, ſav'd by ſpice, like Mummies, many a year,
Dry Bodies of Divinity appear; 152
De Lyra there a dreadful front extends,
And here the groaning ſhelves Philemon bends.
Of theſe twelve volumes, twelve of ampleſt ſize,
Redeem'd from tapers and defrauded pies, 156
Inſpir'd he ſeizes: Theſe an altar raiſe;
An hecatomb of pure, unſully'd lays
That altar crowns: A folio Common-place
Founds the whole pile, of all his works the baſe:
Quartos, octavos, ſhape the leſs'ning pyre; 161
A twiſted Birth-day Ode completes the ſpire.
Then he: Great Tamer of all human art!
Firſt in my care, and ever at my heart;

Dulneſs!

VARIATIONS.

VER. 162. *A twiſted, &c.*] In the former Edd.

And laſt, a little Ajax tips the Spire. W.

Altered for the worſe.

Var. *A little Ajax*] In *duodecimo*, tranſlated from Sophocles by Tibbald, W.

REMARKS.

VER. 152. *Dry Bodies of Divinity*] The impropriety of placing ſuch ſort of books in the library of Cibber, is not to be vindicated.

VER. 153. *De Lyra there*] He was born in Normandy of Jewiſh parents, educated under ſome learned Rabbis, and for many years devoted to Judaiſm. He afterwards was converted to Chriſtianity, and became a Cordelier at Verneuil, 1291. He taught with great reputation at Paris, and was made executor to the will of King Philip's Queen. He died in an advanced age, 1340.

VER. 154. *Philemon Holland,* Doctor in Phyſic. "He tranſlated *ſo many books*, that a man would think he had done *nothing elſe*; inſomuch that he might be called *Tranſlator general of his age.* The books alone of his turning into Engliſh are ſufficient to make a *Country Gentleman* a *complete Library.*" WINSTANLY. W.

Dulneſs! whoſe good old cauſe I yet defend,
With whom my Muſe began, with whom ſhall end,
E'er ſince Sir Fopling's Periwig was Praiſe,
To the laſt honours of the Butt and Bays:
O thou! of Bus'neſs the directing ſoul!
To this our head like byaſs to the bowl,
Which, as more pond'rous, made its aim more true,
Obliquely wadling to the mark in view:
O! ever gracious to perplex'd mankind,
Still ſpread a healing miſt before the mind;
And, leſt we err by Wit's wild dancing light,
Secure us kindly in our native night.

Or,

REMARKS.

VER. 167. *E'er ſince Sir Fopling's Periwig*] The firſt viſible cauſe of the paſſion of the Town for our Hero, was a fair flaxen full-bottom'd Periwig, which, he tells us, he wore in his firſt play of the *Fool in faſhion.* It attracted, in a particular manner, the Friendſhip of Col. Brett, who wanted to purchaſe it. "Whatever contempt (ſays he) Philoſophers may have for a fine Periwig, my friend, who was not to deſpiſe the world, but to live in it, knew very well that ſo material an article of dreſs upon the head of a man of ſenſe, if it became him, could never fail of drawing to him a more partial Regard and Benevolence, than could poſſibly be hoped for in an ill made one. This, perhaps, may ſoften the grave cenſure, which ſo youthful a purchaſe might otherwiſe have laid upon him. In a word, he made his attack upon this Periwig, as your young fellows generally do upon a lady of pleaſure, firſt by a few familiar praiſes of her perſon, and then a civil enquiry into the price of it; and we finiſhed our bargain that night over a bottle." See Life, octavo, p. 303. This remarkable Periwig uſually made its entrance upon the ſtage in a ſedan, brought in by two chairmen with infinite approbation of the audience. W.

IMITATIONS.

VER. 166. *With whom my Muſe began, with whom ſhall end,*]
" A te principium, tibi deſinet."— VIRG. Ecl. viii.
" 'Ἐκ Διὸς ἀρχώμεσθα, καὶ εἰς Δία λήγετε, Μοῖσαι." THEOC.
" Prima dicte mihi, ſumma dicende Camoena." HOR.

Or, if to Wit a Coxcomb make pretence,
Guard the ſure barrier between that and Senſe;
Or quite unravel all the reas'ning thread,
And hang ſome curious cobweb in its ſtead!
As, forc'd from wind-guns, lead itſelf can fly,
And pond'rous ſlugs cut ſwiftly through the ſky;

As

VARIATIONS.

Ver. 177. *Or, if to Wit, &c.*] In the former Edd.

Ah! ſtill o'er Britain ſtretch that peaceful wand,
Which lulls th' Helvetian and Batavian land;
Where rebel to thy throne if Science riſe,
She does but ſhew her coward face and dies:
There thy good Scholiaſts with unweary'd pains
Make Horace flat, and humble Maro's ſtrains:
Here ſtudious I unlucky moderns ſave,
Nor ſleeps one error in its father's grave,
Old puns reſtore, loſt blunders nicely ſeek,
And crucify poor Shakeſpear once a week.
For thee ſupplying, in the worſt of days,
Notes to dull books, and prologues to dull plays;
Not that my quill to critics was confin'd,
My verſe gave ampler leſſons to mankind:
So graveſt precepts may ſucceſsleſs prove,
But ſad examples never fail to move.
As, forc'd from wind-guns, &c. W.

Theſe lines appear to be better than thoſe in the preſent text.

Var. *And crucify poor Shakeſpear once a week.*] For ſome time, once a week or fortnight, he printed in *Miſt's Journal* a ſingle remark or poor conjecture on ſome *word* or *pointing* of *Shakeſpear*, either in his own name, or in letters to himſelf as from others without name. Upon theſe ſomebody made this Epigram:

"'Tis gen'rous, Tibbald! in thee and thy brothers,
To help us thus to read the works of others:
Never for this can juſt returns be ſhown;
For who will help us e'er to read thy own?"

Var. *Notes to dull books, and prologues to dull plays;*] As to *Cook's Heſiod*, where ſometimes a note, and ſometimes even *half* a note, are carefully owned by him: And to *Moore's Comedy* of the *Rival Modes*, and other authors of the ſame rank: Theſe were people who writ about the year 1726. W.

As clocks to weight their nimble motion owe,
The wheels above urg'd by the load below:
Me Emptineſs, and Dulneſs could inſpire,
And were my Elaſticity, and Fire.
Some Demon ſtole my pen (forgive th' offence)
And once betray'd me into common ſenſe:
Elſe all my Proſe and Verſe were much the ſame;
This, proſe on ſtilts; that, poetry fall'n lame.
Did on the ſtage my Fops appear confin'd?
My Life gave ampler leſſons to mankind.
Did the dead Letter unſucceſsful prove;
The briſk Example never fail'd to move.
Yet ſure, had Heav'n decreed to ſave the State,
Heav'n had decreed theſe works a longer date.

Could

VARIATIONS.

VER. 195. *Yet ſure, had Heav'n, &c.*] In the former Edd.

Had Heav'n decreed ſuch works a longer date,
Heav'n had decreed to ſpare the Grubſtreet-ſtate.
But ſee great Settle to the duſt deſcend,
And all thy cauſe and empire at an end!
Could Troy be ſav'd, &c.—— W.

REMARKS.

VER. 181. *As, forc'd from wind-guns, &c.*] The thought of theſe four verſes is found in a poem of our Author's of a very early date (namely written at fourteen years old, and ſoon after printed) to the Author of a poem called *Succeſſio*. W.

VER. 185. *Me Emptineſs,*] This firſt ſpeech of the Hero is full of an impropriety that one could hardly believe our author could fall into; it being contrary to all decorum, character, and probability, that Bays ſhould addreſs the Goddeſs Dullneſs, without

IMITATIONS.

VER. 195. *Had Heav'n decreed, &c.*]

"Me ſi coelicolae voluiſſent ducere vitam,
Has mihi ſervaſſent ſedes."—— VIRG. Aeneid. ii.

Could Troy be ſav'd by any ſingle hand,
This grey-gooſe weapon muſt have made her ſtand.
What can I now? my Fletcher caſt aſide,
Take up the Bible, once my better guide?
Or tread the path by vent'rous Heroes trod,
This Box my Thunder, this right-hand my God?

Or

REMARKS.

without diſguiſing or miſtaking her, as a deſpicable being; and ſhould even call himſelf fool and blockhead. It is in truth outrageouſly unnatural and abſurd. And ſo alſo is another and even more glaring breach of truth and decorum in book iv. v. 210. in making Ariſtarchus, that is, even the great and able Bentley, abuſe himſelf, and laugh at his own labours. Bramſtone has fallen into the ſame abſurdity;

"A Footman I would be in outward ſhew,
In ſenſe and education truly ſo!" Man of Taſte.

VER. 199. *My Fletcher*] A familiar manner of ſpeaking, uſed by modern Critics, of a favourite author. Bays might as juſtly ſpeak thus of Fletcher, as a French Wit did of Tully, ſeeing his works in a library, "Ah! mon cher Ciceron! je le connois bien; c'eſt le même que Marc Tulle." But he had a better title to call Fletcher *his own*, having made ſo free with him. W.

VER. 200. *Take up the Bible, once my better guide?*] When, according to his Father's intention, he had been a *Clergyman*, or (as he thinks himſelf) a *Biſhop* of the Church of England. Hear his own words: "At the time that the fate of K. James, the Prince of Orange, and myſelf, were on the anvil, Providence thought fit to poſtpone mine, 'till theirs were determined: But had my father carried me a month ſooner to the Univerſity, who knows but that purer fountain might have waſhed my Imperfections into a capacity of writing, inſtead of Plays and annual *Odes*, Sermons and *Paſtoral Letters*?" Apology for his Life, chap. iii. W.

IMITATIONS.

VER. 197, 198. *Could Troy be ſav'd—This grey-gooſe weapon*]

——— "Si Pergama dextra
Defendi poſſent, etiam hac defenſa fuiſſent." VIRG. ibid.

VER. 202. *This Box my Thunder, this right hand my God?*]

"Dextra mihi *Deus*, et telum *quod miſſile libro*."
VIRGIL of the Gods of Mezentius.

Or chair'd at White's amidst the Doctors sit,
Teach Oaths to Gamesters, and to Nobles Wit?
Or bidst thou rather party to embrace?
(A friend to Party thou, and all her race;
'Tis the same rope at diff'rent ends they twist;
To Dulness Ridpath is as dear as Mist.)
Shall I, like Curtius, desp'rate in my zeal,
O'er head and ears plunge for the Common-weal?
Or rob Rome's antient geese of all their glories,
And cackling save the Monarchy of Tories?

Hold

REMARKS.

VER. 203. *At* White's *amidst the* Doctors] These Doctors had a modest and upright appearance, no air of overbearing; but, like true Masters of Arts, were only habited in *black* and *white:* They were justly styled *subtiles* and *graves*, but not always *irrefragabiles*, being sometimes examined, and, by a nice distinction, divided and laid open. SCRIBL. *

This learned Critick is to be understood allegorically: The DOCTORS in this place mean no more than *false Dice*, a cant phrase used amongst Gamesters. So the meaning of these four sonorous Lines is only this, "Shall I play fair, or foul?" P.

VER. 208. *Ridpath—Mist.*] George Ridpath, author of a Whig Paper, called the Flying Post; Nathaniel Mist, of a famous Tory Journal. W.

VER 211. *Or rob Rome's ancient geese of all their glories,*] Relates to the well-known story of the geese that saved the Capitol; of which Virgil, Aeneid. viii.

"Atque hic auratis volitans argenteus anser
Porticibus, Gallos in limine adesse canebat."

A passage I have always suspected. Who sees not the antithesis of *auratis* and *argenteus* to be unworthy the Virgilian majesty? And what absurdity to say a goose *sings? canebat.* Virgil gives a contrary character of the voice of this silly bird, in Ecl. ix.

—— "argutos *inter strepere* anser olores."

Read it, therefore, *adesse strepebat.* And why *auratis porticibus?* does not the very verse preceding this inform us,

"Romuleoque recens horrebat regia culmo."

Is

Hold—to the Minister I more incline;
To serve his cause, O Queen! is serving thine.
And see! thy very Gazetteers give o'er,
Even Ralph repents, and Henley writes no more.
What then remains? Ourself. Still, still remain
Cibberian forehead, and Cibberian brain.
This brazen Brightness, to the 'Squire so dear;
This polish'd Hardness, that reflects the Peer:
This arch Absurd, that wit and fool delights;
This Mess, toss'd up of Hockley-hole and White's;
Where Dukes and Butchers join to wreathe my crown,
At once the Bear and Fiddle of the town.

O born

VARIATIONS.

VER. 213. *Hold—to the Minister—*] In the former Edd.

Yes, to my Country I my pen consign,
Yes, from this moment, mighty Mist! am thine. W.

REMARKS.

Is this *thatch* in one line, and *gold* in another, consistent? I scruple not (*repugnantibus omnibus manuscriptis*) to correct it *auritis*. Horace uses the same epithet in the same sense,

—— "*Auritas* fidibus canoris
Ducere quercus."

And to say that *walls have ears* is common even to a proverb.

SCRIBL.

VER. 215. *Gazetteers*] A band of ministerial writers, hired at the price mentioned in the note on book ii. ver. 316. who, on the very day their patron quitted his post, laid down their paper, and declared they would never more meddle in Politics. W.

VER. 217. *What then remains? Ourself.*] An happy parody on the famous MOY of Corneille in his Medea; who unluckily weakened the force of this word by adding, & c'est assez. But the original is, in Seneca's Tragedy of Medea,

—— "Medea superest."

O born in ſin, and forth in folly brought!
Works damn'd, or to be damn'd! (your father's fault)
Go, purify'd by flames aſcend the ſky,
My better and more chriſtian progeny!
Unſtain'd, untouch'd, and yet in maiden ſheets;
While all your ſmutty ſiſters walk the ſtreets.

Ye

VARIATIONS.

Ver. 225. *O born in ſin, &c.*] In the former Edd.

Adieu, my Children! better thus expire
Un-ſtall'd, unſold; thus glorious mount in fire,
Fair without ſpot; than greas'd by grocers hands,
Or ſhipp'd with Ward to Ape-and-monkey lands,
Or wafting ginger, round the ſtreets to run,
And viſit Ale-houſe, where ye firſt begun.
With that he lifted thrice the ſparkling brand,
And thrice he dropp'd it, &c.——— W.

IMITATIONS.

Var. *And viſit Ale-houſe,*] *Waller* on the Navy,

"Thoſe tow'rs of Oak o'er fertile plains may go,
And viſit mountains where they once did grow." W.

REMARKS.

Ver. 225. *O born in ſin, &c.*] This is a tender paſſionate Apoſtrophe to his own works, which he is going to ſacrifice, agreeable to the nature of man in great affliction; and reflecting like a parent on the many miſerable fates to which they would otherwiſe be ſubject. W.

Ver. 228. *My better*] Notwithſtanding all our author's or his commentators efforts, to reduce to contempt Cibber's Apology for his Life, they will never be able to convince ſenſible and

diſpaſſionate

IMITATIONS.

Ver. 229. *Unſtain'd, untouch'd, &c.*]

——— "Faelix Priamëia virgo!
Juſſa mori: quae fortitus non pertulit ullos,
Nec victoris heri tetigit captiva cubile!
Nos, patria incenſa, diverſa per aequora vectae," &c.

Virg. Aeneid. iii.

Ye ſhall not beg, like gratis-given Bland,
Sent with a Paſs, and vagrant through the land;
Nor ſail with Ward, to Ape-and-monkey climes,
Where vile Mundungus trucks for viler rhymes:
Not ſulphur-tipt, emblaze an Alehouſe fire;
Not wrap up Oranges, to pelt your ſire!
O! paſs more innocent, in infant ſtate,
To the mild Limbo of our Father Tate:
Or peaceably forgot, at once be bleſt
In Shadwell's boſom with eternal Reſt!
Soon to that maſs of Nonſenſe to return,
Where things deſtroy'd are ſwept to things unborn.

With

REMARKS.

diſpaſſionate readers, that it is not a work abounding in curious anecdotes, and in characters nicely and accurately drawn, though in a ſtyle indeed ſingular and affected. Swift was ſo highly pleaſed with Cibber's Life, that he ſat up all night to read it, and would not quit it till he had finiſhed the volume; of which, when Cibber was informed, he ſhed tears of joy.

VER. 231. *gratis-given Bland—Sent with a Paſs,*] It was a practice ſo to give the Daily Gazetteer and miniſterial pamphlets (in which this B. was a writer) and to ſend them *Poſt-free* to all the Towns in the Kingdom. W.

Bland, was the Provoſt of Eton.

VER. 233.—*with Ward, to Ape-and-monkey climes,*] "Edward Ward, a very voluminous poet in Hudibraſtic verſe, but beſt known by the London Spy, in proſe. He has of late years kept a public houſe in the City, (but in a genteel way) and with his wit, humour, and good liquor, (ale), afforded his gueſts a pleaſurable entertainment, eſpecially thoſe of the high-church party." JACOB, Lives of Poets, vol. ii. p. 225. Great number of his works were yearly ſold into the Plantations.——Ward, in a book called Apollo's Maggot, declared this account to be a great falſity, proteſting that his public houſe was not in the *City*, but in *Moorfields*. W.

VER. 238—240. *Tate—Shadwell*] Two of his predeceſſors in the Laurel. W.

With that, a Tear (portentous ſign of Grace!)
Stole from the Maſter of the ſev'nfold Face:
And thrice he lifted high the Birth-day brand,
And thrice he dropt it from his quiv'ring hand;
Then lights the ſtructure with averted eyes:
The rolling ſmoke involves the ſacrifice.
The op'ning clouds diſcloſe each work by turns,
Now flames the Cid, and now Perolla burns;

Great

VARIATIONS.

VER. 250. *Now flames the Cid, &c.*] In the former Edd.

Now flames old Memnon, now Rodrigo burns,
In one quick flaſh ſee Proſerpine expire,
And laſt, his own cold Eſchylus took fire.
Then guſh'd the Tears, as from the Trojan's eyes,
When the laſt blaze, &c.

Var. *Now flames old* Memnon, *now* Rodrigo *burns,*
In one quick flaſh ſee Proſerpine *expire.*]

Memnon, a hero in the *Perſian Princeſs*, very apt to take fire, as appears by theſe lines, with which he begins the play,

" By

REMARKS.

VER. 250. *Now flames the Cid, &c.*] In the firſt notes on the Dunciad it was ſaid, that this Author was particularly excellent at Tragedy. " This (ſays he) is as unjuſt as to ſay I could dance on a Rope." But certain it is that he had attempted to dance on this Rope, and fell moſt ſhamefully, having produced no leſs than four Tragedies, (the names of which the Poet preſerves in theſe few lines), the three firſt of them were fairly printed, acted, and damned; the fourth ſuppreſſed in fear of the like treatment. W.

IMITATIONS.

VER. 245. *And thrice he lifted high the Birth-day brand,*] Ovid, of Althea on a like occaſion, burning her offspring:

" Tum conata quater flammis imponere torrem,
Coepta quater tenuit."

VER. 250. *Now flames the Cid, &c.*]

—— " Jam Deïphobi dedit ampla ruinam,
Vulcano ſuperante domus; jam proximus ardet
Ucalegon."—— W.

Great Caesar roars, and hisses in the fires;
King John in silence modestly expires:
No merit now the dear Nonjuror claims,
Moliere's old stubble in a moment flames.

Tears

VARIATIONS.

"By heav'n it fires my frozen blood with rage,
And makes it scald my aged trunk."

Rodrigo, the chief Personage of the *Perfidious Brother*, (a play written between *Tibbald* and a Watch-maker.) The *Rape of Proserpine*, one of the Farces of this Author, in which *Ceres* setting fire to a corn-field, endangered the burning of the Play-house.

Var. *And last, his own cold* Eschylus *took fire.*] He had been (to use an expression of our Poet) *about Eschylus* for ten years, and had received subscriptions for the same, but then went *about* other books. The character of this tragic Poet is Fire and Boldness in a high degree, but our author supposes it very much cooled by the translation; upon sight of a specimen of which was made this Epigram,

"Alas! poor *Eschylus!* unlucky Dog!
Whom once a *Lobster* kill'd, and now a *Log!*"

But this is a grievous error, for *Eschylus* was not slain by the fall of a Lobster on his head, but of a Tortoise, *teste* Val. Max. l. ix. cap. 12. SCRIBL.

REMARKS.

VER. 252. *King John*] He has omitted a fifth tragedy written also by Cibber, *Xerxes*; which being rejected by the Patentees of Drury Lane, was condemned at Lincoln's Inn Theatre; though Betterton and Mrs. Barry acted in it.

VER. 253. *the dear Nonjuror—Moliere's old stubble*] A Comedy threshed out of Moliere's Tartuffe, and so much the Translator's favourite, that he assures us all our author's dislike to it could only arise from *disaffection to the Government*:

"Qui meprise Cotin, n'estime point son Roi,
Et n'a, selon Cotin, ni Dieu, ni foi, ni loi." BOIL.

He assures us, that "when he had the honour to kiss his Majesty's hand upon presenting his dedication of it, he was graciously pleased, out of his Royal bounty, to order him two hundred pounds for it. And this he doubts not *grieved* Mr. P." W.— And probably it did!

Tears guſh'd again, as from pale Priam's eyes,
When the laſt blaze ſent Ilion to the ſkies.

Rouz'd by the light, old Dulneſs heav'd the head,
Then ſnatch'd a ſheet of Thulè from her bed;
Sudden ſhe flies, and whelms it o'er the pyre;
Down ſink the flames, and with a hiſs expire.

Her ample preſence fills up all the place;
A veil of fogs dilates her awful face:
Great in her charms! as when on Shrieves and May'rs
She looks, and breathes herſelf into their airs.

She

REMARKS.

VER. 255. *pale Priam's*] Priam was informed of the fate of Troy, ſays Shakeſpear, by a form ſo *pale*, ſo *woe-begone*; for which laſt epithet, ſaid a certain critic, we ſhould read *Ucalegon.* He was Priam's next neighbour,—proximus ardet Ucalegon. An abſurdity of the very firſt claſs!

VER. 258. *Thulè*] An unfiniſhed poem of that name, of which one ſheet was printed many years ago, by Ambroſe Philips, a northern author. It is an uſual method of putting out a fire, to caſt wet ſheets upon it. Some critics have been of opinion that this ſheet was of the nature of the Aſbeſtos, which cannot be conſumed by fire: But I rather think it an allegorical alluſion to the coldneſs and heavineſs of the writing. W.

Philips, certainly deſerved not to be treated with ſuch acrimonious contempt, if we conſider his epiſtle from Denmark; his imitation of Strada; his tranſlations of Sappho, and Pindar; and his Diſtreſt Mother; though copied indeed from Racine. Pope himſelf commends the Epiſtle from Denmark in his Letters.

IMITATIONS.

VER. 263. *Great in her charms! as when on Shrieves and May'rs*
She looks, and breathes herſelf into their airs.]

" Alma parens confeſſa Deam; qualiſque videri
Coelicolis, et quanta ſolet"—— VIRG. Aen. ii.

" Et laetos oculis afflavit honores." Id. Aen. i.

She bids him wait her to her sacred Dome:
Well pleas'd he enter'd, and confess'd his home.
So, Spirits ending their terrestrial race,
Ascend, and recognize their Native Place.
This the Great Mother dearer held than all
The clubs of Quidnuncs, or her own Guildhall:
Here stood her Opium, here she nurs'd her Owls,
And here she plann'd th' Imperial seat of fools.
  Here to her Chosen all her works she shows;
Prose swell'd to verse, verse loit'ring into prose:
How random thoughts now meaning chance to find,
Now leave all memory of sense behind:
How Prologues into Prefaces decay,
And these to Notes are fritter'd quite away:
How Index-learning turns no student pale,
Yet holds the eel of science by the tail:

How,

VARIATIONS.

After Ver. 268. in the former Edd. followed these two lines,

Raptur'd, he gazes round the dear retreat,
And in sweet numbers celebrates the seat.

Var. *And in sweet numbers celebrates the seat.*] Tibbald writ a Poem called the *Cave of Poverty*, which concludes with a very extraordinary wish, "That some great genius, or man of distinguished merit, may be *starved*, in order to celebrate her power, and describe her Cave." It was printed in octavo, 1715. W.

REMARKS.

Ver. 280. *Eel of science*] Is from the Tale of a Tub.

IMITATIONS.

Ver. 269. *This the Great Mother, &c.*]

"Urbs antiqua fuit———
Quam Juno fertur terris magis omnibus unam
Posthabita coluisse Samo; hic illius arma,
Hic currus fuit: hoc regnum Dea gentibus esse
(Si qua fata sinant) jam tum tenditque fovetque."
Virg. Aeneid. i.

How, with lefs reading than makes felons 'fcape,
Lefs human genius than God gives an ape,
Small thanks to France, and none to Rome or Greece,
A paft, vamp'd, future, old, reviv'd, new piece,
'Twixt Plautus, Fletcher, Shakefpear, and Corneille,
Can make a Cibber, Tibbald, or Ozell.

The

REMARKS.

VER. 286. *Tibbald,*] Lewis Tibbald (as pronounced) or Theobald (as written) was bred an Attorney, and fon to an Attorney (fays Mr. Jacob) of Sittenburn in Kent. He was Author of fome forgotten Plays, Tranflations, and other pieces. He was concerned in a paper called the Cenfor, and a Tranflation of Ovid. "There is a notorious Idiot, one hight Whachum, who from an under fpur-leather to the law, is become an under-ftrapper to the Playhoufe, who hath lately burlefqued the Metamorphofes of Ovid by a vile Tranflation, &c. This fellow is concerned in an impertinent paper called the Cenfor." DENNIS, Rem. on Pope's Hom. p. 9, 10. W.

Ibid. *Ozell.*] "Mr. John Ozell (if we credit Mr. Jacob) did go to fchool in Leicefterfhire, where *fomebody* left him *fomething* to live on, when he fhall retire from bufinefs. He was defigned to be fent to Cambridge, in order for prieflhood; but he chofe rather to be placed in an *office of accounts*, in the City, being qualified for the fame by his fkill in *arithmetic*, and writing the neceffary *hands*. He has obliged the world with many tranflations of French Plays." JACOB, Lives of *Dram. Poets*, p. 198. W.

Mr. Jacob's character of Mr. Ozell feems vaftly fhort of his merits, and he ought to have further juftice done him, having fince fully confuted all Sarcafms on his learning and genius, by an advertifement of Sept. 20, 1729, in a paper called The Weekly Medley, &c. "As to my *learning*, this envious Wretch knew, and every body knows, that the *whole Bench of Bifhops*, not long ago, were pleafed to give me a *purfe of guineas*, for difcovering the erroneous tranflations of the Common-prayer in Portuguefe, Spanifh, French, Italian, &c. As for my *genius*, let Mr. Cleland fhew better verfes in all Pope's works, than Ozell's verfion of Boileau's Lutrin, which the late Lord Halifax was fo pleafed with, that he complimented him with leave to dedicate it to him, &c. Let him fhew better and truer Poetry in the Rape of the

The Goddeſs then, o'er his anointed head,
With myſtic words, the ſacred Opium ſhed.
And lo! her bird (a monſter of a fowl,
Something betwixt a Heideggre and owl)
Perch'd on his crown. "All hail! and hail again,
My ſon! the promis'd land expects thy reign.
Know, Euſden thirſts no more for ſack or praiſe;
He ſleeps among the dull of ancient days;

Safe,

REMARKS.

Lock, than in Ozell's Rape of the Bucket (*la Secchia rapita*). And Mr. Toland and Mr. Gildon publickly declared Ozell's tranſlation of Homer *to be*, as it was *prior*, ſo likewiſe *ſuperior* to Pope's. Surely, ſurely, every man is free to deſerve well of his country!" JOHN OZELL.

We cannot but ſubſcribe to ſuch reverend teſtimonies, as thoſe of the *Bench of Biſhops*, Mr. *Toland*, and Mr. *Gildon*. W.

Ibid. *A Cibber, Tibbald, or Ozell.*] A triumvirate ſurely not of authors on a level. The *firſt* far ſuperior to the other *two*. What did they produce, in any reſpect, equal to the *Careleſs Huſband*, and the *Hiſtory of the Stage*!

VER. 287. *The Goddeſs then,*] There was a poem publiſhed, 1712, entitled Bibliotheca, by Mr. Thomas Newcomb, a friend of Dr. Young, and reprinted in the fifth volume of Nicols's Collection, page 19, in which the Goddeſs *Oblivion* is introduced, ſpeaking and acting, ſo very like the Goddeſs *Dulneſs*, and which throughout bears ſo cloſe and ſtriking a reſemblance to the *Dunciad*, that it is impoſſible Pope ſhould not have ſeen and copied it, though with exquiſite improvements. The expreſſion, o'er his anointed head, is from Mac Fleckno,

"That for anointed Dulneſs he was made."

As alſo is the preceding line, 262;

"His brows thick fogs, inſtead of glories, grace."

VER. 290. *a Heideggre*] A ſtrange bird from Switzerland, and not (as ſome have ſuppoſed) the name of an eminent perſon who was a man of parts, and, as was ſaid of Petronius, *Arbiter Elegantiarum*. W.

Safe, where no Critics damn, no duns molest,
Where wretched Withers, Ward, and Gildon rest,
And high-born Howard, more majestic sire,
With Fool of Quality completes the quire.

Thou,

VARIATIONS.

VER. 293. *Know, Eusden, &c.*] In the former Edd.

" Know, Settle, cloy'd with custard and with praise,
Is gather'd to the dull of ancient days,
Safe where no critics damn, no duns molest,
Where Gildon, Banks, and high-born Howard rest.
I see a King! who leads my chosen sons
To lands that flow with clenches and with puns:
Till each fam'd theatre my empire own;
Till Albion, as Hibernia, bless my throne!
I see! I see!——Then rapt she spoke no more,
God save king Tibbald! Grubstreet alleys roar.
So when Jove's block, &c. W.

REMARKS.

VER. 296. *Withers,*] See on ver. 146.

Ibid. *Gildon*] Charles Gildon, a writer of criticisms and libels of the last age, bred at St. Omer's with the Jesuits; but renouncing popery, he published Blount's books against the Divinity of Christ, the Oracles of Reason, &c. He signalized himself as a critic, having written some very bad Plays; abused Mr. P. very scandalously in an anonymous pamphlet of the life of Mr. Wycherley, printed by Curl; in another, called the New Rehearsal, printed in 1714; in a third, entitled the Complete Art of English Poetry, in two volumes; and others. W.

Ibid. *Withers, Ward,*] It must be confessed, that in this quarrel with mean and contemptible writers, Pope was the aggressor; for it cannot be believed that the initial Letters in the *Bathos*, were placed at random and without design.

VER. 297. *Howard,*] Hon. Edward Howard, author of the British Princes, and a great number of wonderful pieces, celebrated by the late Earls of Dorset and Rochester, Duke of Buckingham, Mr. Waller, &c.

Thou, Cibber! thou, his Laurel ſhalt ſupport,
Folly, my ſon, has ſtill a Friend at Court.
Lift up your Gates, ye Princes, ſee him come!
Sound, ſound ye Viols, be the Cat-call dumb!
Bring, bring the madding Bay, the drunken Vine;
The creeping, dirty, courtly Ivy join.
And thou! his Aid de camp, lead on my ſons,
Light-arm'd with Points, Antitheſes, and Puns.
Let Bawdry, Billingſgate, my daughters dear,
Support his front, and Oaths bring up the rear:
And under his, and under Archer's wing,
Gaming and Grub-ſtreet ſkulk behind the King.

O! when

REMARKS.

VER. 301. *Lift up your Gates,*] I know not what can excuſe this very profane alluſion to a ſublime paſſage in the Pſalms; which was added to the laſt edition of the Dunciad in four books; and this too under the auſpices and direction of Dr. Warburton. So again in Book iii. ver. 126. And alſo again Book iv. ver. 562.

"Dove-like ſhe gathers to her wings again."

And in the Arguments, he talks of giving a Piſgah-ſight of the future fulneſs of her Glory; and even of ſending Prieſts, and Comforters.

VER. 309, 310. *under Archers wing,——Gaming, &c.*] When the Statute againſt Gaming was drawn up, it was repreſented, that the King, by ancient cuſtom, plays at Hazard one night in the year; and therefore a clauſe was inſerted, with an exception as to that particular. Under this pretence, the Groom-porter had a Room appropriated to Gaming all the ſummer the Court was at Kenſington, which his Majeſty accidentally being acquainted of, with a juſt indignation prohibited. It is reported the ſame practice is yet continued wherever the Court reſides, and the Hazard Table there open to all the profeſſed Gameſters in Town.

"*Greateſt* and *juſteſt* SOV'REIGN; know you this?
Alas! no more, than *Thames'* calm *head* can know
Whoſe meads his *arms* drown, or whoſe corn o'erflow."

Donne to Queen Eliz. W.

This practice has been laid aſide for many years.

O! when ſhall riſe a Monarch all our own,
And I, a Nurſing-mother, rock the throne;
'Twixt Prince and People cloſe the curtain draw,
Shade him from Light, and cover him from Law;
Fatten the Courtier, ſtarve the learned band,
And ſuckle Armies, and dry-nurſe the land:
Till Senates nod to Lullabies divine,
And all be ſleep, as at an Ode of thine."

She ceas'd. Then ſwells the Chapel-royal throat:
God ſave king Cibber! mounts in ev'ry note.
Familiar White's, God ſave king Colley! cries;
God ſave king Colley! Drury-lane replies:
To Needham's quick the voice triumphal rode,
But pious Needham dropt the name of God;
Back to the Devil the laſt echoes roll,
And Coll! each Butcher roars at Hockley-hole.

So

REMARKS.

VER. 319. *Chapel-royal*] The Voices and Inſtruments uſed in the ſervice of the Chapel-royal being alſo employed in the performance of the Birth-day and New-year Odes. W.

VER. 324. *But pious Needham*] A Matron of great Fame, and very religious in her way; whoſe conſtant prayer it was, that ſhe might "get enough by her profeſſion to leave it off in time, and make her peace with God." But her fate was not ſo happy; for being convicted, and ſet in the pillory, ſhe was (to the laſting ſhame of all her great Friends and Votaries) ſo ill uſed by the populace, that it put an end to her days. W.

IMITATIONS.

VER. 304. *The creeping, dirty, courtly Ivy join.*]

——— "Quorum Imagines lambunt
Hederae ſequaces." PERS.

VER. 311. *O! when ſhall riſe a Monarch,* &c.] Boileau, Lutrin, Chant. II.

"Helas! qu'eſt devenu cet tems, cet heureux tems,
Où les Rois s'honoroient du nom de Faineans;" &c. W.

So when Jove's block descended from on high,
(As sings thy great forefather Ogilby)
Loud thunder to its bottom shook the bog
And the hoarse nation croak'd, God save King Log!

REMARKS.

VER. 325. *Back to the Devil*] The Devil Tavern in Fleet-street, where these Odes are usually rehearsed before they are performed at Court. Upon which a Wit of those times made this Epigram,

"When Laureates make Odes, Do you ask of what sort?
Do you ask if they're good, or are evil?
You may judge—From the Devil they come to the Court,
And go from the Court to the Devil." W.

The Epigram inserted on this Tavern, is one of the coldest and dullest that can be read. And it is not clear why the Butchers roared out the name of Colley.

VER. 328.—*Ogilby*)—*God save King Log!*] See Ogilby's Esop's Fables, where, in the story of the Frogs and their King, this excellent hemistic is to be found.

Our author manifests here, and elsewhere, a prodigious tenderness for the *bad writers*. We see he selects the only good passage, perhaps, in all that ever Ogilby writ; which shews how candid and patient a reader he must have been.

But how much all indulgence is lost upon these people may appear from the just reflection made on their constant conduct and constant fate, in the following Epigram:

"Ye little Wits, that gleam'd a while,
When Pope vouchsaf'd a ray,
Alas! depriv'd of his kind smile,
How soon ye fade away!

"To compass Phoebus' car about,
Thus empty vapours rise;
Each lends his cloud, to put him out,
That rear'd him to the skies.

"Alas! those skies are not your sphere;
There He shall ever burn:
Weep, weep, and fall! for Earth ye were,
And must to Earth return." W.

THE END OF THE FIRST BOOK.

THE

DUNCIAD.

BOOK THE SECOND.

ARGUMENT.

THE King being proclaimed, the solemnity is graced with public Games *and sports of various kinds; not instituted by the Hero, as by Aeneas in Virgil, but for greater honour by the* Goddess *in person (in like manner as the games Pythia, Isthmia, &c. were anciently said to be ordained by the Gods, and as Thetis herself appearing, according to Homer, Odyss.* xxiv. *proposed the prizes in honour of her son Achilles). Hither flock the Poets and Critics, attended, as is but just, with their Patrons and Booksellers. The Goddess is first pleased, for her disport, to propose games to the* Booksellers, *and setteth up the phantom of a Poet, which they contend to overtake. The Races described, with their divers accidents. Next, the game for a* Poetess. *Then follow the Exercises for the* Poets, *of* tickling, vociferating, diving: *The first holds forth the arts and practices of* Dedicators, *the second of* Disputants *and* fustian Poets, *the third of* profound, dark, *and* dirty Party-writers. *Lastly, for the* Critics, *the Goddess proposes (with great propriety) an Exercise, not of their parts, but their patience, in hearing the works of two voluminous Authors, the one in* verse, *and the other in* prose, *deliberately read,*

without

without ſleeping: The various effects of which, with the ſeveral degrees and manners of their operation, are here ſet forth; till the whole number, not of Critics only, but of ſpectators, actors, and all preſent, fall faſt aſleep; which naturally and neceſſarily ends the games.

BOOK II.

HIGH on a gorgeous ſeat, that far out-ſhone
Henley's gilt tub, or Fleckno's Iriſh throne,
Or that where on her Curls the Public pours,
All-bounteous, fragrant Grains and Golden ſhow'rs,
Great

REMARKS.

Two things there are, upon the ſuppoſition of which the very baſis of all verbal criticiſm is founded and ſupported: The firſt, that an Author could never fail to uſe the *beſt word* on every occaſion; the ſecond, that a Critic cannot chuſe but know *which that is*. This being granted, whenever any word doth not fully content us, we take upon us to conclude, firſt, that the author could *never have uſed it*; and, ſecondly, that he muſt have uſed *that very one*, which we conjecture, in its ſtead.

We cannot, therefore, enough admire the learned Scriblerus for his alteration of the text in the two laſt verſes of the preceding book, which in all the former editions ſtood thus:

" Hoarſe thunder to its bottom ſhook the bog,
And the loud nation croak'd, God ſave king Log!"

He has, with great judgment, tranſpoſed theſe two epithets; putting *hoarſe* to the nation, and *loud* to the thunder: And this being evidently the true reading, he vouchſafed not ſo much as to mention the former; for which aſſertion of the juſt right of a Critic, he merits the acknowledgment of all ſound Commentators. W.

VER. 2. *Henley's gilt tub,*] The pulpit of a Diſſenter is uſually called a Tub; but that of Mr. Orator Henley was covered with velvet,

IMITATIONS.

VER. 1. *High on a gorgeous ſeat,*] Parody of Milton, book ii.

" High on a throne of royal ſtate, that far
Outſhone the wealth of Ormus and of Ind,
Or where the gorgeous Eaſt with richeſt hand
Show'rs on her kings Barbaric pearl and gold,
Satan exalted ſate." W.

Great Cibber ſate: The proud Parnaſſian ſneer,
The conſcious ſimper, and the jealous leer,
Mix on his look: All eyes direct their rays
On him, and crowds turn Coxcombs as they gaze.
His Peers ſhine round him with reflected grace,
New edge their dulneſs, and new bronze their face.

So

REMARKS.

velvet, and adorned with gold. He had alſo a fair altar, and over it this extraordinary inſcription, *The Primitive Euchariſt.* See the hiſtory of this perſon, book iii. W.

Ibid. *or Fleckno's Iriſh throne,*] Richard Fleckno was an Iriſh prieſt, but had laid aſide (as himſelf expreſſed it) the mechanic part of prieſthood. He printed ſome plays, poems, letters, and travels. I doubt not, our author took occaſion to mention him in reſpect to the Poem of Mr. Dryden, to which this bears ſome reſemblance, though of a character more different from it than that of the Aeneid from the Iliad, or the Lutrin of Boileau from the Defait de Bouts rimées of Sarazin. W.

Andrew Marvell wrote a ſatirical poem on Fleckno, with his uſual ſpirit. There is a comedy of Fleckno, 1667, entitled Demoiſſelles a la Mode.

Ver. 3. *Or that where on her Curls the Public pours,*] Edmund Curl ſtood in the pillory at Charing-Croſs, in March 1727-8. "This (ſaith Edmund Curl) is a falſe aſſertion—I had indeed the corporal puniſhment of what the Gentlemen of the long Robe are pleaſed jocoſely to call *mounting the Roſtrum* for one hour: but that ſcene of Action was not in the month of *March*, but in *February*." [*Curliad* 12mo, p. 19.] And of *the Hiſtory of his being toſt in a Blanket*, he ſaith, "Here, *Scriblerus!* thou leeſeth in what thou aſſerteſt concerning the blanket: it was not a *blanket*, but a *rug*." P. 25. Much in the ſame manner Mr. *Cibber* remonſtrated, that his Brothers, at Bedlam, mentioned Book i. were not *Brazen*, but *Blocks*; yet our author let it paſs unaltered, as a trifle that no way altered the relationſhip. W.

Ver. 5. *Great Cibber ſate:*] It is obſervable that in this paſſage the lines run more into one another, than in any other part of our author's works. See lines 5, 7. Perhaps it might be wiſhed he had more frequently done ſo, as it would have added variety to his numbers. Harte and Fenton thought ſo.

So from the Sun's broad beam, in ſhallow urns
Heav'n's twinkling Sparks draw light, and point their
horns.

Not with more glee, by hands Pontific crown'd,
With ſcarlet hats wide-waving circled round,
Rome in her Capitol ſaw Querno ſit,
Thron'd on ſeven hills, the Antichriſt of wit.

And now the Queen, to glad her ſons, proclaims
By herald Hawkers, high heroic Games.
They ſummon all her Race: An endleſs band
Pours forth, and leaves unpeopled half the land.

A motley

REMARKS.

VER. 15. *Rome in her Capitol ſaw Querno ſit,*] Camillo Querno was of Apulia, who hearing the great Encouragement which Leo X. gave to Poëts, travelled to Rome with a harp in his hand, and ſung to it twenty thouſand verſes of a poem called Alexias. He was introduced *as a Buffoon* to Leo, and promoted to the honour of the *Laurel*; a jeſt which the court of Rome and the Pope himſelf entered into ſo far, as to cauſe him to ride on an elephant to the Capitol, and to hold a ſolemn feſtival on his coronation; at which, it is recorded, the Poet himſelf was ſo tranſported as to *weep for joy* *. He was ever after a conſtant frequenter of the Pope's table, drank abundantly, and poured forth verſes without number. PAULUS JOVIUS, Elog. Vir. doct. cap. lxxxii. Some idea of his poetry is given by Fam. Strada, in his Proluſions. W.

VER. 16. *Antichriſt of wit.*] Chaucer, as well as Dante, aſſerted that the Church of Rome was Antichriſt, a notion Boſſuet has taken ſo much pains to refute.

VER. 18. *High heroic Games.*] It is impoſſible to read without ſmiling, the gravity with which Dennis attacks theſe games, and the reaſons he gives for their impropriety. "Is it not monſtrous to imagine they could take place in the maſter ſtreet of a great city; a ſtreet eternally crowded with carriages, carts, coaches, chairs, and men, paſſing in the greateſt hurry about private and public affairs?" Remarks on Dunciad, p. 19. 1729.

---

* See Life of C. C. chap. vi. p. 149.

A motley mixture! in long wigs, in bags,
In ſilks, in crapes, in Garters, and in rags,
From drawing rooms, from colleges, from garrets,
On horſe, on foot, in hacks, and gilded chariots:
All who true Dunces in her cauſe appear'd
And all who knew thoſe Dunces to reward.

Amid that area wide they took their ſtand,
Where the tall May-pole once o'erlook'd the Strand,
But now (ſo ANNE and Piety ordain)
A Church collects the ſaints of Drury-lane.

With Authors, Stationers obey'd the call,
(The field of glory is a field for all).
Glory, and gain, th' induſtrious tribe provoke;
And gentle Dulneſs ever loves a joke.
A Poet's form ſhe plac'd before their eyes,
And bade the nimbleſt racer ſeize the prize;

No

REMARKS.

VER. 35. *A Poet's form*] A clear, energetic, and lively deſcription! eſpecially line 41, and the three ſucceeding ones, of this truly ridiculous Phantom. Dr. Young, who was well acquainted with More, told me the portrait was not over-charged. More was an egregious and inſufferable coxcomb.

IMITATIONS.

VER. 35. *A Poet's form ſhe plac'd before their eyes,*] This is what Juno does to deceive Turnus, Aeneid. x.

"Tum Dea nube cava, tenuem *ſine viribus umbram*
In faciem Aeneae (viſu mirabile monſtrum!)
Dardaniis ornat telis, clypeumque jubaſque
Divini aſſimilat capitis———
——— Dat *inania verba*
Dat *ſine mente ſonum*"———

The reader will obſerve how exactly ſome of theſe verſes ſuit with their allegorical application here to a Plagiary. There ſeems to me a great propriety in this Epiſode, where ſuch an one is imagined by a phantom that deludes the graſp of the expecting Bookſeller. W.

No meagre, muſe-rid mope, aduſt and thin,
In a dun night-gown of his own looſe ſkin;
But ſuch a bulk as no twelve bards could raiſe,
Twelve ſtarv'ling bards of theſe degen'rate days.
All as a partridge plump, full fed, and fair, 41
She form'd this image of well-body'd air;
With pert flat eyes ſhe window'd well its head;
A brain of feathers, and a heart of lead; 44

And

REMARKS.

VER. 39. *But ſuch a bulk*] Parodies are the chief and conſtant ornaments of a mock-heroic poem. The many introduced by our author are made with ſingular pleaſantry, happineſs, and judgment. The ancients, particularly the Athenians, were fond of parodies; eſpecially ſuch as were made on paſſages of Homer, with whoſe works they were ſo familiarly acquainted. In the fourth book of Athenæus, page 134, of Cauſabon's excellent edition, is a parody, conſiſting of more than one hundred verſes, of Matron, whom Euſtathius frequently quotes and praiſes. It is a ridiculous deſcription of a ſupper. See Fabricius, Bib. Græc. p. 354. B. i. It is well known how many parodies Ariſtophanes has given us on Euripides, and other tragedians. Hegemon, ſays Athenæus, in his ninth book, p. 406. was the firſt author very famous for parodies; he was called, Φακη, Lenticula. He was alſo an excellent actor; and the Athenians were ſo fond of him, that one day when news was brought of their defeat in Sicily, they would not quit the theatre, but inſiſted that Hegemon ſhould finiſh the piece. He was a great favourite of Alcibiades; of whom and Hegemon, Athenæus relates a ſtory worth the Reader's peruſal, p. 407. of Cauſabon's edition. There are ſome excellent parodies in the Rehearſal, in Bramſton's Art of Politics, in the Scribleriad, in the Battle of the Wigs, in the Tale of a Tub, and in the works of Fielding; whom it is ſurprizing Dr. Johnſon ſhould call, a barren raſcal.

IMITATIONS.

VER. 39. *But ſuch a bulk as no twelve bards could raiſe,*]

"Vix illud lecti bis ſex——
Quali nunc hominum producit corpora tellus."
VIRG. Aeneid. xii. W.

And empty words ſhe gave, and ſounding ſtrain,
But ſenſeleſs, lifeleſs! idol void and vain!
Never was daſh'd out, at one lucky hit,
A fool, ſo juſt a copy of a wit;
So like, that critics ſaid, and courtiers ſwore,
A Wit it was, and call'd the phantom More.

All

REMARKS.

VER. 47. *Never was daſh'd out, at one lucky hit,*] Our author here ſeems willing to give ſome account of the poſſibility of *Dulneſs* making a Wit (which could be done no other way than by *chance*). The fiction is the more reconciled to probability, by the known ſtory of Apelles, who being at a loſs to expreſs the foam of Alexander's horſe, daſh'd his pencil in deſpair at the picture, and happened to do it by that fortunate ſtroke. W.

VER. 50. *and call'd the phantom More.*] CURL, in his Key to the Dunciad, affirm'd this to be James Moore Smith eſq. and it is probable (conſidering what is ſaid of him in the *Teſtimonies*) that ſome might fancy our author obliged to repreſent this gentleman as a plagiary, or to paſs for one himſelf. His caſe indeed was like that of a man I have heard of, who, as he was ſitting in company, perceived his next neighbour had ſtolen his handkerchief. "Sir, (ſaid the thief, finding himſelf detected), do not expoſe me, I did it for mere want; be ſo good but to take it privately out of my pocket again, and ſay nothing." The honeſt man did ſo, but the other cry'd out, "See, gentlemen, what a thief we have among us! look, he is ſtealing my handkerchief!"

Some time before, he had borrowed of Dr. *Arbuthnot* a paper called an Hiſtorico-phyſical account of the *South-Sea*; and of Mr. *Pope* the Memoirs of a Pariſh Clerk, which for two years he kept; and read to the Rev. Dr. *Young*,—*F. Billers* eſq. and many others, as his own. Being applied to for them, he pretended they were loſt; but there happening to be another copy of the latter, it came out in *Swift* and *Pope*'s Miſcellanies. Upon this, it ſeems, he was ſo far miſtaken as to confeſs his proceeding by an endeavour to hide it: unguardedly printing (in the *Daily Journal* of *April* 3, 1728,) "That the contempt which he and others had for thoſe pieces (which only himſelf had ſhown, and handed

about

All gaze with ardour: Some a poet's name,
Others a ſword-knot and lac'd ſuit inflame.

But

REMARKS.

about as his own) occaſioned their being loſt, and for that cauſe only not returned." A fact, of which as none but he could be conſcious, none but he could be the publiſher of it. The plagiariſms of this perſon gave occaſion to the following Epigram:

"More always ſmiles whenever he recites;
He ſmiles (you think) approving what he writes.
And yet in this no vanity is ſhown;
A modeſt man may like what's not his own."

This young Gentleman's whole misfortune was too inordinate a paſſion to be thought a Wit. Here is a very ſtrong inſtance atteſted by Mr. *Savage*, ſon of the late Earl *Rivers*; who having ſhewn ſome verſes of his in manuſcript to Mr. *Moore*, wherein Mr. *Pope* was called *firſt of the tuneful train*, Mr. *Moore* the next morning ſent to Mr. *Savage* to deſire him to give thoſe verſes another turn, to wit, "That *Pope* might now be the *firſt*, becauſe *Moore* had left him unrival'd in turning his ſtile to Comedy." This was during the rehearſal of the *Rival Modes*, his firſt and only work; the Town condemned it in the action, but he printed it in 1726-7, with this modeſt Motto,

Hic caeſtus, artemque repono.

The ſmaller pieces which we have heard attributed to this author, are, An Epigram on the Bridge at *Blenheim*, by Dr. *Evans*: *Coſmelia*, by Mr. *Pitt*, Mr. *Jones*, &c. The Mock-marriage of a mad Divine, with a Cl— for a Parſon, by Dr. *W.* The Saw-pit, a Simile, by a *Friend*. Certain Phyſical works on Sir *James Baker*; and ſome unown'd Letters, Advertiſements, and Epigrams againſt our author, in the *Daily Journal*.

Notwithſtanding what is here collected of the Perſon imagined by *Curl* to be meant in this place, we cannot be of that opinion; ſince our Poet had certainly no need of vindicating half a dozen verſes to himſelf, which every reader had done for him; ſince the name itſelf is not ſpell'd *Moore*, but *More*; and laſtly, ſince the learned *Scriblerus* has ſo well proved the contrary. W.

Ver. 50. *the phantom More.*] It appears from hence, that this is not the name of a real perſon, but fictitious. *More* from μωρός, *ſtultus*,

But lofty Lintot in the circle rose:
"This prize is mine; who tempt it are my foes;
"With me began this genius, and shall end."
He spoke: and who with Lintot shall contend?

Fear held them mute. Alone, untaught to fear,
Stood dauntless Curl; "Behold that rival here!

"The

REMARKS.

stultus, *μωρία*, *stultitia*, to represent the folly of a plagiary. Thus Erasmus, *Admonuit me* Mori *cognomen tibi*, *quod tam ad* Moriae *vocabulum accedit quam es ipse a re alienus*. Dedication of Moriae Encomium to Sir Tho. More; the farewell of which may be our author's to his plagiary, *Vale*, More! *et moriam tuam gnaviter defende*. Adieu, More! and be sure strongly to defend thy own folly. SCRIBL.

VER. 53. *But lofty Lintot*] We enter here upon the Episode of the Booksellers; Persons, whose names being more known and famous in the learned world than those of the Authors in this poem, do therefore need less explanation. The action of Mr. Lintot here imitates that of Dares in Virgil, rising just in this manner to lay hold on a *Bull*. This eminent Bookseller printed the *Rival Modes* before mentioned. W.

VER. 58. *Stood dauntless Curl*;] We come now to a character of much respect, that of Mr. Edmund Curl. As a plain repetition of great actions is the best praise of them, we shall only say of this eminent man, that he carried the Trade many lengths beyond what it ever before had arrived at; and that he was the envy and admiration of all his profession. He possessed himself of a command over all authors whatever; he caused them to write what he pleased; they could not call their very *Names* their own. He was not only famous among these; he was taken notice of by the *State*, the *Church*, and the *Law*, and received particular marks of distinction from each.

It will be owned that he is here introduced with all possible dignity: He speaks like the intrepid Diomed; he runs like the swift-footed Achilles; if he falls, 'tis like the beloved Nisus; and (what Homer makes to be the chief of all praises) he is *favoured of the Gods*; he says but three words, and his prayer is heard; a Goddess conveys it to the seat of Jupiter: Though he loses the

prize,

"The race by vigour, not by vaunts, is won;
"So take the hindmost, Hell," (he said) and run.
Swift as a bard the Bailiff leaves behind,
He left huge Lintot, and out-strip'd the wind.
As when a dab-chick waddles through the copse
On feet and wings, and flies, and wades, and hops;
So lab'ring on, with shoulders, hands, and head,
Wide as a wind-mill all his figure spread,

With

REMARKS.

prize, he gains the victory; the great Mother herself comforts him, she inspires him with expedients, she honours him with an immortal present (such as Achilles receives from Thetis, and Aeneas from Venus) at once instructive and prophetical: After this he is unrivalled and triumphant.

The tribute our author here pays him is a grateful return for several unmerited obligations: Many weighty animadversions on the public affairs, and many excellent and diverting pieces on private persons, has he given to his name. If ever he owed two verses to any other, he owed Mr. Curl some thousands. He was every day extending his fame, and enlarging his Writings: Witness innumerable instances; but it shall suffice only to mention the *Court Poems*, which he meant to publish as the work of the true writer, a Lady of quality; but being first threatened, and afterwards punished for it by Mr. Pope, he generously transferred it from *her* to *him*, and ever since printed it in his name. The single time that ever he spoke to C. was on that affair, and to that happy incident he owed all the favours since received from him: So true is the saying of Dr. Sydenham, "that any one shall be, at some time or other, the better or the worse, for having but *seen* or *spoken* to a good or bad man." W.

IMITATIONS.

VER. 60. *So take the hindmost, Hell,*]

"Occupet extremum scabies; mihi turpe relinqui est."

HOR. de Arte. W.

VER. 61, &c. Something like this in Homer, Il. x. ver. 220. of Diomed. Two different manners of the same author in his

 similies

With arms expanded Bernard rows his ſtate,
And left-legg'd Jacob ſeems to emulate.
Full in the middle way there ſtood a lake, 69
Which Curl's Corinna chanc'd that morn to make:
(Such was her wont, at early dawn to drop
Her ev'ning cates before his neighbour's ſhop)

Here

REMARKS.

VER. 70. *Curl's Corinna*] This name, it ſeems, was taken by one Mrs. Thomas, who procured ſome private letters of Mr. Pope, while almoſt a boy, to Mr. Cromwell, and ſold them, without the conſent of either of thoſe Gentlemen, to Curl, who printed them in 12mo, 1727. He diſcovered her to be the publiſher, in his Key. p. 11. We only take this opportunity of mentioning the manner in which thoſe letters got abroad, which the author was aſhamed of as very trivial things, full not only of levities, but of wrong judgments of men and books, and only excuſable from the youth and inexperience of the writer. W.

IMITATIONS.

ſimilies are alſo imitated in the two following; the firſt, of the Bailiff, is ſhort, unadorned, and (as the Critics well know) from *familiar life*; the ſecond, of the Water-fowl, more extended, picturesque, and from *rural life*. The 59th verſe is likewiſe a literal tranſlation of one in Homer. W.

VER. 64, 65. *On feet and wings, and flies, and wades, and hops;*
So lab'ring on, with ſhoulders, hands, and head,]

——— "So eagerly the Fiend
O'er bog, o'er ſteep, thro' ſtreight, rough, denſe, or rare,
With head, hands, wings, or feet purſues his way,
And ſwims, or ſinks, or wades, or creeps, or flies."
MILTON, Book ii. W.

VER. 67, 68. *With arms expanded Bernard rows his ſtate,*
And left-legg'd Jacob ſeems to emulate.]

Milton, of the motion of the Swan,

——— "rows
His ſtate with oary feet."

And Dryden, of another's,—*With two left legs*— W.

Here fortun'd Curl to ſlide; loud ſhout the band,
And Bernard! Bernard! rings thro' all the Strand.
Obſcene with filth the miſcreant lies bewray'd,
Fall'n in the plaſh his wickedneſs had laid:

Then

REMARKS.

VER. 75. *Obſcene with filth, &c.*] Though this incident may ſeem too low and baſe for the dignity of an Epic poem, the learned very well know it to be but a copy of Homer and Virgil; the very words ὄνθος and *fimus* are uſed by them, though our poet (in compliance to modern nicety) has remarkably enriched and coloured his language, as well as raiſed the verſification, in this Epiſode, and in the following one of Eliza. Mr. Dryden, in *Mac-Fleckno*, has not ſcrupled to mention the *Morning Toaſt* at which the fiſhes bite in the Thames, *Piſſing Alley*, *Relics of the Bum*, *&c.* but our author is more grave, and (as a fine writer ſays of Virgil in his Georgics) *toſſes about his dung with an air of Majeſty*. If we conſider that the exerciſes of his *Authors* could with juſtice be no higher than *tickling*, *chattering*, *braying*, or *diving*, it was no eaſy matter to invent ſuch games as were proportioned to the meaner degree of *Bookſellers*. In Homer and Virgil, Ajax and Niſus, the perſons drawn in this plight, are *Heroes*; whereas here they are ſuch with whom it had been great impropriety to have joined any but vile ideas; beſides the natural connection there is between Libellers and common Nuiſances. Nevertheleſs I have heard our author own, that this part of his Poem was (as it frequently happens) what coſt him moſt trouble and pleaſed him leaſt; but that he hoped it was excuſeable, ſince levelled at ſuch as underſtand no delicate ſatire: Thus the politeſt men are obliged ſometimes to *ſwear*, when they happen to have to do with porters and oyſter-wenches. W.

IMITATIONS.

VER. 73. *Here fortun'd Curl to ſlide;*]

"Labitur infelix, caeſis ut forte juvencis
Fuſus humum virideſque ſuper madefecerat herbas—
Concidit, immundoque fimo, ſacroque cruore."
VIRGIL, Aeneid. v. of Niſus. W.

VER. 74. *And Bernard! Bernard!*]

—— "Ut littus, Hyla, Hyla, omne ſonaret."
VIRGIL, Ecl. vi. W.

Then firſt (if Poets aught of truth declare)
The caitiff Vaticide conceiv'd a pray'r.
Hear Jove! whoſe name my bards and I adore,
As much at leaſt as any God's, or more;
And him and his, if more devotion warms,
Down with the Bible, up with the Pope's Arms.
A place there is, betwixt earth, air, and ſeas,
Where, from Ambroſia, Jove retires for eaſe.
There in his ſeat two ſpacious vents appear,
On this he ſits, to that he leans his ear,
And hears the various vows of fond mankind;
Some beg an eaſtern, ſome a weſtern wind:
All vain petitions, mounting to the ſky,
With reams abundant this abode ſupply:
Amus'd he reads, and then returns the bills
Sign'd with that Ichor which from Gods diſtils.

In

REMARKS.

VER. 75. *Obſcene*] Do theſe examples juſtify the introduction of ſuch nauſeous and paltry images, or at all diminiſh the diſguſt of the reader? particularly the paſſage which Dryden diſgraced himſelf by writing? Balſac ſeverely cenſured Malherbe for the expreſſion, *excrement de la terre*. This paſſage of Pope reſembles two moſt filthy lines of Eupolis, quoted by Athenæus, page 314. The Commentator, at the end of the note on this paſſage, aſſigns a ſtrange ſort of apology and obligation for uſing oaths. And in truth, the whole note is groſs and indelicate to a degree.

VER. 82. *Down with the Bible, up with the Pope's Arms.*] The Bible, Curl's ſign: the Croſs-keys, Lintot's. W.

VER. 83. See Lucian's Icaro-Menippus; where this fiction is more extended. W.

IMITATIONS.

VER. 83. *A place there is, betwixt earth, air, and ſeas,*]
" Orbe locus medio eſt, inter terraſque, fretumque,
Coeleſteſque plagas"——— OVID. Met. xii. W.

In office here fair Cloacina ſtands,
And miniſters to Jove with pureſt hands.
Forth from the heap ſhe pick'd her Vot'ry's pray'r,
And plac'd it next him, a diſtinction rare!
Oft had the Goddeſs heard her ſervant's call,
From her black grottos near the Temple-wall,
Liſt'ning delighted to the jeſt unclean
Of link-boys vile, and watermen obſcene;
Where as he fiſh'd her nether realms for Wit,
She oft had favour'd him, and favours yet.
Renew'd by ordure's ſympathetic force,
As oil'd with magic juices for the courſe,
Vig'rous he riſes; from th' effluvia ſtrong
Imbibes new life, and ſcours and ſtinks along;
Re-paſſes Lintot, vindicates the race,
Nor heeds the brown diſhonours of his face.

And

REMARKS.

VER. 92. Alludes to Homer, Iliad v.

———ῥέε δ' ἄμβροτον αἷμα Θέοιο,
'Ιχὼρ, οἷος πέρ τε ῥέει μακάρεσσι Θεοῖσιν.

"A ſtream of nect'rous humour iſſuing flow'd,
Sanguine, ſuch as celeſtial ſp'rits may bleed." MILTON. W.

VER. 93. *Cloacina*] The Roman Goddeſs of the common-ſewers. W.

Ibid. *In office here, &c.*] Never were images, abominably low and diſguſting, elevated and expreſſed in finer language, than from hence to verſe 108. What an abuſe of talents to compoſe ſuch lines on ſuch a ſubject?

VER. 101. *Where as he fiſh'd, &c.*] See the preface to Swift's and Pope's Miſcellanies. W.

VER. 104. *As oil'd with magic juices*] Alluding to the opinion that there are ointments uſed by witches to enable them to fly in the air, &c.

IMITATIONS.

VER. 108. *Nor heeds the brown diſhonours of his face.*]

——— "faciem oſtentabat, et udo
Turpia membra fimo"——— VIRG. Aeneid. v. W.

And now the victor ſtretch'd his eager hand
Where the tall Nothing ſtood, or ſeem'd to ſtand;
A ſhapeleſs ſhade, it melted from his ſight,
Like forms in clouds, or viſions of the night.
To ſeize his papers, Curl, was next thy care;
His papers light, fly diverſe, toſt in air;
Songs, ſonnets, epigrams, the winds uplift,
And whiſk 'em back to Evans, Young, and Swift.
Th' embroider'd ſuit at leaſt he deem'd his prey,
That ſuit an unpay'd taylor ſnatch'd away.

No

REMARKS.

VER. 116. *Evans, Young, and Swift.*] Some of thoſe perſons, whoſe writings, epigrams, or jeſts, he had owned. See Note on ver. 50. W.

Dr. Evans was of St. John's College Oxford; author of the Apparition, and of an Epiſtle to Bobart the Botaniſt, entitled, Vertumnus. He was a man of remarkable wit and vivacity, and many of his repartees were long remembered and repeated at Oxford. The apparition was a ſatire on Tindal.

VER. 118. *an unpaid taylor*] This line has been loudly complained of in Miſt, June 8, Dedic. to Sawney, and others, as a moſt inhuman ſatire on the *poverty of Poets:* But it is thought our author will be acquitted by a jury of *Taylors.* To me this inſtance ſeems unluckily choſen; if it be a ſatire on any body, it muſt be on a bad *pay-maſter,* ſince the perſon to whom they have here applied it, was a man of fortune. Not but Poets may well be

jealous

IMITATIONS.

VER. 111. *A ſhapeleſs ſhade, &c.*

——— "Effugit imago
Par levibus ventis, volucrique ſimillima ſomno."
VIRG. Aeneid. vi. W.

VER. 114. *His papers light, fly diverſe, toſt in air;*]

"Carmina ————
turbata volent rapidis ludibria ventis."
VIRG. Aeneid. vi. of the Sibyl's leaves. W.

No rag, no scrap, of all the beau, or wit,
That once so flutter'd, and that once so writ.
  Heav'n rings with laughter: Of the laughter vain,
Dulness, good Queen, repeats the jest again.
Three wicked imps, of her own Grub-street Choir,
She deck'd like Congreve, Addison, and Prior;
Mears, Warner, Wilkins run: delusive thought!
Breval, Bond, Besaleel, the varlets caught.

Curl

REMARKS.

jealous of so great a prerogative as *non-payment*; which Mr. Dennis so far asserts, as boldly to pronounce that, "If Homer himself was not in debt, it was because nobody would trust him." Pref. to Rem. on the Rape of the Lock, p. 15. W.

VER. 124. *like Congreve, Addison, and Prior*;] These authors being such whose names will reach posterity, we shall not give any account of them, but proceed to those of whom it is necessary.—Besaleel Morris was author of some satires on the translators of Homer, with many other things printed in newspapers.—"Bond writ a satire against Mr. P—. Capt. Breval was author of The Confederates, an ingenious dramatic performance to expose Mr. P. Mr. Gay, Dr. Arb. and some ladies of quality," says CURL, Key, p. 11. W.

This is the passage in which our author has mentioned *Prior* with rather more honor than in any other part of his works. Prior was mortified that Pope did not commend his Solomon so highly as he wished.

VER. 125. *Mears, Warner, Wilkins*,] Booksellers and Printers of much anonymous stuff. W

VER. 126. *Breval, Bond, Besaleel*,] I foresee it will be objected from this line, that we were in an error in our assertion on ver. 50. of this book, that More was a fictitious name, since these persons are equally represented by the poet as phantoms. So at first sight it may seem; but be not deceived, reader; these also are not real persons. 'Tis true, Curl declares Breval, a captain, author of a piece called the Confederates; but the same Curl first said it was written by Joseph Gay: Is his second assertion to be credited any more

than

Curl stretches after Gay, but Gay is gone,
He grasps an empty Joseph for a John:
So Proteus, hunted in a nobler shape,
Became, when seiz'd, a puppy, or an ape.
 To him the Goddess: Son! thy grief lay down,
And turn this whole illusion on the town
As the sage dame, experienc'd in her trade,
By names of Toasts retails each batter'd Jade;
(Whence hapless Monsieur much complains at Paris
Of wrongs from Duchesses and Lady Maries;)
Be thine, my stationer! this magic gift;
Cook shall be Prior, and Concanen, Swift:
So shall each hostile name become our own,
And we too boast our Garth and Addison.

With

REMARKS.

than his first? He likewise affirms Bond to be one who writ a satire on our poet. But where is such a satire to be found? where was such a writer ever heard of? As for Besaleel, it carries forgery in the very name; nor is it, as the others are, a surname. Thou may'st depend upon it, no such authors ever lived; all phantoms. SCRIBL.

VER. 131. *Lay down,*] Is one of the most inaccurate expressions in this poem.

VER. 138. *Cook shall be Prior,*] The man here specified writ a thing called The Battle of Poets, in which Philips and Welsted were the Heroes, and Swift and Pope utterly routed. He also published some malevolent things in the British, London, and Daily Journals; and at the same time wrote letters to Mr. Pope, protesting his Innocence. His chief work was a translation of Hesiod, to which Theobald writ notes and half notes, which he carefully owned. W.

Ibid. *And Concanen, Swift:*] In the first edition of this poem there were only asterisks in this place, but the names were since inserted, merely to fill up the verse, and give ease to the ear of the reader. W.

With that she gave him (piteous of his case,
Yet smiling at his rueful length of face)

A shaggy

REMARKS.

VER. 140. *And we too boast our Garth and Addison.*] Nothing is more remarkable than our author's love of praising good writers. He has in this very poem celebrated Mr. Locke, Sir Isaac Newton, Dr. Barrow, Dr. Atterbury, Mr. Dryden, Mr. Congreve, Dr. Garth, Mr. Addison; in a word, almost every man of his time that deserved it; even Cibber himself (presuming him to be author of the Careless Husband). It was very difficult to have that pleasure in a poem on this subject, yet he has found means to insert their panegyric, and has made even Dulness out of her own mouth, pronounce it. It must have been particularly agreeable to him to celebrate Dr. Garth; both as his constant friend, and as he was his predecessor in this kind of satire. The Dispensary attacked the whole body of Apothecaries, a much more useful one undoubtedly than that of the bad poets; if in truth this can be a body, of which no two members ever agreed. It also did, what Mr. Theobald says is unpardonable, drew in *parts* of *private character*, and introduced *persons independent of his subject*. Much more would Boileau have incurred his censure, who left all subjects whatever, on all occasions, to fall upon the bad poets, (which, it is to be feared, would have been more immediately his concern.) But certainly next to commending good writers, the greatest service to learning is to expose the bad, who can only that way be made of any use to it. This truth is very well set forth in these lines addressed to our author:

"The craven Rook, and pert Jackdaw,
(Tho' neither birds of moral kind)
Yet serve, if hang'd, or stuff'd with straw,
To shew us which way blows the wind.

"Thus

IMITATIONS.

VER. 141, 142. ——— *pitious of his case,*
Yet smiling at his rueful length of face.]

——— "Risit pater optimus illi.—
Me liceat casum misereri insontis amici—
Sic fatus, tergum Gaetuli immanae leonis." &c.
VIRG. Aeneid. v. W.

A ſhaggy Tap'ſtry, worthy to be ſpread
On Codrus' old, or Dunton's modern bed;
Inſtructive

REMARKS.

" Thus dirty knaves, or chatt'ring fools,
Strung up by dozens in thy lay,
Teach more by half than Dennis' rules,
And point inſtruction ev'ry way.

" With Egypt's art thy pen may ſtrive;
One potent drop let this but ſhed:
And ev'ry rogue that ſtunk alive,
Becomes a precious mummy dead." W.

VER. 142. *rueful length of face*] " The decrepid perſon or figure of a man are no reflections upon his *Genius*: An honeſt mind will love and eſteem a *man of worth*, though he be deformed or poor. Yet the author of the Dunciad hath libelled a perſon for his *rueful length of face!*" Miſt's Journal, June 8. This *Genius* and *man of worth*, whom an honeſt mind ſhould *love*, is Mr. Curl. True it is, he ſtood in the Pillory, an incident which will lengthen the face of any Man, though it were ever ſo comely, therefore is no reflection on the natural beauty of Mr. Curl. But as to reflections on any man's face, or figure, Mr. Dennis ſaith excellently; " Natural deformity comes not by our fault; 'tis often occaſioned by calamities and diſeaſes, which a man can no more help than a monſter can his deformity. There is no one misfortune, and no one diſeaſe, but what all the reſt of mankind are ſubject to.—But the deformity of this *Author* is viſible, preſent, laſting, unalterable, and peculiar to himſelf. 'Tis the mark of God and Nature upon him, to give us warning that we ſhould hold no ſociety with him, as a creature not of our original, nor of our ſpecies: and they who have refuſed to take this warning which God and nature has given them, and have, in ſpite of it, by a ſenſeleſs preſumption ventured to be familiar with him, have ſeverely ſuffered, &c. 'Tis certain his original is not from Adam, but from the Devil," &c. DENNIS, Character of Mr. P. octavo, 1716.

Admirably it is obſerved by Mr. Dennis againſt Mr. Law, p. 33. " That the language of Billingſgate can never be the language of charity, nor conſequently of Chriſtianity." I ſhould elſe be tempted to uſe the language of a Critic; for what is more provoking to a commentator, than to behold his author thus portray'd? Yet I conſider it really hurts not *him*; whereas to call

Instructive work! whose wry-mouth'd portraiture
Display'd the fates her confessors endure. 146

Earless

REMARKS.

call some others dull, might do them prejudice with a world too apt to believe it: Therefore, though Mr. D. may call another a *little ass* or a *young toad*, far be it from us to call him *a toothless lion*, or an *old serpent*. Indeed, had I written these notes (as once was my intent) in the learned language, I might have given him the appellations of *balatro*, *calceatum caput*, *scurra in triviis*, being phrases in good esteem and frequent usage among the best learned: But in our mother tongue, were I to tax any gentleman of the Dunciad, surely it should be in words not to the vulgar intelligible; whereby christian charity, decency, and good accord among authors, might be preserved. SCRIBL.

The good Scriblerus here, as on all occasions, eminently shews his humanity. But it was far otherwise with the gentlemen of the Dunciad, whose scurrilities were always personal, and of that nature which provoked every honest man but Mr. Pope; yet never to be lamented, since they occasioned the following amiable Verses:

"While Malice, Pope, denies thy page
Its own celestial fire;
While Critics, and while Bards in rage,
Admiring, won't admire:

"While wayward pens thy worth assail,
And envious tongues decry;
These times tho' many a Friend bewail,
These times bewail not I.

"But when the World's loud praise is thine,
And spleen no more shall blame,
When with thy Homer thou shalt shine
In one establish'd fame:

"When none shall rail, and ev'ry lay
Devote a wreath to thee;
That day (for come it will) that day
Shall I lament to see." W.

VER. 143. *A shaggy Tap'stry,*] A sorry kind of Tapestry frequent in old Inns, made of worsted or some coarser stuff;

like

Earleſs on high, ſtood unabaſh'd De Foe,
And Tutchin flagrant from the ſcourge below.
There Ridpath, Roper, cudgell'd might ye view,
The very worſted ſtill look'd black and blue.
Himſelf

REMARKS.

like that which is ſpoken of by Donne——*Faces as frightful as theirs who whip Chriſt in old hangings.* The imagery woven in it alludes to the mantle of Cloanthus, in Aeneid v. W.

VER. 144. *On Codrus' old, or Dunton's modern bed;*] Of Codrus the poet's bed, ſee Juvenal, deſcribing his *poverty* very copiouſly, Sat. iii. ver. 103, &c.

Lectus erat Codro, &c.

" Codrus had but one bed, ſo ſhort to boot,
That his ſhort wife's ſhort legs hung dangling out.
His cupboard's head ſix earthen pitchers grac'd,
Beneath them was his truſty tankard plac'd;
And to ſupport this noble plate, there lay
A bending Chiron, caſt from honeſt clay.
His few Greek books a rotten cheſt contain'd,
Whoſe covers much of mouldineſs complain'd,
Where mice and rats devour'd poetic bread,
And on heroic verſe luxuriouſly were fed.
'Tis true poor Codrus nothing had to boaſt,
And yet poor Codrus all that nothing loſt." DRYDEN.

But Mr. Concanen, in his dedication of the Letters, Advertiſements, &c. to the author of the Dunciad, aſſures us, " that Juvenal never ſatirized the Poverty of Codrus."

John Dunton was a broken bookſeller, and abuſive ſcribler: he writ Neck or Nothing, a violent ſatire on ſome miniſters of ſtate, a libel on the Duke of Devonſhire and the Biſhop of Peterborough, &c. W.

VER. 148. *And Tutchin flagrant from the ſcourge*] John Tutchin, author of ſome vile verſes, and of a weekly paper called The Obſervator: He was ſentenced to be whipped through ſeveral towns in the weſt of England, upon which he petitioned King James II. to be hanged. When that prince died in exile, he wrote an invective againſt his memory, occaſioned by ſome humane elegies on his death. He lived to the time of Queen Anne.

Himſelf among the ſtory'd chiefs he ſpies,
As, from the blanket, high in air he flies,
And oh! (he cry'd) what ſtreet, what lane but knows
Our purgings, pumpings, blanketings, and blows?
In every loom our labours ſhall be ſeen,
And the freſh vomit run for ever green!

See in the circle next, Eliza plac'd,
Two babes of love cloſe clinging to her waiſt;

Fair

REMARKS.

VER. 149. *There Ridpath, Roper,*] Authors of the Flying-poſt and Poſt-boy, two ſcandalous papers on different ſides, for which they equally and alternately deſerved to be cudgelled, and were ſo. W.

Ibid. *Cudgell'd*] It is painful to reflect, that even Dryden once underwent this diſcipline. Mr. Nelſon, whoſe truth cannot be queſtioned, writes thus to Dr. Mapletoft, Jan. 2, 1679; "Your friend and ſchoolfellow Mr. Dryden has been ſeverely beaten for being the ſuppoſed author of a late very abuſive lampoon. There has been a good ſum of money offered to find who ſet them on work; 'tis ſaid they received their orders from the Dutcheſs of Portſmouth, who is concerned in the lampoon."

Line 150 is particularly happy.

VER. 151. *Himſelf among the ſtory'd chiefs he ſpies,*] The hiſtory of Curl's being toſſed in a blanket, and whipped by the Scholars of Weſtminſter, is well known. Of his purging and vomiting, ſee A full and true acccount of a horrid Revenge on the body of Edm. Curl, &c. in Swift and Pope's Miſcellanies. W.

IMITATIONS.

VER. 151. *Himſelf among the ſtory'd chiefs he ſpies,*]
"Se quoque principibus permixtum agnovit Achivis——
Conſtitit, et lacrymans: Quis jam locus, inquit, Achate!
Quae regio in terris noſtri non plena laboris?" VIRG. Aen.i. W.

VER. 156. *And the freſh vomit run for ever green!*] A parody on theſe lines of a late noble author:

"His bleeding arm had furniſh'd all their rooms,
And run for ever purple in the looms." W.

Fair as before her works ſhe ſtands confeſs'd, 159
In flow'rs and pearls by bounteous Kirkall dreſs'd.
The Goddeſs then: "Who beſt can ſend on high
The ſalient ſpout, far-ſtreaming to the ſky;
His

REMARKS.

VER. 157. *See in the circle next, Eliza plac'd*] In this game is expoſed, in the moſt contemptuous manner, the profligate licentiouſneſs of thoſe ſhameleſs ſcribblers (for the moſt part of that ſex, which ought leaſt to be capable of ſuch malice or impudence) who, in libellous Memoirs and Novels, reveal the faults or misfortunes of both ſexes, to the ruin of public fame, or diſturbance of private happineſs. Our good poet (by the whole caſt of his work being obliged not to take off the Irony) where he could not ſhew his indignation, hath ſhewn his contempt, as much as poſſible; having here drawn as vile a picture as could be repreſented in the colours of Epic poeſy. SCRIBL.

Ibid. *Eliza Haywood*; This woman was authoreſs of thoſe moſt ſcandalous books called The Court of Carimania, and the New Utopia. For the *two babes of love*, ſee CURL, KEY, p. 22. But whatever reflection he is pleaſed to throw upon this Lady, ſurely it was what from him ſhe little deſerved, who had celebrated Curl's undertakings for *Reformation of manners*, and declared herſelf "to be ſo perfectly acquainted with the *ſweetneſs of his diſpoſition*, and that *tenderneſs with which he conſidered the errors of his fellow creatures*; that, though ſhe ſhould find the *little inadvertencies* of her *own life* recorded in his papers, ſhe was certain it would be done in ſuch a manner as ſhe could not but approve." Mrs. HAYWOOD, Hiſt. of Clar. printed in the Female Dunciad, p. 18. W.

VER. 160. *Kirkall*, the name of an Engraver. Some of this Lady's works were printed in four volumes in 12mo, with her picture thus dreſſed up before them. W.

VER. 162. *The ſalient ſpout*,] No wit can atone for the meanneſs, filthineſs, and vulgarity, of this conteſt. This Oſborne was the bookſeller

IMITATIONS.

VER. 158. *Two babes of love cloſe clinging to her waiſt*;]
"Creſſa genus, Pholoë, geminique ſub ubere nati."
VIRG. Aeneid. v. W.

His be yon Juno of majeſtic ſize,
With cow-like udders, and with ox-like eyes.
This China Jordan let the chief o'ercome
Repleniſh, not ingloriouſly, at home."
  Oſborne and Curl accept the glorious ſtrife,
(Tho' this his Son diſſuades, and that his Wife.)
One

REMARKS.

bookſeller who purchaſed the great library of the Earl of Oxford, for 13,000 *l.* which, ſays Mr. Oldys, was not more than the binding of the books had coſt. Dr. Johnſon wrote the preface to the catalogue, and is reported, during this employment, to have knocked Oſborne down with a folio in his ſhop. But Johnſon himſelf uſed to ſay, "I beat him for being impertinent to me; but it was in my own chamber, and not in his ſhop."

VER. 167. *Oſborne, Thomas*] A Bookſeller in Gray's Inn, very well qualified by his impudence to act this part; therefore placed here inſtead of a leſs deſerving Predeceſſor. This man publiſhed advertiſements for a year together, pretending to ſell Mr. Pope's Subſcription books of Homer's Iliad at half the price: Of which books he had none, but cut to the ſize of them (which was quarto) the common books in folio, without Copper-plates, on a worſe paper, and never above half the value.

Upon this Advertiſment the Gazetteer harangued thus, July 6, 1739. "How melancholy muſt it be to a writer to be ſo unhappy as to ſee his works hawked for ſale in a manner ſo fatal to his fame!

IMITATIONS.

VER. 163. ——— *yon Juno* ———
With cow-like udders, and with ox-like eyes.]
In alluſion to Homer's Βοῶπις πότνια Ἥρη.

VER. 165. *This China Jordan*]
"Tertius Argolica hac galea contentus abito."
VIRG. Aeneid. vi.

In the games of Homer, Iliad xxiii. there are ſet together, as prizes, a Lady and a Kettle, as in this place Mrs. Haywood and a Jordan. But there the preference in value is given to the Kettle, at which Mad. Dacier is juſtly diſpleaſed. Mrs. H. is here treated with diſtinction, and acknowledged to be the more valuable of the two. W.

One on his manly confidence relies,
One on his vigour and ſuperior ſize.
Firſt Oſborne lean'd againſt his letter'd poſt;
It roſe, and labour'd to a curve at moſt.
So Jove's bright bow diſplays its wat'ry round,
(Sure ſign, that no ſpectator ſhall be drown'd.)
A ſecond effort brought but new diſgrace,
The wild Meander waſh'd the Artiſt's face:
Thus the ſmall jett, which haſty hands unlock,
Spirts in the gard'ner's eyes who turns the cock.
Not ſo from ſhameleſs Curl; impetuous ſpread
The ſtream, and ſmoking flouriſh'd o'er his head.

So

REMARKS.

fame! How, with Honour to yourſelf, and Juſtice to your Subſcribers, can this be done? What an ingratitude to be charged on the *Only honeſt Poet* that lived in 1738! and than whom *Virtue* has not had a *ſhriller Trumpeter* for many ages! That you were once *generally admired and eſteemed* can be denied by none; but that you and your works are now deſpiſed, is verified by *this fact*:" which being utterly falſe, did not indeed much humble the Author, but drew this juſt chaſtiſement on the Bookſeller. W.

VER. 172. IT, is inaccurate, and wants a ſubſtantive.

IMITATIONS.

VER. 169, 170. *One on his manly confidence relies,*
One on his vigour]

"Ille—melior motu, fretuſque juventa;
Hic membris et mole valens." VIRG. Aeneid. v. W.

VER. 173, 174. *So Jove's bright bow*——
(Sure ſign,——]

The words of Homer, of the Rain-bow, in Iliad xi.

——— ἅς τε Κρονίων
Ἐν νέφεϊ στήριξε, τέρας μερόπων ἀνθρώπων.

"Que le fils de Saturne a fondez dans les nües, pour être dans tous les âges une ſigne à tous les mortels." DACIER. W.

So (fam'd like thee for turbulence and horns)
Eridanus his humble fountain ſcorns;
Through half the heav'ns he pours th' exalted urn;
His rapid waters in their paſſage burn.
  Swift as it mounts, all follow with their eyes:
Still happy Impudence obtains the prize.

Thou

REMARKS.

VER. 183. *Through half the heav'ns he pours th' exalted urn*;] In a manuſcript Dunciad (where are ſome marginal corrections of ſome gentlemen ſome time deceaſed) I have found another reading of theſe lines, thus,

And lifts his urn, through half the heav'ns to flow;
His rapid waters in their paſſage *glow*.

This I cannot but think the right: For firſt, though the difference between *burn* and *glow* may ſeem not very material to others, to me I confeſs the latter has an elegance, a *je ne ſçay quoi*, which is much eaſier to be conceived than explained. Secondly, every reader of our poet muſt have obſerved how frequently he uſes this word *glow* in other parts of his works: To inſtance only in his Homer:

(1.) Iliad ix. ver. 726.—" With one reſentment glows.
(2.) Iliad xi. ver. 626.—" There the battle glows.
(3.) Ibid. ver. 985.—" The cloſing fleſh that inſtant ceas'd to glow.

(4.) Iliad

IMITATIONS.

VER. 181, 182. *So (fam'd like thee for turbulence and horns) Eridanus*]

Virgil mentions theſe two qualifications of Eridanus, Georg. iv.

" Et gemina auratus taurino *cornua* vultu,
Eridanus, quo non alius per pinguia culta
In mare purpureum *violentior* influit amnis."

The Poets fabled of this river Eridanus, that it flowed through the ſkies. DENHAM, Cooper's Hill:

" Heav'n her Eridanus no more ſhall boaſt,
Whoſe fame's in thine, like leſſer currents loſt;
Thy nobler ſtream ſhall viſit Jove's abodes,
To ſhine among the ſtars, and bathe the Gods." W.

Thou triumph'ſt, Victor of the high-wrought day,
And the pleas'd dame, ſoft-ſmiling, lead'ſt away.
Oſborne, through perfect modeſty o'ercome,
Crown'd with the Jordan, walks contented home.

But now for Authors nobler palms remain;
Room for my Lord! three jockeys in his train;
Six huntſmen with a ſhout precede his chair:
He grins, and looks broad nonſenſe with a ſtare.
His Honour's meaning Dulneſs thus expreſt,
"He wins this Patron, who can tickle beſt."

He chinks his purſe, and takes his ſeat of ſtate:
With ready quills the Dedicators wait;

Now

REMARKS.

(4.) Iliad xii. ver. 45.—"Encompaſs'd Hector glows.

(5.) Ibid. ver. 475.—"His beating breaſt with gen'rous ardour glows.

(6.) Iliad xviii. ver. 591.—"Another part glow'd with refulgent arms.

(7.) Ibid. ver. 654.—"And curl'd on ſilver props in order glow."

I am afraid of growing too luxuriant in examples, or I could ſtretch this catalogue to a great extent; but theſe are enough to prove his fondneſs for this *beautiful word*, which, therefore, let *all future editions* replace here.

I am aware, after all, that *burn* is the proper word to convey an idea of what was ſaid to be Mr. Curl's condition at this time: But from that very reaſon I infer the direct contrary. For ſurely every *lover of our author* will conclude he had more *humanity* than to inſult a man on ſuch a misfortune or calamity, which could never befal him purely by his *own fault*, but from an unhappy communication with another. This Note is half Mr. THEOBALD, half SCRIBL. It reflects ſhame on both of them.

VER. 187. *the high-wrought day,*] Some affirm this was originally, *well p—ſt day*; but the Poet's decency would not ſuffer it. W.

Nor ſhould the Commentator have written ſuch a note!

Now at his head the dextrous taſk commence,
And, inſtant, fancy feels th' imputed ſenſe;
Now gentle touches wanton o'er his face,
He ſtruts Adonis, and affects grimace:
Rolli the feather to his ear conveys;
Then his nice taſte directs our Operas:
Bentley his mouth with claſſic flatt'ry opes,
And the puff'd orator burſts out in tropes.

But

REMARKS.

VER. 198. *The Dedicators*] Among the innumerable inſtances that might be given of fulſome Dedications, none can exceed that of the courtly Abbé Choiſy, to Madame Maintenon, prefixed to the tranſlation of his *Kempis*, with her picture kneeling before a crucifix, and theſe words of the 44th Pſalm; "Hearken, O Daughter, and conſider."

VER. 203. *Paulo Antonio Rolli*, an Italian Poet, and writer of many Operas in that language, which, partly by the help of his genius, prevailed in England near twenty years. He taught Italian to ſome fine Gentlemen, who affected to direct the Operas. W.

He alſo tranſlated Paradiſe Loſt with ſpirit and elegance; and publiſhed Marchettis' fine tranſlation of Lucretius.

VER. 205. *Bentley his mouth, &c.*] Not ſpoken of the famous Dr. Richard Bentley, but of one Thomas Bentley, a ſmall critic, who aped his uncle in a *little Horace*. The great one was intended to be dedicated to the Lord Halifax, but (on a change of the Miniſtry) was given to the Earl of Oxford; for which reaſon the little one was dedicated to his ſon the Lord Harley. A taſte of his *Claſſic Elocution* may be ſeen in his following Panegyric on the Peace of Utrecht. *Cupimus Patrem tuum, fulgentiſſimum illud Orbis Anglicani jubar*, adorare! *O ingens* Reipublicae *noſtrae columen! O fortunatam tanto* Heroe *Britanniam! Illi tali tantoque viro* DEUM *per* Omnia *adfuiſſe, manumque ejus et mentem direxiſſe*, CERTISSIMUM EST. Hujus *enim* Unius *ferme opera*, aequiſſimis *et* perhonorificiis conditionibus, *diuturno, heu nimium! bello, finem impoſitum videmus. O Diem aeterna memoria digniſſimam! qua terrores Patriae omnes excidit*, Pacemque *diu exoptatam toti fere Europae reſtituit, ille Populi Anglicani Amor, Harleius.*

Thus

But Welſted moſt the Poet's healing balm 207
Strives to extract from his ſoft, giving palm;

Unlucky

VARIATIONS.

VER. 207. in the firſt Edd.
But Oldmixon the Poet's healing balm, &c. W.

REMARKS.

Thus critically (that is, verbally) tranſlated:

"Thy Father, that moſt refulgent ſtar of the Anglican Orb, we much deſire to *adore!* O mighty Column of our *Republic!* Oh Britain, fortunate in ſuch an *Hero!* That to ſuch and ſo great a Man GOD was ever preſent, in *every thing*, and all along directed both his hand and his heart, is a *Moſt Abſolute Certainty!* For it is in a manner by the operation of this *Man alone*, that we behold a *War* (alas! how much too long an one!) brought at length to an end, *on the moſt juſt and moſt honourable Conditions*. Oh Day eternally to be memorated! wherein all the Terrors of his Country were ended, and a PEACE (long wiſhed for by *almoſt all Europe*) was reſtored by HARLEY, the Love and Delight of the People of England."

But that this Gentleman can write in a different ſtyle, may be ſeen in a letter he printed, to Mr. Pope, wherein ſeveral Noble Lords are treated in a moſt extraordinary language, particularly the Lord Bolingbroke abuſed for that very PEACE which he here makes the *ſingle work* of the Earl of Oxford, directed by *God Almighty*. W.

VER. 207. *Welſted*] Leonard Welſted, author of The Triumvirate, or a Letter in verſe from Palemon to Celia at Bath, which was meant for a ſatire on Mr. P. and ſome of his friends, about the year 1718. He writ other things which we cannot remember. Smedley, in his Metamorphoſis of Scriblerus, mentions one, the Hymn of a *Gentleman* to his *Creator*: And there was another in praiſe either of a Cellar, or a Garret. L. W. characterized in the treatiſe Περὶ Βάθους, or the Art of Sinking, as a Didapper, and after as an Eel, is ſaid to be this perſon, by Dennis, Daily Journal of May 11, 1728. He was alſo characterized under another animal, a Mole, by the author of the enſuing Simile, which was handed about at the ſame time:

"Dear Welſted, mark, in dirty hole,
That painful animal, a Mole:

Above

Unlucky Welsted! thy unfeeling master,
The more thou ticklest, gripes his fist the faster.
While thus each hand promotes the pleasing pain,
And quick sensations skip from vein to vein;
A youth unknown to Phoebus, in despair,
Puts his last refuge all in heav'n and pray'r.
What force have pious vows! The Queen of Love
Her sister sends, her vot'ress, from above.
As taught by Venus, Paris learnt the art
To touch Achilles' only tender part;
Secure, through her, the noble prize to carry,
He marches off, his Grace's Secretary.
Now turn to diff'rent sports (the Goddess cries)
And learn, my sons, the wond'rous power of Noise.
To move, to raise, to ravish ev'ry heart,
With Shakespear's nature, or with Johnson's art,

Let

REMARKS.

Above ground never born to grow,
What mighty stir it keeps below?
To make a Mole-hill all this strife,
It digs, pokes, undermines for life.
How proud a little dirt to spread;
Conscious of nothing o'er its head!
Till, lab'ring on for want of eyes,
It blunders into Light—and dies."

You have him again in book iii. ver. 169. W.

VER. 213. *A youth unknown to Phoebus, &c.*] The satire of this episode being levelled at the base flatteries of authors to worthless wealth or greatness, concludes here with an excellent lesson to such men: That although their pens and praises were as exquisite as they conceit of themselves, yet (even in their own mercenary views) a creature unlettered, who serveth the passions, or pimpeth to the pleasures, of such vain, braggart, puff'd Nobility, shall with those patrons be much more inward, and of them much higher rewarded. SCRIBL.

Let others aim: 'Tis yours to ſhake the ſoul
With Thunder rumbling from the muſtard bowl,
With horns and trumpets now to madneſs ſwell,
Now ſink in ſorrows with a tolling bell;
Such happy arts attention can command,
When fancy flags, and ſenſe is at a ſtand.
Improve we theſe. Three Cat-calls be the bribe
Of him, whoſe chatt'ring ſhames the Monkey tribe:
And his this Drum, whoſe hoarſe heroic baſe
Drowns the loud clarion of the braying Aſs.

Now thouſand tongues are heard in one loud din:
The Monkey-mimics ruſh diſcordant in;
'Twas chatt'ring, grinning, mouthing, jabb'ring all,
And Noiſe and Norton, Brangling and Breval,

Dennis

REMARKS.

VER. 226. *With Thunder rumbling from the muſtard bowl,*] The old way of making Thunder and Muſtard were the ſame; but ſince, it is more advantageouſly perform'd by troughs of wood with ſtops in them. Whether Mr. Dennis was the inventor of that improvement, I know not; but it is certain, that being once at a Tragedy of a new author, he fell into a great paſſion at hearing ſome, and cried, "'Sdeath! that is *my* Thunder." W.

VER. 238. *Norton,*] See ver. 417.—*J. Durant Breval,* Author of a very extraordinary Book of Travels, and ſome Poems. See before, Note on ver. 126. W.

IMITATIONS.

VER. 223, 225. *To move, to raiſe, &c.*
Let others aim: 'Tis yours to ſhake, &c.]

"Excudent alii ſpirantia mollius aera,
Credo equidem, vivos ducent de marmore vultus, &c.
Tu regere imperio populos, Romane, memento,
Hae tibi erunt artes"—— W.

Dennis and Diſſonance, and captious Art,
And Snip-ſnap ſhort, and Interruption ſmart,
And Demonſtration thin, and Theſes thick,
And Major, Minor, and Concluſion quick.
Hold (cry'd the Queen) a Cat-call each ſhall win;
Equal your merits! equal is your din!
But that this well-diſputed game may end,
Sound forth, my Brayers, and the welkin rend.
 As when the long-ear'd milky mothers wait
At ſome ſick miſer's triple-bolted gate,
For their defrauded, abſent foals they make
A moan ſo loud, that all the guild awake;
Sore ſighs ſir Gilbert, ſtarting at the bray,
From dreams of millions, and three groats to pay.

So

REMARKS.

VER. 239. *Dennis and Diſſonance,*] "Which two lines, (ſays Harris, in his Philological Enquiries, p. 101.) though truly poetical and humorous, may be ſuſpected by ſome to ſhew their art too conſpicuouſly, and too nearly to reſemble that verſe of old Ennius;

"O Titi, tuti, tati, tibi tanta, tyranna tuliſti."

Alliteration, I muſt add, is a figure too laviſhly uſed by many modern writers; there are beautiful examples of it in Lucretius and Virgil; and Dryden, who had ſo fine and juſt an ear, often adopted it with much ſucceſs. But in his moſt harmonious lines, he ſeldom extended it beyond two words: it is apt to fall into affectation if carried farther.

VER. 247. *Milky mothers*] The epithet is from Spenſer, 36. c. 8.

IMITATIONS.

VER. 243. *a Cat-call each ſhall win,* &c.]

"Non noſtrum inter vos tantas componere lites;
Et vitulâ tu dignus, et hic."— VIRGIL, Ecl. iii. W.

VER. 247. *As when the,* &c.] A ſimile with a long tail, in the manner of Homer. W.

So ſwells each wind-pipe; Aſs intones to Aſs,
Harmonic twang! of leather, horn, and braſs;
Such as from lab'ring lungs th' Enthuſiaſt blows,
High Sound, attemper'd to the vocal noſe;
Or ſuch as bellow from the deep Divine;
There, Webſter! peal'd thy voice, and Whitefield! thine.

But

REMARKS.

VER. 258. *Webſter—and Whitefield!*] The one the writer of a Newſpaper called the *Weekly Miſcellany*; the other a Field-preacher. The Enthuſiaſt thought the only means of advancing Religion was by the New-birth of ſpiritual madneſs: The Bigot, by the old death of fire and faggot: And therefore they agreed in this, though in no other earthly thing, to abuſe all the ſober Clergy. From the ſmall ſucceſs of theſe two extraordinary perſons, we may learn how little hurtful Bigotry and Enthuſiaſm are, while the Civil Magiſtrate prudently forbears to lend his power to the one, to be employed againſt the other. W.

In a letter, of Warburton, preſerved in the Britiſh Muſeum, among Dr. Birch's papers, addreſt to M. Demaizeux, he ſays very pleaſantly; " I have ſeen Whitefield's Journal, and he appears to me to be as mad as ever George Fox the Quaker was. Theſe are very fit Miſſionaries, you will ſay, to propagate the Chriſtian Faith amongſt Infidels. There is another of them, one W. who came over from the ſame Miſſion: He told a friend of mine, that he had lived moſt deliciouſly the laſt ſummer in Georgia, ſleeping under trees, and feeding on boiled maize, ſauced with the aſhes of oak leaves; that he will return thither, and then will caſt off his Engliſh dreſs, and wear a dyed ſkin, like the ſavages, the better to ingratiate himſelf with them. It would be well for virtue and religion, if this humour would lay hold generally of our over-heated bigots, and ſend them to cool themſelves in the Indian marſhes. I fancy that Ven and Webſter would make a very entertaining as well as proper figure in a couple of bear ſkins, and marching in this terror of equipage, like the Pagan prieſts of old.

" Jamque ſacerdotes, primuſque Potitius, ibant
Pellibus in morem cinctis, flammaſque ferebant."

But far o'er all, ſonorous Blackmore's ſtrain;
Walls, ſteeples, ſkies, bray back to him again.
In Tot'nam fields, the brethren, with amaze,
Prick all their ears up, and forget to graze;
Long Chanc'ry-lane retentive rolls the ſound,
And courts to courts return it round and round;
Thames wafts it thence to Rufus' roaring hall,
And Hungerford re-echoes bawl for bawl.
All hail him victor in both gifts of ſong,
Who ſings ſo loudly, and who ſings ſo long.

This

REMARKS.

VER. 268. *Who ſings ſo loudly, and who ſings ſo long.*] A juſt character of Sir Richard Blackmore, knight, who (as Mr. Dryden expreſſeth it)

"Writ to the rumbling of his coach's wheels;"

and

IMITATIONS.

VER. 260. *bray back to him again.*] A figure of ſpeech taken from Virgil:

"Et vox aſſenſu nemorum ingeminata remugit." Georg. iii.

"He hears his num'rous herds low o'er the plain,
While neighb'ring hills *low* back to them again."

COWLEY.

The poet here celebrated, Sir R. B. delighted much in the word *bray*, which he endeavoured to ennoble by applying it to the ſound of *Armour*, *War*, &c. In imitation of him, and ſtrengthened by his authority, our author has here admitted it into Heroic poetry. W.

VER. 262. *Prick all their ears up, and forget to graze;*]

"Immemor herbarum quos eſt mirata juvenca."

VIRGIL, Ecl. viii.

The progreſs of the ſound from place to place, and the ſcenery here of the bordering regions, Tottenham-fields, Chancery-lane, the Thames, Weſtminſter-Hall, and Hungerford-ſtairs, are imitated from Virgil, Aeneid vii. on the ſounding the horn of Alecto:

"Audiit et Triviae longe lacus, audiit amnis
Sulphurea Nar albus aqua, fonteſque Velini." W.

This labour paſt, by Bridewell all deſcend,
(As morning pray'r, and flagellation end)

To

REMARKS.

and whoſe indefatigable Muſe produced no leſs than ſix Epic poems: Prince and King Arthur, twenty books; Eliza, ten; Alfred, twelve; the Redeemer, ſix; beſides Job, in folio; the whole Book of Pſalms; the Creation, ſeven books; Nature of Man, three books; and many more. 'Tis in this ſenſe he is ſtyled afterwards the *everlaſting Blackmore.* Notwithſtanding all which, Mr. Gildon ſeems aſſured, that "this admirable author did not think himſelf upon the *ſame foot* with *Homer.*" Comp. Art of Poetry, vol. i. p. 108.

But how different is the judgment of the author of Characters of the times? p. 25. who ſays, "Sir Richard Blackmore is unfortunate in happening to miſtake his proper talents; and that he has not for many years been *ſo much as named,* or even *thought of* among writers." Even Mr. Dennis differs greatly from his friend Mr. Gildon: "Blackmore's *Action* (ſaith he) has neither unity, nor integrity, nor morality, nor univerſality; and conſequently he can have no *Fable,* and no *Heroic Poem:* His Narration is neither probable, delightful, nor wonderful; his characters have none of the neceſſary qualifications; the things contained in his Narration are neither in their own nature delightful, nor numerous enough, nor rightly diſpoſed, nor ſurpriſing, nor pathetic." —Nay he proceeds ſo far as to ſay Sir Richard has *no Genius;* firſt laying down, "that Genius is cauſed by a *furious joy and pride of ſoul,* on the conception of an *extraordinary Hint.* Many men, (ſays he) have their *Hints,* without theſe motions of *fury* and *pride of ſoul,* becauſe they want fire enough to agitate their ſpirits; and theſe we call cold writers. Others who have a great deal of fire, but have not excellent organs, feel the forementioned *emotions* without the *extraordinary hints;* and theſe we call fuſtian writers. But he declares that Sir Richard had neither the *Hints,* nor the *Motions.*" Remarks on Prince Arthur, octavo, 1696. Preface.

This gentleman, in his firſt works, abuſed the character of Mr. Dryden; and in his laſt, of Mr. Pope, accuſing him in very high and ſober terms of profaneneſs and immorality (Eſſay on Polite Writing, vol. ii. p. 270.) on a mere report from Edm. Curl, that he was author of a Traveſtie on the firſt Pſalm. Mr. Dennis took up the ſame report, but with the addition of what

Sir

To where Fleet-ditch with diſemboguing ſtreams
Rolls the large tribute of dead dogs to Thames,
The

REMARKS.

Sir Richard had neglected, an *Argument to prove it*; which being very curious, we ſhall here tranſcribe. "It was he who burleſqued the Pſalm of David. It is *apparent* to me that Pſalm was burleſqued by a *Popiſh rhymeſter*. Let rhyming perſons who have been brought up *Proteſtants* be otherwiſe what they will, let them be rakes, let them be ſcoundrels, let them be *Atheiſts*, yet education has made an invincible impreſſion on them in behalf of the ſacred writings. But a *Popiſh rhymeſter* has been brought up with a contempt for thoſe ſacred writings; now ſhew me another *Popiſh rhymeſter* but he." This manner of argumentation is uſual with Mr. Dennis; he has employed the ſame againſt Sir Richard himſelf, in a like charge of *Impiety* and *Irreligion*. "All Mr. Blackmore's celeſtial Machines, as they cannot be defended ſo much as by common received opinion, ſo are they directly contrary to the doctrine of the church of England; for the viſible deſcent of an angel muſt be a miracle. Now it is the doctrine of the church of England, that miracles had ceaſed a long time before Prince Arthur came into the world. Now if the doctrine of the church of England be true, as we are obliged to believe, then are all the celeſtial machines in Prince Arthur unſufferable, as wanting not only human, but divine probability. But if the machines are ſufferable, that is, if they have ſo much as divine probability, then it follows of neceſſity that the doctrine of the Church is falſe. So I leave it to every impartial Clergyman to conſider," etc. Preface to the Remarks on Prince Arthur. W.

VER. 270. *As morning pray'r, and flagellation end.*] It is between eleven and twelve in the morning, after church ſervice, that the criminals are whipped in Bridewell.—This is to mark punctually the *time* of the day: Homer does it by the circumſtance of the Judges riſing from court, or of the Labourers dinner; our author by one very proper both to the *Perſons* and the *ſcene* of his poem, which we may remember commenced in the evening of the Lord-mayor's day: The firſt book paſſed in that *night*; the next *morning* the games begin in the Strand, thence along Fleet-ſtreet (places inhabited by Bookſellers), then they proceed by Bridewell towards Fleet-ditch, and laſtly through Ludgate to the City and the Temple of the Goddeſs. W.

The King of dykes! than whom no ſluice of mud
With deeper ſable blots the ſilver flood.
"Here ſtrip, my children! here at once leap in,
Here prove who beſt can daſh through thick and thin,
And who the moſt in love of dirt excel,
Or dark dexterity of groping well.
Who flings moſt filth, and wide pollutes around
The ſtream, be his the Weekly Journals bound;
A pig of lead to him who dives the beſt;
A peck of coals apiece ſhall glad the reſt."

In

REMARKS.

VER. 276, 277, 278. —*Daſh through thick and thin—love of dirt —dark dexterity*] The three chief qualifications of Party-writers: to ſtick at nothing, to delight in flinging dirt, and to ſlander in the dark by gueſs. W.

VER. 280. *the Weekly Journals*] Papers of news and ſcandal intermixed, on different ſides and parties, and frequently ſhifting from one ſide to the other, called the London Journal, Britiſh Journal, Daily Journal, etc. the concealed writers of which for ſome time were Oldmixon, Roome, Arnall, Concanen, and others: perſons never ſeen by our author. W.

VER. 281. *Who dives the beſt*;] The idea of this Game is evidently taken from Lord Dorſet's fine verſes on Howard. I wonder Swift in his Rhapſody on Poetry would venture on the ſame ſubject and idea of diving, after Pope had ſucceeded ſo well:

"For inſtance; when you raſhly think
No Rhymer can like Welſted ſink,
His merits balanc'd you ſhall find,
That Fielding leaves him far behind."

Folio, Ver. 392. 1733.

Little

IMITATIONS.

VER. 273. *The king of dykes, etc.*]
"Fluviorum rex Eridanus,
———quo non alius, per pinguia culta,
In mare purpureum violentior influit amnis." VIRG. W.

In naked majesty Oldmixon stands,
And Milo-like surveys his arms and hands;

Then

REMARKS.

Little did Swift imagine that this very Fielding would hereafter equal him in works of humour, and excel him in drawing and supporting characters, and in the artful conduct and plan of a Comic Epopée.

VER. 282. *A peck of coals apiece*] Our indulgent Poet, whenever he has spoken of any dirty or low work, constantly puts us in mind of the *Poverty* of the offenders, as the only extenuation of such practices. Let any one but remark, when a Thief, a Pickpocket, a Highwayman, or a Knight of the post, are spoken of, how much our hate to those characters is lessened, if they add a *needy* Thief, a *poor* Pickpocket, an *hungry* Highwayman, a *starving* Knight of the post, *etc.* W.

Here again has Swift borrowed from his friend, on the great number of our Scribblers who, he says,

" Computing by their Pecks of Coals,
Amount to just nine thousand souls."

This Rhapsody, and the verses on his own death, are the best of Swift's poetical productions, though they cannot be called true Poetry.

VER. 283. *In naked majesty Oldmixon stands,*] Mr. JOHN OLDMIXON, next to Mr. Dennis, the most ancient Critic of our Nation; an unjust censurer of Mr. Addison in his prose Essay on Criticism, whom also in his imitation of Bouhours (called the Arts of Logic and Rhetoric) he misrepresents in plain matter of fact; for in p. 45, he cites the Spectator as abusing Dr. Swift by name, where there is not the least hint of it; and in p. 304, is so injurious as to suggest that Mr. Addison himself writ that Tatler, No. 43, which says of his own Simile, that " 'Tis as great as ever entered into the mind of man." " In Poetry he was not so happy as laborious, and therefore characterised by the Tatler, No. 62. by the name of *Omicròn* the *Unborn Poet.*" Curl, Key, p. 13. " He writ Dramatic works, and a volume of Poetry consisting of heroic Epistles, etc. some whereof are very well done," said that great Judge Mr. Jacob, in his Lives of Poets, vol. ii. p. 303.

 In

Then ſighing, thus, "And am I now threeſcore?
Ah why, ye Gods! ſhould two and two make four?"
He ſaid, and climb'd a ſtranded lighter's height,
Shot to the black abyſs, and plung'd downright.
The Senior's Judgment all the crowd admire,
Who but to ſink the deeper, roſe the higher.
  Next Smedley div'd; ſlow circles dimpled o'er
The quaking mud, that clos'd, and op'd no more.
All look, all ſigh, and call on Smedley loſt;
Smedley in vain reſounds through all the coaſt.

Then

REMARKS.

In his Eſſay on Criticiſm, and the Arts of Logic and Rhetoric, he frequently reflects on our Author. But the top of his character was a perverter of Hiſtory, in that ſcandalous one of the Stuarts in folio, and his Critical Hiſtory of England, two volumes, octavo. Being employed by Biſhop Kennet, in publiſhing the Hiſtorians in his Collection, he falſified Daniel's Chronicle in numberleſs places. Yet this very man, in the preface to the firſt of theſe books, advanced a *particular fact* to charge three eminent perſons of falſifying the Lord Clarendon's Hiſtory; which fact has been diſproved by Dr. Atterbury, late Biſhop of Rocheſter, then the only ſurvivor of them; and the particular part he pretended to be falſified, produced ſince, after almoſt ninety years, in that noble author's original manuſcript. He was all his life a virulent Party-writer for hire, and received his reward in a ſmall place, which he enjoyed to his death. W.

VER. 291. *Next Smedley div'd*;] In the ſurreptitious editions, this whole Epiſode was applied to an initial letter E—, by whom,

if

IMITATIONS.

VER. 285. *Then ſighing, thus, "And am I now threeſcore? etc.*]
"——Fletque Milon ſenior, cum ſpectat inanes
Herculeis ſimiles, fluidos pendere lacertos." OVID.

VER. 293. *and call on Smedley loſt, etc.*]
"Alcides wept in vain for Hylas loſt,
Hylas, in vain, reſounds through all the coaſt."
Lord ROSCOM. Tranſlat. of VIRGIL's vi^th Ecl.

Then * eſſay'd; ſcarce vaniſh'd out of ſight,
He buoys up inſtant, and returns to light:
He bears no tokens of the ſabler ſtreams,
And mounts far off among the Swans of Thames.
True to the bottom, ſee Concanen creep,
A cold, long-winded, native of the deep:
If

VARIATIONS.

After ver. 298. in the firſt Edit. followed theſe,
Far worſe unhappy D——r ſucceeds,
He ſearch'd for coral, but he gather'd weeds.

REMARKS.

if they meant the Laureate, nothing was more abſurd, no part agreeing with his character. The Allegory evidently demands a perſon dipp'd in ſcandal, and deeply immerſed in dirty work; whereas Mr. Euſden's works rarely offended but by their length and multitude, and accordingly are taxed of nothing elſe in book i. ver. 102. But the perſon here mentioned, an Iriſhman, was author and publiſher of many ſcurrilous pieces, a weekly Whitehall Journal in the year 1722, in the name of Sir James Baker; and particularly whole volumes of Billingſgate againſt Dr. Swift and Mr. Pope, called Gulliveriana and Alexandriana, printed in octavo, 1728. W.

Ver. 295. *Then * eſſay'd;*] A gentleman of genius and ſpirit, who was ſecretly dipt in ſome papers of this kind, on whom our poet beſtows a panegyric inſtead of a ſatire, as deſerving to be better employed than in party quarrels, and perſonal invectives. W.

Suppoſed to be Hill: though this was denied by Pope.

Ver. 299. *Concanen*] Matthew Concanen, an Iriſhman, bred to the law. Smedley (one of his brethren in enmity to Swift) in his Metamorphoſis of Scriblerus, p. 7. accuſes him of "having boaſted of what he had not written, but others had reviſed and done for him." He was author of ſeveral dull and dead ſcurrilities in the Britiſh and London Journals, and in a paper called the Speculatiſt. In a pamphlet, called a Supplement to the Profund, he dealt very unfairly with our poet, not only frequently imputing to him Mr. Broome's verſes (for which he might indeed ſeem in ſome degree accountable, having corrected what that gentleman did) but thoſe of the duke of Buckingham,

 and

If perſeverance gain the Diver's prize,
Not everlaſting Blackmore this denies:
No noiſe, no ſtir, no motion canſt thou make,
Th' unconſcious ſtream ſleeps o'er thee like a lake.
 Next plung'd a feeble, but a deſp'rate pack,
With each a ſickly brother at his back:
Sons of a Day! juſt buoyant on the flood,
Then number'd with the puppies in the mud.
Aſk ye their names? I could as ſoon diſcloſe
The names of theſe blind puppies as of thoſe.
Faſt by, like Niobe (her children gone)
Sits Mother Oſborne, ſtupify'd to ſtone!

And

REMARKS.

and others: To this rare piece ſomebody humourouſly cauſed him to take for his motto, *De profundis clamavi.* He was ſince a hired ſcribler in the Daily Courant, where he poured forth much Billingſgate againſt the Lord Bolingbroke, and others; after which this man was ſurpriſingly promoted to adminiſter Juſtice and Law in Jamaica. W.

This is the Scribler to whom Warburton wrote his famous Letter, publiſhed by Dr. Akenſide; by which it appears, that Concanen was intimately acquainted with Dr. Warburton, in the year 1728, at the time when he publiſhed a Supplement to the Profund.

VER. 306, 307. *With each a ſickly brother at his back: Sons of a day! etc.*] Theſe were daily Papers, a number of which, to leſſen the expence, were printed one on the back of another. W.

—— *at his back*, is a woful conceit!

VER. 311. *like Niobe*] See the ſtory in Ovid, Met. vii. where the miſerable Petrefaction of this old Lady is pathetically deſcribed. W.

VER. 312. *Oſborne,*] A name aſſumed by the eldeſt and graveſt of theſe writers, who at laſt, being aſhamed of his pupils, gave his paper over, and in his age remained ſilent. W.

IMITATIONS.

VER. 302. *Not everlaſting Blackmore.*]

"Nec bonus Eurytion praelato invidit honori," etc.

VIRG. Aeneid.

And Monumental Braſs this record bears,
"Theſe are,—ah no! theſe were the Gazetteers!"

Not

REMARKS.

VER. 314. *Gazetteers!*] We ought not to ſuppreſs that a modern Critic here taxeth the Poet with an Anachroniſm, affirming theſe Gazetteers not to have lived within the time of this poem, and challenging us to produce any ſuch paper of that date. But we may with equal aſſurance aſſert, theſe Gazetteers not to have lived ſince, and challenge all the learned world to produce one ſuch paper at this day. Surely therefore, where the point is ſo obſcure, our author ought not to be cenſured too raſhly. SCRIBL.

Notwithſtanding this affected ignorance of the good Scriblerus, the *Daily Gazetteer* was a title given very properly to certain papers, each of which laſted but a day. Into this, as a common ſink, was received all the traſh, which had been before diſperſed in ſeveral Journals, and circulated at the public expence of the nation. The authors were the ſame obſcure men; though ſometimes relieved by occaſional eſſays from Stateſmen, Courtiers, Biſhops, Deans, and Doctors. The meaner ſort were rewarded with Money; others with Places or Benefices, from an hundred to a thouſand a-year. It appears from the *Report* of the *Secret Committee* for enquiring into the conduct of R. Earl of O. "That no leſs than *fifty thouſand ſeventy-ſeven pounds, eighteen ſhillings,* were paid to Authors and Printers of News-papers, ſuch as Free-Britons, Daily-Courants, Corn-Cutters Journals, Gazetteers, and other political papers, between Feb. 10, 1731, and Feb. 10, 1741." Which ſhews the Benevolence of one Miniſter to have expended, for the current dulneſs of ten years in Britain, double the ſum which gained Louis XIV. ſo much honour, in annual Penſions to Learned men all over Europe. In which, and in a much longer time, not a Penſion at Court, nor Preferment in the Church, or Univerſities, of any Conſideration, was beſtowed on any man diſtinguiſhed for his Learning ſeparately from Party-merit, or Pamphlet-writing. W.

(Perhaps Dr. Warburton, in this laſt ſentence, has carried his cenſure too far.)

It is worth a reflection, that of all the Panegyrics beſtowed by theſe writers on this great Miniſter, not one is at this day ex-

tant

Not ſo bold Arnall; with a weight of ſkull,
Furious he dives, precipitately dull.
Whirlpools and ſtorms his circling arms inveſt,
With all the might of gravitation bleſt.
No crab more active in the dirty dance,
Downward to climb, and backward to advance.
He brings up half the bottom on his head,
And loudly claims the Journals and the Lead.
The plunging Prelate, and his pond'rous Grace,
With holy envy gave one Layman place.

When

REMARKS.

tant or remembered; nor even ſo much credit done to his perſonal character by all they have written, as by one ſhort occaſional compliment of our Author in the Dialogue of One thouſand ſeven hundred and thirty-eight, line 29. W.

VER. 315. *Arnall;*] WILLIAM ARNALL, bred an Attorney, was a perfect Genius in this ſort of work. He began under twenty with furious Party-papers; then ſucceeded Concanen in the Britiſh Journal. At the firſt publication of the Dunciad, he prevailed on the Author not to give him his due place in it, by a letter profeſſing his deteſtation of ſuch practices as his Predeceſſor's. But ſince, by the moſt unexampled inſolence and perſonal abuſe of ſeveral great men, the Poet's particular friends, he moſt amply deſerved a niche in the Temple of Infamy: Witneſs a paper, called the Free-Briton; a Dedication intitled, To the Genuine Blunderer, 1732, and many others. He writ for hire, and valued himſelf upon it; not indeed without cauſe, it appearing by the aforeſaid REPORT, that he received "for Free-"Britons, and other writings, in the ſpace of *four years*, no leſs than *ten thouſand nine hundred and ninety-ſeven pounds, ſix ſhillings and eight-pence,* out of the Treaſury." But frequently, through his fury or folly, he exceeded all the bounds of his commiſſion, and obliged his honourable Patron to diſavow his ſcurrilities. W.

VER. 318. *Gravitation bleſt.*] From Dorſet on Howard, who had ſuch alacrity in Sinking.

When lo! a burſt of thunder ſhook the flood,
Slow roſe a form, in majeſty of Mud;
Shaking the horrors of his ſable brows,
And each ferocious feature grim with ooze.
Greater he looks, and more than mortal ſtares:
Then thus the wonders of the deep declares.
Firſt he relates, how ſinking to the chin,
Smit with his mien, the Mud-nymphs ſuck'd him in:
How young Lutetia, ſofter than the down,
Nigrina black, and Merdamante brown,
Vy'd for his love in jetty bow'rs below,
As Hylas fair was raviſh'd long ago.

Then

REMARKS.

Ver. 323. *The plunging Prelate,*] It was imagined he meant Biſhop Sherlock, whom Bolingbroke attacks ſo violently in the Diſſertation on Parties, for defending the meaſures of Sir Robert Walpole, who was Sherlock's Contemporary at Eton College, and who uſed to relate, that when ſome of the Scholars, going to bathe in the Thames, ſtood ſhivering on the Bank, Sherlock plunged in immediately over his head and ears.

Ver. 331. *Firſt he relates,*] The Adventures of Smedley, and what he ſaw in the Shades below, from thence down to Line 352, are finely imagined, and one of the moſt poetical paſſages in any of his Works.

Ver. 336. *As Hylas fair*] Who was raviſhed by the water-nymphs and drawn into the river. The ſtory is told at large by Valerius Flaccus, lib. iii. Argon. See Virgil, Ecl. vi. W.

But it is better told by Theocritus, Idyll. 13.

IMITATIONS.

Ver. 329. *Greater he looks, and more than mortal ſtares:*]
Virg. Aeneid. vi. of the Sibyl:

" ——majorque videri,
Nec mortale ſonans "——

Then ſung, how ſhown him by the Nut-brown maids
A branch of Styx here riſes from the Shades,
That tinctur'd as it runs with Lethe's ſtreams,
And waſting vapours from the land of dreams,
(As under ſeas Alpheus' ſecret ſluice
Bears Piſa's off'rings to his Arethuſe)
Pours into Thames: and hence the mingled wave
Intoxicates the pert, and lulls the grave:
Here briſker vapours o'er the TEMPLE creep,
There, all from Paul's to Aldgate drink and ſleep.

Thence

REMARKS.

VER. 338. *A branch of Styx, etc.*]

Οἵ τ' ἀμφ' ἱμερτὸν Τιταρήσιον ἔργ' ἐνέμοντο,
Ὅς ῥ' ἐς Πηνειὸν προΐει καλλίῤῥοον ὕδωρ,
Οὐδ' ὅγε Πηνειῷ συμμίσγεται ἀργυροδίνῃ,
Ἀλλά τέ μιν καθύπερθεν ἐπιῤῥέει ἠΰτ' ἔλαιον,
Ὅρκου γὰρ δεινοῦ Στυγος ὕδατός ἐστιν ἀποῤῥώξ.

Homer, Il. ii. Catal.

Of the Land of Dreams in the ſame region, he makes mention, Odyſſ. xxiv. See alſo Lucian's True Hiſtory. *Lethe* and the *Land of Dreams* allegorically repreſent the *Stupefaction* and *viſionary Madneſs* of Poets, equally dull and extravagant. Of Alpheus's water gliding ſecretly under the ſea of Piſa, to mix with thoſe of the Arethuſe in Sicily, ſee Moſchus Idyll. viii. Virg. Ecl x.

" Sic tibi, cum fluctus ſubter labere Sicanos,
Doris amara ſuam non intermiſceat undam."

And again, Aeneid. iii.

" ——Alpheum fama eſt huc, Elidis amnem,
Occultas egiſſe vias ſubter mare, qui nunc
Ore, Arethuſa, tuo Siculis confunditur undis." W.

VER. 341. *Secret ſluice*] Not ſo much from Moſchus or Virgil, as mentioned in the above note, but clearly taken from the Arcades of Milton;

" Divine Alphéus, who, by ſecret ſluſe,
Stole under ſeas to meet his Arethuſe."

Thence to the banks where rev'rend Bards repoſe,
They led him ſoft; each rev'rend Bard aroſe;
And Milbourn chief, deputed by the reſt,
Gave him the caſſock, ſurcingle, and veſt.
" Receive (he ſaid) theſe robes which once were mine,
" Dulneſs is ſacred in a ſound divine."

He ceas'd, and ſpread the robe; the croud confeſs
The rev'rend Flamen in his lengthen'd dreſs.
Around him wide a ſable Army ſtand,
A low-born, cell-bred, ſelfiſh, ſervile band,

Prompt

REMARKS.

VER. 349. *And Milbourn*] Luke Milbourn a Clergyman, the faireſt of Critics; who, when he wrote againſt Mr. Dryden's Virgil, did him juſtice in printing at the ſame time his own tranſlations of him, which were intolerable. His manner of writing has a great reſemblance with that of the Gentlemen of the Dunciad againſt our author, as will be ſeen in the Parallel of Mr. Dryden and him. Append. W.

VER. 355. *Around him wide, etc.*] It is to be hoped that the ſatire in theſe lines will be underſtood in the confined ſenſe in which the Author meant it, of ſuch only of the Clergy, who, though ſolemnly engaged in the ſervice of Religion, dedicate themſelves, for venal and corrupt ends, to the ſervice of Miniſters or Factions; and tho' educated under an entire ignorance of the world, aſpire to interfere in the government of it, and conſequently to diſturb and diſorder it; in which they fall ſhort of their Predeceſſors only by being inveſted with much leſs of that power and authority, which they employed indifferently (as is hinted at in the lines above)

IMITATIONS.

VER. 347. *Thence to the banks, etc.*]

" Tum canit errantem Permeſſi ad flumina Gallum,
Utque viro Phoebi chorus aſſurrexerit omnis;
Ut Linus haec illi divino carmine paſtor,
Floribus atque apio crines ornatus, amaro,
Dixerit, Hos tibi dant calamos, en accipe, Muſae,
Aſcraeo quos ante ſeni"——etc.

Prompt or to guard or ſtab, or ſaint or damn,
Heav'n's Swiſs, who fight for any God, or Man.
  Through Lud's fam'd gates, along the well-known Fleet
Rolls the black troop, and overſhades the ſtreet, 360
'Till ſhow'rs of Sermons, Characters, Eſſays,
In circling fleeces whiten all the ways:
So clouds repleniſh'd from ſome bog below,
Mount in dark volumes, and deſcend in ſnow.
Here ſtopp'd the Goddeſs, and in pomp proclaims,
A gentler exerciſe to cloſe the games. 366
  "Ye Critics! in whoſe heads, as equal ſcales,
"I weigh what author's heavineſs prevails;
"Which

REMARKS.

above) either in ſupporting arbitrary power, or in exciting rebellion; in canonizing the vices of Tyrants, or in blackening the virtues of Patriots; in corrupting religion by ſuperſtition, or betraying it by libertiniſm, as either was thought beſt to ſerve the ends of Policy, or flatter the follies of the Great. *

I fear, notwithſtanding the pains taken by the Commentator, in his note on this paſſage, that it will be thought to contain too general and unmerited a cenſure on the Clergy. The expreſſion is taken from Dryden's Hind and Panther;

"Thoſe Swiſſes fight for any ſide for pay."

VER. 359. *Lud's fam'd gates,*] "King Lud repairing the City, called it after his own name, Lud's Town; the ſtrong gate which he built in the Weſt Part, he likewiſe, for his own honour, named Ludgate. In the year 1260, this gate was beautified with images of Lud and other Kings. Thoſe images in the reign of Edward VI. had their heads ſmitten off, and were otherwiſe defaced by unadviſed folks. Queen Mary did ſet new heads upon their old bodies again. The 28th of Queen Elizabeth the ſame gate was clean taken down, and newly and beautifully builded, with images of Lud and others, as afore." *Stowe's Survey of London.* W.

" Which moſt conduce to ſooth the ſoul in ſlumbers,
" My H—ley's periods, or my Blackmore's numbers;
" Attend the trial we propoſe to make:
" If there be man, who o'er ſuch works can wake,
" Sleep's all-ſubduing charms who dares defy,
" And boaſts Ulyſſes' ear with Argus' eye;
" To him we grant our ampleſt pow'rs to ſit
" Judge of all preſent, paſt, and future wit;
" To cavil, cenſure, dictate, right or wrong,
" Full and eternal privilege of tongue."

Three College Sophs, and three pert Templars came,
The ſame their talents, and their taſtes the ſame;
Each prompt to query, anſwer, and debate,
And ſmit with love of Poeſy and Prate.
The pond'rous books two gentle readers bring;
The heroes ſit, the vulgar form a ring;
The clam'rous croud is huſh'd with mugs of Mum,
Till all tun'd equal, ſend a gen'ral hum.

Then

REMARKS.

VER. 374. See Hom. Odyſſ. xii. Ovid. Met. i.

IMITATIONS.

VER. 380, 381. *The ſame their talents—Each prompt, etc.*]
" Ambo florentes aetatibus, Arcades ambo,
Et certare pares, et reſpondere parati." VIRG. Ecl. vi.

VER. 382. *And ſmit with love of Poeſy and Prate;*]
" Smit with the love of ſacred ſong"—— MILTON.

VER. 384. *The heroes ſit, the vulgar form a ring;*]
" Conſedere duces, et vulgi ſtante corona."
OVID. Met. xiii.

Then mount the Clerks, and in one lazy tone
Through the long, heavy, painful page drawl on;
Soft creeping, words on words, the ſenſe compoſe,
At ev'ry line they ſtretch, they yawn, they doze.
As to ſoft gales top-heavy pines bow low
Their heads, and lift them as they ceaſe to blow:
Thus oft they rear, and oft the head decline,
As breathe, or pauſe, by fits, the airs divine.
And now to this ſide, now to that they nod,
As verſe, or proſe, infuſe the drowzy God.
Thrice Budgel aim'd to ſpeak, but thrice ſuppreſt
By potent Arthur, knock'd his chin and breaſt.
Toland and Tindal, prompt at prieſts to jeer,
Yet ſilent bow'd to *Chriſt's No kingdom here.*

Who

VARIATIONS.

VER. 399. in the firſt Edit. it was,
Collins and Tindal, prompt at Prieſts to jeer.

REMARKS.

VER. 387. *in one lazy tone*] The powerful effects of hearing two dull authors read, deſcribed, from hence to the end of this Book, deſerve great applauſe, for Imagination, Expreſſion, and Elegance; particularly lines 388 to 396.

VER. 397. *Thrice Budgel aim'd to ſpeak,*] Famous for his ſpeeches on many occaſions about the South Sea ſcheme, etc. "He is a very ingenious gentleman, and hath written ſome excellent Epilogues to plays, and *one ſmall* piece on Love, which is very pretty." Jacob, Lives of Poets, vol. ii. p. 289. But this gentleman ſince made himſelf much more eminent, and perſonally well known to the greateſt Stateſmen of all parties, as well as to all the Courts of Law in this nation. W.

VER. 399. *Toland and Tindal,*] Two perſons, not ſo happy as to be obſcure, who writ againſt the Religion of their Country. *Toland,* the Author of the Atheiſt's Liturgy, called *Pantheiſticon,* was a ſpy in pay to Lord Oxford. *Tindal* was author of the *Rights*

of

Who ſate the neareſt, by the words o'ercome,
Slept firſt; the diſtant nodded to the hum.
Then down are roll'd the books; ſtretch'd o'er e'm lies
Each gentle clerk, and mutt'ring ſeals his eyes.
As what a Dutchman plumps into the lakes,
One circle firſt, and then a ſecond makes;
What Dulneſs dropt among her ſons impreſt
Like motion from one circle to the reſt:
So from the mid-moſt the nutation ſpreads
Round and more round, o'er all the *ſea of heads*.

At

REMARKS.

of the Chriſtian Church, and *Chriſtianity as old as the Creation*. He alſo wrote an abuſive pamphlet againſt Earl S——, which was ſuppreſſed, while yet in MS. by an eminent perſon then out of the miniſtry, to whom he ſhewed it, expecting his approbation: This Doctor afterwards publiſhed the ſame piece, *mutatis mutandis*, againſt that very perſon. W.

VER. 400. *Chriſt's No kingdom here*, etc.] This is ſaid by Curl, Key to Dunc. to allude to a ſermon of a reverend Biſhop. W.

It certainly did allude to the famous ſermon of Biſhop Hoadley, whom our Author diſliked on account of ſome letters ſigned Brittanicus in the London Journal, againſt Biſhop Atterbury; whom alſo Hoadley had vigorouſly attacked, for his falſe and perverſe interpretation of that text in St. Paul; "If in this life only we have hope, we are of all men moſt miſerable:" and alſo for a famous ſermon on another ill-underſtood paſſage of Scripture, "Charity ſhall cover a multitude of ſins:" and for his ſermon before the Convocation. Atterbury, I believe, was one of the laſt preachers that ever injudiciouſly urged the authenticity of the Sybilline verſes, as proofs of the coming of our Saviour. Warburton was not of Atterbury's opinion with reſpect to Church-power. See his "Alliance."

IMITATIONS.

VER. 410. *O'er all the ſea of heads*.]

"A waving ſea of heads was round me ſpread,
And ſtill freſh ſtreams the gazing deluge fed."

BLACKM. JOB.

At laſt Centlivre felt her voice to fail,
Motteux himſelf unfiniſh'd left his tale,
Boyer the State, and Law the Stage gave o'er,
Morgan and Mandevil could prate no more;

Norton,

VARIATIONS.

VER. 413. in the firſt Edit. it was,

T——s and T—— the Church and State gave o'er,
Nor *** talked, nor S—— whiſper'd more.

REMARKS.

VER. 411. *Centlivre*] Mrs. Suſanna Centlivre, wife to Mr. Centlivre, Yeoman of the Mouth to his Majeſty. She writ many Plays, and a Song (ſays Mr. Jacob, vol. i. p. 32.) before ſhe was ſeven years old. She alſo writ a Ballad againſt Mr. Pope's Homer, before he began it. W.

VER. 413. *Boyer the State, and Law the Stage gave o'er,*] A. Boyer, a voluminous compiler of Annals, Political Collections, &c.—William Law, A. M. wrote with great zeal againſt the ſtage; Mr. Dennis anſwered with as great: Their books were printed in 1726. Mr. Law affirmed, "The Playhouſe is the temple of the Devil; the peculiar pleaſure of the Devil; where all they who go yield to the Devil; where all the laughter is a laughter among Devils; and all who are there are hearing Muſic in the very Porch of Hell." To which Mr. Dennis replied, that "There is every jot as much difference between a true Play, and one made by a Poetaſter, as between *two religious Books*, the *Bible* and the *Alcoran*." Then he demonſtrates, that "All thoſe who had written againſt the Stage were *Jacobites* and *Non-jurors*; and did it always at a time when ſomething was to be done for the *Pretender*." Mr. Collier publiſhed his Short View when France declared for the Chevalier; and his Diſſuaſive, juſt at the *great ſtorm*, when the devaſtation which that hurricane wrought, had amazed and aſtoniſhed the minds of men, and made them obnoxious to melancholy and deſponding thoughts. Mr. Law took the opportunity to attack the Stage upon the great preparations he heard were making abroad, and which the *Jacobites* flattered themſelves were deſigned in their favour. And as for Mr. Bedford's Serious Remonſtrance, though I know nothing of the time of publiſhing, yet I dare to lay odds it was either upon the Duke d'Aumont's

Norton, from Daniel and Oſtroea ſprung,
Bleſs'd with his father's front, and mother's tongue,
Hung ſilent down his never-bluſhing head;
And all was huſh'd, as Folly's ſelf lay dead.

Thus

REMARKS.

d'Aumont's being at Somerſet-houſe, or upon the *late Rebellion*. DENNIS, Stage defended againſt Mr. Law, p. ult. W.

How Boyer, who was indeed a dull but uſeful writer, offended our author, I have never heard. But indeed moſt of the Scriblers here proſcribed, were of a rank much inferior to the writers whom Boileau thought proper to attack; particularly Quinault, whom he ſo unjuſtly and impotently cenſured. It was ſaid of Boileau, that though he made Vice odious, he never made Virtue amiable. Law was a melancholy Enthuſiaſt, who diſguiſed and miſrepreſented true Religion by dreſſing it up in dark gloomy colours.

VER. 414. *Morgan*] A writer againſt Religion, diſtinguiſhed no otherwiſe from the rabble of his tribe, than by the pompouſneſs of his Title, of a *Moral Philoſopher*. *

Ibid. *Mandevil*] Author of a famous book called *the Fable of the Bees*; written to prove, that Moral Virtue is the invention of knaves, and Chriſtian Virtue the impoſition of fools; and that Vice is neceſſary, and alone ſufficient to render Society flouriſhing and happy. W.

VER. 418. *And all was huſh'd,*] Alluding to the firſt Line of Dryden's Deſcription of Night in the Indian Emperor. A Deſcription which Rhymer produces as a Specimen of the Superiority of Engliſh Poetry, to that of other nations: after quoting the Deſcriptions of Apollonius, Virgil, Arioſto, Taſſo, Marino, Chapelain, and Le Moyne; as if, by one deſcription, ſuch a queſtion could be determined! Rhymer introduces this criticiſm in the preface to his tranſlation of Rapin's Reflexions on Ariſtotle's Poetics; and Rhymer, at that time, gave the Law to all writers, and was appealed to as a ſupreme judge of all works of Taſte and Genius. How well he was qualified for this character, will appear by obſerving, that after making remarks on what he calls our three Epic Poets, Spencer, Davenant, and Cowley, he mentions not one ſyllable of Milton. But Milton was not reliſhed and comprehended either by Rapin or Rhymer.

Thus the ſoft gifts of Sleep conclude the day,
And ſtretch'd on bulks, as uſual, Poets lay.
Why ſhould I ſing, what bards the nightly Muſe
Did ſlumb'ring viſit, and convey to ſtews;
Who prouder march'd, with magiſtrates in ſtate,
To ſome fam'd round-houſe, ever open gate!
How Henley lay inſpir'd beſide a ſink,
And to mere mortals ſeem'd a Prieſt in drink:
While others, timely, to the neighb'ring Fleet
(Haunt of the Muſes) made their ſafe retreat.

REMARKS.

VER. 426. *And to mere mortals ſeem'd a Prieſt in drink:*] This line preſents us with an excellent moral, that we are never to paſs judgment merely by *appearance*; a leſſon to all men, who may happen to ſee a reverend perſon in the like ſituation, not to determine too raſhly: ſince not only the Poets frequently deſcribe a Bard inſpired in this poſture,

"(On Cam's fair bank, where Chaucer lay inſpir'd,"

and the like) but an eminent Caſuiſt tells us, that "if a Prieſt be ſeen in any indecent action, we ought to account it a deception of ſight, or illuſion of the Devil, who ſometimes takes upon him the ſhape of holy men on purpoſe to cauſe ſcandal." SCRIBL.

VER. 427. *Fleet*] A priſon for inſolvent Debtors on the bank of the Ditch. W.

VER. 428. *Haunt of the Muſes*] A moſt happy ſtroke of ſly ſatire, unexpected ſtolen in.

THE END OF THE SECOND BOOK.

THE

DUNCIAD.

BOOK THE THIRD.

ARGUMENT.

AFTER the other persons are disposed in their proper places of rest, the Goddess transports the King to her Temple, and there lays him to slumber with his head on her lap: a position of marvellous virtue, which causes all the Visions of wild enthusiasts, projectors, politicians, inamoratos, castle-builders, chemists, and poets. He is immediately carried on the wings of Fancy and led by a mad Poetical Sibyl to the Elysian shade; *where, on the banks of* Lethe, *the souls of the dull are dipped by* Bavius, *before their entrance into this world. There he is met by the ghost of* Settle, *and by him made acquainted with the wonders of the place, and with those which he himself is destined to perform. He takes him to a* Mount of Vision, *from whence he shews him the past triumphs of the empire of Dulness, then the present, and lastly the future: how small a part of the world was ever conquered by Science, how soon those conquests were stopped, and those very nations again reduced to her dominion. Then distinguishing the Island of* Great Britain, *shews by what aids, by what persons, and by what degrees, it shall be brought to her Empire. Some of the persons he causes to pass in review before his eyes, describing each by his proper figure, character, and qualifications. On a sudden the Scene shifts, and a vast number of miracles and prodigies appear, utterly surprizing and unknown to the King himself, till they are explained to be the wonders of his own reign now commencing. On this subject* Settle *breaks into a congratulation, yet not unmixed with concern, that his own times were but the types of these. He prophecies how first the nation shall be over-run with* Farces, Operas, *and* Shows ; *how the throne of Dulness shall be advanced over the* Theatres, *and set up even at* Court : *then how her Sons shall preside in the seats of* Arts *and* Sciences : *giving a glympse, or Pisgah-sight, of the future Fulness of her Glory, the accomplishment whereof is the subject of the fourth and last book.*

BOOK III.

BUT in her Temple's laſt receſs incloſ'd,
On Dulneſs' lap th' Anointed head repoſ'd.
Him cloſe ſhe curtains round with Vapours blue,
And ſoft beſprinkles with Cimmerian dew.
Then raptures high the ſeat of Senſe o'erflow,
Which only heads refin'd from Reaſon know.
Hence, from the ſtraw where Bedlam's Prophet nods,
He hears loud Oracles, and talks with Gods:
Hence the Fool's Paradiſe, the Stateſman's ſcheme,
The air-built Caſtle, and the golden Dream,
The Maid's romantic wiſh, the Chemiſt's flame,
And Poet's viſion of eternal Fame.

And now, on Fancy's eaſy wing convey'd,
The King deſcending, views th' Elyſian Shade.

A ſlip-

REMARKS.

VER. 5, 6, &c. Hereby is intimated that the following Viſion is no more than the chimera of the dreamer's brain, and not a real or intended ſatire on the preſent Age, doubtleſs more learned, more enlightened, and more abounding with great Genius's in Divinity, Politics, and whatever arts and ſciences, than all the preceding. For fear of any ſuch miſtake of our Poet's honeſt meaning, he hath again, at the end of the Viſion, repeated this monition, ſaying that it all paſſed through the *Ivory gate*, which (according to the Ancients) denoteth Falſity. SCRIBL.

IMITATIONS.

VER. 7, 8. *Hence, from the ſtraw where Bedlam's Prophet nods,*
He hears loud Oracles, and talks with Gods:]

" Et varias audit voces, fruiturque deorum
Colloquio"——— VIRG. Aeneid. viii. W.

A ſlip-ſhod Sibyl led his ſteps along,
In lofty madneſs meditating ſong;
Her treſſes ſtaring from Poetic dreams,
And never waſh'd, but in Caſtalia's ſtreams.
Taylor, their better Charon, lends an oar,
(Once ſwan of Thames, tho' now he ſings no more)
Benlowes, propitious ſtill to blockheads, bows;
And Shadwell nods the Poppy on his brows.

Here,

REMARKS.

VER. 19. *Taylor*] John Taylor the Water-poet, an honeſt man, who owns he learned not ſo much as the Accidence. A rare example of modeſty in a Poet!

> " I muſt confeſs I do want eloquence,
> And never ſcarce did learn my Accidence;
> For having got from *poſſum* to *poſſet*,
> I there was gravel'd, could no farther get."

He wrote fourſcore books in the reign of James I. and Charles I. and afterwards (like Edward Ward) kept an Ale-houſe in Long-Acre. He died in 1654. W.

VER. 21. *Benlowes*] A country gentleman famous for his own bad Poetry, and for patronizing bad Poets, as may be ſeen from many Dedications of Quarles, and others to him. Some of theſe anagram'd his name, *Benlowes* into *Benevolus*: to verify which, he ſpent his whole eſtate upon them. W.

Ibid. *Benlowes— Brown—Mears*] How could he waſte ſo much time, and throw away ſuch charming Poetry on objects ſo very unknown and deſpicable! What a ſtate of anger and irritation muſt his mind (and ſuch a mind!) have been in, during the many hours, nay years, he ſpent in writing the 1670 lines of the Dunciad!

VER. 22. *And Shadwell nods the Poppy, &c.*] Shadwell took Opium for many years, and died of too large a doſe, in the year 1692. W.

IMITATIONS.

VER. 15. *A ſlip-ſhod Sibyl, &c.*]

> " Conclamat Vates ———
> ——— furens antro ſe immiſit aperto." VIRG W.

Here, in a dusky vale where Lethe rolls,
Old Bavius sits, to dip poetic souls,
And blunt the sense, and fit it for a skull
Of solid proof, impenetrably dull:

Instant,

REMARKS.

VER. 24. *Old Bavius sits,*] Bavius was an ancient Poet, celebrated by Virgil for the like cause as Bays by our author, though not in so christian-like a manner: For heathenishly it is declared by Virgil of Bavius, that he ought to be *hated* and *detested* for his evil works; *Qui Bavium non odit*; whereas we have often had occasion to observe our Poet's great *Good Nature* and *Mercifulness* through the whole course of this Poem. SCRIBL.

Mr. Dennis warmly contends, that Bavius was no inconsiderable author; nay, that "He and Maevius had (even in Augustus's days) a very formidable party at Rome, who thought them much superior to Virgil and Horace: For (saith he) I cannot believe they would have fixed that eternal brand upon them, if they had not been coxcombs in more than ordinary credit." Rem. on Pr. Arthur, part ii. c. 1. An argument which, if this poem should last, will conduce to the honour of the gentlemen of the Dunciad. W.

IMITATIONS.

VER. 23. *Here, in a dusky vale, &c.*]

"—— Videt Aeneas in valle reducta
Seclusum nemus ——
Lethaeumque domos placidas qui praenatat amnem, etc.
Hunc circum innumerae gentes," etc.

VIRG. Aeneid. vi. W.

VER. 24. *Old Bavius sits, to dip poetic souls,*] Alluding to the story of Thetis dipping Achilles to render him impenetrable:

"At pater Anchises penitus convalle virenti
Inclusas animas, superumque ad lumen ituras,
Lustrabat"—— VIRG. Aeneid. vi. W.

By no means with an intent to render him impenetrable; but merely in allusion to the passage in Virgil here quoted.

Inſtant, when dipt, away they wing their flight,
Where Brown and Mears unbar the gates of Light,
Demand new bodies, and in Calf's array,
Ruſh to the world, impatient for the day.
Millions and millions on theſe banks he views,
Thick as the ſtars of night, or morning dews,
As thick as bees o'er vernal bloſſoms fly,
As thick as eggs at Ward in Pillory.

Wond'ring

REMARKS.

VER. 28. *Brown and Mears*] Bookſellers, Printers for any body.—The allegory of the ſouls of the dull comiug forth in the form of books, dreſſed in calf's leather, and being let abroad in vaſt numbers by Bookſellers, is ſufficiently intelligible. W.

VER. 34. *Ward in Pillory.*] John Ward of Hackney, Eſq; Member of Parliament, being convicted of forgery, was firſt expelled the Houſe, and then ſentenced to the Pillory on the 17th of February 1727. Mr. Curl (having likewiſe ſtood there) looks upon the mention of ſuch a Gentleman in a ſatire, as a *great act of barbarity*, Key to the Dunc. 3d edit. p. 16. And another author reaſons thus upon it. Durgen, 8vo. p. 11, 12. "How unworthy is it of *Chriſtian Charity* to animate the *rabble* to abuſe a *worthy man* in ſuch a ſituation? What could move the Poet thus to mention a *brave ſufferer*, a *gallant priſoner*, expoſed to the view of all mankind! It was laying aſide his *Senſes*, it was committing a *Crime*, for which the *Law* is *deficient* not to puniſh him! nay, a Crime which *Man can ſcarce forgive*, or *Time efface!* Nothing ſurely could have induced him to it but being bribed by a great Lady," &c. to whom this brave, honeſt, worthy Gentleman was guilty of no offence but Forgery, proved in open Court. But it is evident, this verſe could not be meant of him; it being notorious,

IMITATIONS.

VER. 28. *unbar the gates of Light,*] An Hemiſtic of Milton. W.

VER. 31, 32. *Millions and millions—Thick as the ſtars, &c.*]

"Quam multa in ſilvis autumni frigore primo
Lapſa cadunt folia, aut ad terram gurgite ab alto
Quam multae glomerantur aves," &c.

VIRG. Aen. vi. W

Wond'ring he gaz'd: When lo! a Sage appears,
By his broad ſhoulders known, and length of ears,
Known by the band and ſuit which Settle wore
(His only ſuit) for twice three years before:

All

REMARKS.

rious, that no *Eggs* were thrown at that Gentleman. Perhaps therefore it might be intended of Mr. Edward Ward the Poet, when he ſtood there. W.

VER. 36. *and length of ears,*] This is a *ſophiſtical* reading. I think I may venture to affirm all the Copyiſts are miſtaken here: I believe I may ſay the ſame of the Critics; Dennis, Oldmixon, Welſted have paſſed it in ſilence. I have alſo ſtumbled at it, and wondered how an error ſo manifeſt could eſcape ſuch accurate perſons. I dare aſſert it proceeded originally from the inadvertency of ſome Tranſcriber, whoſe head ran on the *Pillory*, mentioned two lines before; it is therefore amazing that Mr. Curl himſelf ſhould overlook it! Yet that *Scholiaſt* takes not the leaſt notice hereof. That the learned Miſt alſo read it thus, is plain from his ranging this paſſage among thoſe in which our author was blamed for *perſonal Satire* on a *Man's face* (whereof doubtleſs he might take the *ear* to be a part;) ſo likewiſe Concanen, Ralph, the Flying-Poſt, and all the herd of Commentators.—*Tota armenta ſequuntur.*

A very little ſagacity (which all theſe Gentlemen therefore wanted) will reſtore us to the true ſenſe of the Poet, thus,

"By his broad ſhoulders known, and length of *years.*"

See how eaſy a change; of one ſingle letter! That Mr. Settle was old, is moſt certain; but he was (happily) a ſtranger to the *Pillory*. This note partly Mr. THEOBALD's, partly SCRIBL. W.

VER. 37. *Settle*] Elkanah Settle was once a Writer in vogue, as well as Cibber, both for Dramatic Poetry and Politics. Mr. Dennis tells us, that "he was a formidable rival to Mr. Dryden, and that in the Univerſity of Cambridge there were thoſe who gave him the *preference.*" Mr. Welſted goes yet farther in his behalf: "Poor Settle was formerly the *Mighty rival* of Dryden; nay, for *many years*, bore his reputation *above* him." Pref. to his Poems, 8vo. p. 31. And Mr. Milbourn cried out, "How little was Dryden able, even when his blood run high, to defend himſelf againſt Mr. Settle!" Notes on Dryd. Virg. p. 175. Theſe

 are

All as the veſt, appear'd the wearer's frame,
Old in new ſtate, another yet the ſame.
Bland and familiar as in life, begun
Thus the great Father to the greater Son.

Oh born to ſee what none can ſee awake!
Behold the wonders of th' oblivious Lake.
Thou, yet unborn, haſt touch'd this ſacred ſhore;
The hand of Bavius drench'd thee o'er and o'er.
But blind to former as to future fate,
What mortal knows his pre-exiſtent ſtate?
Who knows how long thy tranſmigrating ſoul
Might from Boeotian to Boeotian roll?

How

REMARKS.

are comfortable opinions! and no wonder ſome authors indulge them.

He was author or publiſher of many noted pamphlets in the time of king Charles II. He anſwered all Dryden's political poems; and being cried up on *one ſide*, ſucceeded not a little in his Tragedy of the Empreſs of Morocco (the firſt that was ever printed with Cuts). "Upon this he grew inſolent, the Wits writ againſt his Play, he replied, and the Town judged he had the better. In ſhort, Settle was then thought a very formidable rival to Mr. Dryden; and not only the Town but the Univerſity of Cambridge was divided which to prefer; and in both places the younger ſort inclined to Elkanah." DENNIS, Pref. to Rem. on Hom. W.

VER. 43. *Oh born to ſee*] It ought to be remarked and remembered, that the Speech of Settle, which begins at this line, is uninterruptedly continued to line 224, and ought to be printed as ſuch, without any break in the periods; and, with the interruption of a few lines, at line 230, goes on from line 251 to 338 of this Book.

VER. 50. *Might from Boeotian, &c.*] Boeotia lay under the ridicule of the Wits formerly, as Ireland does now; tho' it produced one of the greateſt Poets, and one of the greateſt Generals of Greece:

"Boeotum craſſo jurares aere natum." HORAT. W.

How many Dutchmen ſhe vouchſaf'd to thrid?
How many ſtages through old Monks ſhe rid?
And all who ſince, in mild benighted days,
Mix'd the Owl's ivy with the Poet's bays.
As man's Meanders to the vital ſpring
Roll all their tides, then back their circles bring;
Or whirligigs, twirl'd round by ſkilful ſwain,
Suck the thread in, then yield it out again:
All nonſenſe thus, of old or modern date,
Shall in thee centre, from thee circulate.
For thus our Queen unfolds to viſion true
Thy mental eye, for thou haſt much to view:
Old ſcenes of glory, times long caſt behind
Shall, firſt recall'd, ruſh forward to thy mind:
Then ſtretch thy ſight o'er all her riſing reign,
And let the paſt and future fire thy brain.

Aſcend this hill, whoſe cloudy point commands
Her boundleſs empire over ſeas and lands

See,

REMARKS.

VER. 67. *Aſcend this hill, &c.*] The ſcenes of this Viſion are remarkable for the order of their appearance. Firſt, from ver. 67 to

IMITATIONS.

VER. 54. *Mix'd the Owl's ivy with the Poet's bays.*]

" ——— ſine tempora circum
Inter victrices hederam tibi ſerpere lauros."
VIRG. Ecl. viii. W.

VER. 61, 62. *For this our Queen unfolds to Viſion true*
Thy mental eye, for thou haſt much to view:]

This has reſemblance to that paſſage in Milton, book xi. where the Angel

" To noble ſights from Adam's eye remov'd
The film; then purg'd with Euphraſie and Rue
The viſual nerve—*For he had much to ſee.*"

There is a general alluſion in what follows to that whole Epiſode. W.

See, round the Poles where keener ſpangles ſhine,
Where ſpices ſmoke beneath the burning Line,
(Earth's wide extremes) her ſable flag diſplay'd,
And all the nations-cover'd in her ſhade!

Far eaſtward caſt thine eye, from whence the Sun
And orient Science their bright courſe begun:
One god-like Monarch all that pride confounds,
He, whoſe long wall the wand'ring Tartar bounds;

Heav'ns!

REMARKS.

to 73, thoſe places of the globe are ſhewn where Science *never* roſe; then, from ver. 74 to 83, thoſe where ſhe was deſtroyed by *Tyranny*; from ver. 85 to 95, by inundations of *Barbarians*; from ver. 96 to 106, by *Superſtition*. Then Rome, the Miſtreſs of Arts, is deſcribed in her degeneracy; and laſtly Britain, the ſcene of the Action of the poem; which furniſhes the occaſion of drawing out the Progeny of Dulneſs in review. W.

It cannot be believed that our author ever dreamt of the order, which the learned Remarker, has ſuppoſed to be obſerved in this viſion. This note is preciſely in the ſtyle and manner of a forced and refined conceit of another eminent Prelate, the good Biſhop of Theſſalonica, Euſtathius: " Aurora was in love with Orion, who was a great Hunter;" by which it was hinted that the morning was the moſt favourable time for Hunting.

VER. 69. *See, round the Poles, &c.*] Almoſt the whole Southern and Northern Continent wrapt in ignorance. W.

VER. 73. Our author favours the opinion that all Sciences came from the Eaſtern nations. W.

See ſelections from Pauw, with curious and valuable Additions by Daniel Webb Eſq. an author who unites profound Philoſophy with fine Taſte.

VER. 74. *Orient Science*] Indoſtan was in all probability the Parent of all the Sciences, that aroſe firſt in the Eaſt. Many new lights will be thrown on this ſubject by the curious inveſtigations of Sir William Jones at Calcutta.——Since this was written, I am ſorry to hear of the loſs the world and his friends (of whom I had the happineſs of being one) have ſuſtained by his death.

Heav'ns! what a pile! whole ages periſh there,
And one bright blaze turns Learning into air.
Thence to the ſouth extend thy gladden'd eyes;
There rival flames with equal glory riſe,
From ſhelves to ſhelves ſee greedy Vulcan roll,
And lick up all their Phyſic of the Soul.
How little, mark! that portion of the ball,
Where, faint at beſt, the beams of Science fall:
Soon as they dawn, from Hyperborean ſkies
Embody'd dark, what clouds of Vandals riſe!

Lo!

REMARKS.

VER. 75. Chi Ho-am-ti Emperor of China, the ſame who built the great wall between China and Tartary, deſtroyed all the books and learned men of that empire. W.

VER. 76. *He, whoſe long wall*] Other nations, ſays Voltaire, fortify their towns; the Chineſe fortified their empire. The great Wall which ſeparated and defended China againſt the Tartars, and which was built an hundred and thirty-ſeven years before our aera, ſubſiſts to this day, on a circumference of five hundred leagues, riſing on the tops of mountains, and deſcending down into precipices, being almoſt every where twenty feet broad and above thirty feet high; a monument ſuperior to the Pyramids of Egypt, both by its utility and its immenſity.

VER. 78. *Into air.*] A very poor expreſſion! and unworthy our author.

VER. 81, 82. The Caliph, Omar I. having conquered Egypt, cauſed his general to burn the Ptolemean library, on the gates of which was this inſcription, ΨΥΧΗΣ ΙΑΤΡΕΙΟΝ, the Phyſic of the Soul. W.

VER. 85. *From Hyperborean ſkies*] The Roman, like other great Empires, having degraded, debaſed, and deſtroyed a great part of the human ſpecies, about the fourth century there ruſhed forth from the North prodigious ſwarms of warlike nations, from regions unknown, to take vengeance on thoſe Tyrants, for the various calamities they had inflicted on mankind. Their mighty

armies

Lo! where Maeotis ſleeps, and hardly flows
The freezing Tanais through a waſte of ſnows,
The North by myriads pours her mighty ſons,
Great nurſe of Goths, of Alans, and of Huns!
See Alaric's ſtern port! the martial frame
Of Genſeric! and Attila's dread name!
See the bold Oſtrogoths on Latium fall;
See the fierce Viſigoths on Spain and Gaul!

See,

REMARKS.

armies could not have been conducted, nor could their victories have been ſo important, without more ſkill, and addreſs, and knowledge, than they are commonly repreſented to have poſſeſſed. When the Goths, it is ſaid, had ſacked Athens, and were going to ſet fire to its libraries, one of their Chiefs diſſuaded them from the deſign, by obſerving to them, that as long as the Greeks were addicted to the Study of Books, they would never apply themſelves to the exerciſe of Arms.

VER. 87. *Lo! where Maeotis*] This is ſaid to be Pope's favourite line of all his Works.

VER. 92. *Attila's dread name!*] At an entertainment given by Attila to the Roman ambaſſadors, two Scythians advanced to him, and recited a poem, in which they celebrated his victories and military virtues. All the Huns fixed their eyes with attention on theſe bards: ſome, remembering their own exploits, exulted with joy; others, feeble with age, burſt into tears, bewailing the decay of their vigour.

See alſo a fine chapter, the 19th of Monteſquieu's Grandeur, &c. for a character of this great hero.

A Poet of Calabria, named Marullus, having written a panegyric on Attila, after he had taken Padua, 451, in which he had called Attila a God, and ſaid he was of Divine Original, Attila, ordering the verſes to be interpreted to him, with indignation ordered the poem to be burnt, and the poet with difficulty eſcaped the ſame puniſhment. See Fabricius, Bibl. Mediae et Infimae Latinitatis, T. 5. The noble painting by Raphael of Attila, St. Peter, and St. Paul, is well known.

See, where the morning gilds the palmy ſhore
(The ſoil that arts and infant letters bore)
His conqu'ring tribes th' Arabian prophet draws,
And ſaving Ignorance enthrones by Laws.
See Chriſtians, Jews, one heavy ſabbath keep,
And all the weſtern world believe and ſleep.

Lo! Rome herſelf, proud miſtreſs now no more
Of arts, but thund'ring againſt heathen lore;
Her grey-hair'd Synods damning books unread,
And Bacon trembling for his brazen head.

Padua,

REMARKS.

VER. 96. *(The ſoil that arts and infant letters bore)*] Phoenicia, Syria, &c. where letters are ſaid to have been invented. In theſe countries Mahomet began his conqueſts. W.

VER. 102. *Thund'ring againſt heathen lore*;] A ſtrong inſtance of this pious rage is placed to Pope Gregory's account. John of Saliſbury gives a very odd encomium of this Pope, at the ſame time that he mentions one of the ſtrongeſt effects of this exceſs of zeal in him: *Doctor ſanctiſſimus ille Gregorius, qui melleo praedicationis imbre totam rigavit et inebriavit eccleſiam; non modo Matheſin juſſit ab aula, ſed, ut traditur a majoribus, incendio dedit probatae lectionis ſcripta, Palatinus quaecunque tenebat Apollo.* And in another place: *Fertur beatus Gregorius bibliothecam combuſſiſſe gentilem; quo divinae paginae gratior eſſet locus, et major authoritas, et diligentia ſtudioſior.* Deſiderius Archbiſhop of Vienna, was ſharply reproved by him for teaching Grammar and Literature, and explaining the Poets; becauſe (ſays this Pope) *In uno ſe ore cum Jovis laudibus Chriſti laudes non capiunt: Et quam grave nefandumque ſit Epiſcopis canere quod nec Laico religioſo conveniat, ipſe conſidera.* He is ſaid, among the reſt, to have burned Livy: *Quia in ſuperſtitionibus et ſacris Romanorum perpetuo verſatur.* The ſame Pope is accuſed by Voſſius, and others, of having cauſed the noble monuments of the old Roman magnificence to be deſtroyed, leſt thoſe who came to Rome ſhould give more attention to Triumphal Arches, &c. than to holy things. Bayle, Dict. W.

Padua, with ſighs, beholds her Livy burn
And ev'n th' Antipodes Vigilius mourn.
See, the Cirque falls, th' unpillar'd Temple nods,
Streets pav'd with Heroes, Tyber choak'd with Gods:
Till Peter's keys ſome chriſt'ned Jove adorn,
And Pan to Moſes lends his pagan horn;
See graceleſs Venus to a Virgin turn'd,
Or Phidias broken, and Apelles burn'd.

Behold

REMARKS.

VER. 108. *Tyber choak'd with Gods:*] The Ruins of Rome are imaged in a ſublimer ſtrain by Akenſide:

" —— Deſolation o'er the graſs-grown ſtreet
Expands her raven wings; and from the gate
Where ſenates once the weal of nations plann'd,
Hiſſes the gliding ſnake through hoary weeds
That claſp the mould'ring column." B. 2. v. 680.

It is obſerved, that interruptions in the periods of learning may be ſometimes favourable to the Arts and Sciences, by breaking the progreſs of authority, and dethroning the uſurpers over human reaſon.

VER. 109. *Till Peter's keys ſome chriſt'ned Jove adorn,*] After the government of Rome devolved to the Popes, their zeal was for ſome time exerted in demoliſhing the heathen Temples and Statues, ſo that the Goths ſcarce deſtroyed more monuments of Antiquity out of rage, than theſe out of devotion. At length they ſpared ſome of the Temples, by converting them to Churches; and ſome of the Statues, by modifying them into images of Saints. In much later times, it was thought neceſſary to change the ſtatues of the Apollo and Pallas, on the tomb of Sannazarius, into David and Judith; the Lyre eaſily became a Harp, and the Gorgon's Head turned to that of Holofernes. W.

VER. 111. *Graceleſs Venus*] Many pleaſing inſtances of this kind are given in Middleton's entertaining Letter from Rome: " As it is, in the Pantheon, (he ſays), 'tis juſt the ſame in all the other heathen Temples that ſtill remain at Rome; they have only pulled down one idol to ſet up another in its place, and changed

Behold yon' Isle, by Palmers, Pilgrims trod,
Men bearded, bald, cowl'd, uncowl'd, shod, unshod,
Peel'd, patch'd, and pyebald, linsey-woolsey brothers,
Grave Mummers! sleeveless some, and shirtless others.
That once was Britain—Happy! had she seen
No fiercer sons, had Easter never been.
In peace, great Goddess, ever be ador'd;
How keen the war, if Dulness draw the sword!
Thus

REMARKS.

changed rather the name than the object of their worship. Thus the little Temple of Vesta, near the Tiber, mentioned by Horace, is now possessed by the Madonna of the Sun; that of Fortuna Virilis, by Mary the Egyptian; that of Saturn (where the public Treasure was anciently kept), by St. Adrian; that of Romulus and Remus, in the Via Sacra, by two other brothers, Cosmas and Damianus; that of Antonine the Godly, by Laurence the Saint: But for my part, I should sooner be tempted out of devotion for Romulus or Antonine, to prostrate myself before their statues, than those of a Laurence or a Damian; and much rather with Pagan Rome give Divine Honours to the Founders of Empires, than with Popish Rome to the Founders of Monasteries." Middleton borrowed much from Les Conformites de Ceremonies modernes avec les Anciennes. A Leyde, 1667.

Ver. 112. *Or Phidias broken,*] Poggius, sitting with a friend on the top of the Capitoline hill, makes a pleasing and eloquent description of the Ruins of Rome, which lay in prospect below him; inserted in the Dialogue de Varietate Fortunae, republished at Paris, 1723; written about the year 1440.

Ver. 117, 118. *Happy!—had Easter never been.*] Wars in England anciently, about the right time of celebrating Easter. W.

IMITATIONS.

Ver. 117, 118. *Happy—had Easter never been.*]
"Et fortunatam, si nunquam armenta fuissent."
Virg. Ecl. vi. W.

Thus visit not thy own! on this blest age
Oh spread thy Influence, but restrain thy Rage.
And see, my son! the hour is on its way,
That lifts our Goddess to imperial sway;
This fav'rite Isle, long sever'd from her reign,
Dove-like, she gathers to her wings again.
Now look thro' Fate! behold the scene she draws!
What aids, what armies to assert her cause!
See all her progeny, illustrious sight!
Behold, and count them, as they rise to light.
As Berecynthia, while her offspring vye
In homage to the Mother of the sky,
Surveys around her, in the blest abode,
An hundred sons, and ev'ry son a God:
Not with less glory mighty Dulness crown'd,
Shall take through Grub-street her triumphant round;
And

REMARKS.

VER. 126. *Dove-like, she gathers*] This is fulfilled in the fourth book. W.

The line is a little prophane.

IMITATIONS.

VER. 127, 129. *Now look through Fate!—See all her progeny, &c.*]

"Nunc age, Dardaniam prolem quae deinde sequatur
Gloria, qui maneant Itala de gente nepotes,
Illustres animas, nostrumque in nomen ituras,
Expediam." VIRG. Aeneid. vi. W.

VER. 131. *As Berecynthia, &c.*]

"Felix prole virûm, qualis Berecynthia mater
Invehitur curru Phrygias turrita per urbes,
Laeta deûm partu, centum complexa nepotes,
Omnes coelicolas, omnes supera alta tenentes."
VIRG. Aeneid. vi. W.

And her Parnaſſus glancing o'er at once,
Behold an hundred ſons, and each a Dunce.
Mark firſt that Youth who takes the foremoſt place,
And thruſts his perſon full into your face.
With all thy Father's virtues bleſt, be born!
And a new Cibber ſhall the ſtage adorn.
  A ſecond ſee, by meeker manners known,
And modeſt as the maid that ſips alone;
From the ſtrong fate of drams if thou get free,
Another Durfey, Ward! ſhall ſing in thee.
Thee ſhall each ale-houſe, thee each gill-houſe mourn,
And anſw'ring gin-ſhops ſowrer ſighs return.
  Jacob, the ſcourge of Grammar, mark with awe,
Nor leſs revere him, blunderbuſs of Law.

Lo!

VARIATIONS.

VER. 149. in the firſt Edit. it was,
Woolſton, the ſcourge of ſcripture, mark with awe!
And mighty Jacob, blunderbuſs of Law! W.

REMARKS.

VER. 138. *And each a Dunce.*] Never was there an happier Parody! merum ſal—heightened by its alluſion to one of the moſt magnificent paſſages in Virgil, Anchiſes ſhewing to Aeneas his future progeny.

IMITATIONS.

VER. 139. *Mark firſt that Youth, &c.*]
" Ille vides, pura juvenis qui nititur haſta,
Proxima ſorte tenet lucis loca"—— VIRG. Aen. vi. W.

VER. 145. *From the ſtrong fate of drams if thou get free,*]
" ——— ſi qua fata aſpera rumpas,
Tu Marcellus eris!" VIRG. Aeneid. vi. W.

VER. 147. *Thee ſhall each ale-houſe, etc.*]
" Te nemus Angitiae, vitrea te Fucinus unda,
Te liquidi flevere lacus." VIRG. Aeneid. viii.
Virgil again, Ecl. x.
" ——— etiam lauri, etiam flevere myricae," &c. W.

Lo P—p—le's brow, tremendous to the town,
Horneck's fierce eye, and Roome's funereal Frown.

Lo

VARIATIONS.

VER. 151. *Lo P—p—le's brow, &c.*] In the former Edd.
Haywood, Centlivre, glories of their race,
Lo Horneck's fierce, and Roome's funereal face. W.

REMARKS.

VER. 149. *Jacob, the ſcourge of Grammar, mark with awe,*] "This *Gentleman* is ſon of a *conſiderable Maltſter* of Romſey in Southamptonſhire, and bred to the Law under a *very eminent Attorney*: Who, between his *more laborious* ſtudies, has *diverted* himſelf with Poetry. He is a great admirer of Poets and their works, which has occaſioned him to try his genius that way.— He has writ in proſe the *Lives* of the *Poets*, *Eſſays*, and a great many Law-books, *The Accompliſh'd Conveyancer*, *Modern Juſtice*," *&c.* GILES JACOB of himſelf, *Lives of Poets*, vol. i. He very groſly, and unprovoked, abuſed in that book the Author's Friend, Mr. *Gay*. W.

VER. 149, 150.

Jacob, *the ſcourge of Grammar, mark with awe,*
Nor leſs revere him, blunderbuſs of Law.]

There may ſeem ſome error in theſe verſes, Mr. Jacob having proved our author to have a *Reſpect* for him, by this undeniable argument. "He had once a *Regard* for my *Judgment*; otherwiſe he would never have ſubſcribed *Two Guineas* to me, for one ſmall Book in octavo." Jacob's Letter to Dennis, printed in Dennis's remarks on the Dunciad, p. 49. Therefore I ſhould think the appellation of *Blunderbuſs* to Mr. Jacob, like that of *Thunderbolt* to Scipio, was meant in his honour.

Mr. Dennis argues the ſame way. "My writings having made great impreſſion on the minds of all ſenſible men, Mr. P. *repented*, and to *give proof of his Repentance*, ſubſcribed to my two Volumes of ſelect Works, and afterwards to my two Volumes of Letters." Ibid. p. 80. We ſhould hence believe, the name of Mr. Dennis hath alſo crept into this poem by ſome miſtake. But from hence, gentle reader! thou may'ſt beware, when thou giveſt thy money

to

IMITATIONS.

VER. 150. Virg. Aeneid. vi.——" duo fulmina belli
Scipiadas, cladem Libyae!" W.

Lo ſneering Goode, half malice and half whim,
A Fiend in glee, ridiculouſly grim. 154
Each Cygnet ſweet, of Bath and Tunbridge race,
Whoſe tuneful whiſtling makes the waters paſs:

Each

REMARKS.

to ſuch Authors, not to flatter thyſelf that thy motives are Good-nature or Charity. W.

VER. 152. *Horneck and Roome*] Theſe two were virulent Party-writers, worthily coupled together, and one would think prophetically, ſince after the publiſhing of this piece, the former dying, the latter ſucceeded him in *Honour* and *Employment*. The firſt was Philip Horneck, Author of a Billingſgate paper, called The High German Doctor. Edward Roome was ſon of an Undertaker for Funerals in Fleet-ſtreet, and writ ſome of the papers called Paſquin, where by malicious Inuendos he endeavoured to repreſent our Author guilty of malevolent practices with a great man then under the proſecution of Parliament. Of this man was made the following Epigram:

" You aſk why Roome diverts you with his jokes,
Yet if he writes, is dull as other folks;
You wonder at it.—This, Sir, is the caſe,
The jeſt is loſt unleſs he prints his face."

Popple was the author of ſome vile Plays and Pamphlets. He publiſhed abuſes on our author in a Paper called the Prompter. W.

Is it ſurpriſing, ſhall I ſay, or mortifying, to ſee the pains and patience of our Author and his Friends who compiled theſe large notes, in tracing out the lives and works of ſuch paultry and forgotten ſcribblers! It is like walking through the darkeſt alleys of the dirtieſt part of St. Giles's. To pull out theſe Literary Cacus's, incendia vana vomentes, from their dark dungeons and deep retreats, was a truly Herculean (though not very Heroic) labour. Theſe, in truth, were Avia picridum loca!

VER 153. *Goode*,] An ill-natured Critic, who writ a ſatire on our Author, called, *The mock Eſop*, and many anonymous Libels in News-papers for hire. W.

VER. 155. *Each Cygnet ſweet*,] Borrowed from two lines of Young's Univerſal Paſſion. S. 6.

" Is there a wit who chants the reigning laſs,
And ſweetly whiſtles as the waters paſs!"

Each Songster, Riddler, ev'ry nameless name,
All crowd, who foremost shall be damn'd to Fame.
Some strain in rhyme; the Muses, on their racks,
Scream like the winding of ten thousand jacks:
Some free from rhyme or reason, rule or check,
Break Priscian's head, and Pegasus's neck;
Down, down they larum, with impetuous whirl,
The Pindars, and the Miltons of a Curl.

Silence, ye Wolves! while Ralph to Cynthia howls,
And makes Night hideous—Answer him, ye Owls!

Sense,

VARIATIONS.

VER. 157. *Each Songster, Riddler, &c.*] In the former Edd.

Lo Bond and Foxton, ev'ry nameless name.

After ver. 158. in the first Edit. followed,

How proud, how pale, how earnest all appear!
How rhymes eternal gingle in their ear! W.

REMARKS.

VER. 157. *Ev'ry nameless name,*] Personal satire, on objects so obscure, is unavoidably attended with the inconvenience of accompanying it with large notes and explanations, which, though tedious, are necessary; and without which it would be unintelligible. Brossette has been forced to use this method in his many notes on the Lutrin, and on the Satires of Boileau.

VER. 165. *Ralph*] James Ralph, a name inserted after the first editions, not known to our Author till he writ a swearing-piece called *Sawney*, very abusive of Dr. Swift, Mr. Gay, and himself. These lines allude to a thing of his, intitled, *Night*, a Poem. This low writer attended his own works with panegyrics in the Journals, and once in particular praised himself highly above Mr. Addison, in wretched remarks upon that Author's

IMITATIONS.

VER. 166. *And makes Night hideous*]

" —— Visit thus the glimpses of the moon,
Making Night hideous"—— SHAKESP. W.

Senſe, ſpeech, and meaſure, living tongues and dead,
Let all give way—and Morris may be read.
Flow, Welſted, flow! like thine inſpirer, Beer,
Tho' ſtale, not ripe; tho' thin, yet never clear;
So

REMARKS.

Author's Account of *Engliſh* Poets, printed in a London Journal, Sept. 1728. He was wholly illiterate, and knew no language, not even *French*. Being adviſed to read the rules of dramatic poetry before he began a play, he ſmiled and replied, "*Shakeſpear* writ without rules." He ended at laſt in the common ſink of all ſuch writers, a political News-paper, to which he was recommended by his friend Arnal, and received a ſmall pittance for pay;—and being detected in writing on both ſides on one and the ſame day, he publickly juſtified the morality of his conduct. W.

He was afterwards patronized by Lord Melcomb, who aſſiſted him in compiling a very curious Hiſtory of England from the Reſtoration to the Revolution, and is frequently mentioned in Lord Melcomb's Diary.

Ver. 168. *Morris.*] *Beſaleel.* See Book ii. W.

Ver. 169. *Flow, Welſted, &c.*] Of this author ſee the Remark on Book ii. ver. 209. But (to be impartial) add to it the following different character of him:

Mr. *Welſted* had, in his youth, raiſed ſo great expectations of his future genius, that there was a *kind of ſtruggle* between the moſt eminent in the two univerſities, which ſhould have the *honour* of his education. To *compound* this, he (*civilly*) became a member of both, and after having paſſed ſome time at the one, he removed to the other. From thence he returned to town, where he became the *darling Expectation* of *all* the polite Writers, whoſe encouragement he acknowledged in his occaſional poems, in a manner that *will make no ſmall part of the Fame* of his protectors. It alſo appears

IMITATIONS.

Ver. 169. *Flow, Welſted, flow! &c.*] Parody on *Denham, Cooper's Hill.*

"O could I flow like thee, and make thy ſtream
My great example, as it is my theme:
Tho' deep, yet clear; tho' gentle, yet not dull;
Strong without rage; without o'erflowing, full!" W.

So ſweetly mawkiſh, and ſo ſmoothly dull;
Heady, not ſtrong; o'erflowing, tho' not full.
Ah Dennis! Gildon ah! what ill-ſtarr'd rage
Divides a friendſhip long confirm'd by age?

Blockheads

REMARKS.

appears from his Works, that he was happy in the patronage of the moſt illuſtrious characters of the preſent age.—Encouraged by ſuch a *Combination* in his favour, he—publiſhed a book of poems, ſome in the *Ovidian*, ſome in the *Horatian* manner, in both which the moſt exquiſite Judges pronounce he even *rival'd his maſters*—His Love verſes have reſcued that way of writing from contempt ——In his Tranſlations, he has given us the very ſoul and ſpirit of his author. His Ode——his Epiſtle——his Verſes——his Love-tale——all, are the *moſt perfect things in all poetry*. WELSTED of *Himſelf, Char. of the Times*, 8vo, 1728, p. 23, 24. It ſhould not be forgot to his honour, that he received at one time the ſum of 500 pounds for ſecret ſervice, among the other excellent authors hired to write anonymouſly for the Miniſtry. See Report of the Secret Committee, &c. in 1742. W.

An ode of merit on the Duke of Marlborough by Welſted, was inſerted in Dodſley's Miſcellanies, at the deſire of Dr. Akenſide, who, I remember, much commended it. The ſimile of Beer is exactly copied from Addiſon in the Freeholder, No. 20.

VER. 173. *Ah Dennis! &c.*] The reader who has ſeen, through the courſe of theſe notes, what a conſtant attendance Mr. Dennis paid our Author and all his works, may perhaps wonder he ſhould be mentioned but twice, and ſo ſlightly touched, in this poem. But in truth he looked upon him with ſome eſteem, for having (more generouſly than all the reſt) *ſet his Name* to ſuch writings. He was alſo a very old man at this time. By his own account of himſelf in Mr. *Jacob's Lives*, he muſt have been above threeſcore, and happily lived many years after. So that he was ſenior to Mr. *Durfey*, who hitherto of all our Poets enjoyed the longeſt bodily life. W.

I was induced, by what Dr. Johnſon has ſaid of Dennis's Criticiſm on Cato, to look into ſome of his other works, in which are ſome remarks not totally contemptible; particularly on Milton; but in a harſh ſtyle and rough manner. Dr. Farmer relates a ſtory of his having aſſaulted and ſtabbed a man in the dark when at Cambridge.

Blockheads with reaſon wicked wits abhor,
But fool with fool is barb'rous civil war.
Embrace, embrace, my ſons! be foes no more!
Nor glad vile Poets with true Critics gore.
 Behold yon Pair, in ſtrict embraces join'd;
How like in manners, and how like in mind!

Equal

REMARKS.

Ver. 179. *Behold yon Pair, &c.*] One of theſe was Author of a weekly paper called *The Grumbler*, as the other was concerned in another called *Paſquin*, in which Mr. *Pope* was abuſed with the Duke of *Buckingham*, and Biſhop of *Rocheſter*. They alſo joined in a piece againſt his firſt undertaking to tranſlate the *Iliad*, intitled *Homerides*, by Sir *Iliad Doggerel*, printed 1715. W.

Of the other works of theſe Gentlemen the world has heard no more, than it would of Mr. *Pope*'s, had their united laudable endeavours diſcouraged him from purſuing his ſtudies. How few good works had ever appear'd (ſince men of true merit are always the leaſt preſuming) had there been always ſuch champions to ſtifle them in their conception? And were it not better for the public, that a million of monſters ſhould come into the world, which are ſure to die as ſoon as born, than that the ſerpents ſhould ſtrangle one *Hercules* in his Cradle? C.

The

IMITATIONS.

Ver. 177. *Embrace, embrace, my ſons! be foes no more!*] Virg. Aeneid. vi.

"—— Ne tanta animis aſſueſcite bella,
Neu patriae validas in viſcera vertite vires:
Tuque prior, tu parce—ſanguis meus!"—— W.

Ver. 179. *Behold yon Pair, in ſtrict embraces join'd;*] Virg. Aeneid. vi.

"Illae autem paribus quas fulgere cernis in armis,
Concordes animae"———

And in the fifth,

"Euryalus, forma inſignis viridique juventa,
Niſus amore pio pueri." W.

Equal in wit, and equally polite,
Shall this a Pasquin, that a Grumbler write;
Like

REMARKS.

The union of these two authors gave occasion to this Epigram,

" Burnet and Ducket, friends in spite,
Came hissing out in verse;
Both were so forward, each would write,
So dull, each hung an A——.
Thus Amphisboena (I have read)
At either end assails;
None knows which leads or which is led,
For both Heads are but Tails."

After many Editions of this poem, the Author thought fit to omit the names of these two persons, whose injury to him was of so old a date. In the verses he omitted, it was said that one of them had a *pious passion* for the other. It was a literal translation of *Virgil, Nisus amore pio pueri*—and there, as in the original, applied to Friendship: That between *Nisus* and *Euryalus* is allowed to make one of the most amiable Episodes in the world, and surely was never interpreted in a perverse sense. But it will astonish the reader to hear, that, on no other occasion than this line, a Dedication was written to that Gentleman to induce him to think something further. " Sir, you are known to have all that affection for the beautiful part of the creation which God and Nature designed——Sir, you have a very fine Lady—and, Sir, you have eight very fine Children,"—&c. [*Dedic. to* Dennis's *Rem. on the Rape of the Lock.*] The truth is, the poor Dedicator's brain was turn'd upon this article: He had taken into his head, that ever since some books were written against the *Stage*, and since the *Italian Opera* had prevailed, the nation was infected with a vice not fit to be named: He went so far as to print upon the subject, and concludes his argument with this remark, " That he cannot help thinking the Obscenity of Plays excusable at this juncture; since, when that execrable sin is spread so wide, it may be of use to the reducing mens minds to the natural desire of women." DENNIS, *Stage defended* against Mr. *Law*, p. 20. Our author solemnly declared, he never heard any creature but the Dedicator mention that Vice and this Gentleman together. W.

Settle, for we must remember that it is he that is still speaking, passes from character to character in a very abrupt incoherent manner.

Like are their merits, like rewards they ſhare,
That ſhines a Conſul, this Commiſſioner.
"But who is he, in cloſet cloſe y-pent.
Of ſober face, with learned duſt beſprent?"
Right well mine eyes arede the myſter wight,
On parchment ſcraps y-fed, and Wormius hight.

To

REMARKS.

manner. Surely not in the manner in which Virgil proceeds in the viſion pointed out in the notes, from the 6th Book of the Aeneid. The Paſquin, mentioned in line 182, was a weekly Paper, and not the comedy written by Fielding, full of humour, pleaſantry, and ſatire, on the miniſtry; and which occaſioned the act of parliament for licenſing plays, an act that met with a very powerful oppoſition at the time.

VER. 184. *That ſhines a* Conſul, *this* Commiſſioner.] Such places were given at this time to ſuch ſort of Writers. W.

VER. 187. *arede*] *Read*, or *peruſe*; though ſometimes uſed for *counſel*. "READE THY READ, *take thy Counſaile*. Thomas Sternhold, in his tranſlation of the firſt Pſalm into Engliſh metre, hath *wiſely* made uſe of this word,

"The man is bleſt that hath not bent
To wicked READ his ear."

But in the laſt ſpurious editions of the ſinging Pſalms the word READ is changed into *men*. I ſay *ſpurious* editions, becauſe not only here, but quite throughout the whole book of Pſalms, are *ſtrange alterations*, all for the worſe; and yet the Title-page ſtands as it uſed to do! and all (which is *abominable* in any book, much more in a ſacred work) is aſcribed to Thomas Sternhold, John Hopkins, and others. I am confident, were Sternhold and Hopkins now living, they would proceed againſt the innovators as cheats.——A liberty, which, to ſay no more of their intolerable alterations, ought by no means to be permitted or approved of by

ſuch

IMITATIONS.

VER. 185. *But who is he, &c.*] Virg. Aeneid. vi. queſtions and anſwers in this manner, of *Numa:*

"Quis procul ille autem ramis inſignis olivae,
Sacra ferens?—noſco crines, incanaque menta," &c. W.

To future ages may thy dulneſs laſt,
As thou preſerv'ſt the dulneſs of the paſt!

There, dim in clouds, the poring Scholiaſts mark,
Wits, who, like owls, ſee only in the dark,

A Lumber-

REMARKS.

ſuch as are for *Uniformity*, and have any regard for the *old* Engliſh Saxon tongue." HEARNE, Gloſſ. on Rob. of Gloc. artic. REDE. W.

VER. 188. Wormius *hight.*] Let not this name, purely fictitious, be conceited to mean the learned *Olaus Wormius*; much leſs (as it was unwarrantably foiſted into the ſurreptitious editions) our own Antiquary Mr. *Thomas Hearne*, who had no way aggrieved our Poet, but on the contrary publiſhed many curious tracts which he hath to his great contentment peruſed.

Moſt rightly are *ancient Words* here employed in ſpeaking of ſuch who ſo greatly delight in the ſame. We may ſay not only rightly, but *wiſely*, yea *excellently*, inaſmuch as for the like practice the like praiſe is given by Mr. Hearne himſelf, Gloſſar. to Rob. of Gloceſter, Artic. BEHETT; "Others ſay BEHIGHT, *promiſed*, and ſo it is uſed *excellently well* by Thomas Norton, in his tranſlation into Metre of the cxvith Pſalm, ver 14.

"I to the Lord will pay my vows
That I to him BEHIGHT,"

Where the modern innovators, not underſtanding the propriety of the word (which is *truly Engliſh*, from the Saxon) have moſt *unwarrantably* alter'd it thus,

"I to the Lord will pay my vows,
With joy and *great delight*." W.

Ibid. *Hight.*] "In Cumberland they ſay to *hight*, for to *promiſe*, or *vow*; but HIGHT, uſually ſignifies *was called*; and ſo it does in the North even to this day, notwithſtanding what is done in Cumberland." HEARNE, ibid. W.

Ibid. *On parchment ſcraps*] In conſideration of the many very accurate and very elegant editions, which Hearne publiſhed of our valuable old Chronicles, which ſhed ſuch a light on Engliſh Hiſtory, he ought not have been ſo ſeverely laſhed as in theſe bitter lines. Every year gives a greater value to theſe books and theſe editions of Hearne; as well as to his Livy and Pliny's Epiſtles.

A Lumberhouſe of books in ev'ry head,
For ever reading, never to be read!
  But, where each Science lifts its modern type,
Hiſt'ry her Pot, Divinity her Pipe,
While proud Philoſophy repines to ſhow,
Diſhoneſt ſight! his breeches rent below;
Imbrown'd with native bronze, lo! Henley ſtands,
Tuning his voice, and balancing his hands.

How

VARIATIONS.

VER. 197. in the firſt Edit. it was,

And proud Philoſophy with breeches tore,
And Engliſh muſic with a diſmal ſcore.
Faſt by in darkneſs palpable inſhrin'd
W—s, B—r, M—n, all the poring kind. W.

REMARKS.

VER. 199. *Lo! Henley ſtands, &c.*] J. Henley the Orator; he preached on the Sundays upon Theological matters, and on the Wedneſdays upon all other ſciences. Each auditor paid one ſhilling. He declaimed ſome years againſt the greateſt perſons, and occaſionally did our Author that honour. WELSTED, in Oratory Tranſactions, No. 1. publiſhed by Henley himſelf, gives the following account of him. "He was born at Melton-Mowbray in Leiceſterſhire. From his own Pariſh ſchool he went to St. John's College in Cambridge. He began there to be uneaſy; for it *ſhock'd* him to find he was *commanded to believe* againſt his own judgment in points of Religion, Philoſophy, &c. for his genius leading him freely to *diſpute all propoſitions*, and *call all points to account*, he was impatient under thoſe fetters of the free born mind——Being admitted to Prieſt's orders, he found the examination very ſhort and ſuperficial, and that it was not *neceſſary to conform to the Chriſtian religion*, in order either to *Deaconſhip*, or *Prieſthood.*" He came to town, and, after having for ſome years been a writer for Bookſellers, he had an ambition to be ſo for Miniſters of ſtate. The only reaſon he did not riſe in the Church, we are told, "was the envy of others, and a diſreliſh entertained of him, becauſe *he was not qualified to be a compleat Spaniel.*"

However,

How fluent nonsense trickles from his tongue!
How sweet the periods, neither said, nor sung!
Still break the benches, Henley! with thy strain,
While Sherlock, Hare, and Gibson preach in vain.
Oh great Restorer of the good old Stage,
Preacher at once, and Zany of thy age!

Oh

REMARKS.

However, he offered the service of his pen to two great men, of opinions and interests directly opposite; by both of whom being rejected, he set up a new Project, and styled himself the *Restorer of ancient Eloquence.* He thought "it as lawful to take a licence from the King and Parliament at one place, as another; at Hicks's-Hall, as at Doctors Commons; so set up his Oratory in Newport-market, Butcher-row. There (says his friend) he had the *assurance* to form a plan, which no mortal ever thought of: he had success against all opposition; challenged his adversaries to fair disputations, and *none would dispute* with him; writ, read, and studied twelve hours a day; composed three dissertations a week on all subjects; undertook to teach in *one year* what schools and Universities teach in *five*; was not terrified by menaces, insults, or satires, but still proceeded, matured his bold scheme, and put the *Church*, and *all that* in *danger*." WELSTED, Narrative in Orat. Transact. No. 1.

After having stood some Prosecutions, he turned his rhetoric to buffoonry upon all public and private occurrences. All this passed in the same room! where sometimes he broke jests, and sometimes that bread which he called the *Primitive Eucharist.*——— This wonderful person struck Medals, which he dispersed as Tickets to his subscribers: The device, a Star rising to the meridian, with this motto, AD SVMMA; and below, INVENIAM VIAM AVT FACIAM. This man had an hundred pounds a year given him for the secret service of a weekly paper of unintelligible nonsense, called the Hyp-Doctor. W.

VER. 204. *Sherlock, Hare, Gibson,*] Bishops of Salisbury, Chichester, and London; whose Sermons and Pastoral Letters did honour to their country as well as stations. *

In the former editions Kennet was named, not Sherlock. The sermons of the latter, though censured by Mr. Church, are master-

pieces

Oh worthy thou of Egypt's wiſe abodes,
A decent prieſt, where monkeys were the gods!
But fate with butchers plac'd thy prieſtly ſtall,
Meek modern faith to murder, hack, and mawl;
And bade thee live, to crown Britannia's praiſe,
In Toland's, Tindal's, and in Woolſton's days.
  Yet oh, my ſons, a father's words attend:
(So may the fates preſerve the ears you lend)
'Tis yours, a Bacon or a Locke to blame,
A Newton's genius, or a Milton's flame:
But oh! with One, immortal One, diſpenſe,
The ſource of Newton's Light, of Bacon's Senſe.
Content, each Emanation of his fires
That beams on earth, each Virtue he inſpires,
Each Art he prompts, each Charm he can create,
Whate'er he gives are given for you to hate.

Perſiſt,

REMARKS.

pieces of argument and eloquence. And his Diſcourſes on Prophecy, and Trial of the Witneſſes, are perhaps the beſt Defences of Chriſtianity in our language.

VER. 207. *Egypt's wiſe abodes,*]

" —— Qualia demens
Egyptus portenta colit." JUVENAL.

Not one of whoſe ſuperſtitions equalled the groſs abſurdity of the doctrine of Tranſubſtantiation. The Egyptian did not make the onion which he eat, and worſhipped. The Bramins are ſhocked at this doctrine, and challenge our miſſionaries to produce any opinion ſo abſurd from their Vedam.

VER. 212. Of *Toland* and *Tindal*, ſee Book ii. *Thomas Woolſton* was an impious madman, who wrote in a moſt inſolent ſtyle againſt the Miracles of the Goſpel, in the years 1726, &c. W.

VER. 219. *Content, each*] Theſe four lines are perhaps the moſt obſcure of any in our poet's writings.

Persist, by all divine in Man unaw'd,
But, "Learn, ye DUNCES! not to scorn your God."
Thus he, for then a ray of Reason stole
Half through the solid darkness of his soul;
But soon the cloud return'd—and thus the Sire:
See now, what Dulness and her Sons admire!
See what the charms, that smite the simple heart
Not touch'd by Nature, and not reach'd by Art.
His never-blushing head he turn'd aside,
(Not half so pleas'd when Goodman prophesy'd)
And look'd, and saw a sable Sorc'rer rise,
Swift to whose hand a winged volume flies:

All

REMARKS.

VER. 231. *His head*] Here is some obscurity. Whose head? *He* is not sufficient; we do not at first perceive it was Cibber. It is a fault in many, even good writers, not to repeat the substantive intended. I must repeat, that it is the faults of good writers only, that are worth noticing.

VER. 232. *Not half so pleas'd when Goodman prophesy'd*] Mr. Cibber tells us, in his Life, p. 149, that Goodman being at the rehearsal of a play, in which he had a part, clapped him on the shoulder, and cried, "If he does not make a good actor, I'll be d——d.—And (says Mr. Cibber) I make it a question, whether Alexander himself, or Charles the twelfth of Sweden, when at the head of their first victorious armies, could feel a greater transport in their bosoms than I did in mine." W.

VER. 233. *A sable Sorc'rer*] Dr. Faustus, the subject of a set of Farces, which lasted in vogue two or three seasons, in which both Playhouses strove to outdo each other for some years. All the extravagancies in the sixteen lines following were introduced

on

IMITATIONS.

VER. 224.—*Learn, ye Dunces! not to scorn your God.*]
"Discite justitiam moniti, et non temnere divos."
VIRG. W.

All ſudden, Gorgons hiſs, and Dragons glare,
And ten-horn'd fiends and Giants ruſh to war.
Hell riſes, Heav'n deſcends, and dance on Earth:
Gods, imps, and monſters, muſic, rage, and mirth,
A fire, a jigg, a battle, and a ball,
Till one wide conflagration ſwallows all.
  Thence a new world to Nature's laws unknown,
Breaks out refulgent, with a heav'n its own:
Another Cynthia her new journey runs,
And other planets circle other ſuns.
The foreſts dance, the rivers upward riſe,
Whales ſport in woods, and dolphins in the ſkies;

And

REMARKS.

on the Stage, and frequented by perſons of the firſt quality in England, to the twentieth and thirtieth time. W.

The ſixteen following lines contain ſome of the moſt forcible and lively deſcriptions any where to be found; and are a perfect pattern of a clear picturesque ſtyle.

VER. 237. *Hell riſes, Heav'n deſcends, and dance on Earth:*] This monſtrous abſurdity was actually repreſented in Tibbald's Rape of Proſerpine. W.

Theſe abſurdities were indeed brought on the ſtage by Tibbald—but not by Cibber; who again and again diſclaimed and deſpiſed them, as may be ſeen in various paſſages of his apology. It is therefore unjuſt to charge him with favouring and promoting ſuch ſpectacles; which for a long time he reſiſted, and was forced, very unwillingly, to gratify by them the depraved appetite of the Public; of which he much and loudly complains.

IMITATIONS.

VER. 244. *And other planets.*]

" —— ſolemque *ſuum*, *ſua* ſidera norunt"——

VIRG. Aeneid. vi. W.

VER. 246. *Whales ſport in woods, and dolphins in the ſkies;*]

" Delphinum ſylvis appingit, fluctibus aprum."

HOR. W.

And laſt, to give the whole creation grace,
Lo! one vaſt Egg produces human race.
  Joy fills his ſoul, joy innocent of thought;
What pow'r, he cries, what pow'r theſe wonders wrought?
Son; what thou ſeek'ſt is in thee! Look, and find
Each Monſter meets his likeneſs in thy mind.
Yet would'ſt thou more? In yonder cloud behold,
Whoſe ſarſenet ſkirts are edg'd with flamy gold,
A matchleſs Youth! his nod theſe worlds controuls,
Wings the red light'ning, and the thunder rolls.
Angel of Dulneſs, ſent to ſcatter round
Her magic charms o'er all unclaſſic ground:
Yon ſtars, yon ſuns, he rears at pleaſure higher,
Illumes their light, and ſets their flames on fire.

Immortal

REMARKS.

VER. 248. *Lo! one vaſt Egg*] In another of theſe Farces Harlequin is hatch'd upon the ſtage, out of a large Egg. W.

IMITATIONS.

VER. 251. *Son; what thou ſeek'ſt is in thee!*]

"Quod petis in te eſt ——
—— Ne te quaeſiveris extra." PERS. W.

VER. 256. *Wings the red light'ning, &c.*] Like Salmoneus in Aeneid. vi.

"Dum flammas Jovis, et ſonitus imitatur Olympi.
—— nimbos, et non imitabile fulmen,
Aere et cornipedum curſu ſimularat equorum." W.

VER. 258. *—O'er all unclaſſic ground:*] Alludes to Mr. Addiſon's verſe, in the praiſes of Italy:

"Poetic fields encompaſs me around,
And ſtill I ſeem to tread on claſſic ground."

As ver. 264. is a parody on a noble one of the ſame author in The Campaign; and ver. 259, 260. on two ſublime verſes of Dr. Y. W.

Immortal Rich! how calm he ſits at eaſe
'Mid ſnows of paper, and fierce hail of peaſe;
And proud his Miſtreſs' orders to perform,
Rides in the whirlwind, and directs the ſtorm.

But lo! to dark encounter in mid air
New wizards riſe; I ſee my Cibber there!
Booth in his cloudy tabernacle ſhrin'd,
On grinning dragons thou ſhalt mount the wind.
Dire is the conflict, diſmal is the dinn,
Here ſhouts all Drury, there all Lincoln's-in;
Contending Theatres our empire raiſe,
Alike their labours, and alike their praiſe.

And are theſe wonders, Son, to thee unknown?
Unknown to thee? Theſe wonders are thy own.
Theſe Fate reſerv'd to grace thy reign divine,
Foreſeen by me, but ah! withheld from mine.
In Lud's old walls tho' long I rul'd, renown'd
Far as loud Bow's ſtupendous bells reſound;

Tho'

VARIATIONS.

After ver. 274. in the former Edit. followed,

For works like theſe let deathleſs Journals tell
"None but thyſelf can be thy parallel." W.

REMARKS.

VER. 261. *Immortal Rich!*] Mr. John Rich, Maſter of the Theatre Royal in Covent-garden, was the firſt that excelled this way. W.

VER. 266. *New wizards*] Yet it is plain from many paſſages in Cibber's Life, that he deſpiſed theſe fooleries and abuſes of the ſtage; and there are many other paſſages in his Life ſtrongly written to the ſame purpoſe. Neither Booth nor Cibber ever degraded themſelves to the appearances mentioned in the two next lines. They were joint managers of the Drury-lane Theatre.

Tho' my own Aldermen confer'd the bays,
To me committing their eternal praiſe,
Their full-fed Heroes, their pacific May'rs,
Their annual trophies, and their monthly wars:
Tho' long my Party built on me their hopes,
For writing Pamphlets, and for roaſting Popes;
Yet lo! in me what authors have to brag on!
Rednc'd at laſt to hiſs in my own dragon.
Avert it, Heav'n! that thou, my Cibber, e'er
Should'ſt wag a ſerpent-tail in Smithfield fair!
Like the vile ſtraw that's blown about the ſtreets,
The needy Poet ſticks to all he meets,

Coach'd,

VARIATIONS.

After ver. 284. In the former Edit. followed,

Diff'rent our parties, but with equal grace
The Goddeſs ſmiles on Whig and Tory race. W.

REMARKS.

VER. 282. *Annual trophies*, on the Lord-mayor's day; and *monthly wars* in the Artillery-ground. W.

Of late years the city militia has been put on a more reſpectable footing.

VER. 283. *Tho' long my Party*] Settle, like moſt Party-writers, was very uncertain in his political principles. He was employed to hold the pen in the *Character* of a *popiſh ſucceſſor*, but afterwards printed his *Narrative* on the other ſide. He had managed the ceremony of a famous Pope-burning on Nov. 17, 1680, then became a trooper in King James's army, at Hounſlow-heath. After the Revolution he kept a booth at Bartholomew-fair, where, in the droll called *St. George for England*, he acted in his old age in a Dragon of green leather of his own invention; he was at laſt taken into the Charter-houſe, and there died, aged ſixty years. W.

VER. 290. *The needy Poet*] Read the following excellent account of the ſtate of modern authors, by one who knew them well:

" It

Coach'd, carted, trod upon, now loose, now fast,
And carry'd off in some Dog's tail at last.

Happier

REMARKS.

"It is not now, as in former times, when men studied long, and passed through the severities of discipline, and the probation of public trials, before they presumed to think themselves qualified for instructors of their countrymen. There is found a nearer way to fame and erudition, and the enclosures of literature are thrown open to every man whom idleness disposes to loiter, or whom pride inclines to set himself in view. The sailor publishes his journal; the farmer writes the process of his annual labour: He that succeeds in his trade thinks his wealth a proof of his understanding, and boldly tutors the public: He that fails, considers his miscarriage as the consequence of a capacity too great for the business of a shop, and amuses himself in the Fleet with writing or translating. The last century imagined, that a man composing in his chariot was an object of curiosity; but how much would the wonder have been increased, by a footman studying behind it? There is now no class of men without its authors, from the peer to the thresher; nor can the sons of literature be confined any longer to Grub-street or Moorfields; they are spread over all the town, and all the country, and fill every stage of habitation, from the cellar to the garret.

"It is well known, that the price of commodities must always fall as the quantity is increased, and that no trade can allow its professors to be multiplied beyond a certain number. The great misery of writers proceeds from their multitude. We easily perceive that in a nation of clothiers, no man could have any cloth to make but for his own back; that in a community of bakers every man must use his own bread; and what can be the case of a nation of authors, but that every man must be content to read his book to himself? For surely it is in vain to hope, that of men labouring at the same occupation, any will prefer the work of his neighbour to his own; yet this expectation, wild as it is, seems to be indulged by many of the writing race; and therefore it can be no wonder that, like all other men who suffer their minds to form inconsiderate hopes, they are harassed and dejected with frequent disappointments.

"If I were to form an adage of misery, or fix the lowest point to which humanity could fall, I should be tempted to name the life

of

Happier thy fortunes! like a rolling ſtone,
Thy giddy dulneſs ſtill ſhall lumber on,
Safe in its heavineſs, ſhall never ſtray,
But lick up ev'ry blockhead in the way.
Thee ſhall the Patriot, thee the Courtier taſte,
And ev'ry year be duller than the laſt.
Till rais'd from booths, to Theatre, to Court,
Her ſeat imperial Dulneſs ſhall tranſport.

Already

VARIATIONS.

VER. 295. *Safe in its heavineſs, &c.*] In the former Edit.

Too ſafe in inborn heavineſs to ſtray;
And lick up ev'ry blockhead in the way.
Thy Dragons, Magiſtrates, and Peers ſhall taſte,
And from each ſhew riſe duller than the laſt.
Till rais'd from booths, &c. W.

REMARKS.

of an author. Many univerſal compariſons there are by which miſery is expreſſed. We talk of a man teazed like a bear at the ſtake, tormented like a toad under a harrow, or hunted like a dog with a ſtick tied to his tail: All theſe are indeed ſtates of uneaſineſs; but what are they to the life of an author! Of an author worried by critics, tormented by his bookſeller, and hunted by his creditors. Yet ſuch muſt be the caſe of many among the retailers of knowledge, while they continue thus to ſwarm over the land; and whether it be by propagation or contagion, produce new writers to heighten the general diſtreſs, to encreaſe confuſion, and haſten famine."

VER. 297. *Thee ſhall the Patriot, thee the Courtier taſte,*] It ſtood in the firſt edition with blanks, ** *and* **. Concanen was ſure, "they muſt needs mean no body but *King GEORGE* and *Queen CAROLINE*; and ſaid he would inſiſt it was ſo, till the Poet cleared himſelf by filling up the blanks otherwiſe, agreeably to the context, and conſiſtent with his *Allegiance*." Pref. to a Collection of verſes, eſſays, letters, &c. againſt Mr. P. printed for A. Moor, p. 6. W.

Already Opera prepares the way,
The ſure fore-runner of her gentle ſway:
Let her thy heart, next Drabs and Dice, engage,
The third mad paſſion of thy doting age.
Teach thou the warbling Polypheme to roar,
And ſcream thyſelf, as none e'er ſcream'd before!
To aid our cauſe, if Heav'n thou can'ſt not bend,
Hell thou ſhalt move; for Fauſtus is our friend:
Pluto with Cato thou for this ſhalt join,
And link the Mourning Bride to Proſerpine.

Grubſtreet!

REMARKS.

VER. 301. *Already Opera*] The Italian Opera is ſaid to owe its origin to a ſacred drama, entitled, Converſione de S. Paölo, ſet to muſic by Franciſco Beverini, a moſt celebrated compoſer at that time, and repreſented before Cardinal Riario, nephew to Pope Sixtus IV, in the Carnival Seaſon of 1480. This was followed by another at the Carnival at Venice, 1485. But in this latter drama was a mixture of comic characters, lawyers, phyſicians, ladies, ſervants, merchants, &c. though on a ſerious ſubject, and entitled, La Verita Raminga.

VER. 305. *Polypheme*] He tranſlated the Italian Opera of Polifemo; but unfortunately loſt the whole jeſt of the ſtory. The Cyclops aſks Ulyſſes his *name*, who tells him his name is *Noma:* After his eye is put out, he roars and calls the Brother Cyclops to his aid: They enquire *who has hurt him?* he anſwers *Noman*; whereupon they all go away again. Our ingenious Tranſlator made Ulyſſes anſwer, *I take no name*, whereby all that followed became unintelligible. Hence it appears that Mr. Cibber (who values himſelf on ſubſcribing to the Engliſh Tranſlation of Homer's Iliad) had not that merit with reſpect to the Odyſſey, or he might have been better inſtructed in the Greek *Pun-ology*. W.

VER. 308, 309. *Fauſtus, Pluto, &c.*] Names of miſerable Farces, which it was the cuſtom to act at the end of the beſt Tragedies, to ſpoil the digeſtion of the audience. W.

Grubſtreet! thy fall ſhould men and Gods conſpire,
Thy ſtage ſhall ſtand, enſure it but from Fire.
Another Eſchylus appears! prepare
For new abortions, all ye pregnant fair!
In flames, like Semele's, be brought to bed,
While op'ning Hell ſpouts wild-fire at your head.

Now Bavius take the poppy from thy brow,
And place it here! here all ye Heroes bow!

'This,

REMARKS.

VER. 312. *enſure it but from Fire.*] In Tibbald's Farce of Proſerpine, a corn-field was ſet on fire: whereupon the other playhouſe had a barn burnt down for the recreation of the ſpectators. They alſo rival'd each other in ſhowing the burnings of hell-fire, in Dr. Fauſtus. W.

VER. 313. *Another Eſchylus appears!*] It is reported of Eſchylus, that when his tragedy of the Furies was acted, the audience were ſo terrified that the children fell into fits, and the big-bellied women miſcarried. W.

On mentioning this abortive attempt of Tibbald to tranſlate the Prometheus, one cannot forbear thinking of the ſpirited and faithful tranſlation which Mr. Potter has given us of this great Father of the Greek Tragedy.

VER. 315. *like Semele's,*] See Ovid. Met. iii. W.

It ſeems ſtrange, that a writer of Congreve's good and claſſical taſte ſhould chooſe Semele for the ſubject of a drama, where the cataſtrophe is ſo very abſurd: the ſtage direction in the laſt act is—"As the cloud which contains Jupiter is arrived juſt over the canopy of Semele, a ſudden and great flaſh of lightning breaks forth, and a clap of loud thunder is heard; when at one inſtant Semele, with the palace, and the whole ſcene, diſappears, and Jupiter re-aſcends ſwiftly." It was with juſtice he took, for a motto to his Opera, theſe words of Seneca—"A naturâ diſcedimus, populo nos damus, nullius rei bono auctori, & in hâc re, ſicut in omnibus, inconſtantiſſimo." I wonder Pope mentioned the ſtory of Semele, as his friend Congreve had introduced it on the ſtage.

This, this is he, foretold by ancient rhymes:
Th' Auguſtus born to bring Saturnian times.
Signs following ſigns lead on the mighty year!
See! the dull ſtars roll round and re-appear.
See, ſee, our own true Phoebus wears the bays!
Our Midas ſits Lord Chancellor of Plays!
On Poets Tombs ſee Benſon's titles writ!
Lo! Ambroſe Philips is prefer'd for Wit!

See

VARIATIONS.

VER. 323. *See, ſee, our own, &c.*] In the former Edit.

Beneath his reign, ſhall Euſden wear the bays,
Cibber preſide Lord Chancellor of plays,
Benſon ſole Judge of Architecture ſit,
And Namby Pamby be prefer'd for Wit!
I ſee, th' unfiniſh'd Dormitory wall,
I ſee the Savoy totter to her fall;
Hibernian Politics, O Swift! thy doom,
And Pope's, tranſlating three whole years with Broome.
Proceed, great days, &c. W.

REMARKS.

VER. 325. *On Poets Tombs ſee Benſon's titles writ!*] W—m Benſon (Surveyor of the Buildings to his Majeſty King George I.) gave in a report to the Lords, that their Houſe and the Painted-chamber adjoining were in immediate danger of falling. Whereupon the Lords met in a committee to appoint ſome other place to ſit in, while the houſe ſhould be taken down. But it being propoſed to cauſe ſome other builders firſt to inſpect it, they found

IMITATIONS.

VER. 319, 320. *This, this is he, foretold by antient rhymes: Th' Auguſtus, &c.*]

" Hic vir, hic eſt! tibi quem promitti ſaepius audis,
Auguſtus Caeſar, divum genus; aurea condet
Secula qui rurſus Latio, regnata per ava
Saturno quondam"——— VIRG. Aeneid. vi.

Saturnian here relates to the age of *Lead*, mentioned book i. ver. 26. W.

See under Ripley rise a new White-hall,
While Jones' and Boyle's united labours fall:
While

REMARKS.

found it in very good condition. The Lords, upon this, were going upon an address to the King against Benson, for such a misrepresentation; but the earl of Sunderland, then secretary, gave them an assurance that his Majesty would remove him, which was done accordingly. In favour of this man, the famous Sir Christopher Wren, who had been Architect to the crown for above fifty years, who built most of the Churches in London, laid the first stone of St. Paul's, and lived to finish it, had been displaced from his employment at the age of near ninety years. W.

Ver. 326. *Ambrose Philips*] "He was (saith Mr. Jacob) one of the wits at Button's, and a justice of the peace;" But he hath since met with higher preferment in Ireland; and a much greater character we have of him in Mr. Gildon's Complete Art of Poetry, vol. i. p. 157. "Indeed he confesses, he dares not set him *quite on the same foot with Virgil*; lest it should *seem* flattery: but he is much mistaken if posterity does not afford him a *greater esteem* than he *at present enjoys*." He endeavoured to create some misunderstanding between our Author and Mr. Addison, whom also soon after he abused as much. His constant cry was, that Mr. P. was an *Enemy to the government*; and in particular he was the avowed author of a report very industriously spread, that he had a hand in a party-paper called the *Examiner*: A falsehood well known to those yet living, who had the direction and publication of it. W.

He proceeded to grosser insults, says Dr. Johnson, and hung up a rod at Button's, with which he threatened to chastise Pope, who appears to be extremely exasperated. It was an honour to Philips to be joined with so excellent a prelate as Dr. Boulter in writing the Freethinker; who, when he was made Primate of Ireland, did not forget the companion of his labours, but took him to Ireland as partaker of his fortune; and making him his secretary, added such preferments as enabled him to represent the county of Armagh in parliament.

Ver. 328. *While Jones' and Boyle's united labours fall*:] At the time when this poem was written, the Banquetting-house of Whitehall, the church and piazza of Covent-garden, and the palace and chapel of Somerset-house, the works of the famous
Inigo

While Wren with ſorrow to the grave deſcends,
Gay dies unpenſion'd with a hundred friends,

Hibernian

REMARKS.

Inigo Jones, had been for many years ſo neglected, as to be in danger of ruin. The portico of Covent-garden church had been juſt then reſtored and beautified at the expence of the Earl of Burlington; who, at the ſame time, by his publication of the deſigns of that great Maſter and Palladio, as well as by many noble buildings of his own, revived the true taſte of Architecture in this Kingdom. W.

VER. 329. *While Wren*] "The length of his life enriched the reigns of ſeveral princes, and diſgraced the laſt of them. A variety of knowledge proclaims the univerſality, a multiplicity of works the abundance, St. Paul's the greatneſs, of Sir Chriſtopher's genius. The nobleſt temple, the largeſt palace, the moſt ſumptuous hoſpital, in ſuch a kingdom as Britain, are all works of the ſame hand. He reſtored London, and recorded its fall. I do not mean to be very minute in the account of Wren, even as an architect. Every circumſtance of his ſtory has been written and repeated. Biſhop Sprat, Anthony Wood, Ward in his Lives of the Greſham Profeſſors, the General Dictionary, and the New Deſcription of London and its Environs, books in the hands of every body, are voluminous on the article of Sir Chriſtopher. In 1680 he was choſen Preſident of the Royal-ſociety; was in two parliaments; was twice married; had two ſons and a daughter; and died in 1723, at the age of ninety-one, having lived to ſee the completion of St. Paul's; a fabric, and an event, which one cannot wonder left ſuch an impreſſion of content on the mind of the good old man, that, being carried to ſee it once a year, it ſeemed to recal a memory that was almoſt deadened to every other uſe. He was buried under his own fabric, with four words that comprehend his merit and his fame: "Si quæras monumentum, circumſpice!" WALPOLE's Anecdotes, 8vo. vol. iii. p. 163.

VER. 330. *Gay dies unpenſion'd, &c.*] See Mr. Gay's fable of the *Hare and many Friends*. This gentleman was early in the friendſhip of our author, which continued to his death. He wrote ſeveral works of humour with great ſucceſs, the Shepherd's Week, Trivia, the What-d'ye-call-it, Fables; and laſtly, the celebrated Beggar's Opera; a piece of ſatire which hit all taſtes

and

Hibernian Politics, O Swift! thy fate;
And Pope's, ten years to comment and translate.

Proceed,

VARIATIONS.

Ver. 331. in the former Editions thus,

—— O Swift! thy doom,
And Pope's, translating ten whole years with Broome.

On which was the following Note: "He concludes his irony with a stroke upon himself: for whoever imagines this a sarcasm on the other ingenious person, is surely mistaken. The opinion our Author had of him was sufficiently shewn by his joining him in the undertaking of the *Odyssey*; in which Mr. Broome having engaged without any previous agreement, discharged his part so much to Mr. Pope's satisfaction, that he gratified him with the full sum of *Five hundred pounds*, and a present of all those books for which his own interest could procure him subscribers, to the value of *One hundred more*. The author only seems to lament, that he was employed in Translation at all." W.

REMARKS.

and degrees of men, from those of the highest quality to the very rabble: That verse of Horace,

"Primores populi arripuit, populumque tributim,"

could never be so justly applied as to this. The vast success of it was unprecedented, and almost incredible: What is related of the wonderful effects of the ancient music or tragedy hardly came up to it: Sophocles and Euripides were less followed and famous. It was acted in London sixty-three days, uninterrupted; and renewed the next season with equal applauses. It spread into all the great towns of England, was played in many places to the thirtieth and fortieth time, at Bath and Bristol fifty, &c. It made its progress into Wales, Scotland, and Ireland, where it was performed twenty-four days together: It was at last acted in Minorca. The fame of it was not confined to the author only; the ladies carried about with them the favourite songs of it in fans; and houses were furnished with it in screens. The person who acted Polly, till then obscure, became all at once the favourite of the town; her pictures were ingraved, and sold in great numbers; her life written, books of letters and verses to her, published; and pamphlets made even of her sayings and jests.

Furthermore,

Proceed, great days! till Learning fly the ſhore,
Till Birch ſhall bluſh with noble blood no more,
Till

REMARKS.

Furthermore, it drove out of England, for that ſeaſon, the Italian Opera, which had carried all before it for ten years. That idol of the Nobility and people, which the great Critic Mr. Dennis by the labours and outcries of a whole life could not overthrow, was demoliſhed by a ſingle ſtroke of this gentleman's pen. This happened in the year 1728. Yet ſo great was his modeſty, that he conſtantly prefixed to all the editions of it this motto, *Nos haec novimus eſſe nihil.* W.

The Dutcheſs of Queenſberry was forbid to appear at Court, on account of her patronizing Mr. Gay, on which occaſion ſhe ſent the following reply to King George II.

"Thurſday, Feb. 27, 1728.

"That the Dutcheſs of Queenſberry is ſurprized, and well pleaſed, that the King hath given her ſo agreeable a command as to ſtay from Court, where ſhe never came for diverſion, but to beſtow a great civility upon the King and Queen. She hopes by ſuch an unprecedented order as this, that the King will ſee as few as he wiſhes at his court (particularly ſuch as dare think or ſpeak the truth). I dare not do otherwiſe, and ought not; nor could I have imagined that it would not have been the higheſt compliment that I could poſſibly pay the King, to endeavour to ſupport truth and innocence in his houſe; particularly when the King and Queen had both told me that they had not read Mr. Gay's play. I have certainly done right then to ſtand to my own word, rather than his Grace of Grafton's, who hath neither made uſe of truth, judgment, or honour, through this whole affair, either for himſelf or his friends.

"C. QUEENSBERRY."

What follows was written by her Grace at the bottom of the copies of the above anſwer, which ſhe gave to her particular friends.

"This is the anſwer I gave in writing to the Vice Chamberlain to read to the King, in anſwer to the meſſage he brought me from the King to refrain coming to court."

Till Thames see Eaton's sons for ever play,
Till Westminster's whole year be holiday,

Till

REMARKS.

VER. 331. *Hibernian Politics, O Swift! thy fate;*] See book i. ver. 26. W.

VER. 332. *And Pope's, ten years to comment and translate.*] The author here plainly laments that he was so long employed in translating and commenting. He began the Iliad in 1713, and finished it in 1719. The Edition of Shakespear (which he undertook merely because no body else would) took up near two years more in the drudgery of comparing impressions, rectifying the Scenery, &c. and the Translation of half the Odyssey employed him from that time to 1725. W.

VER. 333. *Proceed, great days! &c.*] It may perhaps seem incredible, that so great a Revolution in Learning as is here prophesied, should be brought about by such *weak Instruments* as have been [hitherto] described in our poem: But do not thou, gentle reader, rest too secure in thy contempt of these Instruments. Remember what the Dutch stories somewhere relate, that a great part of their Provinces was once overflowed, by a small opening made in one of their dykes by a single *Water-Rat*.

However, that such is not seriously the judgment of our Poet, but that he conceiveth better hopes from the Diligence of our Schools, from the Regularity of our Universities, the Discernment of our Great men, the Accomplishments of our Nobility, the Encouragement of our Patrons, and the Genius of our Writers in all kinds (notwithstanding some few exceptions in each) may plainly be seen from his conclusion; where causing all this vision to pass through the Ivory Gate, he expresly, in the language of Poesy, declares all such imaginations to be wild, ungrounded, and fictitious. SCRIBL.

Ibid. *Proceed, great days! &c.—Till Birch shall blush, &c.*] Another great prophet of Dulness, on this side Styx, promiseth those days to be near at hand. "The Devil (saith he) licensed Bishops to license Masters of Schools to instruct youth in the knowledge of the heathen Gods, their religion, &c. The Schools and Universities will soon be tired and ashamed of Classics, and such trumpery."——HUTCHINSON'S *Use of Reason recovered*, SCRIBL. *

Till Iſis' Elders reel, their pupils ſport,
And Alma mater lie diſſolv'd in Port!
 Enough! enough! the raptur'd Monarch cries;
And through the Iv'ry Gate the Viſion flies.

VARIATIONS.

After ver. 338. in the firſt Edit. were the following lines,
Then when theſe ſigns declare the mighty year,
When the dull ſtars roll round and re-appear;
Let there be darkneſs! (the dread Pow'r ſhall ſay)
All ſhall be darkneſs, as it ne'er were day;
To their firſt Chaos Wit's vain works ſhall fall,
And univerſal Darkneſs cover all. W.

REMARKS.

VER. 339. *Enough! enough!*] "The Dunciad, (ſays Mr. Clarke to Mr. Bowyer), is not ſo much the common-place, as the common-ſhore of Pope's reſentments, where they run off, and are like to do ſo, for life." Letters, p. 562.——What are the ſenſations of a man after reading Gray's Odes and Elegy, and after he has been reading the Dunciad?

VER. 340. *And through the Iv'ry Gate*] See what the truly learned Jortin has ſaid in his Sixth Diſſertation on the ſubject of this Iv'ry Gate. This Sixth Diſſertation very unfortunately produced a Seventh, on the Delicacy of Friendſhip, which it muſt be lamented was ever publiſhed.

IMITATIONS.

VER. 340. *And through the Iv'ry Gate, &c.*]
" Sunt geminae Somni portae; quarum altera fertur
Cornea, qua veris facilis datur exitus umbris;
Altera candenti perfecta nitens elephanto,
Sed falſa ad coelum mittunt inſomnia manes."
VIRG. Aeneid. vi. W.

THE END OF THE THIRD BOOK.

WHEN the firſt complete and correct edition of the Dunciad was publiſhed in quarto, 1729, it conſiſted of three books; and had for its hero Tibbald, a cold, plodding, and taſteleſs writer and critic, who, with great propriety, was choſen, on the death of Settle, by the Goddeſs of Dulneſs, to be the chief inſtrument of that great work which was the ſubject of the poem; namely, "the introduction (as our author expreſſes it) of the loweſt diverſions of the rabble of Smithfield, to be the entertainment of the court and town; the action of the Dunciad being, the removal of the imperial ſeat of Dulneſs from the city to the polite world; as that of the Aeneid is the removal of the empire of Troy to Latium." This was the primary ſubject of the piece. Our author adds, "as Homer, ſinging only the wrath of Achilles, yet includes in his poem the whole hiſtory of the Trojan war, in like manner our poet hath drawn into this ſingle action the whole hiſtory of Dulneſs and her children. To this end, ſhe is repreſented, at the very opening of the poem, taking a view of her forces, which are diſtinguiſhed into theſe three kinds, party-writers, dull poets, and wild critics. A perſon muſt be fixed upon to ſupport this action, who (to agree with the deſign) muſt be ſuch an one as is capable of being all three. This phantom in the poet's mind muſt have a name. He ſeeks for one who hath been concerned in the journals, written bad plays or poems, and publiſhed low criticiſms. He finds his name to be Tibbald, and he becomes of courſe the hero of the poem."

This deſign is carried on, in the firſt book, by a deſcription of the Goddeſs fixing her eye on Tibbald; who, on the evening of a Lord-mayor's day, is repreſented as ſitting penſively in his ſtudy, and apprehending the period of her empire, from the old age of the preſent monarch Settle; and alſo by an account of a ſacrifice he makes of his unſucceſsful works; of the Goddeſs's revealing herſelf to him, announcing the death of Settle that night, anointing and proclaiming him ſucceſſor. It is carried on in the ſecond book, by a deſcription of the various games inſtituted in honour

honour of the new king, in which bookſellers, poets, and critics contend. This deſign is, laſtly, completed in the third book, by the Goddeſs's tranſporting the new king to her temple, laying him in a deep ſlumber on her lap, and conveying him in a viſion to the banks of Lethe, where he meets with the ghoſt of his predeceſſor Settle; who, in a ſpeech that begins at line 35, to almoſt the end of the book, ſhews him the paſt triumphs of the empire of Dulneſs, then the preſent, and laſtly the future: enumerating particularly by what aids, and by what perſons, Great Britain ſhall be forthwith brought to her empire, and propheſying how firſt the nation ſhall be over-run with farces, operas, ſhows; and the throne of Dulneſs advanced over both the theatres: then, how her ſons ſhall preſide in the ſeats of arts and ſciences; till in concluſion, all ſhall return to their original chaos. On hearing which,

Enough! enough! the raptur'd Monarch cries;
And through the Iv'ry Gate the Viſion flies.

With which words, the deſign above recited being perfected, the poem concludes. Thus far all was clear, conſiſtent, and of a piece; and was delivered in ſuch nervous and ſpirited verſification, that the delighted reader had only to lament that ſo many poetical beauties were thrown away on ſuch dirty and deſpicable ſubjects, as were the ſcribblers here proſcribed; who appear like monſters preſerved in the moſt coſtly ſpirits. But in the year 1742, our poet was perſuaded by Dr. Warburton, unhappily enough, to add a fourth book to his finiſhed piece, of ſuch a very different caſt and colour, as to render it at laſt one of the moſt motley compoſitions, that perhaps is any where to be found in the works of ſo exact a writer as Pope. For one great purpoſe of this fourth book (where, by the way, the hero does nothing at all) was to ſatirize and proſcribe infidels and free-thinkers, to leave the ludicrous for the ſerious, Grub-ſtreet for theology, the mock-heroic for metaphyſics: which occaſioned a marvellous mixture and jumble of images and ſentiments, pantomime and philoſophy, journals and moral evidence, Fleet-ditch and the High Priori road, Curl and Clarke.—To ridicule our petulant libertines, and affected minute philoſophers, was doubtleſs a moſt laudable intention; but ſpeaking of the Dunciad as a work of art, in a critical not a religious light, I muſt venture to affirm, that the ſubject of this fourth book was foreign and heterogeneous, and the addition of it as injudicious, ill-placed, and incongruous, as any of thoſe diſſimilar images we meet with in Pulci or Arioſto.

It is like introducing a crucifix into one of Teniers's burlesque conversation-pieces. Some of his most splendid and striking lines are indeed here to be found; but I must beg leave to insist, that they want propriety and decorum, and must wish they had adorned some separate work against irreligion, which would have been worthy the pen of our bitter and immortal satirist.

But neither was this the only alteration the Dunciad was destined to undergo. For in the year 1743, our Author enraged with Cibber (whom he had usually treated with contempt ever since the affair of Three Hours after Marriage) for publishing a ridiculous pamphlet against him, dethroned Tibbald, and made the laureate the hero of his poem. Cibber, with a great stock of levity, vanity, and affectation, had sense, and wit, and humour: And the author of the Careless Husband, was by no means a proper king of the dunces. " His treatise on the stage, (says Mr. Walpole), is inimitable: where an author writes on his own profession, feels it profoundly, and is sensible his readers do not, he is not only excusable, but meritorious, for illuminating the subject by new metaphors, on bolder figures than ordinary. He is the coxcomb that sneers, not he that instructs by appropriated diction." The consequence of this alteration was, that many lines, which exactly suited the heavy character of Tibbald, lost all their grace and propriety when applied to Cibber. Such as,

Sinking from thought to thought, a vast profound!

Such also is the description of his gothic library, for Cibber troubled not himself with Caxton, Wynkyn, and De Lyra. Tibbald, who was an antiquarian, had collected those curious old writers: And to slumber in the Goddess's lap was adapted to his stupidity, not to the vivacity of his successor.

On the whole, the chief fault of the Dunciad, is the violence and vehemence of its satire, and the excessive height to which it is carried; and which therefore I may compare to that marvellous column of boiling water, near Mount Hecla in Iceland, thrown upwards, above ninety feet, by the force of a subterraneous fire. What are the impressions left upon the mind after a perusal of this poem? Contempt, aversion, vexation, and anger. No sentiments that enlarge, ennoble, move, or mend the heart! Insomuch that I know a person, whose name would be an ornament to these papers, if I was suffered to insert it, who, after reading a book of the Dunciad, always sooths himself, as he calls it, by turning to a canto in the Fairy Queen. This is not the case in that very delightful and beautiful poem, Mac Fleenoe, from which Pope

 has

has borrowed ſo many hints, and images, and ideas. But Dryden's poem was the offspring of contempt, and Pope's of indignation: one is full of mirth, and the other of malignity. A vein of pleaſantry is uniformly preſerved through the whole of Mac Flecnoe, and the piece begins and ends in the ſame key. It is natural and obvious to borrow a metaphor from muſic, when we are ſpeaking of a poem whoſe verſification is particularly and exquiſitely ſweet and harmonious. The numbers of the Dunciad, by being much laboured, and encumbered with epithets, have ſomething in them of ſtiffneſs and harſhneſs. Since the total decay of learning and genius was foretold in the Dunciad, how many very excellent pieces of Criticiſm, Poetry, Hiſtory, Philoſophy, and Divinity, have appeared in this country, and to what a degree of perfection has almoſt every art, either uſeful or elegant, been carried!

THE

DUNCIAD.

BOOK THE FOURTH.

ARGUMENT.

THE Poet being, in this Book, to declare the Completion *of the* Prophecies *mentioned at the end of the former, makes a new* Invocation; *as the greater Poets are wont, when some high and worthy matter is to be sung. He shews the Goddess coming in her Majesty, to destroy* Order *and* Science, *and to substitute the* Kingdom of the Dull *upon earth. How she leads captive the* Sciences, *and silenceth the* Muses; *and* what *they be who succeed in their stead. All her Children, by a wonderful attraction, are drawn about her, and bear along with them divers others, who promote her Empire by connivance, weak resistance, or discouragement of Arts; such as Half-wits, tasteless Admirers, vain Pretenders, the Flatterers of Dunces, or the Patrons of them. All these crowd around her; one of them offering to approach her, is driven back by a Rival, but she commends and encourages both. The first who speak in form are the* Genius's *of the* Schools, *who assure her of their care to advance her Cause by confining Youth to* Words, *and keeping them out of the way of real Knowledge. Their Address, and her gracious Answer; with her Charge to them and the Universities. The* Universities *appear by their proper Deputies, and assure her that the same method is observed in the progress of* Education. *The speech of* Aristarchus *on this subject. They are driven off by a band of young Gentlemen returned from* Travel *with their* Tutors; *one of whom delivers to the*

Goddeſs, in a polite oration, an account of the whole Conduct and Fruits of their Travels; *preſenting to her at the ſame time a young nobleman perfectly accompliſhed. She receives him graciouſly, and indues him with the happy quality of* Want of Shame. *She ſees loitering about her a number of* Indolent Perſons *abandoning all buſineſs and duty, and dying with lazineſs: To theſe approaches the Antiquary* Annius, *intreating her to make them* Virtuoſos, *and aſſign them over to him: But* Mummius, *another Antiquary, complaining of his fraudulent proceeding, ſhe finds a method to reconcile their difference. Then enter a Troop of people fantaſtically adorn'd, offering her ſtrange and exotic preſents: Amongſt them, one ſtands forth and demands juſtice on another, who had deprived him of one of the greateſt Curioſities in nature: but he juſtifies himſelf ſo well, that the Goddeſs gives them both her approbation. She recommends to them to find proper employment for the* Indolents *before-mentioned, in the ſtudy of* Butterflies, Shells, Birds-neſts, Moſs, *&c. but with particular caution, not to proceed beyond* Trifles, *to any uſeful or extenſive views of Nature, or of the Author of Nature. Againſt the laſt of theſe apprehenſions, ſhe is ſecured by a hearty Addreſs from the* Minute Philoſophers *and* Free-thinkers, *one of whom ſpeaks in the name of the reſt. The Youth thus inſtructed and principled, are delivered to her in a body, by the hands of* Silenus; *and then admitted to taſte the Cup of the* Magus *her High Prieſt, which cauſes a total oblivion of all Obligations, divine, civil, moral, or rational. To theſe her Adepts ſhe ſends* Prieſts, Attendants, *and* Comforters, *of various kinds; confers on them* Orders *and* Degrees; *and then diſmiſſing them with a ſpeech, confirming to each his* Privileges, *and telling what ſhe expects from each, concludes with a* Yawn *of extraordinary virtue: The Progreſs and Effects whereof on all Orders of men, and the Conſummation of all, in the Reſtoration of* Night *and* Chaos, *conclude the Poem.*

BOOK IV.

YET, yet a moment, one dim Ray of Light
Indulge, dread Chaos, and eternal Night!
Of darkneſs viſible ſo much be lent,
As half to ſhew, half veil the deep Intent.

Ye

REMARKS.

The DUNCIAD, Book IV.] This Book may properly be diſtinguiſhed from the former, by the name of the GREATER DUNCIAD, not ſo indeed in ſize, but in ſubject; and ſo far, contrary to the diſtinction anciently made of the *Greater* and *Leſſer Iliad*. But much are they miſtaken who imagine this Work to be in any wiſe inferior to the former, or of any other hand than of our Poet; of which I am much more certain than that the *Iliad* itſelf was the work of *Solomon*, or the *Batrachomuomachia* of *Homer*, as *Barnes* hath affirmed. BENTL. P.

VER. 1, &c. This is an Invocation of much Piety. The Poet willing to approve himſelf a genuine Son, beginneth by ſhewing (what is ever agreeable to *Dulneſs*) his high reſpect for *Antiquity* and a *Great Family*, how dead or dark ſoever: Next declareth his paſſion for explaining Myſteries; and laſtly, his Impatience to be *re-united* to her. SCRIBL. P. *

It was thought improper to omit the many notes in this fourth book, marked P. * becauſe they were the joint work of Pope and Warburton; and nothing of Mr. Pope's ought to be loſt. The firſt ſixteen lines are particularly elevated and ſtrong. And yet the expreſſion in the third line, "ſo much be lent," is ſomewhat harſh and forced.

VER. 2. *dread Chaos, and eternal Night!*] Invoked, as the Reſtoration of their Empire is the Action of the Poem. P. *

VER. 4. *half to ſhew, half veil the deep Intent.*] This is a great propriety, for a dull Poet can never expreſs himſelf otherwiſe than by *halves*, or imperfectly. SCRIBL. P. *

I underſtand it very differently; the Author in this work had indeed a *deep Intent*; there were in it *Myſteries*, or ἀπόῤῥητα, which

Q 3

Ye Pow'rs! whofe Myfteries reftor'd I fing,
To whom Time bears me on his rapid wing,
Sufpend a while your Force inertly ftrong,
Then take at once the Poet and the Song.
Now flam'd the Dog-ftar's unpropitious ray,
Smote ev'ry Brain, and wither'd ev'ry Bay;
Sick was the Sun, the Owl forfook his bow'r,
The moon-ftruck Prophet felt the madding hour:
Then

REMARKS.

which he durft not fully reveal; and doubtlefs in divers verfes (according to *Milton*)

—"more is meant than meets the ear." Bentl. P. *

Ver. 6. *To whom Time bears me on his rapid wing,*] Fair and foftly, good Poet! (cries the gentle *Scriblerus* on this place.) For fure, in fpite of his unufual modefty, he fhall not travel fo faft toward oblivion, as divers others of more confidence have done: For when I revolve in my mind the catalogue of thofe who have moft boldly promifed to themfelves Immortality, viz. *Pindar*, *Luis Gongora*, *Ronfard*, *Oldham*, Lyrics; *Lycophron*, *Statius*, *Chapman*, *Blackmore*, Heroics; I find the one half to be already dead, and the other in utter darknefs. But it becometh not us, who have taken up the office of his Commentator, to fuffer our Poet thus prodigally to caft away his Life; contrariwife, the more hidden and abftrufe his work is, and the more remote its beauties from common Underftanding, the more it is our duty to draw forth and exalt the fame, in the face of men and angels. Herein fhall we imitate the laudable Spirit of thofe, who have (for this very reafon) delighted to comment on *dark* and *uncouth* Authors, and even on their *darker* Fragments; have preferred *Ennius* to *Virgil*, and have chofen rather to turn the dark Lanthorn of Lycophron, than to trim the everlafting Lamp of *Homer*.

Scribl. P. *

Ver. 7. *Force inertly ftrong,*] Alluding to the *Vis inertiae of Matter*, which, though it really be no Power, is yet the foundation of all the qualities and attributes of that fluggifh fubftance. P. *

Then rose the Seed of Chaos, and of Night,
To blot out Order, and extinguish Light,
Of dull and venal a new World to mold,
And bring Saturnian days of Lead and Gold.

She mounts the Throne: her head a Cloud conceal'd,
In broad Effulgence all below reveal'd,
('Tis thus aspiring Dulness ever shines)
Soft on her lap her Laureat son reclines.

Beneath

REMARKS.

VER. 14. *To blot out* Order, *and extinguish* Light,] The two great ends of her mission; the one in quality of Daughter of *Chaos*, the other as Daughter of *Night*. *Order* here is to be understood extensively, both as civil and moral; the distinctions between high and low in Society, and true and false in Individuals: *Light*, as intellectual only; Wit, Science, Arts. P. *

VER. 15. *Of dull and venal*] The Allegory continued; *dull* referring to the extinction of Light or Science; *venal* to the destruction of Order, or the Truth of things. P. *

Ibid. *a new World*] In reference to the Epicurean opinion, that from the dissolution of the natural World into Night and Chaos, a new one should arise; this the Poet alluding to, in the production of a new moral World, makes it partake of its original Principles. P. *

VER. 16. Lead *and* Gold] *i. e.* dull and venal. P. *

VER. 18. *all below reveal'd,*] It was the opinion of the Ancients, that the Divinities manifested themselves to men by their *Back-parts*. Virg. Aeneid. i. *et* avertens, *rosea cervice refulsit.* But this passage may admit of another exposition.——Vet. Adag. *The higher you climb, the more you shew your A*———. Verified in no instance more than in Dulness aspiring. Emblematized also by an Ape climbing and exposing his posteriors. SCRIBL. P. *

VER. 20. *her Laureat Son reclines.*] With great judgment is it imagined by the Poet, that such a Colleague as Dulness had elected, should sleep upon the Throne, and have very little share in the Action of the Poem. Accordingly he hath done little or nothing from the day of his Anointing; having passed through the second book without taking part in any thing that was transacted about him; and through the third in profound Sleep. Nor ought this,

 well

Beneath her foot-ſtool, *Science* groans in Chains,
And *Wit* dreads Exile, Penalties and Pains.
There foam'd rebellious *Logic*, gagg'd and bound,
There, ſtript, fair *Rhet'ric* languiſh'd on the ground;
His

REMARKS.

well conſidered, to ſeem ſtrange in our days, when ſo many *King-conſorts* have done the like. SCRIBL. P. *

" When I find my Name in the ſatirical works of this Poet, I never look upon it as any malice meant to me, but PROFIT to himſelf. For he conſiders that *my Face* is more *known* than moſt in the nation; and therefore *a Lick at the Laureat* will be a ſure bait *ad captandum vulgus*, to catch little readers." Life of Colley Cibber, ch. ii. W.

Now if it be certain, that the works of our Poet have owed their ſucceſs to this ingenious expedient, we hence derive an unanſwerable argument, that this Fourth DUNCIAD, as well as the former three, hath had the Author's laſt hand, and was by him intended for the preſs: Or elſe to what purpoſe hath he crowned it, as we ſee, by this finiſhing ſtroke, the profitable *Lick at the Laureat?* BENTL. P.

Surely it is not right that the hero ſhould take no part in any thing that was tranſacted about him in the ſecond book; and that in the third book he ſhould be in a profound ſleep.

VER. 21, 22. *Beneath her foot-ſtool, &c.*] We are next preſented with the pictures of thoſe whom the Goddeſs leads in Captivity. *Science* is only depreſſed and confined ſo as to be rendered uſeleſs; but *Wit* or *Genius*, as a more dangerous and active enemy, puniſhed, or driven away: *Dulneſs* being often reconciled in ſome degree with Learning, but never upon any terms with Wit. And accordingly it will be ſeen that ſhe admits ſomething *like* each Science, as Caſuiſtry, Sophiſtry, &c. but nothing like Wit, *Opera* alone ſupplying its place. P. *

Though there are many paſſages in this fourth book of great ſplendor and ſpirit, yet there are many alſo that are disjointed, ununiform, and obſcure; occaſioned by their being taken from materials and fragments of a work he once deſigned to write, on True and Falſe Learning. In the very ſame proportion that he was peculiarly happy and judicious in the fine additions he made to his Rape of the Lock, he was unfortunate and foiled in the additions he made to his Dunciad.

His blunted Arms by *Sophiſtry* are born,
And ſhameleſs *Billingſgate* her Robes adorn.
Morality, by her falſe Guardians drawn,
Chicane in Furs, and *Caſuiſtry* in Lawn,
Gaſps, as they ſtraiten at each end the cord,
And dies, when Dulneſs gives her Page the word.
Mad *Máthesis* alone was unconfin'd,
Too mad for mere material chains to bind,
Now to pure Space lifts her extatic ſtare,
Now running round the Circle, finds its ſquare.
But held in ten-fold bonds the *Muſes* lie,
Watch'd both by Envy's and by Flatt'ry's eye:

There

REMARKS.

VER. 30. *gives her* Page *the word.*] There was a Judge of this name, always ready to hang any man that came in his way; of which he was ſuffered to give a hundred miſerable examples during a long life, even to his dotage——Though the candid *Scriblerus* imagined *Page* here to mean no more than a *Page* or *Mute*, and to allude to the cuſtom of ſtrangling State Criminals in *Turkey* by *Mutes* or *Pages*. A practice more decent than that of *our Page*, who, before he hanged any one, loaded him with reproachful language. SCRIBL. P. *

VER. 31. *Mad* Máthesis] Alluding to the ſtrange Concluſions ſome Mathematicians have deduced from their principles, concerning the *real Quantity of Matter*, the *Reality of Space*, &c. P. *

Is it allowable to make the ſecond ſyllable of Mathĕſis, ſhort? though Prudentius indeed has done ſo.

VER. 34. *running round the* Circle, *finds it ſquare.*] Regards the wild and fruitleſs attempts of *ſquaring the Circle.* P. *

VER. 36. *Watch'd both by* Envy's *and by* Flatt'ry's *eye.*] One of the misfortunes falling on Authors, from the *Act* for ſubjecting *Plays* to the power of a *Licenſer*, being the falſe repreſentations to which they were expoſed, from ſuch as either gratified their envy to Merit, or made their court to Greatneſs, by perverting general reflections againſt Vice into Libels on particular Perſons. P. *

There to her heart ſad Tragedy addreſt
The dagger wont to pierce the Tyrant's breaſt;
But ſober Hiſtory reſtrain'd her rage,
And promiſs'd Vengeance on a barb'rous age.
There ſunk Thalia, nerveleſs, cold, and dead,
Had not her Siſter Satire held her head:
Nor cou'd'ſt thou, CHESTERFIELD! a tear refuſe,
Thou wept'ſt, and with thee wept each gentle Muſe.
When lo! a Harlot form ſoft ſliding by,
With mincing ſtep, ſmall voice, and languid eye:

Foreign

REMARKS.

VER. 43. *Nor cou'd'ſt thou, &c.*] This Noble Perſon in the year 1737, when the Act aforeſaid was brought into the Houſe of Lords, oppoſed it in an excellent ſpeech (ſays Mr. *Cibber*) "with a lively ſpirit, and uncommon eloquence." This ſpeech had the honour to be anſwered by the ſaid Mr. *Cibber*, with a lively ſpirit alſo, and in a manner very uncommon, in the 8th Chapter of his *Life and Manners*. And here, gentle Reader, would I gladly inſert the other ſpeech, whereby thou mighteſt judge between them: but I muſt defer it on account of ſome differences not yet adjuſted between the Noble Author and myſelf, concerning the *True Reading* of certain paſſages. BENTL. P. *

VER. 45. *When lo! a Harlot form*] The Attitude given to this Phantom repreſents the nature and genius of the *Italian* Opera; its affected airs, its effeminate ſounds, and the practice of patching up theſe Operas with favourite ſongs, incoherently put together. Theſe things were ſupported by the ſubſcriptions of the Nobility. This circumſtance, that OPERA ſhould prepare for the opening of the grand Seſſions, was propheſied of in Book iii. ver. 304.

"Already Opera prepares the way,
The ſure fore-runner of her gentle ſway." P. *

Our author had not ſeen the charming Drama's of Metaſtaſio; who is indeed a very fine tragic poet; the plans of ſome of his pieces are conducted with the trueſt art and judgment, which

cannot

Foreign her air, her robe's discordant pride
In patch-work flutt'ring, and her head aside:
By singing Peers up-held on either hand,
She tripp'd and laugh'd, too pretty much to stand;
Cast on the prostrate Nine a scornful look,
Then thus in quaint Recitativo spoke.

O *Cara! Cara!* silence all that train:
Joy to great Chaos! let Division reign:

Chromatic

REMARKS.

cannot be surprising to those who know that this enchanting writer has been excelled by few moderns in genius and in learning. Hear a very serious philosopher asserting, "that nothing can be more deeply affecting than the interesting scenes of the serious Opera; when to good poetry and good music, to the Poetry of Metastasio and the music of Pergolese, is added the execution of a good actor." Essays of ADAM SMITH, p. 159.

See also p. 167, of the Musical Imitations in the same work.

Voltaire thinks more highly of the opera than Pope:

"Ou les beaux vers, la danse, la musique,
L'art de tromper les yeux par les couleures,
L'art plus heureux de seduire les cœurs;
De cent plaisirs font un plaisir unique."

If Pope therefore had lived to read the operas of Metastasio, he would probably have altered his opinion of this species of poetry. And he seems to have not been acquainted with those of Quinault; or perhaps took his opinion concerning them from Boileau. Some are far above love stories; see the incantations of Medea; the opening of Pluto; the speeches of Medusa, Ceres, and Alceste.

VER. 54. *let Division reign:*] Alluding to the false taste of playing tricks with Music with numberless divisions, to the neglect of that harmony which conforms to the Sense, and applies to the Passions. Mr. *Handel* had introduced a great number of Hands, and

IMITATIONS.

VER. 54. *Joy to great Chaos!*]
Joy to great Caesar—The beginning of a famous old Song. W.

Chromatic tortures ſoon ſhall drive them hence,
Break all their nerves, and fritter all their ſenſe:
One Trill ſhall harmonize joy, grief, and rage,
Wake the dull Church, and lull the ranting Stage;
To the ſame notes thy ſons ſhall hum, or ſnore,
And all thy yawning daughters cry, *encore*.
Another Phoebus, thy own Phoebus, reigns,
Joys in my jigs, and dances in my chains.
But ſoon, ah ſoon, Rebellion will commence,
If Muſic meanly borrows aid from Senſe:
Strong in new Arms, lo! Giant HANDEL ſtands,
Like bold Briareus, with a hundred hands;

To

REMARKS.

and more variety of Inſtruments into the Orcheſtra, and employed even Drums and Cannon to make a fuller Chorus; which proved ſo much too manly for the fine Gentlemen of his age, that he was obliged to remove his Muſic into *Ireland*. After which they were reduced, for want of Compoſers, to practiſe the patch-work above-mentioned. P. •

This ſubject is treated with accuracy and taſte in Aviſon's Eſſay on Muſical Expreſſion; and the ſuperiority of Expreſſion to execution, inſiſted on and demonſtrated.

VER. 55. *Chromatic tortures*] The judicious and elegant author of the General Hiſtory of Muſic has given us accurate accounts of every ſpecies of this art, and enriched his work with a variety of curious particulars concerning it, unknown before.

VER. 61. *thy own* Phoebus, *reigns*,]

"Tuus jam regnat Apollo." VIRG.

Not the ancient *Phoebus*, the God of Harmony, but a modern *Phoebus* of *French* extraction, married to the Princeſs *Galimathia*, one of the handmaids of Dulneſs, and an aſſiſtant to Opera. Of whom ſee *Bouhours*, and other Critics of that nation. SCRIBL. P. *

VER. 65. *Giant Handel*] The honor paid to this truly ſublime genius, by the repeated performances of his nobleſt works at

Weſtminſter-

To ſtir, to rouze, to ſhake the Soul he comes,
And Jove's own Thunders follow Mars's Drums.
Arreſt him, Empreſs; or you ſleep no more—
She heard, and drove him to th' Hibernian ſhore.

And now had Fame's poſterior Trumpet blown,
And all the Nations ſummon'd to the Throne.
The young, the old, who feel her inward ſway,
One inſtinct ſeizes, and tranſports away.
None need a guide, by ſure Attraction led,
And ſtrong impulſive gravity of Head:

None

REMARKS.

Weſtminſter-Abbey, under the patronage of the King, will not ſoon be forgotten. The magnificence and accuracy of which performances were beyond compare. It is remarkable, that in the earlier part of his life, Pope was ſo very inſenſible to the charms of muſic, that he once aſked his friend Dr. Arbuthnot, who had a fine ear, "whether, at Lord Burlington's concerts, the rapture which the company expreſſed upon hearing the compoſitions and performance of Handel, did not proceed wholly from affectation?"

Dr. Burney obſerves, v. i. p. 329. that both Dryden and my friend Pitt, have inaccurately and improperly tranſlated the paſſage of Virgil, b. 6. relating to Orpheus, v. 645.

"Obloquitur numeris ſeptem diſcrimina vocum."

VER. 71. *Fame's poſterior Trumpet*] *Poſterior*, viz. her *ſecond* or *more certain* Report: unleſs we imagine this word *poſterior* to relate to the poſition of one of her Trumpets, according to *Hudibras*:

"She blows not both with the ſame Wind,
But one before and one behind;
And therefore modern Authors name
One good, and t'other evil Fame." P. *

VER. 75. *None need a* guide,—*None want a* place,] The ſons of Dulneſs want no inſtructors in ſtudy, nor guides in life: They are their own maſters in all Sciences, and their own Heralds and Introducers into all places. P. *

None want a place, for all their Centre ſound,
Hung to the Goddeſs, and coher'd around.
Not cloſer, orb in orb, conglob'd are ſeen
The buzzing Bees about their duſky Queen.
The gath'ring number, as it moves along,
Involves a vaſt involuntary throng,
Who gently drawn, and ſtruggling leſs and leſs,
Roll in her Vortex, and her pow'r confeſs.
Not thoſe alone who paſſive own her laws,
But who, weak Rebels, more advance her cauſe.
Whate'er of dunce in College or in Town
Sneers at another, in toupee or gown;
Whate'er of mungril no one claſs admits,
A wit with dunces, and a dunce with wits.
Nor abſent they, no members of her ſtate,
Who pay her homage in her ſons, the Great;
Who falſe to Phoebus, bow the knee to Baal;
Or impious, preach his Word without a call.

Patrons,

REMARKS.

VER. 76 to 101.] It ought to be obſerved that here are three claſſes in this aſſembly. The firſt of men abſolutely and avowedly dull, who naturally adhere to the Goddeſs, and are repreſented in the ſimile of the Bees about their Queen. The ſecond involuntarily drawn to her, though not caring to own her influence; from ver. 81 to 90. The third of ſuch as, though not members of her ſtate, yet advance her ſervice by flattering Dulneſs, cultivating miſtaken talents, patronizing vile ſcriblers, diſcouraging living merit, or ſetting up for wits, and men of taſte in arts they underſtand not; from ver. 91 to 101. P. *

VER. 93. *falſe to* Phoebus] Spoken of the ancient and true *Phoebus*; not the *French Phoebus*, who hath no choſen Prieſts or Poets, but equally inſpires any man that pleaſeth to ſing or preach. SCRIBL. P. *

Patrons, who ſneak from living worth to dead,
With-hold the penſion, and ſet up the head;
Or veſt dull Flatt'ry in the ſacred Gown;
Or give from fool to fool the Laurel crown.
And (laſt and worſt) with all the cant of wit,
Without the ſoul, the Muſe's Hypocrit.

There march'd the bard and blockhead, ſide by ſide,
Who rhym'd for hire, and patroniz'd for pride.
Narciſſus, prais'd with all a Parſon's pow'r,
Look'd a white lilly ſunk beneath a ſhow'r.
There mov'd Montalto with ſuperior air;
His ſtretch'd-out arm diſplay'd a Volume fair;
Courtiers and Patriots in two ranks divide,
Through both he paſs'd, and bow'd from ſide to ſide:
But as in graceful act, with awful eye
Compos'd he ſtood, bold Benſon thruſt him by:

On

REMARKS.

VER. 94. *his Word without a call.*] We might have expected an objection to this expreſſion from Dr. Warburton.

VER. 99, 100.

And (laſt and worſt) with all the cant of wit,
Without the ſoul, the Muſe's Hypocrit.]

In this diviſion are reckoned up, 1. The Idolizers of Dulneſs in the Great—2. Ill Judges—3. Ill Writers—4. Ill Patrons. But the *laſt and worſt*, as he juſtly calls him, is the *Muſe's Hypocrite*, who is, as it were, the Epitome of them all. He who thinks the only end of poetry is to amuſe, and the only buſineſs of the poet to be witty; and conſequently who cultivates only ſuch trifling talents in himſelf, and encourages only ſuch in others. *

VER. 103. *Narciſſus, prais'd*] Means Dr. Middleton's laboured encomium on Lord Harvey in his dedication of the Life of Cicero. Had Mr. Pope ever read Dr. Warburton's dedication of his Eſſay on Prodigies, to Sir Robert Sutton?

On two unequal crutches propt he came, 111
Milton's on this, on that one Johnston's name.
The decent Knight retir'd with sober rage,
Withdrew his hand, and clos'd the pompous page.

But

VARIATIONS.

VER. 114. "What! no respect, he cry'd, for SHAKESPEAR'S page?"

REMARKS.

VER. 110. *bold* Benson] This man endeavoured to raise himself to Fame by erecting monuments, striking coins, setting up heads, and procuring translations, of *Milton*; and afterwards by as great passion for one *Arthur Johnston*, a *Scotch* physician's Version of the Psalms, of which he printed many fine Editions. See more of him, Book iii. ver 325. P. *

VER. 112. *Milton's on this,*] Benson is here spoken of too contemptuously. He translated faithfully, if not very poetically, the second book of the Georgics, with useful notes; he printed elegant editions of Johnston's Psalms; he wrote a Discourse on Versification; he rescued his country from the disgrace of having no monument erected to the memory of Milton in Westminster Abbey; he encouraged and urged Pitt to translate the Aeneid; and he gave Dobson a thousand pounds for his Latin translation of Paradise Lost. Dobson had acquired great reputation by his translation of Prior's Solomon, the first book of which he finished when he was a scholar at Winchester College. He had not at that time, as he told me (for I knew him well), read Lucretius, which would have given a richness and force to his verses; the chief fault of which was a monotony, and want of variety of Virgilian pauses. Mr. Pope wished him to translate the Essay on Man; which he began to do, but relinquished on account of the impossibility of imitating its brevity in another language. He has avoided the monotony above mentioned in his Milton; which monotony was occasioned by translating a poem in rhyme. Bishop Hare, a capable judge, used to mention his Solomon as one of the purest pieces of modern Latin poetry. Though he had so much felicity in translating, yet his original poems, of which I have seen many, were very feeble and flat, and contained no mark of genius. He had no great stock of general literature, and was by

But (happy for him as the times went then) 115
Appear'd Apollo's Mayor and Aldermen,

On

REMARKS.

by no means qualified to pronounce on what degree of learning Pope possessed; and I am surprized that Johnson should quote him, as saying, "I found Pope had more learning than I expected."

VER. 113. *The decent* Knight] An eminent person, who was about to publish a very pompous Edition of a great Author *at his own expence.* P. *

VER. 115. *But (happy for him*] These four lines, of which the first is a very indifferent one, were not in the quarto edition of 1743, page 165: But were added on occasion of Sir Thomas Hanmer's edition, printed at Oxford in six large quarto volumes: which edition occasioned a violent quarrel betwixt Sir Thomas and Dr. Warburton, of which the reader may judge by perusing the two curious letters here annexed.

"Milden-hall near Newmarket,
Suffolk, October 28, 1742.

"Dear Sir,

"I have much doubted with myself whether it were proper for me to return an answer to the favour of your letter, till after hearing again from you or Dr. Shippen. There seem to arise some difficulties with respect to the design of printing a new edition of Shakespeare, and I beg it may be laid aside, if you are not fully satisfied, that some advantage may arise from it to the university; for I have no end in view to myself to make me desire it. I am satisfied there is no edition coming or likely to come from Warburton, but it is a report raised to serve some little purpose or other, of which I see there are many on foot. I have reason to know that gentleman is very angry with me, for a cause of which I think I have no reason to be ashamed, or he to be proud. My acquaintance with him began upon an application from himself, and at his request the present bishop of Salisbury introduced him to me for this purpose only, as was then declared, that as he had many observations upon Shakespeare then lying by him, over and above those printed in Theobald's book, he much desired to communicate them to me, that I might judge whether any of them worthy to be added to those emendations, which he understood I had long been making upon that author. I received

 his

On whom three hundred gold-capt youths await,
To lug the pond'rous volume off in ſtate.

When

REMARKS.

his offer with all the civility I could: upon which a long correſpondence began by letters, in which he explained his ſenſe upon many paſſages, which ſometimes I thought juſt, but moſtly wild and out of the way. Afterwards he made a journey hither on purpoſe to ſee my books; he ſtaid about a week with me, and had the inſpection of them: and, all this while I had no ſuſpicion of any other deſign, in all the pains he took, but to perfect a correct text in Shakeſpeare, of which he ſeemed very fond. But not long after, the views of intereſt began to ſhew themſelves, ſeveral hints were dropt of the advantage he might receive from publiſhing the work thus corrected; but as I had no thoughts at all of making it public, ſo I was more averſe to yield to it in ſuch a manner as was likely to produce a paltry edition, by making it the means only of getting a greater ſum of money by it. Upon this, he flew into a great rage, and there is an end of the ſtory; with which I have thought it beſt to make you acquainted, that, as you mention the working of his friends, you may judge the better of what you ſee and hear from them, and may make what uſe you pleaſe of the truth of facts, which I have now laid before you.

"As to my own particular, I have no aim to purſue in this affair: I propoſe neither honour, reward, or thanks, and ſhould be very well pleaſed to have the books continue upon their ſhelf, in my own private cloſet. If it is thought they may be of uſe or pleaſure to the public, I am willing to part with them out of my hands, and to add, for the honour of Shakeſpeare, ſome decorations and embelliſhments at my own expence. It will be an unexpected pleaſure to me, if they can be made in any degree profitable to the univerſity, to which I ſhall always retain a gratitude, a regard, and reverence; but that I may end as I began, I beg the favour of you, if upon more mature conſideration among yourſelves, you ſee reaſon to diſcourage you from proceeding in this affair, that you will give it over, and not look upon yourſelves to be the more obliged to proſecute it from any ſteps already taken with,

"Sir, your moſt humble and obedient ſervant,

"THO. HANMER."

The

When Dulneſs, ſmiling—" Thus revive the wits!
But murder firſt, and mince them all to bits;
As

REMARKS.

The biſhop's ſtrictures on this charge, which were deſigned to be printed in the Biographia Britannica, if the ſheet had not been cancelled, are as follow:

" Sir Thomas Hanmer's letter from Milden-hall to Oxford, Oct. 28, 1742, is one continued falſehood from beginning to end.

" It is falſe that my acquaintance with him began upon an application from me to him. It began on an application of the preſent biſhop of London to me, in behalf of Sir T. Hanmer; and, as I underſtood, at Sir T. Hanmer's deſire. The thing ſpeaks itſelf. It was publicly known that I had written notes on Shakeſpear, becauſe part of them were printed; few people knew that Sir T. Hanmer had: I certainly did not know; nor, indeed, whether he was living or dead.

" The falſehood is ſtill viler (becauſe it ſculks only under an inſinuation) that I made a journey to him to Milden-hall, without invitation: whereas it was at his earneſt and repeated requeſt, as appears by his letters, which I have ſtill by me.

" It is falſe that the views of intereſt began to ſhew themſelves in me to this *diſintereſted gentleman.* My reſentment at Sir Thomas H.'s behaviour began on the following occaſion: a bookſeller in London, of the beſt reputation, had wrote me word, that Sir Thomas Hanmer had been with him, to propoſe his printing an edition of Shakeſpear on the following conditions; of its being pompouſly printed with cuts, (as it afterwards was at Oxford) at the expence of the ſaid bookſeller, who, beſides, ſhould pay one hundred guineas, or ſome ſuch ſum, to a friend of his, (Sir T. Hanmer's) who had tranſcribed the *gloſſary* for him. But the bookſeller, underſtanding that he made uſe of many of my notes, and that I knew nothing of the project, thought fit to ſend me this account. On which, I wrote to Sir Th. Hanmer, upbraiding him with his behaviour, and demanding, out of his hands, all the letters I had written to him on the ſubject; which he unwillingly complied with, after cavilling about the right of property in thoſe letters, for which he had (he ſaid) paid the poſtage.

" When the bookſeller would not deal with him on theſe terms, he applied to the univerſity of Oxford; and was at the expence of his purſe in procuring cuts for his edition; and at the expence of

As erſt Medea (cruel, ſo to ſave!)
A new Edition of old Aeſon gave;
Let ſtandard Authors, thus, like trophies born,
Appear more glorious as more hack'd and torn.
And you, my Critics! in the chequer'd ſhade,
Admire new light through holes yourſelves have made.
  Leave not a foot of verſe, a foot of ſtone,
A Page, a Grave, that they can call their own;

But

REMARKS.

his reputation in employing a number of my emendations on the text, without my knowledge or conſent: and this behaviour was what occaſioned Mr. Pope's perpetuating the memory of the Oxford edition of Shakeſpear in the *Dunciad*.

"This is a true and exact account of the whole affair, which I never thought worth while afterwards to complain of, but to the biſhop of London, at whoſe deſire I lent Sir Thomas Hanmer my aſſiſtance: nor ſhould ever have revived it, but for the publication of this ſcandalous letter, *ſent from Oxford to this Philip Nichols*, to be inſerted in the Biographia Britannica.

"Jan. 29, 1761. W. GLOUCESTER."

VER. 119. "*Thus revive, &c.*] The Goddeſs applauds the practice of tacking the obſcure names of Perſons not eminent in any branch of learning, to thoſe of the moſt diſtinguiſhed Writers; either by printing *Editions* of their works with impertinent alterations of their Text, as in the former inſtances; or by ſetting up *Monuments* diſgraced with their own vile names and inſcriptions, as in the latter. P. *

VER. 122. *old* Aeſon] Of whom Ovid (very applicable to theſe reſtored authors)

"Aeſon *miratur*,
"Diſſimilemque animum *ſubiit*"— P. *

VER. 125. *the chequer'd ſhade,*] An expreſſion of Milton.

IMITATIONS.

VER. 126. *Admire new light, &c.*]

"The Soul's dark cottage, batter'd and decay'd,
"Lets in new light, through chinks that time has made."
WALLER. W.

But ſpread, my ſons, your glory thin or thick,
On paſſive paper, or on ſolid brick.
So by each Bard an Alderman ſhall ſit,
A heavy Lord ſhall hang at ev'ry Wit,
And while on Fame's triumphal Car they ride,
Some Slave of mine be pinion'd to their ſide."

Now crowds on crowds around the Goddeſs preſs,
Each eager to preſent the firſt Addreſs.
Dunce ſcorning Dunce beholds the next advance,
But Fop ſhews Fop ſuperior complaiſance.

REMARKS.

VER. 128. *A Page, a Grave,*] For what leſs than a Grave can be granted to a dead author? or what leſs than a Page can be afforded a living one? P. *

Pagina, not *Pediſſequus*. A Page of a Book, not a Servant, Follower, or Attendant; no Poet having had a *Page* ſince the death of Mr. Thomas Durfey. SCRIBL. P. *

VER. 131. *So by each Bard an Alderman, &c.*] Vide the *Tombs of the Poets*, Editio Weſtmonaſterienſis. P. *

Alluding to the monument erected for Butler, the Author of *Hudibras*, by Alderman Barber. W.

VER. 132. *A heavy* LORD *ſhall hang at ev'ry Wit,*] Ariſtarchus thinks the common reading LORD not LOAD right: and that the author himſelf had been ſtruggling with, and but juſt ſhaken off his *Load*, when he wrote the following Epigram:

My LORD complains, that Pope, ſtark mad with gardens,
Has lopt three trees the value of three farthings:
" But he's my neighbour," cries the peer polite,
" And if he'll viſit me, I'll wave my right."
What! on Compulſion? and againſt my Will,
A Lord's acquaintance? Let him file his Bill. *

The concluding line alludes to a famous one of Auguſtus Caeſar, in ſome groſs verſes.—The Lord is ſaid to be his next neighbour, the then Lord Radnor.

When lo! a Spectre roſe, whoſe index-hand
Held forth the Virtue of the dreadful wand;
His beaver'd brow a birchen garland wears,
Dropping with Infant's blood, and Mother's tears.
O'er ev'ry vein a ſhudd'ring horror runs;
Eton and Winton ſhake through all their Sons.
All Fleſh is humbled, Weſtminſter's bold race
Shrink, and confeſs the Genius of the place:
The pale Boy-Senator yet tingling ſtands,
And holds his breeches cloſe with both his hands.
Then thus. Since Man from beaſt by Words is known,
Words are Man's province, Words we teach alone.

When

REMARKS.

VER. 148. *And holds his breeches*] An effect of Fear, ſomewhat like this, is deſcribed in the viith Aeneid,

"Contremuit nemus——
Et trepidae matres preſſere ad pectora natos."

nothing being ſo natural in any apprehenſion, as to lay cloſe hold on whatever is ſuppoſed to be moſt in danger. But let it not be imagined the author would inſinuate theſe youthful Senators (though ſo lately come from ſchool) to be under the undue influence of any *Maſter*. SCRIBL. P. *

VER. 150. *Words we teach alone.*] Here is a groſs miſrepreſentation of a fact, eaſily confuted by a great cloud of witneſſes. When he made this aſſertion, our poet muſt have been very ill-informed of what is conſtantly taught in our great ſchools. To read, to interpret, to tranſlate the beſt poets, orators, and hiſtorians,

IMITATIONS.

VER. 142. *Dropping with Infant's blood, &c.*]

"Fi ſt Moloch, horrid King, beſmear'd with blood
Of human Sacrifice, and parents tears." MILTON. W.

When Reaſon doubtful, like the Samian letter,
Points him two ways, the narrower is the better.
Plac'd at the door of Learning, youth to guide,
We never ſuffer it to ſtand too wide.
To aſk, to gueſs, to know, as they commence,
As Fancy opens the quick ſprings of Senſe, 156

We

REMARKS.

rians, of the beſt ages; that is, thoſe authors, "that ſupply moſt axioms of prudence, moſt principles of moral truth, moſt examples of virtue and integrity, moſt materials for converſation;" cannot be called confining youth to words alone, and keeping them out of the way of real knowledge. And as to plying the memory, and loading the brain, as in verſe 157, it was the opinion of Milton, and is a practice in our great ſeminaries, "that if paſſages from the heroic poems, orations, and tragedies of the ancients, were ſolemnly pronounced, with right accent and grace, they would endue the ſcholars even with the ſpirit and vigour of Demoſthenes or Cicero, Euripides or Sophocles." The illuſtrious names of Wyndham, Talbot, Murray, and Pulteney, which our Author himſelf immediately adds, and which catalogue might be much enlarged with the names of many great ſtateſmen, lawyers, and divines, paſt and preſent, are a ſtrong confutation of this opprobrious and futile objection. Perhaps he adopted this falſe opinion from that idle book on education, which Locke diſgraced himſelf by writing; who ſeems never to have read the ſecond chapter of the firſt book of Quintilian on this ſubject; and which is as much ſuperior in ſtrength of reaſoning, as it is in elegance of ſtyle, to the treatiſe of our great Britiſh philoſopher.

VER. 151. *like the Samian letter,*] The letter Y, uſed by Pythagoras as an emblem of the different roads of Virtue and Vice,

"Et tibi quae Samios diduxit litera ramos." PERS. P. *

VER. 153. *Plac'd at the door, &c.*] This circumſtance of the *Genius Loci* (with that of the Index-hand before) ſeems to be an alluſion to the *Table of Cebes*, where the Genius of Human Nature points out the road to be purſued by thoſe juſt entering into life. Ὁ δὲ γέρων ὁ ἄνω ἑστηκὼς, ἔχων χάρτην τινα ἐν τῇ χειρὶ, και τῇ ἑτέρᾳ ὥσπερ δεικνύων, τὶς οὗτος Δαίμων καλεῖται, &c. P. *

We ply the Memory, we load the brain,
Blind rebel Wit, and double chain on chain,
Confine the thought, to exercife the breath;
And keep them in the pale of Words till death.
Whate'er the talents, or howe'er defign'd,
We hang one jingling padlock on the mind:
A Poet the firft day he dips his quill;
And what the laft? a very Poet ftill.
Pity! the charm works only in our wall,
Loft, loft too foon in yonder Houfe or Hall.
There truant WYNDHAM ev'ry Mufe gave o'er,
There TALBOT funk, and was a Wit no more!
How fweet an Ovid, MURRAY was our boaft!
How many Martials were in PULTNEY loft!
Elfe fure fome Bard, to our eternal praife,
In twice ten thoufand rhyming nights and days,
Had reach'd the Work, the All that mortal can;
And South beheld that Mafter-piece of Man.

Oh

REMARKS.

VER. 159. *to exercife the breath*;] By obliging them to get the claffic poets by heart, which furnifhes them with endlefs matter for Converfation and Verbal amufement for their whole lives. P. *

VER. 162. *We hang one jingling padlock, &c.*] For youth being ufed like Pack-horfes, and beaten under a heavy load of words, left they fhould tire, their inftructors contrive to make the words jingle in rhyme or metre. *

This is a conceit equally falfe, frigid, and far-fetched.

VER. 166. *in yonder* Houfe *or* Hall.] Weftminfter-hall and the Houfe of Commons. *

VER. 174. *that Mafter-piece of Man.*] Viz. an *Epigram*. The famous Dr. *South* ufed to declare that a perfect Epigram was as difficult

Oh (cry'd the Goddeſs) for ſome pedant Reign!
Some gentle JAMES, to bleſs the land again; 176

To

REMARKS.

difficult a performance as an Epic Poem. And the Critics ſay, "an Epic Poem is the greateſt work human nature is capable of." P. *

VER. 175. *Oh (cry'd the Goddeſs) &c.*] The matter under debate, is how to confine men to words, for life. The inſtructors of youth ſhew how well they do their parts; but complain that when men come into the world they are apt to forget their learning, and turn themſelves to uſeful knowledge. This was an evil that wanted to be redreſſed. And this the Goddeſs aſſures them will need a more extenſive Tyranny than that of Grammar-ſchools. She therefore points out to them the remedy, in her wiſhes for *arbitrary Power*; whoſe intereſt it being to keep men from the ſtudy of *things*, will encourage the propagation of *words* and *ſounds*; and, to make all ſure, ſhe wiſhes for another *Pedant Monarch*. The ſooner to obtain ſo great a bleſſing, ſhe is willing even for once to violate the fundamental principle of her politics, in having her ſons taught at leaſt *one thing*; but that which compriſes all, the *Doctrine of Divine Right.*

Nothing can be juſter than the obſervation here inſinuated, that no branch of Learning thrives well under arbitrary Government but the *verbal.* The reaſons are evident. It is unſafe under ſuch Governments to cultivate the ſtudy of *things*, eſpecially things of importance. Beſides, when men have loſt their public virtue, they naturally delight in trifles, if their private morals ſecure them from vice. Hence ſo great a cloud of Scholiaſts and Grammarians ſo ſoon overſpread Greece and Italy, when once thoſe famous lights of the World had loſt their Liberties. Another reaſon is the *encouragement* which arbitrary Governments give to the ſtudy of *words*, in order to buſy and amuſe active Geniuſes, who might otherwiſe prove troubleſome and inquiſitive. Thus when Cardinal Richelieu had deſtroyed the poor remains of Gallic liberty, and made the ſupreme Court of Parliament merely *miniſterial*, he inſtituted the *French Academy*, for the perfecting their language. What was ſaid upon that occaſion, by a brave Magiſtrate, when the letters patent of its erection came to be verified in the Parliament of Paris, deſerves to be remembered: He told the

aſſembly,

To ſtick the Doctor's Chair into the Throne,
Give law to Words, or war with Words alone,
Senates and Courts with Greek and Latin rule,
And turn the Council to a Grammar School!
For ſure, if Dulneſs ſees a grateful Day,
'Tis in the ſhade of Arbitrary Sway.

O!

REMARKS.

aſſembly, that *it put him in mind how an Emperor of Rome once treated his Senate*; *who, when he had deprived them of the direction of Public matters, ſent a meſſage to them in form, for their opinion about the beſt Sauce for a Turbot.* *

VER. 176. *Some gentle* JAMES, *&c.*] Wilſon tells us that this King, *James* the Firſt, took upon himſelf to teach the Latin tongue to Car, Earl of Somerſet; and that Gondomar the Spaniſh Ambaſſador would ſpeak falſe Latin to him, on purpoſe to give him the pleaſure of correcting it, whereby he wrought himſelf into his good graces.

This great prince was the firſt who aſſumed the title of *Sacred Majeſty*, which his loyal Clergy transfer'd from *God* to *Him*. "The principles of Paſſive Obedience and Non-reſiſtance (ſays the Author of the Diſſertation on Parties, Letter 8.), which before his time had ſkulk'd perhaps in ſome old Homily, were talked, written, and preached into vogue in that inglorious reign." P. *

King James prevailed on Camden to alter ſome paſſages in the firſt part of his hiſtory, for which Thuanus reproached him.

VER. 181, 182. *if Dulneſs ſees a grateful Day,—'Tis in the ſhade of* Arbitrary Sway.] And grateful it is in Dulneſs to make this confeſſion. I will not ſay ſhe alludes to that celebrated verſe of Claudian,

"nunquam *Libertas* gratior exſtat
Quam ſub *Rege pio*;"

But this I will ſay, that the words *Liberty* and *Monarchy* have been frequently confounded and miſtaken one for the other, by the graveſt authors. I ſhould therefore conjecture, that the genuine reading of the forecited verſe was thus,

"nunquam *Libertas* gratior exſtat
Quam ſub *Lege pia*,"

and

O! if my sons may learn one earthly thing,
Teach but that one, sufficient for a King;
That which my Priests, and mine alone, maintain,
Which, as it dies, or lives, we fall, or reign:
May you, my Cam, and Isis, preach it long!
"The RIGHT DIVINE of Kings to govern wrong."
  Prompt at the call, around the Goddess roll
Broad hats, and hoods, and caps, a sable shoal:
Thick

REMARKS.

and that *Rege* was the reading only of Dulness herself: And therefore she might allude to it. SCRIBL.

I judge quite otherwise of this passage: The genuine reading is *Libertas* and *Rege:* So Claudian gave it. But the error lies in the verb: It should be *exit,* not *exstat,* and then the meaning will be, that Liberty was never *lost,* or *went away* with so good a grace, as under a good King: it being without doubt a tenfold shame to lose it under a bad one.

This further leads me to animadvert upon a most grievous piece of nonsense to be found in all the Editions of the Author of the Dunciad himself. A most capital one it is, and owing to the confusion mentioned above by Scriblerus, of the two words *Liberty* and *Monarchy*. Essay on Crit.

> "Nature, like *Monarchy,* is but restrain'd
> By the same Laws herself at first ordain'd."

Who sees not, it should be, *Nature, like* Liberty? Correct it therefore *repugnantibus omnibus* (even though the Author himself should oppugn) in all the impressions which have been, or shall be, made of his works. BENTL. P. *

VER. 183. *O! if my sons may learn*] The doctrines of true Whiggism, as it is called, were never placed in a stronger light, or set off with more forcible language, than in this and the five following lines. What will the disciples of Hobbes or Filmer, say to this passage?

VER. 189. *Prompt at the call,—Aristotle's friends.*] The Author, with great propriety, hath made these, who were so *prompt, at the call* of Dulness, to become preachers of the Divine Right of Kings,

Thick and more thick the black blockade extends,
A hundred head of Ariſtotle's friends.
Nor wert thou, Iſis! wanting to the day,
[Tho' Chriſt-church long kept prudiſhly away.]
Each ſtaunch Polemic, ſtubborn as a rock,
Each fierce Logician, ſtill expelling Locke,

Came

REMARKS.

Kings, to be the *friends* of *Ariſtotle*; for this philoſopher, in his *Politics*, hath laid it down as a principle, that ſome men were by nature made to ſerve, and others to command. *

VER. 192. *of Ariſtotle's friends.*] Let thoſe who wantonly and ignorantly condemn the philoſophy of Ariſtotle, carefully read the truly learned treatiſe of the late James Harris eſq. entitled, Philoſophical Arrangements; where they may ſee in what manner the preceptor of Alexander the Great arranged his pupil's ideas, ſo that they might not cauſe confuſion for want of accurate diſpoſition.

VER. 194. [*Tho' Chriſt-church*] This line is doubtleſs ſpurious, and foiſted in by the impertinence of the Editor; and accordingly we have put it between Hooks. For I affirm this College came as early as any other, by its *proper Deputies*; nor did any College pay homage to Dulneſs in its *whole Body*. BENTL. P. *

VER. 196. *ſtill expelling* Locke,] In the year 1703 there was a meeting of the heads of the Univerſity of *Oxford* to cenſure Mr. Locke's Eſſay on Human Underſtanding, and to forbid the reading it. See his Letters in the laſt Edit. of his works. P. *

Such was the fate of this *new Philoſophy* at Oxford. The *new Theology* of Eraſmus met with pretty much the ſame treatment, a Century or two before, in the Univerſity of *Cambridge*. See Dr. Knight's Life of Eraſmus, p. 137.—But our obnoxious *Eſſayiſt* had given ſcandal to the Scholiaſtic ſpirit of Anthony Wood, the famed Oxford Hiſtorian, long before; who, in the Journal of his own life, has furniſhed us with this curious anecdote. "April 23d, 1663, I began a Courſe of Chymiſtry, [in Oxford] under the noted Chimiſt and *Roſicruſian*, Peter Sthael of Straſburg in Royal Pruſſia. The club conſiſted of ten at leaſt, whereof was JOHN LOCK, of Chriſt Church, afterwards a noted Writer. This John

Lock

Came whip and ſpur, and daſh'd through thin and thick
On German Crouzaz, and Dutch Burgerſdyck.
As many quit the ſtreams that murm'ring fall
To lull the ſons of Marg'ret and Clare-hall,
Where Bentley late tempeſtuous wont to ſport
In troubled waters, but now ſleeps in Port.

Before

REMARKS.

Lock was a man of a turbulent ſpirit, clamorous, and never contented. The Club wrote, and took notes from the mouth of their Maſter: but the ſaid John Lock ſcorned to do it: ſo that while every man beſides were writing, he would be prating and troubleſome." *

Whatever might have been the caſe in the year 1703, certain I am, that Locke's Eſſay has been univerſally read and recommended at Oxford, for above fifty years laſt paſt.

Ver. 198. *Crouzaz,*] Author of a very abſurd and abuſive Commentary on the *Eſſay on Man.* *

Ibid. *On German* Crouzaz, *and Dutch* Burgerſdyck.] There ſeems to be an improbability that the Doctors and Heads of Houſes ſhould ride on horſeback, who, of late days, being gouty or unwieldy, have kept their coaches. But theſe are horſes of great ſtrength, and fit to carry any weight, as their German and Dutch extraction may manifeſt; and very famous we may conclude, being honoured with *Names,* as were the horſes Pegaſus and Bucephalus. Scribl. P. *

Ver. 199. *the ſtreams*] The river Cam, running by the walls of theſe Colleges, which are particularly famous for their ſkill in Diſputation. P. *

Ver. 200. *To lull the ſons*] Dr. Hurd in his Dialogues on Early Travel, is of a quite contrary opinion, and has vindicated the utility of an univerſity education; yet ſome have thought it a little inconſiſtent, that Locke ſhould be the perſon introduced as a defender of this diſcipline, who ſuffered by a very unjuſt expulſion from the Univerſity of Oxford. It is mortifying to behold ſuch a man as Dr. Fell baſely obedient to the arbitrary Orders of a miniſter, Lord Sunderland, on that occaſion.

Ver. 202. *ſleeps in Port.*] viz. "Now retired into harbour, after the tempeſts that had long agitated his ſociety." So *Scriblerus.*

But

Before them march'd that awful Ariſtarch;
Plow'd was his front with many a deep Remark:
His Hat, which never vail'd to human pride,
Walker with rev'rence took, and lay'd aſide.
Low bow'd the reſt: He, kingly, did but nod;
So upright Quakers pleaſe both Man and God.
Miſtreſs! diſmiſs that rabble from your throne:
Avaunt—is Ariſtarchus yet unknown?
Thy mighty Scholiaſt, whoſe unweary'd pains
Made Horace dull, and humbled Milton's ſtrains.

Turn

REMARKS.

But the learned *Scipio Maffei* underſtands it of a certain Wine called *Port*, from *Oporto*, a city of Portugal, of which this Profeſſor invited him to drink abundantly. Scip. Maff. *De Compotationibus Academicis.* P. *

Ver. 205. *His Hat, &c.—So upright Quakers pleaſe both Man and God.*] The *Hat-worſhip*, as the Quakers call it, is an abomination to that ſect: yet, where it is neceſſary to pay that reſpect to man (as in the Courts of Juſtice and Houſes of Parliament) they have, to avoid offence, and yet not violate their conſcience, permitted other people to uncover them. P. *

Ver. 210. *Ariſtarchus*] A famous Commentator, and Corrector of Homer, whoſe name hath been frequently uſed to ſignify a complete Critic. The compliment paid by our author to this eminent Profeſſor, in applying to him ſo great a name, was the reaſon that he hath omitted to comment on this part which contains his own praiſes. We ſhall therefore ſupply that loſs to our beſt ability. Scribl. P. *

IMITATIONS.

Ver. 207. —*He, kingly, did but nod*;] Milton,
———" He, kingly, from his State
" Declin'd not"——— W.

Ver. 210. —*is* Ariſtarchus *yet unknown?*]
——" Sic notus *Ulyſſes!*" Virg.
" Doſt thou not feel me, *Rome?*" Ben Johnson. W.

Turn what they will to Verſe, their toil is vain,
Critics like me ſhall make it Proſe again.
Roman and Greek Grammarians! know your Better:
Author of ſomething yet more great than Letter:
While tow'ring o'er your Alphabet, like Saul,
Stands our Digamma, and o'ertops them all.
  'Tis true, on Words is ſtill our whole debate,
Diſpute of *Me* or *Te*, of *aut* or *at*,
To ſound or ſink in *cano*, O or A,
Or give up Cicero to C or K.

Let

REMARKS.

VER. 214. *Critics like me*] This is the line in which, contrary to nature, character, and decorum, Bentley is made to condemn and ridicule himſelf, and his own labours. Beſides, his Horace ought not to be ranked with his Milton, as containing many acute remarks and happy emendations; and therefore, did not make Horace dull.

VER. 217, 218. *While tow'ring o'er your Alphabet, like Saul, —Stands our* Digamma,] Alludes to the boaſted reſtoration of the Eolic Digamma, in his long projected Edition of Homer. He calls it *ſomething more than Letter*, from the enormous figure it would make among the other letters, being one Gamma ſet upon the ſhoulders of another. P. *

VER. 220. *Diſpute of* Me *or* Te, *of* aut *or* at,] It is remarkable that there is an old Greek epigram of Herodicus, quoted by Athenaeus in his fifth book, page 112. Baſileae apud J. Valderum, 1635, Folio; ridiculing verbal criticiſm, in a manner exactly reſembling theſe lines, of Pope, which it is not at all probable he had ever read. The two ſecond lines follow:

"Γωνιοβόμβυκες, μονοσύλλαβοι· οἷσι μέμηλε,
Το σφῖν, καὶ σφωῖν, και το μὶν, ἤδε τὸ νὶν."

IMITATIONS.

VER. 215. *Roman and Greek* Grammarians, &c.] Imitated from Propertius ſpeaking of the Aeneid.

"*Cedite*, Romani *ſcriptores*, *cedite* Graii!
Neſcio quid majus *naſcitur Iliade*." W.

Let Freind affect to ſpeak as Terence ſpoke,
And Alſop never but like Horace joke:
From me, what Virgil, Pliny may deny,
Manilius or Solinus ſhall ſupply:
For Attic Phraſe in Plato let them ſeek,
I poach in Suidas for unlicens'd Greek.
In ancient Senſe if any needs will deal,
Be ſure I give them Fragments, not a Meal;
What Gellius or Stobaeus haſh'd before,
Or chew'd by blind old Scholiaſts o'er and o'er.
The critic Eye, that microſcope of Wit,
Sees hairs and pores, examines bit by bit:

How

REMARKS.

VER. 223, 224. *Freind—Alſop*] Dr. Robert Freind, maſter of Weſtminſter-ſchool, and canon of Chriſt-church——Dr. Anthony Alſop, a happy imitator of the Horatian ſtyle. P. *

Not only in odes but in ſome Aeſopic fables.

VER. 226. *Manilius or Solinus*] Some Critics having had it in their choice to comment either on Virgil or Manilius, Pliny or Solinus, have choſen the worſe author, the more freely to diſplay their critical talents. P. *

VER. 228. *&c. Suidas, Gellius, Stobaeus*] The firſt a Dictionary-writer of impertinent facts and barbarous words; the ſecond a minute Critic; the third a collector, who gave his Common-place book to the public, where we happen to find much Mince-meat of good old Authors. P. *

All theſe three writers abound in uſeful and elegant remarks, and in facts, which, but for their collections, would have been loſt and unknown; and therefore deſerved not this ridicule, eſpecially from a poet who, as Dr. Jortin obſerves, knew very little of their works. Burman, Kuſter, and Waſſe, mentioned verſe 237, were men of real and uſeful erudition.

VER. 232. *Or chew'd by blind old Scholiaſts o'er and o'er.*] Theſe men taking the ſame things eternally from the mouth of one another. P. *

How parts relate to parts, or they to whole,
The body's harmony, the beaming ſoul,
Are things which Kuſter, Burman, Waſſe ſhall ſee,
When Man's whole frame is obvious to a *Flea*.

Ah, think not, Miſtreſs! more true Dulneſs lies
In Folly's Cap, than Wiſdom's grave diſguiſe.
Like buoys, that never ſink into the flood,
On Learning's ſurface we but lie and nod.
Thine is the genuine head of many a houſe,
And much Divinity without a Νοῦς.

Nor

REMARKS.

VER. 239, 240. *Ah, think not, Miſtreſs, &c.—In Folly's Cap, &c.*] By this it appears, that the Dunces and Fops, mentioned ver. 139, 140. had a contention for the Goddeſs's favour on this great day. *Thoſe* got the ſtart; but *Theſe* make it up by their Spokeſman in the next ſpeech. It ſeems as if Ariſtarchus here firſt ſaw him advancing with his fair Pupil. SCRIBL. *

VER. 243. *Thine is the genuine*] It has been ſuggeſted that Dr. Warburton inſerted ſome lines of his own compoſition in this fourth book of the Dunciad, which the poet wrote at his earneſt requeſt; and theſe two verſes, as containing ſome common cant words peculiar to the univerſity, are mentioned as ſome of them: As alſo the following,

"As erſt Medea cruel ſo to ſave,
A new Edition of old Oeſon gave."

And the calling the members of the Univerſity of Oxford,

"Apollo's May'r and Aldermen,"

is ſaid to be one of Dr. Warburton's witticiſms. For the truth of this aſſertion I cannot vouch.

VER. 244. *And much Divinity without a* Νοῦ.] A word much affected by the learned Ariſtarchus in common converſation, to ſignify *Genius* or natural *acumen*. But this paſſage has a farther view: Νοῦς was the Platonic term for *Mind*, or the *firſt cauſe*; and that ſyſtem of Divinity is here hinted at which terminates in blind Nature, without a Νοῦς: ſuch as the Poet afterwards deſcribes (ſpeaking of the dream of one of theſe later Platoniſts)

Or that bright Image *to our Fancy draw,*
Which Theocles *in raptur'd Viſion ſaw,*
That Nature——*&c.* P. *

Nor could a BARROW work on ev'ry block,
Nor has one ATTERBURY ſpoil'd the flock.
See! ſtill thy own, the heavy Canon roll,
And Metaphyſic ſmokes involve the Pole.
For thee we dim the eyes, and ſtuff the head
With all ſuch reading as was never read:
For thee explain a thing till all men doubt it,
And write about it, Goddeſs, and about it:

So

REMARKS.

VER. 245, 246. *Barrow, Atterbury*] Iſaac Barrow, Maſter of Trinity; Francis Atterbury, Dean of Chriſt-church; both great Genuiſes and eloquent Preachers; one more converſant in the ſublime Geometry, the other in claſſical Learning; but who equally made it their care to advance the polite Arts in their ſeveral Societies. P. *

No compoſitions can be more different than the ſermons of theſe two eminent divines. If there be more eloquence and taſte in the diſcourſes of Atterbury, there is certainly more matter, more penetration, more knowledge of human nature, in thoſe of Barrow.

VER. 247. *the heavy Canon*] Canon here, if ſpoken of *Artillery*, is in the plural number; if of the *Canons of the Houſe*, in the ſingular, and meant only of *one*: in which caſe I ſuſpect the *Pole* to be a falſe reading, and that it ſhould be the *Poll*, or *Head* of that Canon. It may be objected, that this is a mere *Paranomaſia* or *Pun*. But what of that? Is any figure of Speech more appoſite to our gentle Goddeſs, or more frequently uſed by her and her Children, eſpecially of the Univerſity? Doubtleſs it better ſuits the Character of Dulneſs, yea of a Doctor, than that of an Angel; yet *Milton* feared not to put a conſiderable quantity into the mouths of his. It hath indeed been obſerved, that they were the Devil's Angels, as if he did it to ſuggeſt that the Devil was the Author as well of falſe Wit, as of falſe Religion, and that the Father of Lies was alſo the Father of Puns. But this is idle: It muſt be owned to be a Chriſtian practice; uſed in the primitive times by ſome of the Fathers, and in the latter by moſt of the Sons of the Church; till the debauched reign of Charles the ſecond, when the ſhameful Paſſion for *Wit* overthrew every thing: and even then the beſt Writers admitted it, provided it was obſcene, under the name of the *Double entendre*. SCRIBL. P. *

So ſpins the ſilk-worm ſmall its ſlender ſtore,
And labours till it clouds itſelf all o'er.
  What tho' we let ſome better ſort of fool
Thrid ev'ry ſcience, run through ev'ry ſchool?
Never by tumbler through the hoops was ſhown
Such ſkill in paſſing all, and touching none.
He may indeed (if ſober all this time)
Plague with Diſpute, or perſecute with Rhyme.
We only furniſh what he cannot uſe,
Or wed to what he muſt divorce, a Muſe:
Full in the midſt of Euclid dip at once,
And petrify a Genius to a Dunce:
Or ſet on Metaphyſic ground to prance,
Show all his paces, not a ſtep advance.
With the ſame CEMENT, ever ſure to bind,
We bring to one dead level every mind.
Then take him to devellop, if you can,
And hew the Block off, and get out the Man.

But

REMARKS.

VER. 257. *Never by tumbler*] Theſe two verſes are verbatim from an epigram of Dr. Evans, of St. John's College, Oxford; given to my father twenty years before the Dunciad was written. The Parentheſis, in v. 259, (if ſober all this time) is a poor expletive.

VER. 264. *petrify a* Genius] Thoſe who have no Genius, employed in works of imagination; thoſe who have, in abſtract ſciences. P. *

VER. 266. *not a ſtep advance.*] He has condeſcended to borrow this illuſtration on metaphyſicians, from Lord Hervey's Obſervations on Alciphron.

VER. 267. *With the ſame Cement,*] A cement bringing to a level, is not a pure metaphor: and take him to devellop, v. 269. is hard.

But wherefore waſte I words? I ſee advance
Whore, Pupil, and lac'd Governor from France.
Walker! our hat—nor more he deign'd to ſay,
But, ſtern as Ajax' ſpectre, ſtrode away.
In flow'd at once a gay embroider'd race,
And titt'ring puſh'd the Pedants off the place:

Some

REMARKS.

VER. 270. *And hew the Block off,*] A notion of Ariſtotle, that there was originally in every block of marble, a Statue, which would appear on the removal of the ſuperfluous parts. P. *

VER. 272. *lac'd Governor*] Why *lac'd?* Becauſe Gold and Silver are neceſſary trimming to denote the dreſs of a perſon of rank; and the Governor muſt be ſuppoſed ſo, in foreign countries, to be admitted into courts and other places of fair reception. But how comes Ariſtarchus to know at ſight that this Governor came from France? Know? Why, by his laced coat. SCRIBL. P. *

Ibid. *Whore, Pupil, and lac'd Governor*] Some Critics have objected to the order here, being of opinion that the Governor ſhould have the preference before the Whore, if not before the Pupil: But were he ſo placed, it might be thought to inſinuate that the Governor led the Pupil to the Whore: and were the Pupil placed firſt, he might be ſuppoſed to lead the Governor to her. But our impartial Poet, as he is drawing their picture, repreſents them in the order in which they are generally ſeen; namely, the Pupil between the Whore and the Governor; but placeth the Whore firſt, as ſhe uſually governs both the other. P. *

Ibid. *Whore, Pupil,*] Meaning the late Duke of Kingſton, and his celebrated miſtreſs, Mad. De La Touche.

VER. 274. *ſtern as Ajax' ſpectre, ſtrode away.*] See Homer, Odyſſ. xi. where the Ghoſt of Ajax turns ſullenly from Ulyſſes the *Traveller,* who had ſucceeded againſt him in the diſpute for the arms of Achilles. There had been the ſame contention between the *Travelling,* and the *Univerſity* Tutor, for the ſpoils of our young heroes; and faſhion adjudged it to the former; ſo that this might well occaſion the *ſullen dignity in departure,* which Longinus ſo much admired. SCRIBL. *

VER. 276. *And titt'ring puſh'd, &c.*] HOR.
"Rideat et pulſet laſciva decentius aetas." P. *

Some would have ſpoken, but the voice was drown'd
By the French horn, or by the op'ning hound.
The firſt came forwards with an eaſy mien,
As if he ſaw St. James's and the Queen.
When thus th' attendant Orator begun,
Receive, great Empreſs! thy accompliſh'd Son:
Thine from the birth, and ſacred from the rod,
A dauntleſs infant! never ſcar'd with God.
The Sire ſaw, one by one his Virtues wake:
The Mother begg'd the bleſſing of a Rake.
Thou gav'ſt that Ripeneſs, which ſo ſoon began,
And ceas'd ſo ſoon, he ne'er was Boy, nor Man,
Through School and College, thy kind cloud o'er-caſt,
Safe and unſeen the young Aeneas paſt:

Thence

REMARKS.

VER. 280. *As if he ſaw* St. James's] Reflecting on the diſreſpectful and indecent Behaviour of ſeveral forward young perſons in the Preſence, ſo offenſive to all ſerious men, and to none more than the good Scriblerus. P. *

VER. 281. *th' attendant Orator*] The Governor aboveſaid. The Poet gives him no particular name; being unwilling, I preſume, to offend or do injuſtice to any, by celebrating one only with whom this character agrees, in preference to ſo many who equally deſerve it. SCRIBL. P. *

VER. 290. *unſeen the young* Aeneas *paſt: Thence burſting glorious,*] See Virg. Aeneid. i.

"At Venus obſcuro gradientes aëre ſepſit,
Et multo nebulae circum Dea fudit amictu,
Cernere ne quis eos;—1. neu quis contingere poſſit;
2. Molirive moram;—aut 3. veniendi poſcere cauſas."

Where he enumerates the cauſes why his mother took this care of him: to wit, 1. that no body might touch or correct him: 2.

might

IMITATIONS.

VER. 284. *A dauntleſs infant! never ſcar'd with God.*]
——" ſine Dis animoſus Infans." HOR. W.

Thence burſting glorious, all at once let down,
Stunn'd with his giddy Larum half the town.
Intrepid then, o'er ſeas and lands he flew:
Europe he ſaw, and Europe ſaw him too.
There all thy gifts and graces we diſplay,
Thou, only thou, directing all our way!
To where the Seine, obſequious as ſhe runs,
Pours at great Bourbon's feet her ſilken ſons;
Or Tyber, now no longer Roman, rolls,
Vain of Italian Arts, Italian Souls:
To happy Convents, boſom'd deep in vines,
Where ſlumber Abbots, purple as their wines:
To iſles of fragrance, lilly-ſilver'd vales,
Diffuſing languor in the panting gales:
To lands of ſinging, or of dancing ſlaves,
Love-whiſp'ring woods, and lute-reſounding waves.

But

REMARKS.

might ſtop or detain him: 3. examine him about the progreſs he had made, or ſo much as gueſs why he came there. P. *

VER. 294. *Europe he ſaw,*] The pernicious effects of too early travelling are here ridiculed and expoſed with equal good ſenſe, and charming poetry.

VER. 301. *To happy Convents,*] I cannot forbear ſaying, though indeed every reader of taſte will perceive the thing, that Pope has never written, nor indeed does our language afford, ſix more delicious lines. The three compound epithets, which are more in number than he ever has uſed ſo near each other, have a fine effect, and are moſt happily conſtructed. So alſo is greatly-daring, in line 318.. Verſe 302, Abbots, purple as their wines, is from Rouſſeau the Poet.

VER. 303. *lilly-ſilver'd vales,*] Tuberoſes. W.

VER. 305. *To lands of—dancing ſlaves,*] In the year 1413, when the City of Paris was in the utmoſt deſolation, in the murders and proſcriptions of the Great, by the uncontrouled fury of

a mad

But chief her ſhrine where naked Venus keeps,
And Cupids ride the Lion of the Deeps;
Where, eas'd of Fleets, the Adriatic main
Wafts the ſmooth Eunuch and enamour'd ſwain.
Led by my hand, he ſaunter'd Europe round,
And gather'd ev'ry Vice on Chriſtian ground;
Saw ev'ry Court, heard ev'ry King declare
His royal Senſe, of Op'ra's or the Fair;
The Stews and Palace equally explor'd,
Intrigu'd with glory, and with ſpirit whor'd;
Try'd all *hors-d'oeuvres*, all *liqueurs* defin'd;
Judicious drank, and greatly-daring din'd;

Dropt

REMARKS.

a mad Populace, who had deſtroyed one half of the Court, and had kept the other half, with the King and Dauphin, Priſoners in the Palace, devoted to deſtruction. At this dreadful juncture, the inſolence of one Jacqueville, the Captain of the Mob, has been the occaſion of bringing down to us a circumſtance very declarative of the ſingular temper of this gay Nation. As that Fellow, with his Guards at his heels, was going his rounds, to ſee that the work of ruin went on without interruption, when he came to the Palace he went abruptly up into the apartments, where he found the Dauphin and the principal Lords and Ladies of the Court dancing, as in the midſt of Peace and Security: on which, with the air of a Cato, he reproached them for the levity of their behaviour, at a time when the reſt of the Court were languiſhing in the Dungeons of the Common Priſons. W.

VER. 308. *And Cupids ride the Lion of the Deeps*;] The winged Lion, the Arms of Venice. This Republic heretofore the moſt conſiderable in Europe, for her Naval Force and the extent of her Commerce; now illuſtrious for her *Carnivals*. P. *

VER. 313. *ev'ry King declare*] Another of his many ſarcaſms on kings. Verſe 316. for intriguing with glory, ſee his friend Lord Cheſterfield's Letters.

Dropt the dull lumber of the Latin ſtore,
Spoil'd his own language, and acquir'd no more;
All Claſſic learning loſt on Claſſic ground;
And laſt turn'd *Air*, the Echo of a Sound!
See now, half-cur'd, and perfectly well-bred,
With nothing but a Solo in his head;
As much Eſtate, and Principle, and Wit,
As Janſen, Fleetwood, Cibber ſhall think fit;
Stol'n from a Duel, follow'd by a Nun,
And, if a Borough chuſe him not, undone;
See, to my country happy I reſtore
This glorious Youth, and add one Venus more.
Her too receive (for her my ſoul adores)
So may the ſons of ſons of ſons of whores,

Prop

REMARKS.

VER. 318. *greatly-daring din'd*;] It being indeed no ſmall riſque to eat through thoſe extraordinary compoſitions, whoſe diſguiſed ingredients are generally unknown to the gueſts, and highly inflammatory and unwholeſome. P. *

VER. 324. *With nothing but a* Solo *in his head*;] With nothing but a *Solo?* Why, if it be a *Solo*, how ſhould there be any thing elſe? Palpable tautology! Read boldly an *Opera*, which is enough of conſcience for ſuch a head as has loſt all its Latin. BENTL. P. *

VER. 326. *Janſen, Fleetwood, Cibber,*] Three very eminent perſons, all Managers of *Plays*; who, though not Governors by profeſſion, had, each in his way, concerned themſelves in the Education of Youth: and regulated their *Wits*, their *Morals*, or their *Finances*, at that period of their age which is the moſt important, their entrance into the polite world. Of the laſt of theſe, and his Talents for this end, ſee Book i. ver. 199, &c. P. *

VER. 328. *And, if a Borough chuſe him*] A ſevere ſtroke on ſome parts of the Engliſh Parliament.

IMITATIONS.

VER. 332. *So may the ſons of ſons, &c.*]
"Et nati natorum, et qui naſcentur ab illis." VIRG. W.

Prop thine, O Empreſs! like each neighbour Throne,
And make a long Poſterity thy own.
Pleas'd, ſhe accepts the Hero, and the Dame,
Wraps in her Veil, and frees from ſenſe of Shame.
  Then look'd, and ſaw a lazy, lolling ſort,
Unſeen at Church, at Senate, or at Court,
Of ever-liſtleſs Loit'rers, that attend
No Cauſe, no Truſt, no Duty, and no Friend.
Thee too, my Paridel! ſhe mark'd thee there,
Stretch'd on the rack of a too eaſy chair,
And heard thy everlaſting yawn confeſs
The Pains and Penalties of Idleneſs.
She pity'd! but her Pity only ſhed
Benigner influence on thy nodding head.

But

REMARKS.

VER. 331. *Her to receive, &c.*] This confirms what the learned Scriblerus advanced in his note on ver. 272, that the Governor, as well as the Pupil, had particular intereſt in this lady. P. *

VER. 333. *like each neighbour Throne,*] A line ſomewhat obſcure; but ſeeming to contain a very extenſive piece of ſatire.

VER. 341. *Thee too, my* Paridel!] The Poet ſeems to ſpeak of this young gentleman with great affection. The name is taken from Spenſer, who gives it to a *wandering courtly 'Squire*, that travelled about for the ſame reaſon, for which many young Squires are now fond of travelling, and eſpecially to *Paris*. P. *

IMITATIONS.

VER. 342. *Stretch'd on the rack——*
And heard, &c.]

" Sedet, *aeternumque ſedebit*,
Infelix Theſeus, Phlegyaſque *miſerrimus* omnes
Admonet"—— VIRG. W

But Annius, crafty Seer, with ebon wand,
And well-diſſembled em'rald on his hand,
Falſe as his Gems, and canker'd as his Coins,
Came, cramm'd with capon, from where Pollio dines.
Soft, as the wily Fox is ſeen to creep,
Where baſk on ſunny banks the ſimple ſheep,
Walk round and round, now prying here, now there,
So he; but pious, whiſper'd firſt his pray'r.
Grant, gracious Goddeſs, grant me ſtill to cheat!
O may thy cloud ſtill cover the deceit!
Thy choicer miſts on this aſſembly ſhed,
But pour them thickeſt on the noble head.
So ſhall each youth, aſſiſted by our eyes,
See other Caeſars, other Homers riſe;

Through

REMARKS.

Ver. 347. *Annius,*] The name taken from Annius the Monk of Viterbo, famous for many Impoſitions and Forgeries of ancient manuſcripts and inſcriptions, which he was prompted to by mere Vanity; but our Annius had a more ſubſtantial motive. P. *

The ſudden appearance of this character, whom we never heard of before, makes this paſſage very obſcure. By Annius, was meant Sir Andrew Fountaine.

Ver. 355. ſtill *to cheat,*] Some read *ſkill,* but this is frivolous; for Annius hath that ſkill already; or if he had not, *ſkill* were not wanting to cheat ſuch perſons. Bentl. P. *

IMITATIONS.

Ver. 355. ——*grant me ſtill to cheat!*
O may thy cloud ſtill cover the deceit!]

"——Da, pulchra Laverna,
Da mihi fallere——
Noctem peccatis et fraudibus objice nubem." Hor. W.

Through twilight Ages hunt th' Athenian fowl,
Which Chalcis, Gods; and mortals call an Owl;
Now ſee an Attys, now a Cecrops clear,
Nay, Mahomet! the Pigeon at thine ear;
Be rich in ancient braſs, tho' not in gold,
And keep his Lares, though his houſe be ſold;
To heedleſs Phoebe his fair bride poſtpone,
Honour a Syrian Prince above his own;
Lord of an Otho, if I vouch it true;
Bleſt in one Niger, till he knows of two.
Mummius o'erheard him; Mummius, Fool-renown'd,
Who like his Cheops ſtinks above the ground,
Fierce

REMARKS.

VER. 361. *hunt th' Athenian fowl,*] The Owl ſtamp'd on the reverſe on the ancient money of Athens.

Which Chalcis *Gods, and Mortals call an* Owl,

is the verſe by which Hobbes renders that of Homer,

Χαλκίδα κικλήσκουσι Θεοὶ, ἄνδρες δὲ Κύμινδιν. P. *

VER. 363. *Attys and Cecrops.*] The firſt King of Athens, of whom it is hard to ſuppoſe any Coins are extant; but not ſo improbable as what follows, that there ſhould be any of Mahomet, who forbad all Images; and the ſtory of whoſe pigeon was a monkiſh fable. Nevertheleſs one of theſe Annius's made a counterfeit medal of that Impoſtor, now in the poſſeſſion of a learned Nobleman. P. *

VER. 371. *Mummius*] This name is not merely an alluſion to the Mummies he was ſo fond of, but probably referred to the Roman General of that name, who burned Corinth, and committed the curious Statues to the Captain of a Ship, aſſuring him, "that if any were loſt or broken, he ſhould procure others to be made in their ſtead:" by which it ſhould ſeem (whatever may be pretended) that Mummius was no Virtuoſo. P. *

Who, or from whence, was Mummius? we know as little of him, thus abruptly brought out, as of Annius in the preceding paſſage, ver. 347. It is painful, but neceſſary, to make an obſervation

Fierce as a ſtartled Adder, ſwell'd, and ſaid,
Rattling an ancient Siſtrum at his head:
Speak'ſt thou of Syrian Princes? Traitor baſe!
Mine, Goddeſs! mine is all the horned race. 376

True,

REMARKS.

ſervation on ſuch a fault in our poet. To ſay the name alluded to Egyptian Mummies, is frigid enough! I have been lately informed, that by Mummius was meant Dr. Mead, a man too learned and too liberal to be thus ſatirized.

Ibid. —*Fool-renown'd,*] A compound epithet in the Greek manner, *renown'd by fools*, or *renown'd for making fools*. P. *

VER. 372. *Cheops*] A King of Egypt, whoſe body was certainly to be known, as being buried alone in his Pyramid, and is therefore more genuine than any of the Cleopatra's. This Royal Mummy, being ſtolen by a wild Arab, was purchaſed by the Conſul of Alexandria, and tranſmitted to the Muſeum of Mummius; for proof of which he brings a paſſage in Sandys's Travels; where that accurate and learned Voyager aſſures us that he ſaw the Sepulchre empty, which agrees exactly (ſaith he) with the time of the theft above-mentioned.—But he omits to obſerve that Herodotus tells us it was empty in his time. P. *

VER. 375. *Speak'ſt thou of Syrian Princes? &c.*] The ſtrange ſtory following, which may be taken for a fiction of the Poet, is juſtified by a true relation in Spon's Voyages. Vaillant (who wrote the Hiſtory of the Syrian Kings, as it is to be found on medals) coming from the Levant, (where he had been collecting various coins), and being purſued by a Corſaire of Sallee, ſwallowed down twenty gold metals. A ſudden Bouraſque freed him from the Rover, and he got ſafe to land with the medals in his belly. On his road to Avignon he met two Phyſicians, of whom he demanded aſſiſtance. One adviſed purgations, the other vomits. In this uncertainty he took neither, but purſued his way to Lyons; where he found his ancient friend the famous Phyſician and Antiquary, Dufour, to whom he related his adventure. Dufour, without ſtaying to enquire about the uneaſy ſymptoms of the burthen he carried, firſt aſked him, *whether the Medals were of the higher Empire?* He aſſured him they were. Dufour was raviſhed with the hope of poſſeſſing ſo rare a treaſure; he bargained with him on the ſpot for the moſt curious of them; and was to recover them at his own expence. P. *

True, he had wit, to make their value riſe;
From fooliſh Greeks to ſteal them, was as wiſe;
More glorious yet, from barb'rous hands to keep,
When Sallee Rovers chac'd him on the deep.
Then taught by Hermes, and divinely bold,
Down his own throat he riſqu'd the Grecian gold,
Receiv'd each Demi-God, with pious care,
Deep in his Entrails—I rever'd them there,
I bought them, ſhrouded in that living ſhrine,
And, at their ſecond birth, they iſſue mine.

Witneſs great Ammon! by whoſe horns I ſwore,
(Reply'd ſoft Annius) this our paunch before
Still bears them, faithful; and that thus I eat,
Is to refund the Medals with the meat.
To prove me, Goddeſs! clear of all deſign,
Bid me with Pollio ſup, as well as dine:
There all the Learn'd ſhall at the labour ſtand,
And Douglas lend his ſoft, obſtetric hand.

The

REMARKS.

VER. 387. *Witneſs great* Ammon!] Jupiter Ammon is called to witneſs, as the father of Alexander, to whom thoſe Kings ſucceeded in the diviſion of the Macedonian Empire, and whoſe *Horns* they wore on their Medals. P. *

VER. 394. *Douglas*] A Phyſician of great learning and no leſs taſte; above all, curious in what related to HORACE; of whom he collected every Edition, Tranſlation, and Comment, to the number of ſeveral hundred volumes. P. *

IMITATIONS.

VER. 383. *Received each Demi-God.*]
" Emiſſumque ima de ſede Typhoëa terrae
Coelitibus feciſſe metum; cunctoſque dediſſe,
Terga fugae: donec feſſos Aegyptia tellus
Ceperit"—— OVID. W.

The Goddeſs ſmiling ſeem'd to give conſent;
So back to Pollio, hand in hand, they went.
Then thick as Locuſts black'ning all the ground,
A tribe, with weeds and ſhells fantaſtic crown'd,
Each with ſome wond'rous gift approach'd the Pow'r,
A Neſt, a Toad, a Fungus, or a Flow'r.
But far the foremoſt, two, with earneſt zeal,
And aſpect ardent to the Throne appeal.

The firſt thus open'd: Hear thy ſuppliant's call,
Great Queen, and common Mother of us all!
Fair from its humble bed I rear'd this Flow'r,
Suckled, and chear'd, with air, and ſun, and ſhow'r.

Soft

REMARKS.

VER. 397. *Then thick as Locuſts*] This tranſition is too haſty and abrupt.

VER. 403. *Hear thy ſuppliant's call,*] The character and ſpeech of the Floriſt in this paſſage, and thoſe of the Butterfly Hunter, verſe 421 to verſe 436, cannot eſcape the attention and applauſe of the elegant and judicious reader. Why, therefore, it will be ſaid, point them out? Verſe 418, where no carnation fades, is particularly happy and appropriated to the character of the perſon ſpeaking.

IMITATIONS.

VER. 405. *Fair from its humble bed, &c.—nam'd it* Caroline:
Each maid cry'd, charming! *and each youth,* divine!
Now proſtrate! dead! behold that Caroline:
No maid cries, charming! *and no youth,* divine;]

Theſe verſes are tranſlated from Catullus, Epith.

"Ut flos in ſeptis ſecretus naſcitur hortis,
Quam mulcent aurae, firmat Sol, educat imber,
Multi illum pueri, multae optavere puellae:
Idem quum tenui carptus defloruit ungui,
Nulli illum pueri, nullae optavere puellae," &c. W.

It is alſo elegantly tranſlated by Arioſto.

Soft on the paper ruff its leaves I ſpread,
Bright with the gilded button tipt its head.
Then thron'd in glaſs, and nam'd it CAROLINE:
Each maid cry'd, Charming! and each youth Divine!
Did Nature's pencil ever blend ſuch rays,
Such vary'd light in one promiſcuous blaze?
Now proſtrate! dead! behold that Caroline:
No maid cries, Charming! and no youth, Divine!
And lo the wretch! whoſe vile, whoſe inſect luſt
Lay'd this gay daughter of the Spring in duſt.
Oh puniſh him, or to th' Elyſian ſhades
Diſmiſs my ſoul, where no Carnation fades.
He ceas'd, and wept. With innocence of mien,
Th' Accus'd ſtood forth, and thus addreſs'd the Queen.
  Of all th' enamel'd race, whoſe ſilv'ry wing
Waves to the tepid Zephyrs of the ſpring,
Or ſwims along the fluid atmoſphere,
Once brighteſt ſhin'd this child of Heat and Air.
I ſaw, and ſtarted from its vernal bow'r,
The riſing game, and chac'd from flow'r to flow'r.

It

REMARKS.

VER. 409. *and nam'd it* Caroline:] It is a compliment which the Floriſts uſually pay to Princes and great perſonages, to give their names to the moſt curious Flowers of their raiſing: Some have been very jealous of vindicating this honour; but none more than that ambitious Gardener at Hammerſmith, who cauſed his Favourite to be painted on his Sign, with this inſcription, *This is* My *Queen Caroline.* P. *

IMITATIONS.

VER. 421. *Of all th' enamel'd race,*] The Poet ſeems to have an eye to Spenſer, Muiopotmos.

" Of all the race of ſilver-winged Flies
Which do poſſeſs the Empire of the Air." W.

It fled, I follow'd; now in hope, now pain;
It ſtopt, I ſtopt; it mov'd, I mov'd again.
At laſt it fix'd, 'twas on what plant it pleas'd,
And where it fix'd the beauteous bird I ſeiz'd:
Roſe or Carnation was below my care;
I meddle, Goddeſs! only in my ſphere.
I tell the naked fact without diſguiſe,
And, to excuſe it, need but ſhew the prize;
Whoſe ſpoils this paper offers to your eye,
Fair ev'n in death! this peerleſs *Butterfly*.

My ſons! (ſhe anſwer'd) both have done your parts:
Live happy both, and long promote our arts.
But hear a Mother, when ſhe recommends
To your fraternal care, our ſleeping friends.
The common Soul, of Heav'n's more frugal make,
Serves but to keep fools pert, and knaves awake:
A drowzy Watchman, that juſt gives a knock,
And breaks our reſt, to tell us what's a clock.
Yet by ſome object ev'ry brain is ſtirr'd;
The dull may waken to a Humming-bird;

The

VARIATIONS.

VER. 441. *The common Soul, &c.*] In the firſt Edit. thus,

Of Souls the greater part, Heav'n's common make,
Serve but to keep fools pert, and knaves awake;
And moſt but find that centinel of God,
A drowzy Watchman in the land of Nod. W.

REMARKS.

VER. 440. *our ſleeping friends.*] Of whom ſee v. 345, above. W.

IMITATIONS.

VER. 427, 428. *It fled, I follow'd, &c.*]

"—— I ſtarted back,
It ſtarted back; but pleas'd I ſoon return'd,
Pleas'd it return'd as ſoon"—— MILTON. W.

The most recluse, discreetly open'd, find
Congenial matter in the Cockle-kind;
The mind, in Metaphysics at a loss,
May wander in a wilderness of Moss;
The head that turns at superlunar things,
Poiz'd with a tail, may steer on Wilkins' wings.
O! would the Sons of Men once think their Eyes
And Reason giv'n them but to study *Flies!*
See Nature in some partial narrow shape,
And let the Author of the Whole escape:
Learn but to trifle; or, who most observe,
To wonder at their Maker, not to serve.

Be

REMARKS.

VER. 450. *a wilderness of Moss;*] Of which the aturalists count I can't tell how many hundred species. P. *

VER. 452. Wilkins' *wings.*] One of the first Projectors of the Royal Society; who, among many enlarged and useful notions, entertained the extravagant hope of a possibility to fly to the Moon; which has put some volatile Geniuses upon making wings for that purpose. P. *

VER. 453. *O! would the Sons of Men, etc.*] This is the third speech of the Goddess to her Supplicants, and completes the whole of what she had to give in instruction on this important occasion, concerning *Learning*, *Civil Society*, and *Religion*. In the first speech, ver. 119, to her Editors and conceited Critics, she directs how to deprave Wit and discredit fine Writers. In her second, ver. 175, to the Educators of Youth, she shews them how all civil duties may be extinguished, in that one doctrine of Divine Hereditary Right. And in this third, she charges the investigators of Nature to amuse themselves in trifles, and rest in second causes, with a total disregard of the first. This being all that Dulness can wish, is all she needs to say; and we may apply to her (as the Poet hath managed it) what hath been said of true Wit, that *She neither says too little, nor too much.* P. *

Be that my taſk (replies a gloomy Clerk,
Sworn foe to Myſt'ry, yet divinely dark;
Whoſe pious hope aſpires to ſee the day
When Moral Evidence ſhall quite decay,
And damns implicit faith, and holy lies,
Prompt to impoſe, and fond to dogmatize:)
Let others creep by timid ſteps, and ſlow,
On plain Experience lay foundations low,

By

REMARKS.

VER. 459. *a gloomy Clerk,*] The Epithet *gloomy* in this line may ſeem the ſame with that of *dark* in the next. But *gloomy* relates to the uncomfortable and diſaſtrous condition of an irreligious Sceptic; whereas *dark* alludes only to his puzzled and embroiled Syſtems. P. *

VER. 462. *When Moral Evidence ſhall quite decay,*] Alluding to a ridiculous and abſurd way of ſome Mathematicians, in calculating the gradual decay of Moral Evidence by mathematical proportions: according to which calculation, in about fifty years it will be no longer probable, that Julius Caeſar was in Gaul, or died in the Senate Houſe. See *Craig's Theologiae Chriſtianae Principia Mathematica.*——But as it ſeems evident, that facts of a thouſand years old, for inſtance, are now as probable as they were five hundred years ago; it is plain that in fifty more they quite diſappear, it muſt be owing, not to their Arguments, but to the extraordinary Power of our Goddeſs; for whoſe help therefore they are bound to pray. P. *

VER. 465—68. *Let others creep—through Nature led.*] In theſe lines are deſcribed the *Diſpoſition* of the rational Inquirer; and the *means* and *end* of Knowledge. With regard to his *diſpoſition,* the contemplation of the works of God with human faculties muſt needs make a modeſt and ſenſible man timorous and fearful; and that will naturally direct him to the right *means* of acquiring the little knowledge his faculties are capable of comprehending, namely *plain and ſure experience*; which though it ſupports only an humble *foundation,* and permits only a very ſlow progreſs, yet it leads, ſurely, to the *end,* the diſcovery of the *God of Nature.* W.

This

By common ſenſe to common knowledge bred,
And laſt, to Nature's Cauſe through Nature led.
All-ſeeing in thy miſts, we want no guide,
Mother of Arrogance, and Source of Pride!
We nobly take the high Priori Road,
And reaſon downward, till we doubt of God:

Make

REMARKS.

This note may well remind us of what Lord Bacon finely ſays on the ſubject of ſtrained interpretations: "Wines which at the firſt treading run gently, are pleaſanter than thoſe which are forced by the wine preſs; for theſe taſte of the ſtone and of the huſk of the grape.

VER. 471. *the high Priori Road,*] Thoſe who, from the effects in this viſible world, deduce the Eternal Power and Godhead of the Firſt Cauſe, though they cannot attain to an adequate idea of the Deity, yet diſcover ſo much of him, as enables them to ſee the end of their Creation, and the means of their Happineſs: whereas they who take this high Priori Road (ſuch as Hobbes, Spinoſa, Des Cartes, and ſome better Reaſoners) for one that goes right, ten loſe themſelves in Miſts, or ramble after Viſions, which deprive them of all ſight of their end, and miſlead them in the choice of the means. P. *

He alludes to Dr. Clarke's famous Demonſtrations of the Attributes of God, a book which Bolingbroke, who hated Clarke becauſe he was a favourite of Queen Caroline, impotently attacked. In Bolingbroke's works are many paſſages in ridicule of this Queen's pretences to underſtand philoſophy, and religious controverſies, and particularly the controverſies relating to the Trinity.

Dr. Clarke and Woolaſton conſidered moral obligation as ariſing from the eſſential differences and relations of things; Shafteſbury and Hutcheſon, as ariſing from the moral ſenſe; and the generality of divines, as ariſing ſolely from the will of God. On theſe three principles practical morality has been built by theſe different writers. "Thus has God been pleaſed (ſays the Author of the Divine Legation) to give three different excitements to the practice of virtue; that men, as he finely adds, of all ranks, conſtitutions, and educations, might find their account in one or other of them; ſomething that would hit their palate, ſatisfy

their

Make Nature ſtill incroach upon his plan;
And ſhove him off as far as e'er we can:
Thruſt ſome Mechanic Cauſe into his place;
Or bind in Matter, or diffuſe in Space.
Or, at one bound, o'erleaping all his laws,
Make God Man's Image, Man the final Cauſe,

Find

REMARKS.

their reaſon, or ſubdue their will.—But this admirable proviſion for the ſupport of virtue, hath been in ſome meaſure defeated by its pretended advocates, who have ſacrilegiouſly untwiſted this three-fold cord, and each, running away with the part he eſteemed the ſtrongeſt, hath affixed that to the throne of God, as the golden chain that is to unite and to draw all to it." Book i. p. 39. firſt edition.

VER. 473. *Make Nature ſtill*] This relates to ſuch as, being aſhamed to aſſert a mere Mechanic Cauſe, and yet unwilling to forſake it entirely, have had recourſe to a certain *Plaſtic Nature, Elaſtic Fluid, Subtile Matter, &c.*] P. *

VER. 475. *Thruſt ſome* Mechanic Cauſe *into its place,*
Or bind in Matter, *or diffuſe in* Space.]

The firſt of theſe Follies is that of Des Cartes; the ſecond of Hobbes; the third of ſome ſucceeding Philoſophers. P. *

VER. 478, &c.
Make God Man's Image, Man the final Cauſe,
Find Virtue local, *all* Relation *ſcorn,*
See all in Self—]

Here the Poet, from the errors relating to a Deity in *natural* Philoſophy, deſcends to thoſe in *moral.* Man was made according to *God's Image:* but this falſe Theology, meaſuring his attributes by ours, makes God after *Man's Image:* this proceeds from the imperfection of his *Reaſon.* The next, of imagining himſelf the final Cauſe, is the effect of his *Pride:* as the making Virtue and Vice arbitrary, and Morality the impoſition of the Magiſtrate, is of the *Corruption* of his *heart.* Hence he centers every thing in *himſelf.* The Progreſs of Dulneſs herein differing from that of Madneſs; this ends in *ſeeing all in God*; the other in *ſeeing all in Self.* P. *

Find Virtue local, all Relation ſcorn,
See all in *Self*, and but for Self be born:
Of nought ſo certain as our *Reaſon* ſtill,
Of nought ſo doubtful as of *Soul* and *Will*.
Oh hide the God ſtill more! and make us ſee
Such as Lucretius drew, a God like Thee:
Wrapt up in Self, a God without a Thought,
Regardleſs of our merit or default.
Or that bright Image to our fancy draw,
Which Theocles in raptur'd viſion ſaw,

While

REMARKS.

VER. 481. *Of nought ſo certain as our* Reaſon *ſtill,*] Of which we have moſt cauſe to be diffident. *Of nought ſo doubtful as of* Soul *and* Will; *i. e.* the Exiſtence of our Soul, and the Freedom of our Will; the two things moſt ſelf-evident. P. *

VER. 484. *Such as Lucretius drew,*] Lib. i. ver. 57.

"Omnis enim per ſe Divam natura neceſſe eſt
Immortali aevo *ſumma cum pace* fruatur,
Semota ab noſtris rebus, *ſummotaque* longe——
Nec bene pro *merites* capitur, nec tangitur *ira*;"

from whence the two verſes following are tranſlated; and wonderfully agree with the character of our Goddeſs. SCRIBL. P. *

VER. 487. *Or that* bright Image] *Bright Image* was the title given by the later Platoniſts to that Viſion of *Nature*, which they had formed out of their own fancy; ſo bright, that they called it Αὔτοπτον Ἄγαλμα, or the *Self-ſeen Image*, *i. e.* ſeen by its own light. *

Ibid. *Or that bright Image*] i. e. Let it be either the *Chance-God* of Epicurus, or the FATE, of this Goddeſs. *

VER. 488. *Which* Theocles *in raptur'd Viſion ſaw,*] Thus this Philoſopher calls upon his Friend, to partake with him in theſe Viſions:

"To-morrow, when the Eaſtern Sun
With his firſt Beams adorns the front
Of yonder Hill, if you're content
To wander with me in the Woods you ſee,
We will purſue thoſe Loves of ours,
By favour of the Sylvan Nymphs:

 and

While through Poetic ſcenes the Genius roves,
Or wanders wild in Academic Groves;
That Nature our Society adores,
Where Tindal dictates, and Silenus ſnores.

Rous'd

REMARKS.

and invoking firſt the *Genius* of the *Place*, we'll try to obtain at leaſt ſome faint and diſtant view of the *Sovereign Genius* and *firſt Beauty*." Charact. Vol. ii. page 245.

This *Genius* is thus apoſtrophized (pag. 345.) by the ſame Philoſopher:

" —— O glorious *Nature!*
Supremely fair, and ſovereignly good!
All-loving, and all-lovely! all-divine!
Wiſe Subſtitute of Providence! *impower'd*
Creatreſs! or *impow'ring Deity*,
Supreme Creator!
Thee I invoke, and thee alone adore."

Sir *Iſaac Newton* diſtinguiſhes between theſe two in a very different manner. (Princ. Schol. gen. ſub fin.)——*Hunc cognoſcimus ſolummodo per proprietates ſuas et attributa, et per ſapientiſſimas et optimas rerum ſtructuras, et cauſas finales; veneramur autem et colimus ob dominium.* Deus *etenim ſine dominio, providentia, et cauſis finalibus, nihil aliud eſt quam* Fatum *et* Natura. P. *

The manifeſt injuſtice of introducing Shafteſbury, who was a rigid deiſt, though not a Chriſtian, and who wrote ſo ſtrongly in favour of an intelligent firſt cauſe, has been before noticed in the remarks on the Eſſay on Man. Dr. Berkley was the firſt author, who printed in his Alciphron ſome paſſages of Shafteſbury, which certainly border on the bombaſt, as blank verſes. In the London Journal, May 18, 1732, there is a vindication of Shafteſbury againſt Alciphron, ſuppoſed by Biſhop Hoadley.

Ver. 489. *roves,—Or wanders wild in Academic Groves;*] "Above all things I lov'd *Eaſe*, and of all Philoſophers thoſe who reaſoned moſt *at their Eaſe*, and were never angry or diſturb'd, as thoſe call'd *Sceptics* never were. I look'd upon this kind of Philoſophy as the *prettieſt, agreeableſt, roving Exerciſe of the mind*, poſſible to be imagined." Vol. ii. p. 206. P. *

Ver. 491. *That Nature our Society adores,*] See the *Pantheiſticon*, with its liturgy and rubrics, compoſed by *Toland*; which

very

Rous'd at his name, up rose the bowzy Sire,
And shook from out his Pipe the seeds of fire;
Then snapt his box, and strok'd his belly down:
Rosy and rev'rend, tho' without a Gown.
Bland and familiar to the throne he came,
Led up the Youth, and call'd the Goddess *Dame*.
Then thus. From Priestcraft happily set free,
Lo! every finish'd Son returns to thee:
First slave to Words, then vassal to a Name,
Then dupe to Party; child and man the same:

Bounded

REMARKS.

very lately, for the Edification of the *Society*, has been translated into English, and publickly sold by the Booksellers of London and Westminster. *

VER. 492. *Silenus*] Mr. Thomas Gordon.—Silenus was an Epicurean Philosopher, as appears from Virgil, Eclog. vi. where he sings the principles of that Philosophy in his drink. P. *

By Silenus he means Gordon, the translator of Tacitus; which translation he made in an affected, hard, abrupt, and inharmonious style, under the notion of imitating the pregnant brevity of the original, crowded as it is, with sense and matter. He also was the publisher of the Independent Whig, and obtained a lucrative place under government. Lord Monboddo has certainly been too severe in his animadversions on Tacitus. Let us pardon his affected style, for his weighty matter.

VER. 494. *seeds of fire*;] The Epicurean language, *Semina rerum*, or Atoms. Virg. Eclog. vi. *Semina ignis—semina flammae*. P.*

VER. 501. *First slave to Words*, &c.] A recapitulation of the whole Course of modern Education described in this book, which confines Youth to the study of *Words* only in Schools; subjects them to the authority of *Systems* in the Universities; and deludes them with the names of *Party-distinctions* in the World. All equally concurring to narrow the Understanding, and establish Slavery and Error in Literature, Philosophy, and Politics. The whole finished in modern FREE-THINKING; the completion of whatever is vain, wrong, and destructive to the happiness of mankind, as it establishes *Self-love* for the sole Principle of Action. P.*

Bounded by Nature, narrow'd ſtill by Art,
A trifling head, and a contracted heart.
Thus bred, thus taught, how many have I ſeen,
Smiling on all, and ſmil'd on by a Queen?
Mark'd out for Honours, honour'd for their Birth,
To thee the moſt rebellious things on earth:
Now to thy gentle ſhadow all are ſhrunk,
All melted down, in Penſion, or in Punk!
So K* ſo B** ſneak'd into the grave,
A Monarch's half, and half a Harlot's ſlave.
Poor W** nipt in Folly's broadeſt bloom,
Who praiſes now? his Chaplain on his Tomb.
Then take them all, oh take them to thy breaſt!
Thy *Magus*, Goddeſs! ſhall perform the reſt.
  With that, a WIZARD OLD his *Cup* extends;
Which whoſo taſtes, forgets his former friends,

Sire,

REMARKS.

VER. 506. *ſmil'd on by a Queen?*] i.e. This Queen or Goddeſs of Dulneſs. W.

But it certainly was intended as a ſly and ſatirical ſtroke on Queen Caroline, and did not relate to the Goddeſs of Dulneſs.

VER. 511. *So K* ſo B**, poor W.*] It is vain to enquire the names that belong to theſe initial letters. Some of the fineſt paſſages in Abſalom and Architophel, one of Dryden's capital poems, though concerning perſons of far more conſequence and importance, are now already unknown; and the ſatire has loſt all its force and poignancy.

VER. 517. *his Cup—Which whoſo taſtes, &c.*] *The Cup of Self-love,* which cauſes a total oblivion of the obligations of Friendſhip,

or

IMITATIONS.

VER. 518. *Which whoſo taſtes, forgets his former friends,—Sire, &c.*] Homer of the Nepenthe, Odyſſ. iv.

Αὐτίκ' ἄρ' εις οἶνον βάλε φάρμακον, ἔνθεν ἔπινον
Νηπενθης τ' ἀχολόν τι, κακων ἐπίληθον ἁπαντων.

Sire, Ancestors, Himself. One casts his eyes
Up to a *Star*, and like Endymion dies:
A *Feather*, shooting from another's head,
Extracts his brain; and Principle is fled;
Lost is his God, his Country, ev'ry thing;
And nothing left but Homage to a King!
The vulgar herd turn off to roll with Hogs,
To run with Horses, or to hunt with Dogs;

But

REMARKS.

or Honour; and of the Service of God or our Country; all sacrificed to Vain-glory, Court-worship, or the yet meaner considerations of Lucre and brutal pleasures. From ver. 520 to 528. P. *

Ibid. *With that, a Wizard*] The greater mysteries, mentioned in a remark of Warburton on this passage, have no more to do with the Dunciad, than they have with the sixth book of the Aeneid. All that can be collected about the mysteries is to be found in Meursius's Collections on this subject, in the 27 vol. Folio, of Graevius' and Gronovius's Thesaur. From which collections Warburton borrowed largely in his famous dissertation on this subject, which has been so completely refuted by Gibbon.

VER. 523, 524. *Lost is his God, his Country—And nothing left but Homage to a King!*] So strange as this must seem to a mere English reader, the famous Mons. de la Bruyere declares it to be the character of every good subject in a Monarchy: "Where (says he) *there is no such thing as Love of our Country*, the Interest, the Glory, and the Service of the *Prince*, supply its place." *De la Republique*, chap. x.

Of this duty another celebrated *French* Author speaks, indeed, a little more disrespectfully; which, for that reason, we shall not translate, but give in his own words, "L'Amour de la Patrie, le grand motif des prémiers Heros, n'est plus regardé que comme une Chimêre; l'idée du Service du Roi, etendüe jusqu'à l'oubli de tout autre Principe, tient lieu de ce qu' on appelloit autrefois Grandeur d'Ame & Fidelité." *Boulainvilliers Hist. des Anciens Parlements de France, &c.*—And a much greater man than either of them, the Cardinal de Retz, speaking of a conversation he had with the Regente, Anne of Austria, makes this observation on the Court,—"Je connus en cet endroit, qu'il est impossible que la Cour conçoive ce que c'est LE PUBLIC. La flatterie, qui en est la peste, l'infecte toujours à un tel point, qu'elle lui cause un *delire incurable* sur cet article." *

But, ſad example! never to eſcape
Their Infamy; ſtill keep the human ſhape.
  But ſhe, good Goddeſs, ſent to ev'ry child
Firm Impudence, or Stupefaction mild;
And ſtraight ſucceeded, leaving ſhame no room,
Cibberian forehead, or Cimmerian gloom.
  Kind Self-conceit to ſome her glaſs applies,
Which no one looks in with another's eyes:
But as the Flatt'rer or Dependent paint,
Beholds himſelf a Patriot, Chief, or Saint.
  On other's Int'reſt her gay liv'ry flings,
Int'reſt, that waves on Party-colour'd wings:
Turn'd to the Sun, ſhe caſts a thouſand dyes,
And, as ſhe turns, the colours fall or riſe.
  Others the Syren Siſters warble round,
And empty heads conſole with empty ſound.
No more, alas! the voice of Fame they hear,
The balm of Dulneſs trickling in their ear.

Great

REMARKS.

VER. 528. *keep the human ſhape.*] Few pieces of ſatire are more finely imagined, than the Circe of Gelli, (copied from Plutarch), in which the men transformed into beaſts, refuſe to return again into the human ſhape, and be again ſubject to the follies and miſeries of that ſpecies of animals. The 526th line contains a moſt ſevere invective on horſe-racing and hunting; and perhaps an invective too ſevere.

VER. 529. *But ſhe, good Goddeſs, &c.*] The only comfort ſuch people can receive, muſt be owing in ſome ſhape or other to Dulneſs; which makes one ſort ſtupid, another impudent; gives Self-conceit to ſome, ariſing from the flatteries of their dependants; preſents the falſe colours of Intereſt to others, and buſies or amuſes the reſt with idle Pleaſures or Senſualities, till they become eaſy under any infamy. Each of which ſpecies is here ſhadowed under allegorical perſons. P. *

Great C**, H**, P**, R**, K*,
Why all your Toils? your Sons have learn'd to sing.
How quick Ambition hastes to ridicule!
The Sire is made a Peer, the Son a Fool.
On some, a Priest succinct in amice white
Attends; all flesh is nothing in his sight!
Beeves, at his touch, at once to jelly turn,
And the huge Boar is shrunk into an Urn:
The board with specious miracles he loads,
Turns Hares to Larks, and Pigeons into Toads.
Another (for in all what one can shine?)
Explains the *Seve* and *Verdeur* of the Vine.
What cannot copious Sacrifice attone?
Thy Treufles, Perigord! thy Hams, Bayonne!
With French Libation, and Italian Strain,
Wash Bladen white, and expiate Hays's stain.

KNIGHT

REMARKS.

VER. 556. Seve *and* Verdeur] French Terms relating to Wines, which signify their flavour and poignancy.

"Et je gagerois que chez le Commandeur
Villandri priseroit sa *Seve* et sa *Verdeur*." DEPREAUX.

St. Evremont has a very pathetic letter to a *Nobleman in disgrace*, advising him to seek Comfort in a *good Table*; and particularly to be attentive to *these qualities* in his Champaigne. P. *

VER. 560. *Bladen—Hays*] Names of Gamesters. Bladen is a black man. ROBERT KNIGHT Cashier of the South-sea Company, who fled from England in 1720 (afterwards pardoned in 1742.)—These lived with the utmost magnificence at Paris, and kept open tables frequented by persons of the first Quality of England, and even by Princes of the Blood of France. P. *

The former Note of—*Bladen is a black man*, is very absurd. The Manuscript text is here partly obliterated, and doubtless could only have been—"*Wash* Blackmoors *white*" alluding to a known Proverb. SCRIBL. P. *

Colonel

Knight lifts the head, for what are crouds undone,
To three eſſential Partridges in one?
Gone ev'ry bluſh, and ſilent all reproach,
Contending Princes mount them in their Coach.
Next bidding all draw near on bended knees,
The Queen confers her *Titles* and *Degrees*.
Her children firſt of more diſtinguiſh'd ſort,
Who ſtudy Shakeſpear at the Inns of Court,

Impale

REMARKS.

Colonel Martin Bladen, was a man of ſome literature, and tranſlated Cæſar's Commentaries. I never could learn that he had offended Pope. He was uncle to my dear and lamented friend Mr. William Collins the Poet, to whom he left an eſtate, which he did not get poſſeſſion of till his faculties were deranged and he could not enjoy it. I remember Collins told me that Bladen had given to Voltaire, all that account of Camoëns inſerted in his eſſay on the Epic Poets of all Nations, and that Voltaire ſeemed before entirely ignorant of the name and character of Camoëns.

Ver. 562. *To three eſſential Partridges*] It cannot be denied that this is a ſarcaſm on one of the myſteries of the Chriſtian Religion.

Ver. 567. *Her children firſt of more diſtinguiſh'd ſort,*
Who ſtudy Shakeſpear *at the Inns of Court,*]

Ill would that Scholiaſt diſcharge his duty, who ſhould neglect to honour thoſe whom Dulness has *diſtinguiſhed:* or ſuffer them to lie forgotten, when their rare modeſty would have left them nameleſs. Let us not, therefore, overlook the ſervices which have been done her Cauſe, by one Mr. Thomas Edwards, a *Gentleman*, as he is pleaſed to call himſelf, of *Lincoln's Inn*; but, in reality, a Gentleman only of the Dunciad; or, to ſpeak him better, in the plain language of our honeſt Anceſtors to ſuch muſhrooms, *A Gentleman of the laſt Edition:* who nobly eluding the ſolicitude of his careful Father, very early retained himſelf in the cauſe of *Dulneſs* againſt *Shakeſpear*; and with the wit and learning of his Anceſtor *Tom Thimble* in the *Rehearſal*, and with the air of good nature and politeneſs of *Caliban* in the *Tempeſt*, hath now happily finiſhed the *Dunce's Progreſs*, in perſonal abuſe. For a Libeller is nothing but a Grubſtreet Critic run to Seed.

Scribl. *

This attack on Mr. Edwards is not of weight ſufficient to weaken the effects of his excellent Canons of Criticiſm.

Impale a Glow-worm, or Vertú profeſs,
Shine in the dignity of F. R. S.
Some, deep Free-Maſons, join the ſilent race
Worthy to fill Pythagoras's place :
Some Botaniſts, or Floriſts at the leaſt,
Or iſſue Members of an Annual feaſt.
Nor paſs the meaneſt unregarded, one
Roſe a Gregorian, one a Gormogon.
The laſt, not leaſt in honour or applauſe,
Iſis and Cam made DOCTORS of her LAWS.
  Then, bleſſing all, Go, Children of my care!
To Practice now from Theory repair.
All my commands are eaſy, ſhort, and full :
My Sons! be proud, be ſelfiſh, and be dull.

Guard

REMARKS.

VER. 570. *Shine in the dignity*] A line taken from Bramſton's Man of Taſte ; a ſatire in which Bramſton has been guilty of the indecorum and abſurdity of making his hero laugh at himſelf and his own follies.

VER. 571. *Some, deep Free-Maſons, join the ſilent race*] The Poet all along expreſſes a very particular concern for this *ſilent Race:* He has here provided, that in caſe they will not waken or open (as was before propoſed) to a *Humming-bird,* or a *Cockle,* yet at worſt they may be made Free-Maſons ; where *Taciturnity* is the only eſſential qualification, as it was the chief of the diſciples of Pythagoras. P. *

VER. 576. *a Gregorian, one a Gormogon.*] A ſort of Lay-brothers, two of the innumerable *Slips* from the Root of the Free-Maſons. P. *

VER. 578. *Iſis and Cam*] When we conſider on whom the Univerſities have ſometimes conferred degrees, we muſt wiſh that Pope and Warburton had been made doctors at Oxford.

VER. 582. *be ſelfiſh, and be dull.*] From Dryden's Abſalom and Architophel, " With this prophetic bleſſing, Be thou dull."

Guard my Prerogative, aſſert my Throne :
This Nod confirms each Privilege your own.
The Cap and Switch be ſacred to his Grace ;
With Staff and Pumps the Marquis lead the Race ;
From Stage to Stage the licens'd Earl may run,
Pair'd with his Fellow-Charioteer the Sun ;
The learned Baron Butterflies deſign,
Or draw to ſilk Arachne's ſubtile line ;

The

REMARKS.

VER. 584. *each* Privilege *your own*, *&c.*] This ſpeech of Dulneſs to her Sons at parting may poſſibly fall ſhort of the Reader's expectation ; who may imagine the Goddeſs might give them a Charge of more conſequence ; and, from ſuch a Theory as is before delivered, incite them to the practice of ſomething more extraordinary, than to perſonate Running-Footmen, Jockeys, Stage-Coachmen, &c.

But if it be well conſidered, that whatever inclination her ſons might have to do miſchief, they are generally rendered harmleſs by their Inability ; and that it is the common effect of Dulneſs (even in her greateſt efforts) to defeat her own deſign ; the Poet, I am perſuaded, will be juſtified, and it will be allowed, that theſe worthy perſons, in their ſeveral ranks, do as much as can be well expected from them. P. *

VER. 589. *The learned Baron*] Evidently taken from Young's Univerſal Paſſion, ſatire 1.

" By this inſpir'd (O ne'er to be forgot)
Some lords have learnt to ſpell, and ſome to knot."

The trifling employments and amuſements of ſome men of quality cannot be more finely or more juſtly expoſed. The dance of the judges, mentioned at ver. 591. is not of this ſort, is not of a piece with the reſt, and aroſe from another cauſe. And yet, though ſome men of rank may merit the ridicule in the above verſes, 585, &c. yet candour muſt allow, that a great number deſerve not this ſarcaſm.

VER. 590. *Arachne's ſubtile line* ;] This is one of the moſt ingenious employments aſſigned,—and therefore recommended only to Peers of Learning. Of weaving gray-ſilk Stockings of the Webs of Spiders, ſee the Philoſoph. Tranſact. P. *

The Judge to dance his brother Sergeant call;
The Senator at Cricket urge the Ball;
The Biſhop ſtow (Pontific Luxury!)
An hundred Souls of Turkeys in a pie;
The ſturdy Squire to Gallic maſters ſtoop,
And drown his Lands and Manors in a Soupe.
Others import yet nobler arts from France,
Teach Kings to fiddle, and make Senates dance.
Perhaps more high ſome daring ſon may ſoar,
Proud to my liſt to add one Monarch more;
And nobly conſcious, Princes are but things
Born for Firſt Miniſters, as Slaves for Kings,
Tyrant ſupreme! ſhall three Eſtates command,
And MAKE ONE MIGHTY DUNCIAD OF THE LAND!
  More ſhe had ſpoke, but yawn'd—All Nature nods:
What Mortal can reſiſt the Yawn of Gods?

Churches

REMARKS.

VER. 591. *The Judge to dance his brother Sergeant call*;] Alluding perhaps to that ancient and ſolemn *Dance* intitled, *A Call of Sergeants*. P. *

VER. 598. *Teach Kings to fiddle*,] An ancient amuſement of Sovereign Princes, (viz.) Achilles, Alexander, Nero; though deſpiſed by Themiſtocles, who was a Republican.—*Make Senates dance*, either after their Prince, or to Pontoiſe, or Siberia. P. *

Ibid. *make Senates dance*.] Alludes to the frequent baniſhments of the parliaments of France, when they exerted a noble ſpirit of oppoſition to deſpotic power. In the Annual Regiſters of thoſe times, are many ſpirited remarks on theſe baniſhments by a man of great genius.

VER. 602. *Princes are but things*] The making miniſters of more real importance than princes, is admirably ſevere.

VER. 606. *What Mortal can reſiſt the Yawn of Gods?*] This verſe is truly Homerical; as is the concluſion of the Action, where

the

Churches and Chapels inftantly it reach'd;
(St. James's firft, for leaden G—— preach'd)
Then catch'd the Schools; the Hall fcarce kept awake;
The Convocation gap'd, but could not fpeak: 610
Loft

REMARKS.

the great Mother compofes all, in the fame manner as Minerva at the period of the Odyffey.——It may indeed feem a very fingular Epitafis of a Poem, to end as this does, with a GREAT YAWN; but we muft confider it as the *Yawn of a God*, and of powerful effects. Nor is it out of nature; moft long and grave Counfels concluding in this very manner: Nor yet without authority, the incomparable Spencer having ended one of the moft confiderable of his works with a ROAR; but then it is the *Roar of a Lion*, the effects whereof (as here of the *Yawn*) are defcribed as the Cataftrophe of the Poem. P. *

VER. 607. *Churches and Chapels, &c.*] The Progrefs of this Yawn is judicious, natural, and worthy to be noted. Firft it feizeth the Churches and Chapels; then catcheth the Schools, where, though the boys be unwilling to fleep, the Mafters are not: Next Weftminfter-hall, much more hard indeed to fubdue, and not totally put to filence even by the Goddefs: then the Convocation, which though *extremely defirous to fpeak*, yet cannot: Even the Houfe of Commons, juftly called the Senfe of the Nation, is *loft* (that is to fay *fufpended*) during the Yawn (far be it from our Author to fuggeft it could be loft any longer!) but it fpreadeth at large over all the reft of the Kingdom, to fuch a degree, that Palinurus himfelf (though as incapable of fleeping as Jupiter himfelf) yet noddeth for a moment: the effect of which, though ever fo momentary, could not but caufe fome relaxation, for the time, in all public affairs. SCRIBL. P. *

VER. 608. *for leaden G——*] He meant Dr. Gilbert, Bifhop of Salifbury. He had never given Pope any particular offence; but he had attacked Dr. King of Oxford, whom Pope much refpected. And this attack was made in a rude and rough manner.

VER. 610. *The Convocation gap'd, but could not fpeak:*] Implying a great defire fo to do, as the learned Scholiaft on the place rightly obferves. Therefore, beware, Reader, left thou take this *Gape* for a *Yawn*, which is attended with no defire, but
to

Loſt was the Nation's Senſe, nor could be found,
While the long ſolemn Uniſon went round:
Wide, and more wide, it ſpread o'er all the realm;
Ev'n Palinurus nodded at the Helm:
" The Vapour mild o'er each Committee crept;
Unfiniſh'd Treaties in each Office ſlept;
And Chiefleſs Armies doz'd out the Campaign;
And Navies yawn'd for Orders on the Main."
O Muſe! relate (for you can tell alone,
Wits have ſhort Memories, and Dunces none)
Relate,

REMARKS.

to go to reſt: by no means the diſpoſition of the Convocation; whoſe melancholy caſe in ſhort is this: She was, as is *reported*, infected with the general influence of the Goddeſs; and while ſhe was yawning careleſly at her eaſe, a wanton Courtier took her at advantage, and in the very nick, clap'd a *Gag* into her mouth. Well therefore may we know her meaning by her *gaping*; and this diſtreſsful poſture which our poet here deſcribes, is juſt as ſhe ſtands at this day, a ſad example of the effects of Dulneſs and Malice unchecked and deſpiſed. BENTL. *

VER. 615, 618. Theſe Verſes were written many years ago, and may be found in the State Poems of that time. So that Scriblerus is miſtaken, or whoever elſe have imagined this Poem of a freſher date. P. *

VER. 619. *O muſe! relate*] Mr. Gray's opinion of this fourth book was as follows: " The genii of operas and ſchools, with their attendants, the pleas of the virtuoſo's and floriſts, and the yawn of Dulneſs in the end, are as fine as any thing he has written. The metaphyſician's part is to me the worſt; and here and there a few ill-expreſſed lines, and ſome hardly intelligible."

VER. 620. *Wits have ſhort Memories,*] This ſeemeth to be the reaſon why the Poets, whenever they give us a Catalogue, conſtantly call for help on the Muſes, who, as the Daughters of *Memory*, are obliged not to forget any thing. So Homer, Iliad ii.

Πληθὺν δ' ὐκ ἂν ἐγὼ μυθήσομαι ὐδ' ὀνομήνω,
Εἰ μὴ Ὀλυμπιάδες Μȣσαι, Διὸς αἰγιόχοιο
Θυγατέρες, μνησαίαθ'——

Relate, who firſt, who laſt reſign'd to reſt;
Whoſe Heads ſhe partly, whoſe completely bleſt;
What Charms could Faction, what Ambition lull,
The Venal quiet, and intrance the Dull;
Till drown'd was Senſe, and Shame, and Right, and
Wrong—
O ſing, and huſh the Nations with thy Song!

* * * * * * *

In vain, in vain,—the all-compoſing Hour
Reſiſtleſs falls: The Muſe obeys the Pow'r.
She comes! ſhe comes! the ſable Throne behold
Of *Night* Primeval, and of *Chaos* old!
Before her, *Fancy*'s gilded clouds decay,
And all its varying Rain-bows die away.
Wit ſhoots in vain its momentary fires,
The meteor drops, and in a flaſh expires.
As one by one, at dread Medea's ſtrain,
The ſick'ning ſtars fade off th' ethereal plain;

As

REMARKS.

And Virg. Aeneid. vii.

"Et meminiſtis enim, Divae, et memorare poteſtis:
Ad nos vix tenuis famae perlabitur aura."

But our Poet had yet another reaſon for putting this taſk upon the Muſe, that, all beſides being *aſleep*, ſhe only could relate what paſſed. SCRIBL. P. *

IMITATIONS.

VER. 621. *Relate, who firſt, who laſt reſign'd to reſt;*
Whoſe Heads ſhe partly, whoſe completely bleſt.]

"Quem telo primum, quem poſtremum *aſpera Virgo*
Dejicis? aut quot humi *morientia corpora* fundis?"
VIRG. W.

As Argus' eyes, by Hermes' wand oppreſt,
Clos'd one by one to everlaſting reſt;
Thus at her felt approach, and ſecret might,
Art after *Art* goes out, and all is Night.
See ſkulking *Truth* to her old cavern fled,
Mountains of Caſuiſtry heap'd o'er her head!
Philoſophy, that lean'd on Heav'n before,
Shrinks to her ſecond cauſe, and is no more.

Phyſic

VARIATIONS.

Ver. 643. In the former Edit. it ſtood thus,
" Philoſophy, that reach'd the Heav'ns *before*,
Shrinks to her hidden cauſe, *and is no more!*" W.

REMARKS.

Ver. 643. Philoſophy, *that lean'd on Heav'n*] Philoſophy has at length brought things to that paſs, as to have it eſteemed unphiloſophical to reſt in the *firſt cauſe*; as if its buſineſs were an endleſs indagation of cauſe after cauſe, without ever coming to the Firſt. So that to avoid this unlearned diſgrace, ſome of the propagators of our beſt philoſophy have had recourſe to the contrivance here hinted at. For this philoſophy, which is founded on the principle of *Gravitation*, firſt conſidered that property in matter as ſomething extrinſical to it, and impreſſed by God upon it. Which fairly and modeſtly coming up to the firſt Cauſe, was puſhing natural enquiries as far as they ſhould go. But this ſtopping, though at the extent of our ideas, and on the maxim of the great founder of this Philoſophy, *Bacon*, who ſays, *Circa ultimates rerum fruſtranea eſt inquiſitio*, was miſtaken by foreign philoſopher as recurring to the *occult qualities* of the Peripatetics; whoſe ſenſe is thus delivered by a great Poet, whom, indeed, it more became than a Philoſopher.

" Sed

IMITATIONS.

Ver. 637. *As Argus' eyes, &c.*]
" Et quamvis ſopor eſt oculorum parte receptus,
Parte tamen vigilat——
Vidit Cyllenius omnes
Succubuiſſe oculos," &c. Ovid. Met. ii. W.

Physic of *Metaphysic* begs defence, 645
And *Metaphysic* calls for aid on *Sense*!

See

REMARKS.

" Sed gravitas etiam crescat, dum corpora centro
Accedunt propius. *Videor mihi cernere terrâ*
Emergens quidquid caliginis ac tenebrarum
Pellaei Juvenis Doctor conjecerat olim
In Physicae studium." Anti-Lucr.

To avoid which imaginary discredit to the new theory, it was thought proper to seek for the *cause* of *gravitation* in a certain *subtile matter* or *elastic fluid*, which pervaded all body. By this means, instead of really advancing in natural enquiries, we were brought back again, by this ingenious expedient, to an unsatisfactory *second cause*:

" Philosophy, that *lean'd* on Heav'n before,
Shrinks to her *second cause*, and is no more.

For it might still, by the same kind of objection, be asked, what was the *cause* of that *elasticity*? See this folly censured, ver. 475. and confuted in the following words of an excellent Philosopher, who having demonstrated the absolute impossibility of any *subtile matter* or *elastic fluid's* being able to perform the office here assigned to it, as it must impel every particle of matter an infinite number of different ways at once, and incessantly, goes on thus, " When it is said that *the higher we rise in the* SCALE OF NATURE *towards the supreme cause, the views we have from Philosophy appear more beautiful and extensive*; we may observe that *the scale of material causes* in philosophy is not like *the rising scale of Beings* in the creation: though the supposed *scale* here seems to have been taken from that. In the *scale of* BEINGS, the beginning is low: and every species rises in perfection as we ascend: There is an amazing variety, from dead matter, to living spirit: nor does the gradation end there. This is full of instruction and delight: we see ourselves in the middle of the *scale*, and are certain of rising higher, as rational beings were not made for utter extinction. But it is not so in a *scale of material* CAUSES. There are no degrees of perfection in matter. All matter is equally an unactive substance, that resists a change of its state. The higher we had ascended in *such a scale*, we should have met with the more obscurity. We see it is so in reality to those who pretend to mount this way. The *first sort of matter* might perhaps have been seen easily; the

second,

See *Myſtery* to *Mathematics* fly!
In vain! they gaze, turn giddy, rave, and die.

Religion

REMARKS.

ſecond, but darkly; and the *third,* not at all. This had been the way for the Deity to conceal himſelf: And this is the view which this philoſophy endeavours to give us. It is equivocal language to ſpeak of riſing towards the *ſupreme cauſe through a ſcale of material cauſes.* No Philoſophy ever yet diſcovered the ſecond ſtep of the *ſcale.* I ſee a ſtone fall. I am certain there is but one ſtep here. A *fluid* that impreſſed a cruſhing force on a ſmall piece of matter, would have as much overcome my ſtrength to wade through it, as if I had endeavoured to walk in the bottom of an ocean of Mercury, or ſomething more denſe. Thus we ſee their ſecond ſtep is a fiction, to divert the attention, and ſet us a gazing at ſomething that cannot be ſeen. The views that we have from this Philoſophy are indeed very dark and myſterious. Philoſophers ſpeak of *not excluding the Deity out of nature,* as of a favour: But they endeavour to *exclude* him from every thing we can point out, to diſcover him. They endeavour to make us eaſy, by telling us, *he is every where active, and every where preſent:* But at the ſame time they try to reſtrain his activity, to quadrate with their hypotheſis; and make him preſent only that SUBTILE MATTER may exerciſe his power and knowledge. Nothing can derogate more from the Government and Influences of the Deity."—BAXTER. *Appendix to his Inquiry into the nature of the human ſoul,* p. 194. * W.

VER. 645, 646. Phyſic *of* Metaphyſic, *&c.*—*And* Metaphyſic *calls, &c.*] Certain writers, as Malbranche, Norris, and Berkley, have thought it of importance, in order to ſecure the exiſtence of the *ſoul,* to bring in queſtion the reality of *body:* which they have attempted to do by a very refined *metaphyſical* reaſoning: While others of the ſame party, in order to perſuade us of the neceſſity of a Revelation which promiſes immortality, have been as anxious to prove that thoſe qualities which are commonly ſuppoſed to belong only to an immaterial Being are but the reſult from certain diſpoſitions of the particles of matter, and conſequently that the ſoul is naturally mortal. Thus, between their different reaſonings, theſe good men have left us neither Soul nor Body; nor the Sciences of Phyſics and Metaphyſics the leaſt ſupport, by making them depend upon, and go a begging to, one another. * W.

Religion bluſhing veils her ſacred fires,
And unawares *Morality* expires.
Nor *public* Flame, nor *private*, dares to ſhine;
Nor *human* Spark is left, nor Glimpſe *divine!*
Lo! thy dread Empire, CHAOS! is reſtor'd;
Light dies before thy uncreating word:
Thy hand, great Anarch! lets the curtain fall;
And univerſal Darkneſs buries All.

REMARKS.

VER. 654. *thy uncreating word:*] After this noble and energetic line, the expreſſion in the next, of—"lets the curtain fall," is an unhappy deſcent in ſtyle and imagery.

By the AUTHOR

A DECLARATION.

WHEREAS certain Haberdaſhers of Points and Particles, being inſtigated by the ſpirit of Pride, and aſſuming to themſelves the name of Critics and Reſtorers, have taken upon them to adulterate the common and current ſenſe of our Glorious Anceſtors, Poets of this Realm, by clipping, coining, defacing the images, mixing their own baſe allay, or otherwiſe falſifying the ſame; which they publiſh, utter, and vend as genuine: The ſaid Haberdaſhers having no right thereto, as neither heirs, executors, adminiſtrators, aſſigns, or in any ſort related to ſuch Poets, to all or any of them; Now We, having carefully revised this our Dunciad,[a] beginning with the words The Mighty Mother, and ending with the words buries All, containing the entire sum of One thousand seven hundred and fifty-four verses, declare every word, figure, point, and comma of this impression to be authentic: And do therefore strictly enjoin and forbid any person or persons whatsoever, to erase, reverse, put between hooks, or by any other means, directly or indirectly, change or mangle any of them. And we do hereby earnestly exhort all our brethren to follow this our Example, which we heartily wish our great Predecessors had heretofore set, as a remedy and

[a] Read thus confidently, instead of "beginning with the word *Books*, and ending with the word *flies*," as formerly it stood: Read also, "containing the entire sum of *one thousand seven hundred and fifty-four* verses," instead of "*one thousand and twelve* lines;" such being the initial and final words, and such the true and entire contents of this poem.

Thou art to know, Reader! that the first Edition thereof, like that of Milton, was never seen by the Author, (though living and not blind:) The Editor himself confessed as much in his Preface: And no two poems were ever published in so arbitrary a manner. The Editor of this, had as boldly suppressed whole Passages, yea the entire last book, as the Editor of Paradise Lost, added and augmented. Milton himself gave but *ten* books, his Editor *twelve*; this Author gave *four* books, his Editor only *three*. But we have happily done justice to both; and presume we shall live in this our last labour, as long as in any of our others. BENTL.

and prevention of all such abuses. Provided always, that nothing in this Declaration shall be construed to limit the lawful and undoubted right of every subject of this Realm, to judge, censure, or condemn, in the whole or in part, any Poem or Poet whatsoever.

Given under our hand at London this third Day of January, in the Year of our Lord one thousand seven hundred thirty and two.

Declarat' cor' me,
JOHN BARBER, Mayor.

and prevention of all
always, that nothing in
be construed to limit the
right of every subject of t
censure, or condemn, in
any Poem or [illegible] what

[illegible] under our ha
Day of Janu
Lord one
thirty and tw

Declared before me,
John Barber, Mayor.

APPENDIX.

PREFACE

Prefixed to the five first imperfect Editions of the DUNCIAD, in three books, printed at DUBLIN and LONDON, in octavo and duodecimo, 1727.

The PUBLISHER [a] to the READER.

IT will be found a true observation, though somewhat surprizing, that when any scandal is vented against a man of the highest distinction and character, either in the state or literature, the public in general afford

[a] *The Publisher*] Who he was is uncertain; but Edward Ward tells us, in his preface to Durgen, "that most judges are of opinion this preface is not of English extraction, but Hibernian," &c. He means it was written by Dr. Swift, who, whether the publisher or not, may be said in a sort to be author of the Poem. For when he, together with Mr. Pope (for reasons specified in the preface to their Miscellanies) determined to own the most trifling pieces in which they had any hand, and to destroy all that remained in their power; the first sketch of this poem was snatched from the fire by Dr. Swift, who persuaded his friend to proceed in it, and to him it was therefore inscribed. But the occasion of printing it was as follows:

There was published in those Miscellanies, a Treatise of the Bathos, or Art of Sinking in Poetry, in which was a chapter, where the species of bad writers were ranged in classes, and initial letters of names prefixed, for the most part at Random. But such

afford it a most quiet reception; and the large part accept it as favourably as if it were some kindness done to themselves: whereas if a known scoundrel or blockhead but chance to be touched upon, a whole legion is up in arms, and it becomes the common cause of all scriblers, booksellers, and printers whatsoever.

Not to search too deeply into the reason hereof, I will only observe as a fact, that every week for these two months past, the town has been persecuted with [b] pamphlets, advertisements, letters, and weekly essays,

such was the Number of poets eminent in that art, that some one or other took every letter to himself. All fell into so violent a fury, that for half a year, or more, the common Newspapers (in most of which they had some property, as being hired writers) were filled with the most abusive falsehoods and scurrilities they could possibly devise; a liberty no ways to be wondered at in those people, and in those papers, that, for many years, during the uncontrouled Licence of the press, had aspersed almost all the great characters of the age; and this with impunity, their own persons and names being utterly secret and obscure. This gave Mr. Pope the thought, that he had now some opportunity of doing good, by detecting and dragging into light these common enemies of mankind; since to invalidate this universal slander, it sufficed to shew what contemptible men were the authors of it. He was not without hopes, that by manifesting the dulness of those who had only malice to recommend them; either the booksellers would not find their account in employing them, or the men themselves, when discovered, want courage to proceed in so unlawful an occupation. This it was that gave birth to the Dunciad; and he thought it an happiness, that by the late flood of slander on himself, he had acquired such a peculiar right over their Names as was necessary to his design. W.

[b] *Pamphlets, advertisements,* &c.] See the list of those anonymous papers, with their dates and authors annexed, inserted before the Poem. W.

essays, not only against the wit and writings, but against the character and person of Mr. Pope. And that of all those men who have received pleasure from his works, (which by modest computation may be about a [c] hundred thousand in these kingdoms of England and Ireland; not to mention Jersey, Guernsey, the Orcades, those in the new world, and foreigners who have translated him into their languages) of all this number not a man hath stood up to say one word in his defence.

The only exception is the [d] author of the following poem, who doubtless had either a better insight into the grounds of this clamour, or a better opinion of Mr. Pope's integrity, joined with a greater personal love for him, than any other of his numerous friends and admirers.

Farther, that he was in his peculiar intimacy, appears from the knowledge he manifests of the most private

[c] *About a hundred thousand*] It is surprizing with what stupidity this preface, which is almost a continued irony, was taken by those authors. All such passages as these were understood by Curl, Cook, Cibber, and others, to be serious. Here the Laureate (Letter to Mr. Pope, p. 9.) "Though I grant the Dunciad a better poem of its kind than ever was writ; yet when I read it with those *vain glorious* encumbrances of Notes and Remarks upon it, &c.——it is amazing, that you, who have writ with such masterly spirit upon the ruling Passion, should be so blind a slave to your own, as not to see how far a *low avarice of Praise*," &c. (taking it for granted that the notes of Scriblerus and others, were the author's own.) W.

[d] *The author of the following poem*, &c.] A very plain irony, speaking of Mr. Pope himself. W.

private authors of all the anonymous pieces againſt him, and from his having in this poem attacked [e] no man living, who had not before printed, or publiſhed, ſome ſcandal againſt this gentleman.

How I came poſſeſt of it, is no concern to the reader; but it would have been a wrong to him had I detained the publication; ſince thoſe names which are its chief ornaments die off daily ſo faſt, as muſt render it too ſoon unintelligible. If it provoke the author to give us a more perfect edition, I have my end.

Who he is I cannot ſay, and (which is a great pity) there is certainly [f] nothing in his ſtyle and manner of writing, which can diſtinguiſh or diſcover him: For if it bears any reſemblance to that of Mr. Pope, 'tis not improbable but it might be done on purpoſe, with a view to have it paſs for his. But by the frequency of his alluſions to Virgil, and a laboured (not to ſay affected) *ſhortneſs* in imitation of him, I ſhould think him more an admirer of the Roman poet than of the Grecian, and in that not of the ſame taſte with his friend.

I have

[e] The publiſher in theſe words went a little too far: but it is certain whatever names the reader finds that are unknown to him, are of ſuch: and the exception is only of two or three, whoſe dulneſs, impudent ſcurrilities, or ſelf-conceit, all mankind agreed to have juſtly entitled them to a place in the Dunciad. W.

[f] *There is certainly nothing in his ſtyle, &c.*] This irony had ſmall effect in concealing the author. The Dunciad, imperfect as it was, had not been publiſhed two days, but the whole Town gave it to Mr. Pope. W.

I have been well informed, that this work was the labour of full [g] six years of his life, and that he wholly retired himself from all the avocations and pleasures of the world, to attend diligently to its correction and perfection; and six years more he intended to bestow upon it, as it should seem by this verse of Statius, which was cited at the head of his manuscript,

Oh mihi bissenos multum vigilata per annos,
Duncia [h] *!*

Hence also we learn the true title of the poem; which with the same certainty as we call that of Homer the Iliad, of Virgil the Aeneid, of Camoens the Lusiad, we may pronounce, could have been, and can be no other than

The DUNCIAD.

It

[g] *The labour of full six years, &c.*] This also was honestly and seriously believed by divers gentlemen of the Dunciad. J. Ralph, pref. to Sawney: "We are told it was the labour of six years, with the utmost assiduity and application: It is no great compliment to the author's sense, to have employed so large a part of his life," &c. So also Ward, pref. to Durgen: "The Dunciad, as the publisher very wisely confesses, cost the author six years retirement from all the pleasures of life; though it is somewhat difficult to conceive, from either its bulk or beauty, that it could be so long in hatching, &c. But the length of time and closeness of application were mentioned to prepossess the reader with a good opinion of it."

They just as well understood what Scriblerus said of the Poem. W.

[h] The prefacer to Curl's Key, p. 3. took this word to be really in Statius: "By a quibble on the word *Duncia*, the *Dunciad* is formed." Mr. Ward also follows him in the same opinion." W.

It is ſtyled *Heroic*, as being *doubly* ſo; not only with reſpect to its nature, which, according to the beſt rules of the ancients, and ſtricteſt ideas of the moderns, is critically ſuch; but alſo with regard to the heroical diſpoſition and high courage of the writer, who dared to ſtir up ſuch a formidable, irritable, and implacable race of mortals.

There may ariſe ſome obſcurity in chronology from the *Names* in the poem, by the inevitable removal of ſome authors, and inſertion of others, in their niches. For whoever will conſider the unity of the whole deſign, will be ſenſible, that the *poem was not made for theſe authors, but theſe authors for the poem.* I ſhould judge that they were clapped in as they roſe, freſh and freſh, and changed from day to day; in like manner as when the old boughs wither, we thruſt new ones into a chimney.

I would not have the reader too much troubled or anxious, if he cannot decypher them; ſince when he ſhall have found them out, he will probably know no more of the perſons than before.

Yet we judged it better to preſerve them as they are, than to change them for fictitious names; by which the ſatire would only be multiplied, and applied to many inſtead of one. Had the Hero, for inſtance, been called Codrus, how many would have affirmed him to have been Mr. T. Mr. E. Sir R. B. &c. but now all that unjuſt ſcandal is ſaved by calling him by a name, which by good luck happens to be that of a real perſon.

II.

A LIST of BOOKS, PAPERS, and VERSES, in which our Author was abufed, before the Publication of the DUNCIAD; with the true Names of the Authors.

REFLECTIONS critical and fatyrical on a late Rhapfody, called, An Effay on Criticifm. By Mr. Dennis, printed by B. Lintot, price 6d.

A new Rehearfal, or Bays the younger; containing an Examen of Mr. Rowe's plays, and a word or two on Mr. Pope's Rape of the Lock. Anon. [By Charles Gildon] printed for J. Roberts, 1714, price 1s.

Homerides, or a Letter to Mr. Pope, occafioned by his intended tranflation of Homer. By Sir Iliad Dogrel [Tho. Burnet and G. Ducket, efquires] printed for W. Wilkins, 1715, price 9d.

Æfop at the Bear-garden; a vifion, in imitation of the Temple of Fame, by Mr. Prefton. Sold by John Morphew, 1715, price 6d.

The Catholic Poet, or Proteftant Barnaby's Sorrowful Lamentation; a Ballad about Homer's Iliad. By Mrs. Centlivre, and others, 1715, price 1d.

An Epilogue to a Puppet-fhew at Bath, concerning the faid Iliad. By George Ducket, efq; printed by E. Curl.

A complete Key to the What d'ye call it. Anon. [By Griffin a player, ſuperviſed by Mr. Th——] printed by J. Roberts, 1715.

A true character of Mr. P. and his writings, in a letter to a friend. Anon. [Dennis] printed for S. Popping, 1716, price 3d.

The Confederates, a Farce. By Joſeph Gay [J. D. Breval] printed for R. Burleigh, 1717, price 1s.

Remarks upon Mr. Pope's tranſlation of Homer; with two letters concerning the Windſor Foreſt, and the Temple of Fame. By Mr. Dennis, printed for E. Curl, 1717, price 1s. 6d.

Satires on the tranſlators of Homer, Mr. P. and Mr. T. Anon. [Bez. Morris] 1717, price 6d.

The Triumvirate; or, a Letter from Palaemon to Celia at Bath. Anon. [Leonard Welſted] 1711, folio, price 1s.

The Battle of Poets; an heroic poem. By Tho. Cooke, printed for J. Roberts, folio, 1725.

Memoirs of Lilliput. Anon. [Eliza Haywood] octavo, printed in 1727.

An Eſſay on Criticiſm, in proſe. By the Author of the Critical Hiſtory of England [J. Oldmixon] octavo, printed 1728.

Gulliveriana and Alexandriana; with an ample preface and critique on Swift and Pope's Miſcellanies. By Jonathan Smedley, printed by J. Roberts, octavo, 1728.

Characters of the Times; or, an account of the writings, characters, &c. of several gentlemen libelled by S— and P—, in a late Miscellany, octavo, 1728.

Remarks on Mr. Pope's Rape of the Lock, in letters to a friend. By Mr. Dennis; written in 1724, though not printed till 1728, octavo.

Verses, Letters, Essays, or Advertisements, in the Public Prints.

British Journal, Nov. 25, 1727. A Letter on Swift and Pope's Miscellanies. [Writ by M. Concanen.]

Daily Journal, March 18, 1728. A Letter by Philomauri. James-Moore Smith.

Id. March 29. A Letter about Thersites; accusing the author of disaffection to the Government. By James-Moore Smith.

Mist's Weekly Journal, March 30. An Essay on the Arts of a Poet's sinking in reputation; or, a Supplement to the Art of Sinking in Poetry. [Supposed by Mr. Theobald.]

Daily Journal, April 3. A Letter under the name of Philo-ditto. By James-Moore Smith.

Flying Post, April 4. A Letter against Gulliver and Mr. P. [By Mr. Oldmixon.]

Daily Journal, April 5. An Auction of Goods at Twickenham. By James-Moore Smith.

The Flying Post, April 6. A Fragment of a Treatise upon Swift and Pope. By Mr. Oldmixon.

The Senator, April 9. On the ſame. By Edward Roome.

Daily Journal, April 8. Advertiſement by James-Moore Smith.

Flying Poſt, April 13. Verſes againſt Dr. Swift, and againſt Mr. P—'s Homer. By J. Oldmixon.

Daily Journal, April 23. Letter about the tranſlation of the character of Therſites in Homer. By Thomas Cooke, &c.

Miſt's Weekly Journal, April 27. A Letter of Lewis Theobald.

Daily Journal, May 11. A Letter againſt Mr. P. at large. Anon. [John Dennis.]

All theſe were afterwards reprinted in a pamphlet, entituled, a Collection of all the Verſes, Eſſays, Letters, and Advertiſements occaſioned by Mr. Pope and Swift's Miſcellanies, prefaced by Concanen, Anonymous, octavo, and printed for A. Moore, 1728, price 1 s. Others of an elder date, having lain as waſte Paper many years, were, upon the publication of the Dunciad, brought out, and their Authors betrayed by the mercenary Bookſellers (in hopes of ſome poſſibility of vending a few) by advertiſing them in this manner——"The Confederates, a farce. By Capt. Breval (for which he was put into the Dunciad.) An Epilogue to Powel's Puppet-ſhow. By Col. Ducket (for which he was put into the Dunciad.) Eſſays, &c. By Sir Richard Blackmore. (N. B. It was for a paſſage of this book that Sir Richard was put into the Dunciad.)" And ſo of others.

An Eſſay on the Dunciad, octavo, printed for J. Roberts. [In this book, p. 9. it was formally declared, " That the complaint of the aforeſaid Libels and Advertiſements was forged and untrue; that all mouths had been ſilent, except in Mr. Pope's praiſe; and nothing againſt him publiſhed, but by Mr. Theobald."]

Sawney, in blank verſe, occaſioned by the Dunciad; with a Critique on that poem. By J. Ralph [a perſon never mentioned in it at firſt, but inſerted after] printed for J. Roberts, octavo.

A complete Key to the Dunciad. By E. Curl. 12mo. price 6d.

A ſecond and third edition of the ſame, with additions, 12mo.

The Popiad. By E. Curl, extracted from J. Dennis, Sir Richard Blackmore, &c. 12mo. price 6d.

The Curliad. By the ſame E. Curl.

The Female Dunciad. Collected by the ſame Mr. Curl, 12mo. price 6d. With the Metamorphoſis of P. into a ſtinging Nettle. By Mr. Foxton, 12mo.

The Metamorphoſis of Scriblerus into Snarlerus. By J. Smedley, printed for A. Moore, folio, price 6d.

The Dunciad diſſected. By Curl and Mrs. Thomas, 12mo.

An Eſſay on the Taſte and Writings of the preſent times. Said to be writ by a gentleman of C. C. C. Oxon, printed for J. Roberts, octavo.

The Arts of Logic and Rhetoric, partly taken from Bouhours, with new Reflections, &c. By John Oldmixon, octavo.

Remarks on the Dunciad. By Mr. Dennis, dedicated to Theobald, octavo.

A Supplement to the Profund. Anon. By Matthew Concanen, octavo.

Miſt's Weekly Journal, June 8. A long Letter, ſign'd W. A. Writ by ſome or other of the Club of Theobald, Dennis, Moore, Concanen, Cooke, who for ſome time held conſtant weekly meetings for theſe kind of performances.

Daily Journal, June 11. A Letter ſigned Philoſcriblerus, on the name of Pope—Letter to Mr. Theobald, in verſe, ſigned B. M. [Bezaleel Morris] againſt Mr. P—. Many other little epigrams about this time in the ſame papers, by James Moore, and others.

Miſt's Journal, June 22. A Letter by Lewis Theobald.

Flying Poſt, Auguſt 8. Letter on Pope and Swift.

Daily Journal, Auguſt 8. Letter charging the Author of the Dunciad with Treaſon.

Durgen: a plain ſatire on a pompous ſatiriſt. By Edward Ward, with a little of James Moore.

Apollo's Maggot in his Cups. By E. Ward.

Gulliveriana

Gulliveriana ſecunda. Being a Collection of many of the Libels in the Newſpapers, like the former Volume, under the ſame title, by Smedley. Advertiſed in the Craftſman, Nov. 9, 1728, with this remarkable promiſe, that " *any thing* which *any body* ſhould ſend as Mr. Pope's or Dr. Swift's, ſhould be inſerted and publiſhed as theirs."

Pope Alexander's ſupremacy and infallibility examined, &c. By George Ducket, and John Dennis, quarto.

Dean Jonathan's Paraphraſe on the 4th chapter of Geneſis. Writ by E. Roome, folio, 1729.

Labeo. A paper of verſes by Leonard Welſted, which after came into *One Epiſtle*, and was publiſhed by James Moore, quarto, 1730. Another part of it came out in Welſted's own name, under the juſt title of Dulneſs and Scandal, folio, 1731.

There have been ſince publiſhed,

Verſes on the Imitator of Horace. By a Lady [or between a Lady, a Lord, and a Court-Squire.] Printed for J. Roberts, folio.

An Epiſtle from a Nobleman to a Doctor of Divinity, from Hampton court [Lord H——y.] Printed for J. Roberts alſo, folio.

A Letter from Mr. Cibber to Mr. Pope. Printed for W. Lewis in Covent Garden, octavo.

III.

ADVERTISEMENT

To the FIRST EDITION with Notes, in Quarto, 1729.

IT will be ſufficient to ſay of this edition, that the reader has here a much more correct and complete copy of the DUNCIAD, than has hitherto appeared. I cannot anſwer but ſome miſtakes may have ſlipt into it, but a vaſt number of others will be prevented by the names being now not only ſet at length, but juſtified by the authorities and reaſons given. I make no doubt, the author's own motive to uſe real rather than feigned names, was his care to preſerve the innocent from any falſe application; whereas in the former editions, which had no more than the initial letters, he was made, by keys printed here, to hurt the inoffenſive; and (what was worſe) to abuſe his friends, by an impreſſion at Dublin.

The commentary which attends this poem was ſent me from ſeveral hands, and conſequently muſt be unequally written; yet will have one advantage over moſt commentaries, that it is not made upon conjectures, or at a remote diſtance of time: And the reader cannot but derive one pleaſure from the very

Obſcurity

Obſcurity of the perſons it treats of, that it partakes of the nature of a *Secret*, which moſt people love to be let into, though the men or the things be ever ſo inconſiderable or trivial.

Of the *Perſons* it was judged proper to give ſome account: For ſince it is only in this monument that they muſt expect to ſurvive (and here ſurvive they will, as long as the Engliſh tongue ſhall remain ſuch as it was in the reigns of Queen ANNE and King GEORGE,) it ſeemed but humanity to beſtow a word or two upon each, juſt to tell what he was, what he writ, when he lived, and when he died.

If a word or two more are added upon the chief offenders, 'tis only as a paper pinned upon the breaſt, to mark the enormities for which they ſuffered; leſt the correction only ſhould be remembered, and the crime forgotten.

In ſome articles it was thought ſufficient, barely to tranſcribe from Jacob, Curl, and other writers of their own rank, who were much better acquainted with them than any of the authors of this comment can pretend to be. Moſt of them had drawn each other's characters on certain occaſions; but the few here inſerted are all that could be ſaved from the general deſtruction of ſuch works.

Of the part of Scriblerus I need ſay nothing; his manner is well enough known, and approved by all but thoſe who are too much concerned to be judges.

The

The Imitations of the Ancients are added to gratify thofe who either never read, or may have forgotten them; together with fome of the parodies and allufions to the moft excellent of the Moderns. If, from the frequency of the former, any man think the poem too much a Cento, our poet will but appear to have done the fame thing in jeft which Boileau did in earneft; and upon which Vida, Fracaftorius, and many of the moft eminent Latin poets, profeffedly valued themfelves.

IV.

ADVERTISEMENT

To the FIRST EDITION of the FOURTH BOOK of the DUNCIAD, when printed feparately in the Year 1742.

WE apprehend it can be deemed no injury to the author of the three firft books of the Dunciad, that we publifh this Fourth. It was found merely by accident, in taking a furvey of the *Library* of a late eminent nobleman; but in fo blotted a condition, and in fo many detached pieces, as plainly fhewed it to be not only *incorrect*, but *unfinifhed*. That the author

author of the three firſt books had a deſign to extend and complete his poem in this manner, appears from the diſſertation prefixed to it, where it is ſaid, that *the deſign is more extenſive, and that we may expect other epiſodes to complete it:* And from the declaration in the argument to the third book, that *the accompliſhment of the prophecies therein would be the theme hereafter of a greater Dunciad.* But whether or no he be the author of this, we declare ourſelves ignorant. If he be, we are no more to be blamed for the publication of it, than Tucca and Varius for that of the laſt ſix books of the Aeneid, though perhaps inferior to the former.

If any perſon be poſſeſſed of a more perfect copy of this work, or of any other fragments of it, and will communicate them to the publiſher, we ſhall make the next edition more complete: In which we alſo promiſe to inſert any *Criticiſms* that ſhall be publiſhed (if at all to the purpoſe) with the *Names* of the *Authors*; or any letter ſent us (though not to the purpoſe) ſhall yet be printed under the title of *Epiſtolae Obſcurorum Virorum*; which, together with ſome others of the ſame kind formerly laid by for that end, may make no unpleaſant addition to the future impreſſions of this poem.

V.

ADVERTISEMENT

To the complete Edition of 1743.

I have long had a design of giving some sort of Notes on the works of this poet. Before I had the happiness of his acquaintance, I had written a commentary on his *Essay on Man*, and have since finished another on the *Essay on Criticism*. There was one already on the *Dunciad*, which had met with general approbation: but I still thought some additions were wanting (of a more serious kind) to the humorous notes of *Scriblerus*, and even to those written by Mr. *Cleland*, Dr. *Arbuthnot*, and others. I had lately the pleasure to pass some months with the author in the country, where I prevailed upon him to do what I had long desired, and favour me with his explanation of several passages in his works. It happened, that just at that juncture was published a ridiculous book against him, full of Personal Reflection, which furnished him with a lucky opportunity of improving *This Poem*, by giving it the only thing it wanted, a *more considerable Hero*. He was always sensible of its defect in that particular, and owned he had let it pass with the Hero it had, purely for want of a better; not entertaining the least expectation that such an one was reserved for this Post, as has since obtained the *Laurel*: But since that had happened,

happened, he could no longer deny this juſtice either to *him* or the *Dunciad.*

And yet I will venture to ſay, there was another motive which had ſtill more weight with our Author: This perſon was one, who from every Folly (not to ſay Vice) of which another would be aſhamed, has conſtantly derived a *Vanity*; and therefore was the *man in the world who would leaſt be hurt by it.*

W. W.

VI.

ADVERTISEMENT

Printed in the JOURNALS, 1730.

WHEREAS, upon occaſion of certain Pieces relating to the Gentlemen of the Dunciad, ſome have been willing to ſuggeſt, as if they looked upon them as an *abuſe*: we can do no leſs than own, it is our opinion, that to call theſe Gentlemen *bad authors* is no ſort of *abuſe*, but a great *truth.* We cannot alter this opinion without ſome reaſon; but we promiſe to do it in reſpect to every perſon who thinks it an injury to be repreſented as no *Wit*, or *Poet*, provided he procures a Certificate of his being really ſuch, from any *three of his companions* in the Dunciad, or from Mr. *Dennis ſingly*, who is eſteemed equal to any three of the number.

VII.

A PARALLEL OF THE CHARACTERS OF Mr. DRYDEN and Mr. POPE,

As drawn by certain of their Contemporaries.

Mr. DRYDEN,

HIS POLITICS, RELIGION, MORALS.

MR. Dryden is a mere renegado from monarchy, poetry, and good ſenſe [a]. A true Republican ſon of monarchical Church [b]. A Republican Atheiſt [c]. Dryden was from the beginning an ἀλλοπρόσαλλος, and I doubt not will continue ſo to the laſt [d].

In the poem called *Abſalom* and *Achitophel* are notoriouſly traduced, The KING, the QUEEN, the LORDS, and GENTLEMEN, not only their honourable perſons expoſed,

[a] Milbourn on Dryden's Virgil, 8vo. 1698. p. 6.
[b] Page 38. [c] Page 192. [d] Page 8.

VII.

A PARALLEL OF THE CHARACTERS OF Mr. POPE and Mr. DRYDEN,

As drawn by certain of their Contemporaries.

Mr. POPE,

His Politics, Religion, Morals.

Mr. Pope is an open and mortal enemy to his country, and the commonwealth of learning [a]. Some call him a popish whig, which is directly inconsistent [b]. Pope, as a papist, must be a tory and high flyer [c]. He is both a whig and tory [d].

He hath made it his custom to cackle to more than one party in their own sentiments [e].

In

[a] Dennis Rem. on the Rape of the Lock, pref. p. xii.
[b] Dunciad dissected. [c] Pref. to Gulliveriana.
[d] Dennis, Character of Mr. P.
[e] Theobald, Letter in Mist's Journal, June 22, 1728.

exposed, but the whole NATION and its REPRESENTATIVES notoriously libelled. It is *scandalum magnatum*, yea of MAJESTY itself [e].

He looks upon God's gospel as a foolish fable, like the Pope, to whom he is a pitiful purveyor [f]. His very Christianity may be questioned [g]. He ought to expect more severity than other men, as he is most unmerciful in his reflections on others [h]. With as good a right as his Holiness, he sets up for poetical infallibility [i].

Mr. DRYDEN only a Versifier.

His whole Libel is all bad matter, beautify'd (which is all that can be said of it) with good metre [k]. Mr. Dryden's genius did not appear in any thing more than his Versification, and whether he is to be ennobled for that only, is a question [l].

Mr. DRYDEN's VIRGIL.

Tonson calls it *Dryden's Virgil*, to shew that this is not that Virgil so admired in the Augustean age; but a Virgil of another stamp, a silly, impertinent, nonsensical

[e] Whip and Key, 4to, printed for R. Janeway, 1682. Preface.
[f] Ibid. [g] Milbourn, p. 9. [h] Ibid. p. 175.
[i] Page 39. [k] Whip and Key, Pref.
[l] Oldmixon, Essay on Criticism, p. 84.

In his Miscellanies the Persons abused are, The KING, the QUEEN, his late MAJESTY, both Houses of PARLIAMENT, the Privy-Council, the Bench of BISHOPS, the Established CHURCH, the present MINISTRY, &c. To make Sense of some passages, they must be construed into ROYAL SCANDAL [f].

He is a Popish Rhymester, bred up with a contempt of the Sacred Writings [g]. His Religion allows him to destroy Heretics, not only with his pen, but with fire and sword; and such were all those unhappy Wits whom he sacrificed to his accursed Popish Principles [h]. It deserved Vengeance to suggest, that Mr. Pope had less infallibility than his Namesake at Rome [i].

Mr. POPE only a Versifier.

The smooth numbers of the Dunciad are all that recommend it, nor has it any other merit [k]. It must be owned that he hath got a notable knack of rhyming and writing smooth verse [l].

Mr. POPE's HOMER.

The Homer which Lintot prints, does not talk like Homer, but like Pope; and he who translated him, one

[f] List at the end of a Collection of Verses, Letters, Advertisements, 8vo. Printed for A. More, 1728, and the Preface to it, p. 6.

[g] Dennis's Rem. on Homer, p. 27.

[h] Preface to Gulliveriana, p. 11.

[i] Dedication to the Collection of Verses, Letters, &c. p. 9.

[k] Mist's Journal of June 8, 1728.

[l] Character of Mr. P. and Dennis on Hom.

ſenſical writer [m]. None but a Bavius, a Maevius, or a Bathyllus, carped at Virgil; and none but ſuch unthinking Vermin admire his Tranſlator [n]. It is true, ſoft and eaſy lines might become Ovid's Epiſtles or Art of Love—But Virgil, who is all great and majeſtic, &c. requires ſtrength of lines, weight of words, and cloſeneſs of expreſſion; not an ambling Muſe running on Carpet-ground, and ſhod as lightly as a Newmarket-racer.—He has numberleſs faults in his Author's meaning, and in propriety of expreſſion [o].

Mr. DRYDEN underſtood no Greek nor Latin.

Mr. Dryden was once, I have heard, at Weſtminſter-ſchool: Dr. Buſby would have whipt him for ſo childiſh a Paraphraſe [p]. The meaneſt Pedant in England would whip a Lubber of twelve for conſtruing ſo abſurdly [q]. The Tranſlator is mad, every line betrays his Stupidity [r]. The faults are innumerable, and convince me that Mr. Dryden did not, or would not underſtand his Author [s]. This ſhews how fit Mr. D. may be to tranſlate *Homer!* A miſtake in a ſingle letter might fall on the Printer well enough, but εἴχωρ for ἰχὼρ muſt be the error of the Author: Nor had he art enough to correct it at the Preſs [t]. Mr. Dryden writes for the Court Ladies——He writes for the Ladies, and not for uſe [u].

The

[m] Milbourn, page 2. [n] Page 35. [o] Page 22, and 102.
[p] Milbourn, p. 72. [q] Page 203. [r] Page 78.
[s] Page 206. [t] Page 19. [u] Page 144, 190.

one would ſwear, had a Hill in Tipperary for his Parnaſſus, and a Puddle in ſome Bog for his Hippocrene [m]. He has no admirers among thoſe that can diſtinguiſh, diſcern, and judge [n].

He hath a knack at ſmooth verſe, but without either Genius or good Senſe, or any tolerable knowledge of Engliſh. The qualities which diſtinguiſh Homer are the beauties of his Diction and the Harmony of his Verſification.——But this little Author, who is ſo much in vogue, has neither Senſe in his Thoughts, nor Engliſh in his Expreſſions [o].

Mr. POPE underſtood no Greek.

He hath undertaken to tranſlate Homer from the Greek, of which he knows not one word, into Engliſh, of which he underſtands as little [p]. I wonder how this Gentleman would look, ſhould it be diſcovered, that he has not tranſlated ten verſes together in any book of Homer with juſtice to the Poet, and yet he dares reproach his fellow-writers with not underſtanding Greek [q]. He has ſtuck ſo little to his Original as to have his knowledge in Greek called in queſtion [r]. I ſhould be glad to know which it is of all Homer's Excellencies which has ſo delighted the Ladies, and the Gentlemen who judge like Ladies [s].

But

[m] Dennis Rem. on Pope's Homer, p. 12. [n] Ibid. p. 14.
[o] Character of Mr. P. p. 17. and Remarks on Homer, p. 91.
[p] Dennis's Rem. on Homer, p. 12. [q] Daily Journ. April 23, 1728. [r] Suppl. to the Profund Pref.
[s] Oldmixon, Eſſay on Criticiſm, p. 66.

The Tranſlator puts in a little burleſque now and then into Virgil, for a Ragoût to his cheated Subſcribers [w].

Mr. DRYDEN tricked his Subſcribers.

I wonder that any man, who could not but be conſcious of his own unfitneſs for it, ſhould go to amuſe the learned world with ſuch an undertaking! A man ought to value his Reputation more than money; and not to hope that thoſe who can read for themſelves, will be impoſed upon, merely by a partially and unſeaſonably celebrated Name [x]. *Poetis quidlibet audendi* ſhall be Mr. Dryden's Motto, though it ſhould extend to picking of Pockets [y].

Names beſtowed on Mr. DRYDEN.

An Ape.] A crafty Ape dreſt up in a gaudy gown——Whips put into an Ape's paw, to play pranks with—None but Apiſh and Papiſh brats will heed him [z].

An Ass.] A Camel will take upon him no more burden than is ſufficient for his ſtrength, but there is another beaſt that crouches under all [a].

A Frog.] Poet Squab endued with Poet Maro's Spirit! an ugly, croaking kind of Vermin, which would ſwell to the bulk of an Ox [b].

A Coward.]

[w] Page 67. [x] Page 192. [y] Page 125.
[z] Whip and Key, Pref. [a] Milb. p. 105. [b] Page 11.

But he has a notable talent at Burlesque; his genius slides so naturally into it, that he had burlesqued Homer without designing it [t].

Mr. POPE tricked his Subscribers.

'Tis indeed somewhat bold, and almost prodigious, for a single man to undertake such a work: But 'tis too late to dissuade by demonstrating the madness of the Project. The Subscribers expectations have been raised in proportion to what their Pockets have been drained of [u]. Pope has been concerned in Jobs, and hired out his Name to Booksellers [w].

Names bestowed on Mr. POPE.

An Ape.] Let us take the initial letter of his Christian name, and the initial and final letters of his surname, viz. APE, and they give you the same Idea of an Ape as his Face [x], &c.

An Ass.] It is my duty to pull off the Lion's skin from this little Ass [y].

A Frog.] A squab short Gentleman—a little creature, that, like the Frog in the Fable, swells, and is angry that it is not allowed to be as big as an ox [z].

A Coward.]

[t] Dennis's Rem. p. 28. [u] Homerides, p. 1, &c. [w] British Journ. Nov. 25, 1727. [x] Dennis, Daily Journal, May 11, 1728. [y] Dennis, Rem. on Hom. Pref. [z] Dennis's Rem. on the Rape of the Lock, Pref. p. 9.

A COWARD.] A Clinias or a Damaetas, or a Man of Mr. Dryden's own Courage [c].

A KNAVE.] Mr. Dryden has heard of Paul, the Knave of Jesus Christ: And, if I mistake not, I've read somewhere of John Dryden, Servant to his Majesty [d].

A FOOL.] Had he not been such a self-conceited Fool [e].—Some great Poets are positive Blockheads [f].

A THING.] So little a Thing as Mr. Dryden [g].

[c] Page 176. [d] Page 57. [e] Whip and Key, Pref.
[f] Milbourn, p. 34. [g] Ibid. p. 35.

A Coward.] A lurking way-laying coward [a].

A Knave.] He is one whom God and Nature have marked for want of common honesty [b].

A Fool.] Great Fools will be christened by the names of great Poets, and Pope will be called Homer [c].

A Thing.] A little abject Thing [d].

[a] Char. of Mr. P. page 3.
[b] Ibid.
[c] Dennis, Rem. on Homer, p. 37.
[d] Ibid. p. 8.

A COWARD.] A lurking way-laying coward [a].

A KNAVE.] He is one whom God and Nature have marked for want of common honesty [b].

A FOOL.] Great Fools will be christened by the names of great Poets, and Pope will be called Homer [c].

A THING.] A little abject Thing [d].

[a] Char. of Mr. P. page 3. [b] Ibid.
[c] Dennis, Rem. on Homer, p. 37. [d] Ibid. p. 8.

INDEX

OF

PERSONS celebrated in this POEM.

[The firſt Number ſhews the Book, the ſecond the Verse.]

A

Ambrose Philips, i. 105. iii. 326.
Attila, iii. 92.
Alaric, iii. 91.
Alma Mater, iii. 338.
Annius, an Antiquary, iv. 347.
Arnal, William, ii. 315.

B

Blackmore, Sir Richard, i. 104. ii. 268.
Beſaleel Morris, ii. 126. iii. 168.
Banks, i. 146.
Broome, ibid.
Bond, ii. 126.
Brown, iii. 28.
Bladen, iv. 560.
Budgel, Eſq. ii. 397.
Bentley, Richard, iv. 201.
Bentley, Thomas, ii. 205.
Boyer, Abel, ii. 413.
Bland, a Gazetteer, i. 231.
Breval, J. Durant, ii. 126. 238.
Benlowes, iii. 21.
Bavius, ibid.
Burmannus, iv. 237.
Benſon, William, Eſq. iii. 325. iv. 110.
Burgerſdick, iv. 198.
Boeotians, iii. 50.
Bruin and Bears, i. 101.
Bear and Fiddle, i. 224.

C

Cibber, Colley, Hero of the Poem, paſſim.
Cibber, jun. iii. 139. 326.
Caxton, William, i. 149.
Curl, Edm. i. 40. ii. 3. 58. 167, &c.
Cooke, Thomas, ii. 138.
Concanen, Matthew, ii. 299.
Centlivre, Suſannah, ii. 411.
Caeſar in Egypt, i. 251.
Chi Ho-amti, emperor of China, iii. 75.
Crouzaz, iv. 198.
Codrus, ii. 144.

D

De Foe, Daniel, i. 103. ii. 147.
De Foe, Norton, ii. 415.
De Lyra, or Harpsfield, i. 153.
Dennis, John, i. 106. ii. 239. iii. 173.
Dunton, John, ii. 144.
Durfey, iii. 146.
Dutchmen, ii. 405. iii. 51.
Doctors, at White's, i. 203.
Douglas, iv. 394.

Euſden,

INDEX.

E

Eusden, Laurence, Poet Laureate, i. 104.
Eliza Haywood, ii. 157, &c.

F

Fleckno, Richard, ii. 2.
Faustus, Dr. iii. 233.
Fleetwood, iv. 326.
Free-Masons, iv. 576.
French Cook, iv. 553.

G

Gildon, Charles, i. 296.
Goode, Barn. iii. 153.
Goths, iii. 90.
Gazetteers, i. 215. ii. 314.
Gregorians and Gormogons, iv. 575.

H

Holland, Philemon, i. 154.
Hearne, Thomas, iii. 185.
Horneck, Philip, iii. 152.
Haywood, Eliza, ii. 157, &c.
Howard, Edward, i. 297.
Henley, John, the Orator, ii. 2. 425. iii. 199, &c.
Huns, iii. 90.
Heywood, John, i. 98.
Harpsfield, i. 153.
Hays, iv. 560.

J

John, King, i. 252.
James I. iv. 176.
Jacob, Giles, iii. 149.
Janssen, a gamester, iv. 326.

K

Knight, Robert, iv. 561.
Kuster, iv. 237.

L

Lintot, Bernard, i. 40. ii. 53.
Law, William, ii. 413.
Log, King, i. lin. ult.

M

More, James, ii. 50, &c.
Morris, Besaleel, ii. 126. iii. 168.
Mist, Nathaniel, i. 208.
Milbourn, Luke, ii. 349.
Mahomet, iii. 97.
Mears, William, ii. 125. iii. 28.
Motteux, Peter, ii. 412.
Monks, iii. 52.
Mandevil, ii. 414.
Morgan, ibid.
Montalto, iv. 105.
Mummius, an antiquary, iv. 371.

N

Newcastle, Duchess of, i. 141.
Nonjuror, i. 253.

O

Ogilvy, John, i. 141. 328.
Oldmixon, John, ii. 283.
Ozell, John, i. 285.
Ostrogoths, iii. 93.
Omar, the Caliph, iii. 81.
Owls, i. 271. 290. iii. 54.
——Athenian, iv. 362.
Osborne, bookseller, ii. 167.
Osborne, mother, ii. 312.

P

Prynn, William, i. 103.
Philips, Ambrose, i. 105. iii. 326.
Paridel, iv. 341.

Quarles,

INDEX.

Q

Quarles, Francis, i. 140.
Querno, Camillo, ii. 15.

R

Ralph, James, i. 216. iii. 165.
Roome, Edward, iii. 152.
Ridley, Tho. iii. 327.
Ridpath, George, i. 208. ii. 149.
Roper, Abel, ii. 149.
Rich, iii. 261.

S

Settle, Elkanah, i. 90. 146. iii. 37.
Smedley, Jonathan, ii. 291, &c.
Shadwell, Thomas, i. 240. iii. 22.
Scholiasts, iv. 231.
Silenus, iv. 492.
Sooterkins, i. 126.

T

Tate, i. 105. 238.
Theobald, or Tibbald, i. 133, 286.
Tutchin, John, ii. 148.
Toland, John, ii. 399. iii. 212.
Tindal, Dr. ii. 399. iii. 212. iv, 492.
Taylor, John, the Water-Poet, iii. 19.

V

Vandals, iii. 86.
Visigoths, iii. 94.

W

Walpole [late Sir Robert] praised by our Author, ii. 314.
Withers, George, i. 296.
Wynkin de Werde, i. 149.
Ward, Edward, i. 233. iii. 34.
Webster, ii. 258.
Whitfield, ibid.
Warner, Thomas, ii. 125.
Wilkins, ibid.
Welsted, Leonard, ii. 207. iii. 170.
Woolston, Thomas, iii. 212.
Wormius, iii. 188.
Wasse, iv. 237.
Walker, Hat-bearer to Bentley, iv. 206. 273.

THAT the Reader may ſee at one view, the nature, conduct, and coherence of this Poem, how perfect it was in three books, and how much it ſuffered, and was disfigured, by a fourth book, and by a new hero, the Dunciad is here added, as it ſtood in the quarto edition, 1728.

THAT the Reader may see at one view, the nature, conduct, and coherence of this Poem, how perfect it *was* in three books, and how much it suffered, and *was* disfigured, by a fourth book, and by a new hero, the Dunciad is here added, as it stood in the quarto edition, 1728.

THE

DUNCIAD:

TO

DR. JONATHAN SWIFT.

Argument to Book the First.

THE Propofition, the Invocation, and the Infcription. Then the Original of the great Empire of Dulnefs, *and caufe of the continuance thereof. The beloved feat of the Goddefs is defcribed, with her chief attendants and officers, her functions, operations, and effects. Then the poem haftes into the midft of things, prefenting her on the evening of a Lord Mayor's day, revolving the long fucceffion of her fons, and the glories paft and to come. She fixes her eye on* Tibbald *to be the inftrument of that great event which is the Subject of the poem. He is defcribed penfive in his ftudy, giving up the caufe, and apprehending the period of her empire from the old age of the prefent monarch* Settle: *Wherefore debating whether to betake himfelf to Law or Politicks, he raifes an altar of proper books, and (making firft his folemn prayer and declaration) purpofes thereon to facrifice all his unfuccefsful writings. As the pile is kindled, the Goddefs beholding the flame from her ſeat, flies in perſon and puts it out, by caſting upon it the poem of* Thule. *She forthwith reveals herſelf to him, tranſports him to her Temple, unfolds her arts, and initiates him into her myſteries; then announcing the death of* Settle *that night, anoints, and proclaims him Succeſſor.*

BOOK I.

BOOKS and the Man I ſing, the firſt who brings
The Smithfield Muſes to the Ear of Kings.
Say great Patricians! (ſince yourſelves inſpire
Theſe wond'rous works: ſo Jove and Fate require)
Say from what cauſe, in vain decry'd and curſt,
Still Dunce the ſecond reigns like Dunce the firſt.
In eldeſt time, e'er mortals writ or read,
E'er Pallas iſſu'd from the Thund'rer's head,
Dulneſs o'er all poſſeſs'd her antient right,
Daughter of Chaos and eternal Night:
Fate in their dotage this fair ideot gave,
Groſs as her ſire, and as her mother grave,
Laborious, heavy, buſy, bold, and blind,
She rul'd in native Anarchy, the mind.
Still her old empire to confirm, ſhe tries,
For born a Goddeſs, Dulneſs never dies.
O THOU! whatever Title pleaſe thine ear,
Dean, Drapier, Bickerſtaff, or Gulliver,
Whether thou chuſe Cervantes' ſerious air,
Or laugh and ſhake in Rab'lais eaſy Chair,
Or praiſe the Court, or magnify Mankind,
Or thy griev'd Country's copper chains unbind;
From thy Bæotia tho' Her Pow'r retires,
Grieve not, my SWIFT at ought our realm acquires,

Here pleas'd behold her mighty wings out-ſpread,
To hatch a new Saturnian Age of Lead.
  Where wave the tatter'd enſigns of Rag-fair,
A yawning ruin hangs and nods in air;
Keen, hollow winds howl thro' the bleak receſs,
Emblem of Muſic caus'd by Emptineſs.
Here in one bed two ſhiv'ring Siſters lye,
The Cave of Poverty and Poetry.
This, the Great Mother dearer held than all
The clubs of Quidnunc's, or her own Guild-hall.
Here ſtood her Opium, here ſhe nurs'd her Owls,
And deſtin'd here the imperial ſeat of fools.
Hence ſprings each weekly Muſe, the living boaſt
Of Curl's chaſte preſs, and Lintot's rubric poſt,
Hence hymning Tyburn's elegiac lay,
Hence the ſoft ſing-ſong on Cecilia's day,
Sepulchral Lyes, our holy walls to grace,
And New-year Odes, and all the Grubſtreet race.
  'Twas here in clouded majeſty ſhe ſhone;
Four guardian Virtues, round, ſupport her throne;
Fierce champion Fortitude, that knows no fears
Of hiſſes, blows, or want, or loſs of ears:
Calm Temperance, whoſe bleſſings thoſe partake
Who hunger, and who thirſt, for ſcribling ſake:
Prudence, whoſe glaſs preſents th' approaching jayl:
Poetic Juſtice, with her lifted ſcale;
Where, in nice balance, truth with gold ſhe weighs,
And ſolid pudding againſt empty praiſe.
  Here ſhe beholds the Chaos dark and deep,
Where, nameleſs Somethings in their cauſes ſleep,

Till

Till genial Jacob, or a warm Third-day
Call forth each maſs, a poem, or a play:
How hints, like ſpawn, ſcarce quick in embryo lie,
How new-born nonſenſe firſt is taught to cry,
Maggots half-form'd, in rhyme exactly meet,
And learn to crawl upon poetic feet.
Here one poor word a hundred clenches makes,
And ductile dulneſs new meanders takes;
There motley Images her fancy ſtrike,
Figures ill-pair'd, and Similies unlike.
She ſees a Mob of Metaphors advance,
Pleas'd with the madneſs of the mazy dance:
How Tragedy and Comedy embrace;
How Farce and Epic get a jumbled race;
How Time himſelf ſtands ſtill at her command,
Realms ſhift their place, and Ocean turns to land.
Here gay Deſcription Ægypt glads with ſhow'rs,
Or gives to Zembla fruits, to Barca flow'rs;
Glitt'ring with ice here hoary hills are ſeen,
There painted vallies of eternal green,
On cold December fragrant chaplets blow,
And heavy harveſts nod beneath the ſnow.

All theſe and more, the cloud-compelling Queen
Beholds thro' fogs, that magnify the ſcene:
She, tinſel'd o'er in robes of varying hues,
With ſelf-applauſe her wild creation views,
Sees momentary monſters riſe and fall,
And with her own fools-colours gilds them all.

'Twas on the day, when Thorold, rich and grave,
Like Cimon triumph'd both on land and wave:

(Pomps without guilt, of bloodlefs fwords and maces,
Glad chains, warm furs, broad banners, and broad faces)
Now Night defcending, the proud fcene was o'er,
But liv'd, in Settle's numbers, one day more.
Now May'rs and Shrieves all hufh'd and fatiate lay,
Yet eat, in dreams, the cuftard of the day;
While penfive Poets painful vigils keep,
Sleeplefs themfelves to give their readers fleep.
Much to the mindful Queen the feaft recalls
What City Swans once fung within the walls;
Much fhe revolves their arts, their ancient praife,
And fure fucceffion down from *Heywood*'s days.
She faw with joy the line immortal run,
Each fire impreft and glaring in his fon;
So watchful Bruin forms with plaftic care
Each growing lump, and brings it to a Bear.
She faw old *Pryn* in reftlefs *Daniel* fhine,
And *Eufden* eke out *Blackmore*'s endlefs line;
She faw flow *Philips* creep like *Tate*'s poor page,
And all the mighty Mad in *Dennis* rage.
In each fhe marks her image full expreft,
But chief, in *Tibbald*'s monfter breeding breaft;
Sees Gods with Dæmons in ftrange league ingage,
And earth, and heav'n, and hell her battles wage.
She ey'd the Bard, where fupperlefs he fate,
And pin'd, unconfcious of his rifing fate;
Studious he fate, with all his books around,
Sinking from thought to thought, a vaft profound!

Plung'd

Plung'd for his ſenſe, but found no bottom there;
Then writ, and flounder'd on, in mere deſpair.
He roll'd his eyes that witneſs'd huge diſmay,
Where yet unpawn'd, much learned lumber lay:
Volumes, whoſe ſize the ſpace exactly fill'd,
Or which fond authors were ſo good to gild,
Or where, by ſculpture made for ever known,
The page admires new beauties, not its own.
Here ſwells the ſhelf with Ogilby the great:
There, ſtamp'd with arms, *Newcaſtle* ſhines compleat:
Here all his ſuff'ring brotherhood retire,
And 'ſcape the martyrdom of jakes and fire;
A *Gothic* Vatican! of *Greece* and *Rome*
Well purg'd, and worthy *Withers*, *Quarles*, and *Blome*.
  But high above, more ſolid Learning ſhone,
The Claſſics of an Age that heard of none;
There *Caxton* ſlept, with *Wynkin* at his ſide,
One claſp'd in wood, and one in ſtrong cow-hide,
There, ſav'd by ſpice, like mummies, many a year,
Old Bodies of Philoſophy appear:
De Lyra there a dreadful front extends,
And here, the groaning ſhelves *Philemon* bends.
  Of theſe, twelve volumes, twelve of ampleſt ſize,
Redeem'd from tapers and defrauded pyes,
Inſpir'd he ſeizes: Theſe an altar raiſe:
An hecatomb of pure, unſully'd lays
That altar crowns; A folio Common-place
Founds the whole pyle, of all his works the baſe;
Quarto's, octavo's, ſhape the leſs'ning pyre;
And laſt, a little *Ajax* tips the ſpire.

Then he. Great Tamer of all human art!
Firſt in my care, and neareſt at my heart:
Dulneſs! whoſe good old cauſe I yet defend,
With whom my Muſe began, with whom ſhall end!
O thou, of buſineſs the directing ſoul,
To human heads like byaſs to the bowl,
Which as more pond'rous makes their aim more true,
Obliquely wadling to the mark in view.
O ever gracious to perplex'd mankind!
Who ſpread a healing miſt before the mind,
And, leſt we err by Wit's wild, dancing light,
Secure us kindly in our native night.
Ah! ſtill o'er *Britain* ſtretch that peaceful wand,
Which lulls th' *Helvetian* and *Batavian* land;
Where rebel to thy throne if Science riſe,
She does but ſhew her coward face and dies;
There, thy good Scholiaſts with unweary'd pains
Make *Horace* flat, and humble *Maro*'s ſtrains:
Here ſtudious I unlucky moderns ſave,
Nor ſleeps one error in its father's grave,
Old puns reſtore, loſt blunders nicely ſeek,
And crucify poor *Shakeſpear* once a week.
For thee I dim theſe eyes, and ſtuff this head,
With all ſuch reading as was never read;
For thee ſupplying, in the worſt of days,
Notes to dull books, and prologues to dull plays;
For thee explain a thing till all men doubt it,
And write about it, Goddeſs, and about it;
So ſpins the ſilk-worm ſmall its ſlender ſtore,
And labours, 'till it clouds itſelf all o'er.

Not that my quill to Critiques was confin'd,
My Verſe gave ampler leſſons to mankind;
So graveſt precepts may ſucceſsleſs prove,
But ſad examples never fail to move.
As forc'd from wind-guns, lead itſelf can fly,
And pond'rous ſlugs cut ſwiftly thro' the ſky:
As clocks to weight their nimble motion owe,
The wheels above urg'd by the load below;
Me, emptineſs and dulneſs could inſpire,
And were my elaſticity and fire.
Had Heav'n decreed ſuch works a longer date,
Heav'n had decreed to ſpare the *Grubſtreet*-ſtate.
But ſee great *Settle* to the duſt deſcend,
And all thy cauſe and empire at an end!
Cou'd *Troy* be ſav'd by any ſingle hand,
His grey-gooſe weapon muſt have made her ſtand.
But what can I? my *Flaccus* caſt aſide,
Take up th' Attorney's (once my better) guide?
Or rob the *Roman* geeſe of all their glories,
And ſave the ſtate by cackling to the Tories?
Yes, to my Country I my pen conſign,
Yes, from this moment, mighty *Miſt!* am thine,
And rival, *Curtius!* of thy fame and zeal,
O'er head and ears plunge for the publick weal.
Adieu my children! better thus expire
Unſtall'd, unſold, thus glorious mount in fire
Fair without ſpot; than greas'd by grocer's hands,
Or ſhip'd with *Ward* to ape and monkey lands,
Or wafting ginger, round the ſtreets to go,
And viſit alehouſe where ye firſt did grow.

With

With that, he lifted thrice the ſparkling brand,
And thrice he dropt it from his quiv'ring hand:
Then lights the ſtructure, with averted eyes;
The rowling ſmokes involve the ſacrifice.
The opening clouds diſcloſe each work by turns,
Now flames old *Memnon*, now *Rodrigo* burns,
In one quick flaſh ſee *Proſerpine* expire,
And laſt, his own cold *Æſchylus* took fire.
Then guſh'd the tears, as from the *Trojan*'s eyes
When the laſt blaze ſent *Ilion* to the ſkies.

Rowz'd by the light, old Dulneſs heav'd the head;
Then ſnatch'd a ſheet of *Thulè* from her bed,
Sudden ſhe flies, and whelms it o'er the pyre,
Down ſink the flames, and with a hiſs expire.

Her ample preſence fills up all the place;
A veil of fogs dilates her awful face:
Great in her charms! as when on Shrieves and May'rs
She looks, and breathes herſelf into their airs.
She bids him wait her to the ſacred Dome;
Well-pleas'd he enter'd, and confeſs'd his home:
So Spirits ending their terreſtrial race,
Aſcend and recognize their native place.
Raptur'd, he gazes round the dear retreat,
And in ſweet numbers celebrates the ſeat.

Here to her Choſen all her works ſhe ſhews;
Proſe ſwell'd to verſe, Verſe loitring into proſe;
How random thoughts now meaning chance to find,
Now leave all memory of ſenſe behind:
How prologues into prefaces decay,
And theſe to notes are fritter'd quite away.

How

How index-learning turns no ſtudent pale,
Yet holds the eel of ſcience by the tail.
How, with leſs reading than makes felons 'ſcape,
Leſs human genius than God gives an ape,
Small thanks to *France*, and none to *Rome* or *Greece*,
A paſt, vamp'd, future, old, reviv'd, new piece,
'Twixt *Plautus*, *Fletcher*, *Congreve*, and *Corneille*,
Can make a *Cibber*, *Johnſon*, or *Ozell*.
The Goddeſs then, o'er his anointed head,
With myſtic words, the ſacred Opium ſhed;
And lo! her bird, a monſter of a fowl!
Something betwixt a *Heideggre* and owl,
Perch'd on his crown. All hail! and hail again,
My ſon! the promis'd land expects thy reign.
Know, *Settle* cloy'd with cuſtard, and with praiſe,
Is gather'd to the dull of antient days,
Safe, where no Critics damn, no duns moleſt,
Where wretched *Withers*, *Banks*, and *Gildon* reſt,
And high-born *Howard*, more majeſtic ſire,
Impatient waits, till * * grace the quire.
I ſee a Chief, who leads my choſen ſons,
All arm'd with points, antitheſes and puns!
I ſee a Monarch, proud my race to own!
A Nurſing-mother, born to rock the throne!
Schools, courts, and ſenates ſhall my laws obey,
Till *Albion*, as *Hibernia*, bleſs my ſway.
She ceas'd: her owls reſponſive clap the wing,
And *Grubſtreet* garrets roar, God ſave the king.

So

So when *Jove*'s block deſcended from on high,
(As ſings thy great forefather, *Ogilby*,)
Loud thunder to its bottom ſhook the bog,
And the hoarſe nation croak'd, God ſave King Log.

END OF THE FIRST BOOK.

THE

DUNCIAD.

Argument to Book the Second.

THE King being proclaimed, the ſolemnity is graced with publick games and ſports of various kinds; not inſtituted by the Hero, as by Æneas *in* Virgil, *but for greater honour by the Goddeſs in perſon (in like manner as the games* Pythia, Iſthmia, *&c. were anciently ſaid to be by the Gods, and as* Thetis *herſelf appearing, according to* Homer Odyſſ. 24. *propoſed the prizes in honour of her ſon* Achilles). *Hither flock the Poets and Criticks, attended, as is but juſt, with their Patrons and* Bookſellers. *The Goddeſs is firſt pleaſed for her diſport to propoſe games to the* Bookſellers, *and ſetteth up the phantom of a Poet which they contend to overtake. The Races deſcribed, with their divers accidents: next, the Game for a* Poeteſs: *then follow the exerciſes for the* Poets, *of* tickling, vociferating, diving: *the firſt holds forth the arts and practices of Dedicators, the ſecond of Diſputants and fuſtian Poets, the third of profound, dark, and dirty Authors. Laſtly, for the* Critics, *the Goddeſs propoſes (with great propriety) an exerciſe not of their parts, but their patience; in hearing the works of two voluminous authors, one in verſe and the other in proſe, deliberately read, without ſleeping: The*

various

various effects of which, with the several degrees and manners of their operation, are here set forth: till the whole number, not of critics only, but of spectators, actors, and all present, fall fast asleep, which naturally and necessarily ends the games.

BOOK II.

HIGH on a gorgeous ſeat, that far out-ſhone
Henley's gilt tub, or *Fleckno*'s *Iriſh* throne,
Or that, where on her *Curls* the public pours,
All-bounteous, fragrant grains, and golden ſhow'rs:
Great *Tibbald* nods: The proud *Parnaſſian* ſneer,
The conſcious ſimper, and the jealous leer,
Mix on his look. All eyes direct their rays
On him, and crowds grow fooliſh as they gaze.
Not with more glee, by hands pontific crown'd,
With ſcarlet hats, wide waving, circled round,
Rome in her capitol ſaw *Querno* ſit,
Thron'd on ſev'n hills, the Antichriſt of wit.
  To grace this honour'd day, the Queen proclaims
By herald hawkers, high heroic games.
She ſummons all her ſons: An endleſs band
Pours forth, and leaves unpeopled half the land;
A motley mixture! in long wigs, in bags,
In ſilks, in crapes, in garters, and in rags,
From drawing rooms, from colleges, from garrets,
On horſe, on foot, in hacks, and gilded chariots,
All who true dunces in her cauſe appear'd,
And all who knew thoſe dunces to reward.
  Amid that Area wide ſhe took her ſtand,
Where the tall May-pole once o'er look'd the *Strand*.

But

But now, ſo Anne and Piety ordain,
A church collects the ſaints of *Drury-lane*.
With authors, Stationers obey'd the call,
The field of glory is a field for all;
Glory, and gain, th' induſtrious tribe provoke;
And gentle Dulneſs ever loves a joke.
A Poet's form ſhe plac'd before their eyes,
And bad the nimbleſt racer ſeize the prize;
No meagre, muſe-rid mope, aduſt and thin,
In a dun night-gown of his own looſe ſkin,
But ſuch a bulk as no twelve bards could raiſe,
Twelve ſtarveling bards of theſe degen'rate days.
All as a partridge plump, full-fed, and fair,
She form'd this image of well-bodied air,
With pert flat eyes ſhe window'd well its head,
A brain of feathers, and a heart of lead,
And empty words ſhe gave, and ſounding ſtrain,
But ſenſeleſs, lifeleſs! idol void and vain!
Never was daſh'd out, at one lucky hit,
A fool, ſo juſt a copy of a wit;
So like, that critics ſaid, and courtiers ſwore,
A Wit it was, and call'd the phantom *More*.
All gaze with ardour: ſome, a poet's name,
Others, a ſword-knot and lac'd ſuit inflame.
But lofty *Lintot* in the circle roſe;
"This prize is mine; who tempt it, are my foes:
With me began this genius, and ſhall end."
He ſpoke, and who with *Lintot* ſhall contend!
Fear held them mute. Alone untaught to fear
Stood dauntleſs *Curl*, "Behold that rival here!

The

The race by vigor, not by vaunts is won;
So take the hindmoſt Hell——He ſaid, and run.
Swift as a bard the bailiff leaves behind,
He left huge *Lintot*, and out-ſtrip'd the wind.
As when a dab-chick waddles thro' the copſe,
On feet, and wings, and flies, and wades, and hops;
So lab'ring on, with ſhoulders, hands, and head,
Wide as a windmill all his figure ſpread,
With legs expanded *Bernard* urg'd the race,
And ſeem'd to emulate great *Jacob*'s pace.
Full in the middle way there ſtood a lake,
Which *Curl*'s *Corinna* chanc'd that morn to make:
(Such was her won't, at early dawn to drop
Her evening cates before his neighbour's ſhop,)
Here fortun'd *Curl* to ſlide; loud ſhout the band,
And *Bernard! Bernard!* rings thro' all the *Strand*.
Obſcene with filth the miſcreant lies bewray'd,
Fal'n in the plaſh his wickedneſs had laid:
Then firſt (if poets aught of truth declare)
The caitiff Vaticide conceiv'd a prayer.
  Hear *Jove!* whoſe name my bards and I adore,
As much at leaſt as any God's, or more;
And him and his if more devotion warms,
Down with the Bible, up with the Pope's Arms.
  A place there is, betwixt earth, air and ſeas,
Where from *Ambroſia*, *Jove* retires for eaſe.
There in his ſeat two ſpacious vents appear,
On this he ſits, to that he leans his ear,
And hears the various vows of fond mankind,
Some beg an eaſtern, ſome a weſtern wind:

All vain petitions, mounting to the ſky,
With reams abundant this abode ſupply;
Amus'd he reads, and then returns the bills
Sign'd with that Ichor which from Gods diſtils.
In office here fair *Cloacina* ſtands,
And miniſters to *Jove* with pureſt-hands;
Forth from the heap ſhe pick'd her vot'ry's pray'r,
And plac'd it next him, a diſtinction rare!
(Oft, as he fiſh'd her nether realms for wit,
The Goddeſs favour'd him, and favours yet)
Renew'd by ordure's ſympathetic force,
As oil'd with magic juices for the courſe,
Vig'rous he riſes, from th' effluvia ſtrong
Imbibes new-life and ſcours and ſtinks along:
Re-paſſes *Lintot*, vindicates the race,
Nor heeds the brown diſhonours of his face.
And now the victor ſtretch'd his eager hand
Where the tall Nothing ſtood, or ſeem'd to ſtand;
A ſhapeleſs ſhade, it melted from his ſight,
Like forms in clouds, or viſions of the night!
To ſeize his papers, *Curl*, was next thy care;
His papers light, fly diverſe, toſt in air:
Songs, ſonnets, epigrams the winds uplift,
And whiſk 'em back to *Evans*, *Younge*, and *Swift*.
Th' embroider'd ſuit, at leaſt, he deem'd his prey;
That ſuit, an unpay'd taylor ſnatch'd away!
No rag, no ſcrap, of all the beau, or wit,
That once ſo flutter'd, and that once ſo writ.
Heav'n rings with laughter: Of the laughter vain,
Dulneſs, good Queen, repeats the jeſt again.

Three

Three wicked imps of her own *Grubſtreet* choir,
She deck'd like *Congreve*, *Addiſon* and *Prior*;
Mears, *Warner*, *Wilkins* run: deluſive thought!
Breval, *Beſaleel*, *Bond*, the varlets caught.
Curl ſtretches after *Gay*, but *Gay* is gone,
He graſps an empty *Joſeph* for a *John*:
So *Proteus*, hunted in a nobler ſhape,
Became, when ſeiz'd, a puppy, or an ape.
  To him the Goddeſs. Son! thy grief lay down,
And turn this whole illuſion on the town.
As the ſage dame, experienc'd in her trade,
By names of Toaſts retails each batter'd jade,
(Whence hapleſs Monſieur much complains at *Paris*
Of wrongs from Ducheſſes and Lady *Mary*'s)
Be thine, my ſtationer! this magic gift;
Cook ſhall be *Prior*, and *Concanen*, *Swift*;
So ſhall each hoſtile name become our own,
And we too boaſt our *Garth* and *Addiſon*.
  With that, ſhe gave him (piteous of his caſe,
Yet ſmiling at his ruful length of face)
A ſhaggy tap'ſtry, worthy to be ſpread
On *Codrus*' old, or *Dunton*'s modern bed;
Inſtructive work! whoſe wry mouth'd portraiture
Diſplay'd the fates her confeſſors endure.
Ear-leſs on high, ſtood un-abaſh'd *Defoe*,
And *Tuchin* flagrant from the ſcourge, below:
There *Ridpath*, *Roper*, cudgell'd might ye view,
The very worſted ſtill look'd black and blue:
Himſelf among the ſtoried Chiefs he ſpies,
As from the blanket high in air he flies,

And oh! (he cry'd) what ſtreet, what lane but knows
Our purgings, pumpings, blanketings and blows?
In ev'ry loom our labours ſhall be ſeen,
And the freſh vomit run for ever green!
  See in the circle next, *Eliza* plac'd;
Two babes of love cloſe clinging to her waſte;
Fair as before her works ſhe ſtands confeſs'd,
In flow'rs and pearls by bounteous *Kirkall* dreſs'd.
The Goddeſs then: " Who beſt can ſend on high
The ſalient ſpout, far-ſtreaming to the ſky:
His be yon *Juno* of majeſtic ſize,
With cow-like udders, and with ox-like eyes.
This *China*-Jordan, let the chief o'ercome
Repleniſh, not ingloriouſly, at home."
  Chapman and *Curl* accept the glorious ſtrife,
(Tho' one his ſon diſſuades, and one his wife)
This on his manly confidence relies,
That on his vigour and ſuperior ſize.
Firſt *Chapman* lean'd againſt his letter'd poſt;
It roſe, and labour'd to a curve at moſt.
So *Jove*'s bright bow diſplays its watry round,
(Sure ſign, that no ſpectator ſhall be drown'd)
A ſecond effort brought but new diſgrace,
The wild *Mæander* waſh'd the Artiſt's face:
Thus the ſmall jett which haſty hands unlock,
Spirts in the gardner's eyes who turns the cock.
Not ſo from ſhameleſs *Curl*; impetuous ſpread
The ſtream, and ſmoaking, flouriſh'd o'er his head.
So, (fam'd like thee for turbulence and horns,)
Eridanus his humble fountain ſcorns;

Thro'

Thro' half the heav'ns he pours th' exalted urn;
His rapid waters in their paſſage burn.
Swift as it mounts, all follow with their eyes;
Still happy Impudence obtains the prize.
Thou triumph'ſt, Victor of the high-wrought day,
And the pleas'd dame, ſoft-ſmiling leads away.
Chapman, thro' perfect modeſty o'ercome,
Crown'd with the Jordan, walks contented home.
But now for Authors nobler palms remain;
Room for my Lord! three Jockeys in his train:
Six huntſmen with a ſhout precede his chair;
He grins, and looks broad nonſenſe with a ſtare.
His honour'd meaning Dulneſs thus expreſt;
" He wins this Patron who can tickle beſt."
He chinks his purſe, and takes his ſeat of ſtate:
With ready quills the Dedicators wait,
Now at his head the dext'rous taſk commence,
And inſtant, fancy feels th' imputed ſenſe;
Now gentle touches wanton o'er his face,
He ſtruts *Adonis*, and affects grimace:
Rolli the feather to his ear conveys,
Then his nice taſte directs our Opera's:
Bentley his mouth with claſſic flatt'ry opes,
And the puff'd orator burſts out in tropes.
But *Welſted* moſt the poet's healing balm
Strives to extract, from his ſoft, giving palm;
Unlucky *Welſted!* thy unfeeling maſter,
The more thou tickleſt, gripes his fiſt the faſter.
While thus each hand promotes the pleaſing pain,
And quick ſenſations ſkip from vein to vein,

A youth unknown to *Phœbus*, in deſpair,
Puts his laſt refuge all in heav'n and pray'r.
What force have pious vows? the Queen of Love
His Siſter ſends, her vot'reſs, from above.
As taught by *Venus*, *Paris* learnt the art
To touch *Achilles'* only tender part;
Secure, thro' her, the noble prize to carry,
He marches off, his Grace's Secretary.

Now turn to diff'rent ſports (the Goddeſs cries)
And learn, my ſons, the wond'rous pow'r of Noiſe.
To move, to raiſe, to raviſh ev'ry heart,
With *Shakeſpear*'s nature, or with *Johnſon*'s art,
Let others aim: 'Tis yours to ſhake the ſoul
With Thunder rumbling from the muſtard bowl,
With horns and trumpets now to madneſs ſwell,
Now ſink in ſorrows with a tolling Bell,
Such happy arts attention can command,
When fancy flags, and ſenſe is at a ſtand.
Improve we theſe. Three Cat-calls be the bribe,
Of him, whoſe chatt'ring ſhames the Monkey tribe,
And his this Drum, whoſe hoarſe heroic baſe
Drowns the loud clarion of the braying Aſs.

Now thouſand tongues are heard in one loud din:
The Monkey-mimicks ruſh diſcordant in:
'Twas chatt'ring, grinning, mouthing, jabb'ring all,
And Noiſe, and *Norton*, Brangling, and *Breval*,
Dennis, and Diſſonance; and captious art,
And ſnip-ſnap ſhort, and interruption ſmart.
Hold (cry'd the Queen) A Cat-call each ſhall win,
Equal your merits! equal is your din!

But

But that this well-diſputed game may end,
Sound forth, my Brayers, and the welkin rend.

As when the long-ear'd milky mothers wait
At ſome ſick miſer's triple-bolted gate,
For their defrauded, abſent foals they make
A moan ſo loud, that all the Guild awake;
Sore ſighs Sir *Gilbert*, ſtarting, at the bray,
From dreams of millions, and three groats to pay!
So ſwells each wind-pipe; Aſs intones to Aſs,
Harmonic twang, of leather, horn, and braſs;
Such, as from lab'ring lungs th' Enthuſiaſt blows,
High ſounds, attempted to the vocal noſe.
But far o'er all, ſonorous *Blackmore*'s ſtrain;
Walls, ſteeples, ſkies, bray back to him again:
In *Tot'nam* fields, the brethren with amaze
Prick all their ears up, and forget to graze;
Long *Chanc'ry-lane* retentive rolls the ſound,
And courts to courts return it round and round:
Thames wafts it thence to *Rufus*' roaring hall,
And *Hungerford* re-ecchoes bawl for bawl.
All hail him victor in both gifts of ſong,
Who ſings ſo loudly, and who ſings ſo long.

This labour paſt, by *Bridewell* all deſcend,
(As morning-pray'r and flagellation end)
To where *Fleet-ditch* with diſemboguing ſtreams
Rolls the large tribute of dead dogs to *Thames*,
The King of dykes! than whom no ſluice of mud
With deeper ſable blots the ſilver flood.
" Here ſtrip my children! here at once leap in!
Here prove who beſt can daſh thro' thick and thin,

And who the moſt in love of dirt excel,
Or dark dexterity of groping well.
Who flings moſt filth, and wide pollutes around
The ſtream, be his the Weekly Journals bound;
A pig of lead to him who dives the beſt:
A peck of coals a-piece ſhall glad the reſt."

In naked majeſty *Oldmixon* ſtands,
And *Milo*-like, ſurveys his arms and hands,
Then ſighing, thus. "And am I now threeſcore?
Ah why, ye Gods! ſhould two and two make four?
He ſaid, and climb'd a ſtranded Lighter's height,
Shot to the black abyſs, and plung'd down-right.
The Senior's judgment all the crowd admire,
Who but to ſink the deeper, roſe the higher.

Next *Smedley* div'd; ſlow circles dimpled o'er
The quaking mud, that clos'd, and op'd no more.
All look, all ſigh, and call on *Smedley* loſt;
Smedley in vain reſounds thro' all the coaſt.

Then * eſſay'd; ſcarce vaniſh'd out of ſight,
He buoys up inſtant, and returns to light:
He bears no token of the ſabler ſtreams,
And mounts far off among the Swans of *Thames*.

True to the bottom, ſee *Concanen* creep,
A cold, long-winded, native of the deep!
If perſeverance gain the Diver's prize,
Not everlaſting *Blackmore* this denies:
No noiſe, no ſtir, no motion can'ſt thou make,
Th' unconſcious flood ſleeps o'er thee like a lake.

Not ſo bold *Arnall*; with a weight of ſcull,
Furious he ſinks, precipitately dull.

Whirlpools

Whirlpools and storms his circling arm invest,
With all the might of gravitation blest.
No crab more active in the dirty dance,
Downward to climb, and backward to advance.
He brings up half the bottom on his head,
And loudly claims the Journals and the Lead.
  Sudden, a burst of thunder shook the flood:
Lo *Smedley* rose in majesty of mud!
Shaking the horrors of his ample brows,
And each ferocious feature grim with ooze.
Greater he looks, and more than mortal stares;
Then thus the wonders of the deep declares.
  First he relates, how sinking to the chin,
Smit with his mien, the mud-nymphs suck'd him in:
How young *Lutetia*, softer than the down,
Nigrina black, and *Merdamante* brown,
Vy'd for his love in jetty bow'rs below;
As *Hylas* fair was ravish'd long ago.
Then sung, how shown him by the nut-brown maids
A branch of *Styx* here rises from the Shades,
That tinctur'd as it runs with *Lethe*'s streams,
And wafting vapours from the land of Dreams,
(As under seas *Alphæus*' secret sluice
Bears *Pisa*'s offerings to his *Arethuse*)
Pours into *Thames*: Each City bowl is full
Of the mixt wave, and all who drink grow dull.
How to the banks where bards departed doze,
They led him soft; how all the bards arose,
Taylor, sweet Swan of *Thames*, majestic bows,
And *Shadwell* nods the poppy on his brows;

While

While *Milbourn* there, deputed by the reſt,
Gave him the caſſock, ſurcingle, and veſt;
And "Take (he ſaid) theſe robes which once were mine,
Dulneſs is ſacred in a ſound Divine."
He ceas'd, and ſhow'd the robe; the crowd confeſs
The rev'rend *Flamen* in his lengthen'd dreſs.
Slow moves the Goddeſs from the ſable flood,
(Her Prieſt preceding) thro' the gates of *Lud*.
Her Critics there ſhe ſummons, and proclaims
A gentler exerciſe to cloſe the games.
Here you! in whoſe grave heads, as equal ſcales,
I weigh what author's heavineſs prevails;
Which moſt conduce to ſooth the ſoul in ſlumbers,
My *Henley*'s periods, or my *Blackmore*'s numbers?
Attend the trial we propoſe to make:
If there be man who o'er ſuch works can wake,
Sleep's all ſubduing charms who dares defy,
And boaſts *Ulyſſes*' ear with *Argus*' eye;
To him we grant our ampleſt pow'rs to ſit
Judge of all preſent, paſt, and future wit,
To cavil, cenſure, dictate, right or wrong,
Full, and eternal privilege of tongue.
Three *Cambridge* Sophs and three pert Templars came,
The ſame their talents, and their taſtes the ſame,
Each prompt to query, anſwer, and debate,
And ſmit with love of Poeſy and Prate,
The pond'rous books two gentle readers bring,
The heroes ſit; the vulgar form a ring.

The

The clam'rous crowd is hush'd with mugs of Mum,
Till all tun'd equal, send a gen'ral hum.
Then mount the clerks, and in one lazy tone,
Thro' the long, heavy, painful page, drawl on;
Soft creeping, words on words, the sense compose,
At ev'ry line, they stretch, they yawn, they doze.
As to soft gales top-heavy pines bow low
Their heads, and lift them as they cease to blow;
Thus oft they rear, and oft the head decline,
As breathe, or pause, by fits, the airs divine:
And now to this side, now to that, they nod,
As verse, or prose, infuse the drowzy God.
Thrice *Budgel* aim'd to speak, but thrice supprest
By potent *Arthur*, knock'd his chin and breast.
Toland and *Tindal*, prompt at priests to jeer,
Yet silent bow'd to Christ's No kingdom here.
Who sate the nearest, by the words o'ercome
Slept first, the distant nodded to the hum.
Then down are roll'd the books; stretch'd o'er 'em lies
Each gentle clerk, and mutt'ring seals his eyes.
At what a *Dutchman* plumps into the lakes,
One circle first, and then a second makes,
What Dulness dropt among her sons imprest
Like motion, from one circle to the rest;
So from the mid-most the nutation spreads
Round, and more round, o'er all the sea of heads.
At last *Centlivre* felt her voice to fail,
Motteux himself unfinish'd left his tale,
Boyer the State, and *Law* the Stage gave o'er,
Nor *Kelsey* talk'd, nor *Naso* whisper'd more;

Norton, from *Daniel* and *Oſtræa* ſprung,
Bleſs'd with his father's front, and mother's tongue,
Hung ſilent down his never-bluſhing head;
And all was huſh'd, as Folly's ſelf lay dead.

Thus the ſoft gifts of Sleep conclude the day,
And ſtretch'd on bulks, as uſual, Poets lay.
Why ſhould I ſing what bards the nightly Muſe
Did ſlumbring viſit, and convey to ſtews:
Who prouder march'd, with magiſtrates in ſtate,
To ſome fam'd round-houſe, ever open gate:
How *Laurus* lay inſpir'd beſide a ſink,
And to mere mortals ſeem'd a Prieſt in drink:
While others, timely, to the neighbouring Fleet
(Haunt of the Muſes) made their ſafe retreat.

THE END OF THE SECOND BOOK.

THE DUNCIAD.

ARGUMENT to BOOK the THIRD.

AFTER the other perſons are diſpoſed in their proper places of reſt, the Goddeſs tranſports the King to her Temple, and there lays him to ſlumber with his head on her lap; a poſition of marvellous virtue, which cauſes all the Viſions of wild enthuſiaſts, projectors, politicians, inamoratos, caſtle-builders, chymiſts, and poets. He is immediately carried on the wings of Fancy to the Elyzian *ſhade; where on the banks of* Lethe *the ſouls of the dull are dipped by* Bavius, *before their entrance into this world. There he is met by the ghoſt of* Settle, *and by him made acquainted with the wonders of the place, and with thoſe which he is himſelf deſtined to perform. He takes him to a* Mount *of* Viſion, *from whence he ſhews him the paſt triumphs of the Empire of Dulneſs, then the preſent, and laſtly the future: How ſmall a part of the world was ever conquered by* Science, *how ſoon thoſe conqueſts were ſtopped, and thoſe very nations again reduced to her dominion. Then diſtinguiſhing the Iſland of* Great Britain, *ſhews by what aids, and by what perſons, it ſhall be forthwith brought to her empire. Theſe he cauſes to paſs in review before his eyes, deſcribing each by his proper figure, character, and qualifications. On a ſudden the*

the ſcene ſhifts, and a vaſt number of miracles and prodigies appear, utterly ſurprizing and unknown to the King himſelf, till they are explained to be the wonders of his own reign now commencing. On this ſubject Settle *breaks into a congratulation, yet not unmixed with concern, that his own times were but the types of theſe. He prophecies how firſt the nation ſhall be over-run with Farces, Operas, and Shows; and the throne of Dulneſs advanced over both the Theatres; then how her ſons ſhall preſide in the ſeats of Arts and Sciences, till in concluſion all ſhall return to their original Chaos: A ſcene, of which the preſent Action of the Dunciad is but a Type or Foretaſte, giving a Glympſe, or* Piſgah-ſight *of the promiſed Fulneſs of her Glory; the accompliſhment whereof will, in all probability, hereafter be the Theme of many other and greater Dunciads.*

BOOK III.

BUT in her Temple's laſt receſs inclos'd,
On Dulneſs' lap th' Anointed head repos'd.
Him cloſe ſhe curtain'd round with vapours blue,
And ſoft beſprinkled with *Cimmerian* dew.
Then raptures high the ſeat of ſenſe o'erflow,
Which only heads refin'd from reaſon know.
Hence, from the ſtraw where *Bedlam*'s Prophet nods,
He hears loud Oracles, and talks with Gods:
Hence the Fool's paradiſe, the Stateſman's ſcheme,
The air-built Caſtle, and the golden Dream,
The Maid's romantic wiſh, the Chymiſt's flame,
And Poet's viſion of eternal fame.
And now, on Fancy's eaſy wing convey'd,
The King deſcended to th' *Elyzian* Shade.
There, in a duſky vale where *Lethe* rolls,
Old *Bavius* ſits, to dip poetic Souls,
And blunt the ſenſe, and fit it for a ſcull
Of ſolid proof, impenetrably dull:
Inſtant when dipt, away they wing their flight,
Where *Brown* and *Mears* unbar the gates of Light,
Demand new bodies, and in Calf's array,
Ruſh to the world, impatient for the day.
Millions and millions on theſe banks he views,
Thick as the ſtars of night, and morning dews,

As thick as bees o'er vernal bloſſoms fly,
As thick as eggs at *Ward* in Pillory.
Wond'ring he gaz'd: When lo! a Sage appears,
By his broad ſhoulders known, and length of ears,
Known by the band and ſuit which *Settle* wore,
(His only ſuit) for twice three years before:
All as the veſt, appear'd the wearer's frame,
Old in new ſtate, another yet the ſame.
Bland and familiar as in life, begun
Thus the great Father to the greater Son.
Oh born to ſee what none can ſee awake!
Behold the wonders of th' oblivious Lake.
Thou, yet unborn, haſt touch'd this ſacred ſhore;
The hand of *Bavius* drench'd thee o'er and o'er.
But blind to former, as to future Fate,
What mortal knows his pre-exiſtent ſtate?
Who knows how long, thy tranſmigrating ſoul
Might from *Bœotian* to *Bœotian* roll!
How many *Dutchmen* ſhe vouchſaf'd to thrid?
How many ſtages thro' old Monks ſhe rid?
And all who ſince, in mild benighted days,
Mix'd the Owl's ivy with the Poet's bays?
As man's mæanders to the vital ſpring
Roll all their tydes, then back their circles bring;
Or whirligigs, twirl'd round by ſkilful ſwain,
Suck the thread in, then yield it out again:
All nonſenſe thus, of old or modern date,
Shall in thee center, from thee circulate.
For this, our Queen unfolds to viſion true
Thy mental eye, for thou haſt much to view:

Old ſcenes of glory, times long caſt behind
Shall firſt recall'd, ruſh forward to thy mind;
Then ſtretch thy ſight o'er all her riſing reign,
And let the paſt and future fire thy brain.
 Aſcend this hill, whoſe cloudy point commands
Her boundleſs empire over ſeas and lands.
See round the Poles where keener ſpangles ſhine,
Where ſpices ſmoke beneath the burning Line,
(Earth's wide extreams) her ſable flag diſplay'd;
And all the nations cover'd in her ſhade!
 Far eaſtward caſt thine eye, from whence the Sun
And orient Science at a birth begun.
One god-like Monarch all that pride confounds,
He, whoſe long wall the wand'ring *Tartar* bounds.
Heav'ns! what a pile? whole ages periſh there:
And one bright blaze turns Learning into air.
 Thence to the ſouth extend thy gladden'd eyes;
There rival flames with equal glory riſe,
From ſhelves to ſhelves ſee greedy *Vulcan* roll,
And lick up all their Phyſick of the ſoul.
 How little, mark! that portion of the ball,
Where, faint at beſt, the beams of Science fall;
Soon as they dawn, from *Hyperborean* ſkies,
Embody'd dark, what clouds of *Vandals* riſe!
Lo where *Mæotis* ſleeps, and hardly flows
The freezing *Tanais* thro' a waſte of ſnows,
The North by myriads pours her mighty ſons,
Great nurſe of *Goths*, of *Alans*, and of *Huns*.
See *Alaric*'s ſtern port! the martial frame
Of *Genſeric!* and *Attila*'s dread name!

See, the bold *Oſtrogoths* on *Latium* fall;
See, the fierce *Viſigoths* on *Spain* and *Gaul*.
See, where the morning gilds the palmy ſhore
(The ſoil that arts and infant letters bore)
His conqu'ring tribes th' *Arabian* prophet draws,
And ſaving Ignorance enthrones by Laws.
See Chriſtians, Jews, one heavy ſabbath keep;
And all the Weſtern world believe and ſleep.

Lo *Rome* herſelf, proud miſtreſs now no more
Of arts, but thund'ring againſt heathen lore;
Her gray-hair'd Synods damning books unread,
And *Bacon* trembling for his brazen head;
Padua with ſighs beholds her *Livy* burn,
And ev'n th' *Antipodes Virgilius* mourn.
See, the Cirque falls, th' unpillar'd Temple nods,
Streets pav'd with Heroes, *Tyber* choak'd with Gods:
'Till *Peter*'s keys ſome chriſten'd *Jove* adorn,
And *Pan* to *Moſes* lends his pagan horn;
See graceleſs *Venus* to a Virgin turn'd,
Or *Phidias* broken, and *Apelles* burn'd.

Behold yon' Iſle, by Palmers, Pilgrims trod,
Men bearded, bald, cowl'd, uncowl'd, ſhod, unſhod,
Peel'd, patch'd, and pyebald, linſey-woolſey brothers,
Grave mummers! ſleeveleſs ſome, and ſhirtleſs others.
That once was *Britain*—Happy! had ſhe ſeen
No fiercer ſons, had *Eaſter* never been!
In peace, great Goddeſs, ever be ador'd;
How keen the war, if Dulneſs draw the ſword?
Thus viſit not thy own! on this bleſt age
Oh ſpread thy Influence, but reſtrain thy Rage.

And ſee! my ſon, the hour is on its way,
That lifts our Goddeſs to imperial ſway;
This fav'rite Iſle, long ſever'd from her reign,
Dove like, ſhe gathers to her wings again.
Now look thro' Fate! behold the ſcene ſhe draws!
What aids, what armies, to aſſert her cauſe?
See all her progeny, illuſtrious ſight!
Behold, and count them, as they riſe to light.
As *Berecynthia*, while her off-ſpring vye
In homage, to the Mother of the ſky,
Surveys around her in the bleſt abode
A hundred ſons, and every ſon a God:
Not with leſs glory mighty Dulneſs crown'd
Shall take thro' *Grubſtreet* her triumphant round,
And her *Parnaſſus* glancing o'er at once,
Behold a hundred ſons, and each a dunce.
Mark firſt that youth who takes the foremoſt place,
And thruſts his perſon full into your face.
With all thy father's virtues bleſt, be born!
And a new *Cibber* ſhall the ſtage adorn.
A ſecond ſee, by meeker manners known,
And modeſt as the maid that ſips alone;
From the ſtrong fate of drams if thou get free,
Another *Durfey*, *Ward!* ſhall ſing in thee.
Thee ſhall each Ale-houſe, thee each Gill-houſe mourn,
And anſw'ring Gin-ſhops ſowrer ſighs return.
Lo next two ſlip-ſhod Muſes traipſe along,
In lofty madneſs, meditating ſong,
With treſſes ſtaring from poetic dreams,
And never waſh'd, but in *Caſtalia*'s ſtreams:

Haywood, *Centlivre*, glories of their race!
Lo *Horneck*'s fierce, and *Room*'s funereal face;
Lo ſneering *Goode*, half malice and half whim,
A fiend in glee, ridiculouſly grim.
Jacob, the ſcourge of Grammar, mark with awe,
Nor leſs revere him, blunderbuſs of Law.
Lo *Bond* and *Foxton*, ev'ry nameleſs name,
All crowd, who foremoſt ſhall be damn'd to fame.
Some ſtrain in rhyme; the Muſes, on their racks,
Scream like the winding of ten thouſand jacks:
Some free from rhyme or reaſon, rule or check,
Break *Priſcian*'s head, and *Pegaſus*'s neck;
Down, down they larum, with impetuous whirl,
The *Pindars*, and the *Miltons* of a *Curl*.

Silence, ye Wolves! while *Ralph* to *Cynthia* howls,
And makes Night hideous—Anſwer him ye Owls!

Senſe, ſpeech, and meaſure, living tongues and dead,
Let all give way—and *Morris* may be read.

Flow *Welſted*, flow! like thine inſpirer Beer,
Tho' ſtale, not ripe; tho' thin, yet never clear;
So ſweetly mawkiſh, and ſo ſmoothly dull;
Heady, not ſtrong; and foaming, tho' not full.

Ah *Dennis!* *Gildon* ah! what ill-ſtarr'd rage
Divides a friendſhip long confirm'd by age?
Blockheads with reaſon wicked wits abhor,
But fool with fool is barb'rous civil war.
Embrace, embrace my ſons! be foes no more!
Nor glad vile Poets with true Critics gore.

Behold yon Pair, in ſtrict embraces join'd;
How like in manners, and how like in mind!

Fam'd

Fam'd for good nature, *Burnet*, and for truth;
Ducket for pious paſſion to the youth.
Equal in wit, and equally polite,
Shall this a *Paſquin*, that a *Grumbler* write;
Like are their merits, like rewards they ſhare.
That ſhines a Conſul, this Commiſſioner.

"But who is he, in cloſet cloſe y pent,
Of ſober face, with learned duſt beſprent?
Right well mine eyes arede the myſter wight,
On parchment ſcraps y fed, and *Wormius* hight."
To future ages may thy dulneſs laſt,
As thou preſerv'ſt the dulneſs of the paſt!

There, dim in clouds, the poreing Scholiaſts mark,
Wits, who like owls ſee only in the dark,
A Lumberhouſe of books in ev'ry head,
For ever reading, never to be read!

But, where each Science lifts its modern type,
Hiſt'ry her Pot, Divinity his Pipe,
While proud Philoſophy repines to ſhow
Diſhoneſt ſight! his breeches rent below;
Imbrown'd with native bronze, lo *Henley* ſtands,
Tuning his voice, and balancing his hands,
How fluent nonſenſe trickles from his tongue!
How ſweet the periods, neither ſaid nor ſung!
Still break the benches, *Henley!* with thy ſtrain,
While *Kennet*, *Hare*, and *Gibſon* preach in vain.
Oh great Reſtorer of the good old Stage,
Preacher at once, and *Zany* of thy age!
Oh worthy thou of *Ægypt*'s wiſe abodes,
A decent prieſt, where monkeys were the gods!

But fate with butchers plac'd thy prieſtly ſtall,
Meek modern faith to murder, hack, and mawl;
And bade thee live, to crown *Britannia*'s praiſe,
In *Toland*'s, *Tindal*'s, and in *Woolſton*'s days.
Yet oh my ſons! a father's words attend:
(So may the fates preſerve the ears you lend)
'Tis yours, a *Bacon* or a *Locke* to blame,
A *Newton*'s Genius, or a *Milton*'s flame:
But O! with one, immortal One diſpenſe,
The ſource of *Newton*'s Light, of *Bacon*'s Senſe!
Content, each Emanation of his fires
That beams on earth, each Virtue he inſpires,
Each Art he prompts, each Charm he can create,
Whate'er he gives, are giv'n for you to hate.
Perſiſt, by all divine in Man un-aw'd,
But learn, ye Dunces! not to ſcorn your God.
Thus he, for then a ray of Reaſon ſtole
Half thro' the ſolid darkneſs of his ſoul;
But ſoon the cloud return'd—and thus the Sire:
See now, what Dulneſs and her ſons admire!
See what the charms that ſmite the ſimple heart,
Not touch'd by nature, and not reach'd by art.
He look'd, and ſaw a ſable Sorc'rer riſe,
Swift to whoſe hand a winged volume flies:
All ſudden, Gorgons hiſs, and dragons glare,
And ten-horn'd fiends and Giants ruſh to war.
Hell riſes, Heav'n deſcends, and dance on Earth,
Gods, imps, and monſters, muſic, rage, and mirth,
A fire, a jigg, a battle, and a ball,
Till one wide conflagration ſwallows all.

Thence

Thence a new world to Nature's laws unknown,
Breaks out refulgent, with a heav'n its own.
Another *Cynthia* her new journey runs,
And other planets circle other ſuns:
The foreſts dance, the rivers upward riſe,
Whales ſport in woods, and dolphins in the ſkies;
And laſt, to give the whole creation grace,
Lo! one vaſt Egg produces human race.
Joy fills his ſoul, joy innocent of thought:
What pow'r, he cries, what pow'r theſe wonders wrought?
Son! what thou ſeek'ſt is in thee. Look, and find
Each monſter meets his likeneſs in thy mind.
Yet would'ſt thou more? In yonder cloud behold,
Whoſe ſarcenet ſkirts are edg'd with flamy gold,
A matchleſs youth! His nod theſe worlds controuls,
Wings the red lightning, and the thunder rolls.
Angel of Dulneſs, ſent to ſcatter round
Her magic charms o'er all unclaſſic ground:
Yon ſtars, yon ſuns, he rears at pleaſure higher,
Illumes their light, and ſets their flames on fire.
Immortal *Rich!* how calm he ſits at eaſe
Mid ſnows of paper, and fierce hail of peaſe;
And proud his miſtreſs' orders to perform,
Rides in the whirlwind, and directs the ſtorm.
But lo! to dark encounter in mid air
New wizards riſe: here *Booth*, and *Cibber* there:
Booth in his cloudy tabernacle ſhrin'd,
On grinning dragons *Cibber* mounts the wind:

Dire

Dire is the conflict, dismal is the din,
Here shouts all *Drury*, there all *Lincolns-Inn*;
Contending Theatres our empire raise,
Alike their labours, and alike their praise.

And are these wonders, Son, to thee unknown?
Unknown to thee? These wonders are thy own.
For works like these let deathless Journals tell,
" None but thyself can be thy parallel."
These, Fate reserv'd to grace thy reign divine,
Foreseen by me, but ah! withheld from mine.
In *Lud*'s old walls tho' long I rul'd renown'd,
Far, as loud *Bow*'s stupendous bells resound;
Tho' my own Aldermen conferr'd my bays,
To me committing their eternal praise,
Their full-fed Heroes, their pacific May'rs,
Their annual trophies, and their monthly wars:
Tho' long my Party built on me their hopes,
For writing pamphlets, and for roasting Popes;
(Diff'rent our parties, but with equal grace
The Goddess smiles on Whig and Tory race,
'Tis the same rope at several ends they twist,
To Dulness, *Ridpath* is as dear as *Mist*.)
Yet lo! in me what authors have to brag on!
Reduc'd at last to hiss in my own dragon.
Avert it, heav'n! that thou or *Cibber* e'er
Should wag two serpent-tails in *Smithfield* fair.
Like the vile straw that's blown about the streets,
The needy Poet sticks to all he meets,
Coach'd, carted, trod upon, now loose, now fast,
And carry'd off in some Dog's tail at last.

Happier

Happier thy fortunes! like a rolling ſtone,
Thy giddy dulneſs ſtill ſhall lumber on,
Safe in its heavineſs can never ſtray,
And licks up every blockhead in the way.
Thy dragons Magiſtrates and Peers ſhall taſte,
And from each ſhow riſe duller than the laſt;
Till rais'd from Booths to Theatre, to Court,
Her ſeat imperial, Dulneſs ſhall tranſport.
Already Opera prepares the way,
The ſure fore-runner of her gentle ſway.
To aid her cauſe, if heav'n thou can'ſt not bend,
Hell thou ſhalt move; for *Fauſtus* is thy friend:
Pluto with *Cato* thou for her ſhalt join,
And link the *Mourning Bride* to *Proſerpine.*
Grubſtreet! thy fall ſhould men and Gods conſpire,
Thy ſtage ſhall ſtand, enſure it but from fire,
Another *Æſchylus* appears! prepare
For new abortions, all ye pregnant fair!
In flames, like *Semele's*, be brought to bed,
While opening Hell ſpouts wild-fire at your head.
Now *Bavius* take the poppy from thy brow,
And place it here! here all ye Heroes bow!
This, this is he, foretold by ancient rhymes:
Th' *Auguſtus*, born to bring Saturnian times:
Beneath his reign, ſhall *Euſden* wear the bays,
Cibber preſide, Lord-Chancellor of Plays.
Benſon ſole judge of architecture ſit,
And *Ambroſe Philips* be preferr'd for wit!
While naked mourns the Dormitory wall,
And *Jones* and *Boyle's* united labours fall,

While *Wren* with ſorrow to the grave deſcends,
Gay dies unpenſion'd with a hundred friends,
Hibernian politicks, O *Swift*, thy fate,
And *Pope*'s whole years to comment and tranſlate.

Proceed great days! till learning fly the ſhore,
Till birch ſhall bluſh with noble blood no more,
Till *Thames* ſee *Eton*'s ſons for ever play,
Till *Weſtminſter*'s whole year be holiday;
Till *Iſis*' elders reel, their pupils ſport;
And *Alma Mater* lye diſſolv'd in port!

Signs following ſigns lead on the mighty year;
See! the dull ſtar roll round and re-appear.
She comes! the cloud-compelling Pow'r, behold!
With Night primæval, and with Chaos old.
Lo! the great Anarch's ancient reign reſtor'd;
Light dies before her uncreating word.
As one by one, at dread *Medæa*'s ſtrain,
The ſick'ning ſtars fade off th' æthereal plain;
As *Argus*' eyes, by *Hermes* wand oppreſt,
Clos'd one by one to everlaſting reſt;
Thus at her felt approach, and ſecret might,
Art after art goes out, and all is night.
See ſculking Truth in her old cavern lye,
Secur'd by mountains of heap'd caſuiſtry:
Philoſophy, that touch'd the heav'ns before,
Shrinks to her hidden cauſe, and is no more:
See Phyſic beg the Stagyrite's defence!
See Metaphyſic call for aid on ſenſe!
See myſtery to Mathematics fly;
In vain! they gaze, turn giddy, rave, and die.

Thy

Thy hand, great Dulneſs! lets the curtain fall,
And univerſal darkneſs buries all.
  Enough! enough! the raptur'd monarch cries;
And thro' the Ivory gate the viſion flies.

END OF THE FIFTH VOLUME.

www.ingramcontent.com/pod-product-compliance
Lightning Source LLC
Chambersburg PA
CBHW021544110726
47902CB00004B/1014
9783337100759